Men, Law and Gender

Essays on the 'Man' of Law

Richard Collier

Routledge
Taylor & Francis Group

a GlassHouse book

First published 2010
by Routledge
2 Park Square, Milton Park, Abingdon, Oxon, OX14 4RN

Simultaneously published in the USA and Canada
by Routledge
711 Third Avenue, New York, NY 10017

A GlassHouse book
Routledge is an imprint of the Taylor & Francis Group, an informa business

First issued in paperback 2011

© 2010 Richard Collier

Typeset in Sabon by
Taylor & Francis Books

British Library Cataloguing in Publication Data
A catalogue record for this book is available from the British Library

Library of Congress Cataloguing in Publication Data
Collier, Richard.
Men, law, and gender : rethinking the 'man' of law / Richard Collier.
p. cm.
"Simultaneously published in the USA and Canada."
Includes bibliographical references and index.

ISBN 978-1-904385-49-3
1. Sex and law.   2. Men – Legal status, laws, etc.   3. Masculinity.   4.
Fathers – Legal status, laws, etc. – Great Britain.   5. Law students – Great
Britain – Social aspects.   6. Lawyers – Great Britain – Social aspects.   I. Title.
K380.C65 2010
346.01'3 – dc22
2009026300

ISBN13: 978-0-415-68572-6 (pbk)
ISBN13: 978-1-904385-49-3 (hbk)
ISBN13: 978-0-203-86212-4 (ebk)

Men, Law and Gender

Essays on the 'Man' of Law

What does it mean to speak of 'men' as a gender category in relation to law? How does law relate to masculinities? This book presents the first comprehensive overview and critical assessment of the relationship between men, law and gender, outlining the contours of the 'man' of law across diverse areas of legal and social policy.

Written in a theoretically informed, yet accessible style, *Men, Law and Gender* provides an introduction to the study of law and masculinities whilst calling for a richer, more nuanced conceptual framework in which men's legal practices and subjectivities might be approached. Building on recent sociological work concerned with the relational nature of gender and personal life, Richard Collier argues that social, cultural and economic changes have reshaped ideas about men and masculinities in ways that have significant implications for law. Bringing together voices and disciplines that are rarely considered together, he explores the way ideas about men have been contested and politicised in the legal arena. This includes original empirical studies of male lawyers, the legal profession and fathers' rights and law reform, alongside discussions of university law schools and legal academics, family policy and parenting cultures.

This innovative, timely and important text provides a unique insight into the relationship between law, men and masculinities. It will be required reading for academics and students in law and legal theory, socio-legal studies, gender studies, sociology and social policy, as well as policy-makers and others concerned with the changing nature of gender relations.

Richard Collier is Professor of Law at the University of Newcastle, UK.

Contents

Acknowledgements

I have presented, over the years, many papers at conferences, workshops and staff seminars drawing on research conducted for this book, and I would like to thank all who have commented and asked me to speak, in particular those who have kindly supported my work as a Visiting Scholar.

I would like to thank Colin Perrin and his colleagues at Routledge who have worked on this book and have shown such great patience as each deadline passed. I would like to express my especial thanks to Sally Sheldon. Chapters 5 and 7 of this book develop themes discussed in previous collaborations with Sally and I would like to acknowledge both the influence of this work and my discussions with her, as well as her insights, generosity and understanding, in shaping the ideas about law, men and gender presented here. Any errors and oversights are, of course, my own.

I would like to acknowledge the financial support and assistance provided by the following. Discussion in chapter 6 draws on an empirical project funded by the British Academy, 'Male Lawyers and the Negotiation of Work and Family Commitments' (SG-31920) and I would like to thank and acknowledge the support of all the men and women who participated in this project and agreed to be interviewed. Chapter 7 presents preliminary findings from a study of the UK fathers' rights movement funded by the British Academy/Leverhulme Trust Thank Offer to Britain Fellowship (TOB06–07/SRF2005.88 & SG42903) and parts of the discussion in chapters 1 and 5 draw on work undertaken during a period of research leave funded by the AHRC (RL/AN8065/APN16739). In relation to chapter 7, I would also especially like to acknowledge and thank all the individual men and women who agreed to be interviewed and gave up their time to participate in this project. I hope the argument presented reflects key themes that emerged and succeeds in setting out, even to some degree, how it might be possible to chart a way through the often highly polarised debates in this area.

Some parts of the book contain substantially revised versions of material that has appeared elsewhere and I am grateful to the publishers for the permission to reproduce them here, in particular, notably: R. Collier, 'Be Smart, Be Successful, Be Yourself...': Representations of the Training Contract and the Trainee Solicitor in Advertising by Large Law Firms', 12(1) *International*

Journal of the Legal Profession (2005), pp 51–92; R. Collier, '"We're All Socio-Legal Now?": Legal Education, Scholarship and the Global Knowledge Economy – Reflections on the UK Experience', 26(4) *Sydney Law Review* (2004), pp 503–37; R. Collier, 'Fathers 4 Justice, Law and the New Politics of Fatherhood', 17(4) *Child and Family Law Quarterly* (2005), pp 1–29; R. Collier, 'Reflections on the Relationship Between Law and Masculinities: Rethinking The "Man Question"', 56 *Current Legal Problems* (2003), pp 345–402. All references to previously published work have been appropriately cited.

Finally, I would like to dedicate this book to Fiona Coleman, Rosie Collier and my mother, Nancy, with my love.

Richard Collier
18/6/09

Introduction

In 1995, I published a book entitled *Masculinity, Law and the Family*, the first words of which were as follows:

> Why another book on masculinity? It is becoming difficult to keep up with the books and articles exploring the social construction of masculinity. Each week, it seems, sees the publication of another. Yet amongst this now considerable literature ... there are few texts which take as the specific object of study the relationship between masculinity *and law*.[1]

Over the past fifteen years or so, a rich picture has emerged within legal studies of the 'man' or, rather, as we shall see, the 'men' of legal discourse. Across diverse areas of law, work has sought to unpack the way in which ideas about men and gender have been understood, constructed or otherwise depicted. Gender struggles involving law have, of course, a long and well-documented history. Yet a legal-political terrain premised on particular beliefs about men and masculinity has, I shall argue in this book, been reshaped by the embedding in law of models of universal formal equality, by ideas of gender neutrality and rights discourses. Law has become a key site of conflict for a series of contemporary contestations around the 'historical collapse of the legitimacy of patriarchal power'.[2] The debates about law, men and gender discussed in the following chapters illustrate, in different ways, to adopt Raewyn Connell's term, crisis tendencies that have arisen around the legitimacy of gender relations in late modern societies. This book explores the uncertain, contradictory effects of these changes, and how legal feminism and the development of pro-feminist praxis alike have sought to question what it means to speak of 'men' as a gender category in relation to law, the 'Man' of law of my title.[3]

---

[1] R. Collier, *Masculinity, Law and the Family*, London: Routledge, 1995, p 1, original emphasis.

[2] R. W. Connell, *Masculinities*, Cambridge: Polity, 1995, p 85.

[3] A similar approach has informed interrogations of the 'man question', whether in relation to law or feminist thought: for example, K. E. Ferguson, *The Man Question: Visions of Subjectivity in Feminist Theory*, Berkeley, University of California Press, 1993; N. Dowd, *The Man Question: Feminist Jurisprudence, Masculinities and Law*, New York: New York University Press, forthcoming; A. Howe, *Sex, Violence and Crime: Foucault and the 'Man' Question*, London: Routledge Cavendish, 2009.

Discussion of the relationship between law, men and gender, we shall see, raises questions about diverse aspects of social life, the variable and contested meanings that attach to gender, the structures of feeling that shape our lives. In the chapters to follow, I investigate a diverse range of discursive frameworks, different areas within which ideas about men's identities and experiences have been understood in law. I shall consider university law schools and legal academics, images of lawyers and work-life balance in the legal profession, the development of family policy and parenting cultures and the connections between the politics of law reform and the dynamics of separation. The way in which ideas about men become contested and politicised in the legal arena is a theme reflected in both recent feminist work and pro-feminist studies of masculinities. In chapter 1, I will explore how subjectivity and the idea of a distinctive masculine gender identity – what it means, for example, to be 'man' within specific, grounded contexts – is a culturally constituted category, neither wholly dependent on nor set apart from biology. I question, in particular, binary oppositions bound up with a form of thinking about men and masculinity that is, in certain respects at least, increasingly obsolete. Conceptual debates have moved far beyond the sexual divisions through which ideas about law, men and gender had, in the past, been understood, with new conceptual tools emerging that provide new possibilities for a more nuanced and multi-layered engagement with this gendered subject. Across each of the following chapters, I shall argue, there is no such thing as an essential or intrinsic 'male' or 'masculine' identity. Men's identities are constituted, rather, through diverse and socially contingent practices that may themselves be contradictory, 'practices that people socially categorised as men reproduce through their agency within contexts of power'.[4]

Building on recent sociological work, I seek to integrate, in particular, an appreciation, at both a theoretical and political level, of the complexity and contradictory nature of personal life.[5] This will involve questioning, at different moments, how ideas about social class, race, ethnicity and vulnerability, intimacy and emotion have informed ideas about masculinity in law. Studies of law and gender, I suggest, have much to gain from incorporating a more complex account of the gendered male subject and the interconnected nature of the lives of women, children and men. Equally, public policies based on outmoded stereotypes of both sexes, we shall see, are unlikely to address the very real problems both women and men can face, problems I address in this book across a wide range of legal policy debates. What is required, I argue, is a re-theorising of men's identities by looking critically at, and beyond, the term 'masculinities' in ways

---

[4] F. Ashe, *The New Politics of Masculinity Men, Power and Resistance*, (Routledge Innovations in Political Theory) London: Routledge, 2007, p. 159

[5] C. Smart, *Personal Life: New Directions in Sociological Thinking*, Cambridge: Polity, 2007; also J. Eekelaar, *Family Law and Personal Life*, Oxford: OUP, 2006. See chapter 1, pp 44–46.

that might produce a richer, more nuanced conceptual framework in which men's practices, subjectivities and bodies can be approached.

It is unsurprising given the relational nature of gender identities and gender categories (masculinity/femininity and so forth) that a significant reconfiguration of ideas about gender should have had important implications for understandings of power between men and women. The case of fathers' rights politics, for example, discussed in chapter 7, illustrates in a particularly clear way the contradictory nature of some recent changes around law with regard to questions of equality and power. At various points in this book, we will see how law has reproduced heterosexist, gendered frameworks premised on problematic ideas about 'authentic' masculine identity and experience. In certain legal contexts, this has led to the embrace of standpoints that can all too often result in 'a dehumanizing of other groups and a corresponding withering of empathy and emotional relatedness within the self'.[6] Collective mobilisation around law, we shall see, can in a certain context become a strategy for the maintenance of power.

At the same time, however, it is also important to recognise how new configurations of gender have profoundly reshaped a political terrain around equality, rights and responsibility in law, doing so in far-reaching and unpredictable ways. Whether in relation to these debates around fathers' rights and law reform (chapter 7), men's parenting in social policy (chapter 5), changes in the legal profession (chapters 4 and 6) or in universities and their law schools (chapters 2 and 3), reducing developments to the level of a backlash to feminism, for example, offers little 'in terms of conceptual clarity or theoretical usefulness'.[7] Equally, these social changes and men's responses to them cannot be simply reduced to an 'anti-woman' sentiment, the reassertion of patriarchal privilege. In chapter 1, looking at feminism's interrogation of masculinity in legal studies, I will explore how a historical association of heterosexual, middle-class, white men with ideas about power and the reproduction of gender inequality in law linked men to certain beliefs about the masculine culture of law. These ideas about law and masculinity continue to resonate powerfully within certain contexts in the legal arena. This does not mean, however, 'that explorations of men's identities have to be based only on negative aspects ... or framed through analyses of men as constituting a 'social problem'[8] (as in, for example, the analysis of family policy to be discussed in chapter 5). Men's lives are, as will be discussed within this book, more complex than would be indicated by the deployment of hegemonic masculinity within much of this work on men, a concept that itself stands in an increasingly uneasy relation to the multi-dimensional nature of men's engagements with and relationships to law discussed in these pages.

---

[6] R.W. Connell and J.W. Messerschmidt, 'Hegemonic Masculinity: Rethinking the Concept', *Gender and Society*, 2005, vol 19(6), p 852.7

[7] Ashe, op cit, 2007, p 159.

[8] Ashe, op cit, 2007, p 159.

Paying attention to these 'practices within the category of men', therefore, to follow a recent reading by Fidelma Ashe, 'does not mean side-stepping questions of power or accountability'.[9] It does however point to the need for a more complex account of men's identities in contemporary society.

In the chapters to follow I will explore how ideas about affect and emotion, memory, intimacy, love and commitment inform men's experiences and personal lives in contexts around law. I do so, however, in a way that is not set apart from a consideration of gender relations and power. As the discussion of contemporary work on men and gender considered in chapter 1 will illustrate, emotions, experiences and subjectivities can be seen *as* effects of power whilst, at the same time, having the potential to produce oppositional practices and resistances (including to dominant masculinities).[10] That is why, building on earlier studies in this area,[11] it is important to note the complex, situated nature of the investments individual men and women can have in gender categories. The allure of particular ideas about legal practice, for example, considered in chapters 4 and 6 in the context of the legal profession, of a 'legal lifestyle' and certain kind of commitment to being a 'successful' lawyer, can be more complex than any reference to the masculine nature of law would allow. Ideas of masculinity are deeply contested in debates about the legal profession, about universities and their law schools, in relation to ideas about men's work, family practices, intimacy and emotional lives. The nature of these gendered investments and social commitments can be fluid and contradictory, and it is significant that 'the internal complexities of masculinities has only gradually come into focus as a research issue'.[12] In terms of the perceived costs, as well as the benefits, that attach to gendered identities, meanwhile, 'without treating men as objects of pity, we should recognise that hegemonic masculinity does not necessarily translate into a satisfying experience of life'.[13] Even a cursory look at the contemporary debates in the legal field, including those to be discussed in this book, illustrates how this is the case.

To raise these questions about law, men and gender, therefore, is not to efface issues of power. Far from it, whether at a theoretical level (chapter 1), in relation to the changes in legal education and research (chapters 2 and 3), the legal profession (chapters 4 and 6) and family policy and men's parenting (chapters 5 and 7), I locate questions about men's agency (what men do) within networks of power. This can be contrasted with engagements with men and gender, law and policy, where there often appears to be something more akin to a celebration or refusal of men and masculinity premised on the idea that there exists an essential 'male' identity among people who are identified within a

---

[9] Ashe, op cit, 2007, p 159.
[10] See further chapter 1.
[11] R. Collier, *Masculinities, Crime and Criminology: Men, Heterosexuality and the Criminal(ised) Other*, London: Sage, 1998: Connell and Messerschmidt, op cit, 2005, p 829.
[12] Connell and Messerschmidt, op cit, 2005, p 852.
[13] Connell and Messerschmidt, op cit, 2005, p 852.

particular society as 'men'. Such identities, I will argue in chapter 1, do not exist prior to social practices and, therefore, the adoption of simplistic 'male positive' and 'anti-male' standpoints alike makes, as Ashe has argued, little sense.[14] Many of the questions about law raised in this book will cut across categories of men, women and children, involving theilisation of contrasting interests and loyalties, different concepts of family and intimacy, diverse practices of care and a wide range of beliefs about the scope of legal rights and responsibilities. We are dealing with the heterogeneous nature of social practices in which progressive and regressive forms of gender politics can, we shall see, interact and co-exist in specific legal contexts, cutting across traditional political terrains in uncertain ways. This point has much to offer in developing an oppositional gender politics in the field of law, as well as in challenging the existing frameworks through which these gender relations have been understood.

The time is, I believe, propitious for a book such as this and I wish to locate this work, at the outset, in the context of broader engagements with the relationship between law and gender. Writing in 2004 in the *Australian Feminist Law Journal* Margaret Thornton spoke of her wish to begin 'a conversation which I hope others will join so that we might discursively constitute a new episteme of feminist legal theory that is linked to the political'.[15] Asking whether 'the conjunction of postmodernism and neo-liberalism' might add up 'to post-feminism',[16] Thornton sought to question whether the institutional base of feminist legal scholarship may be 'disappearing beneath our feet'. Linking to themes and concerns I discuss in each of the following chapters, what is necessary, she suggested, is a return to 'political engagement, rather than introspection', to discourage 'an exclusive focus upon individual and micro-political sites ... disconnected from *the broader political picture*'.[17] 'Clinging to the universals of the past' Thornton concludes, cannot 'save legal academic feminism'. Rather, she suggests, it is important to locate developments in feminist legal studies in the context of 'a particular politico-historical moment'.[18] This is a moment, I will argue in this book, in which the political terrain around law and masculinity has been reshaped by an amalgam of social, legal, cultural and technological developments.

In contributing to this new episteme of legal theory, therefore, in the sense depicted by Thornton, what follows re-examines the 'broader political picture' marked by a new constellation of ideas about the relationship between law, men and gender. As such, and challenging all too often untested claims about the nature of masculine identity, this book does not present a linear narrative

[14] Ashe, op cit, 2007, p 159.
[15] M. Thornton, 'Neoliberal Melancholia: The Case of Feminist Legal Scholarship', *Australian Feminist Law Journal*, 2004, vol 20, pp 7 and 22.
[16] Thornton, op cit, 2004, p 21.
[17] Thornton, op cit, 2004, p 21, my emphasis.
[18] Thornton, op cit, 2004, p 21.

of progression in the study of law and gender. Rather, following Thornton, I historically contextualise accounts that have sought to explore the relationship between men and law. I will question the extent to which the very model(s) of and approaches to masculinity dominant within much legal study in the past, including strands of feminist legal scholarship, can be seen as the product a particular 'episteme' – one whose time, if it has not already passed, then is at least, I shall suggest, open to question. In so doing, bringing together voices and disciplines that do not always speak together, I wish to push the boundaries of enquiry and adopt a rather different lens through which it might be possible to explore voices, histories, emotions and issues hitherto silent in many accounts of law and gender.

Chapter 1

Men, masculinities and law

The 'man question' in legal studies

Introduction

This chapter 'sets the scene' for the discussions to follow in this book. It does so by considering a concept central to studies of law, men and gender – masculinities. The argument is structured around three sections. In the first, I introduce and overview core themes within the 'masculinity turn' in legal scholarship over the past two decades. Distinctive intellectual and political influences, I suggest, provide the backdrop for the study of masculinities and law and, throughout the chapter, I draw on examples from two areas in which this engagement with masculinities has been particularly developed; the field of Family Law and studies of law, crime and criminology. The first section provides the reader with knowledge of the kinds of arguments that have been made about the relationship between law and masculinity and the diverse subjects that have been addressed in this work.

The second section shifts the focus towards the conceptualisation of masculinity within legal studies. I examine the strengths and weaknesses of two of the main sociological and social-psychological approaches that have influenced these writings on men and gender. First, an engagement with hegemonic masculinity, an approach in which law is accorded a particular place in the reproduction of gender relations and position within the social structure. Second, encounters between law, discourse and the idea of the male (masculine) subject, what has been referred to in some accounts as a psychosocial account of men and masculinities.[1] In the third, and final, section, I chart a way through these perspectives, suggesting there is a pressing need to rethink the relationship between law, men and gender in the light of social changes discussed in this book and theoretical developments that have taken place in

---

[1] The transition between these two perspectives is discussed by J. Hood-Williams, 'Gender, Masculinities and Crime: From Structures to Psyches', *Theoretical Criminology*, 2001, vol 5, p 37. See further W. Cealey Harrison and J. Hood-Williams, *Beyond Sex and Gender*, London: Sage, 2002.

law and other disciplines. This chapter, in summary, explores how legal scholarship has sought to engage with the gender of men, the 'man question' or 'man of law' of my title, outlining a general context for the studies of law, men and gender to follow. It provides the backdrop against which the analyses of the following chapters will be developed; of university law schools and legal education, (chapters 2 and 3), men, gender and the legal profession (chapters 4 and 6), of men, law and social policy (chapter 5) and the politics of parenting, law and gender (chapter 7).

Contexts: the 'masculinity turn' in legal scholarship

Interrogation of the relationship between masculinities and law within legal studies has occurred at a nexus of developments that, although interconnected, draw on distinct theoretical and political trajectories in terms of how both law and masculinity have been conceptualised at different historical moments. The most significant influence – not only on law, but on the analysis of masculinity throughout the social sciences, arts and humanities – has been that of feminism; or, in relation to legal studies, the now well-established body of work sometimes referred to as legal feminism (or, more accurately, legal feminisms).[2] In this section, I outline how masculinity has been approached within feminist legal studies, detailing the kinds of areas explored and the arguments made. I proceed to discuss how an engagement with law has informed the critical study of men and masculinities, drawing out points of similarity, and difference, with these feminist conceptualisations of 'the man of law'.

Men, masculinities and feminist legal studies

In approaching how feminist legal scholarship has sought to address masculinity, it is helpful to recall something of the history of the concept. The roots of an engagement with masculinity in social studies can be found in the distinction between sex and gender and, more specifically, in a body of post-war social-psychological research concerned with the relationship between sex roles and gender identity. Biological sex is here seen as something serving to augment, but not to determine, the gender identity for each sex; that is, masculinity in the case of the male sex, femininity in the case of female sex. A person's gendered subjectivity, their sense of maleness or femaleness, is understood in this model to be a result of largely post-natal psychological influences able, in some cases at least, to completely override the biological 'fact' of a person's genital, chromosomal or hormonal sex (resulting in, for example, the

---

[2] These feminist engagements with men and masculinities are considered throughout this book.

phenomenon of the transsexual).[3] Within this frame of analysis, sex and gender are conceptually differentiated. Sex is deployed to describe the innate biological characteristics of humans. It is something 'of the body'. Gender, and with it masculinity as a descriptor of the gender of men, relates, in contrast, to social characteristics and usages which are socially/culturally associated with one sex or the other.[4] This, broadly, constitutes the dominant frame of analysis within which an interrogation of masculinity has developed in both sociology and legal studies.

The functionalist analyses that emerged from the 1950s onwards, adopting this kind of approach to sex/gender, can be seen, in retrospect, to constitute a 'pre-history' of contemporary masculinity theory.[5] A central problem with such accounts, feminist scholars later argued, concerned the way in which an overarching methodological individualism served to negate any questioning of the social structure, the gendered nature of a contingent, socially constituted public/private divide[6] and, in particular, the crucial issue of the social power of men relative to women. When masculinity was addressed in this pre-history, rather, it all too often appeared as something that could be measured on a scale (as in studies of androgyny), or else as something individually possessed.[7] Within the feminist texts that began to impact profoundly on the social sciences throughout the 1970s and 1980s, in contrast, a concern to challenge the structural power of men served to reframe the way in which masculinity was understood. In turn, the development of a distinctive feminist legal scholarship during this period has utilised the concept of masculinity in a number of different ways in

[3] For detailed discussion of these issues, A. Sharpe, *Transgender Jurisprudence: Dysphoric Bodies of Law*, London: Cavendish, 2002.

[4] R. Stoller, *Sex and Gender Vol 1: On the Development of Masculinity and Femininity*, London: Karnac Books, 1984; J. Archer and B. Lloyd, *Sex and Gender*, Cambridge: Cambridge University Press, 1985; Cealey Harrison and Hood-Williams, op cit, 2002, ch 3.

[5] On the 'intellectually disorganized, erratic and incoherent' nature of the earlier sex role research, T. Carrigan, R. Connell and J. Lee, 'Towards a New Sociology of Masculinity', *Theory and Society*, 1985, vol 14, p 551, at p 553. On the 'male sex role', J. H. Pleck, 'The Male Sex Role: Problems, Definitions and Sources of Change', *Journal of Social Issues*, 1976, vol 32, p 55; M. Komarovsky, 'Functional Analysis of Sex Roles', *American Sociological Review*, 1950, vol 15, p 508; R. Brannon, 'The Male Sex Role: Our Culture's Blueprint for Manhood and What It's Done for Us Lately' in D. David and R. Brannon (eds), *The Forty-Nine Per Cent Majority: The Male Sex Role*, Reading, Mass: Addison Wesley, 1976. For an overview of this early literature R.W.Connell, *Gender and Power*, Cambridge: Polity, 1987.

[6] K. O'Donovan, *Sexual Divisions in Law*, London: Weidenfeld & Nicolson, 1985; M. Thornton (ed.), *Public and Private: Feminist Legal Debates*, Melbourne: OUP, 1995; S. Boyd (ed.), *Challenging the Public/Private Divide: Feminism, Law and Public Policy*, Toronto: University of Toronto Press, 1997; J. B. Elshtain, *Public Man, Private Woman*, Oxford: Wiley Blackwell, 1982.

[7] Carrigan et al., op cit, 1985. On androgyny note, for example, S. Bem, 'Probing the Promise of Androgyny' in A. G. Kaplan and J. P. Bean (eds), *Beyond Sex Role Stereotypes: Readings Towards a Psychology of Androgyny*, Boston: Little Brown, 1976. On the impact of this early masculinity theory on accounts of law and crime see N. Naffine, *Female Crime: The Construction of Women in Criminology*, Sydney: Allen and Unwin, 1987; N. Naffine, 'The Masculinity-Femininity Hypothesis', *British Journal of Sociology*, 1985, vol 25, p 365.

seeking to account for the relationship between women, men and the power of law.

It is important to sound two notes of caution at this point. First, the project of feminist legal studies has long been – and, of course, remains – contentious, not least in terms of an epistemological foundation around the notion of a unified subject 'Woman'.[8] In the following, I will be using, for heuristic purposes, the idea of distinctive phases to feminist scholarship. Such an argument is, I recognise, problematic in its tendency to categorise together a vast and diverse body of work, and assume that a linear narrative (one of progress?) underscores what is, in fact, a far more complex (and contested) history.[9] Second, it is important to recall that earlier pre-feminist sociogenic sex-role accounts of masculinity themselves raised themes that recur within later feminist and pro-feminist studies. Thus, there is an intriguing degree of continuity in this work on masculinity, not least a depiction of masculinity as something at once fragile, precarious and marked by anxiety (notably in relation to (hetero)sexuality); and, simultaneously, as something natural, taken for granted and defined repeatedly in relation to what it is *not*: not feminine, 'unmanly' or homosexual.[10]

Notwithstanding the above, it is possible to identify three principal areas within which an engagement with masculinity has figured in feminist legal scholarship. These are, first, in the exploration of the gendered nature of legal *practices and institutions*, second, in a critique of legal *methods and reasoning* and, third, in studies of the construction of gender and sexuality within *legal discourse*. In relation to each, I shall now suggest, there exist revealing similarities, and differences, in how masculinity has been conceptualised. Each, importantly, raises issues which, I shall proceed to argue in section two, speak to more fundamental ambiguities about the meaning of masculinity as it has been deployed in relation to the study of law.

Legal practices and institutions

The concept of masculinity has been used extensively within analyses of a wide range of institutions and practices relating to diverse aspects of law and legal

---

[8] See further C. Smart, *Feminism and the Power of Law*, London: Routledge, 1989; C. Smart, 'The Woman of Legal Discourse', *Social and Legal Studies*, 1992, vol 1, p 29; N. Lacey, *Unspeakable Subjects: Feminist Essays in Legal and Social Theory*, Oxford: Hart Publications, 1998; N. Naffine, 'In Praise of Legal Feminism', *Legal Studies*, 2002, p 71; J. Conaghan, 'Reassessing the Feminist Theoretical Project in Law', *Journal of Law and Society*, 2000, vol 27, p 351. See below, p 19.

[9] N. Naffine, *Law and the Sexes: Explorations in Feminist Jurisprudence*, Sydney: Allen and Unwin, 1990, ch 1.

[10] Contrast H. M. Hacker, 'The New Burdens of Masculinity', *Marriage and Family Living*, 1957, vol 3, p 227; R. E. Hartley, 'Sex Role Pressures and the Socialisation of the Male Child' in J. Pleck and J. Sawyer (eds), *Men and Masculinity*, Englewood Cliffs, NJ: Prentice Hall, 1974.

regulation. It has informed, for example, we shall see later in this book, studies of the work of solicitors, barristers and the judiciary; the courts, the police and prison service; legal education, the law school and the legislature, as well as the administration of criminal and civil justice more generally. Questions about masculinity have been addressed in theoretical engagements with law and policy debates about gender equality and discrimination that bear upon many aspects of legal practice and employment. The legal profession, for example, has seen a heightened focus on issues of diversity and equality prompted, at least in part, by well-documented shifts in the number of women entering law (chapters 2, 3, 4 and 6). This work has raised important questions about the gendered cultures of law (see below), the social effects of 'what men do' within specific, situated contexts, and the consequences of these actions for women, children and for men themselves. In relation to university law schools (chapters 2 and 3) and the contemporary legal profession (chapters 4 and 6), legal institutions have been seen as being marked by systemic gendered inequalities in ways that connect to ideas about the masculine nature of law. Attention has been paid, for example, to the gendered nature of professional commitment, disparities in pay and promotion and the ongoing relative absence of women in senior positions, notwithstanding a gender transformation at the point of entry to law.[11]

At the same time, if we look more closely then we will see that a reframing of masculinity as a social problem has come to pervade many areas of law and policy and is, I will argue in this book, reshaping ideas about gender and equality in relation to legal institutions and practices in far-reaching ways. Broader attempts within the study of men and masculinities to depict, in Raewyn Connell's terms, the 'big picture'[12] of gender hierarchies in the public sphere[13] meanwhile, reveals that men have historically dominated not just the institutions of law but also government, business and the 'world of work' generally. This has been described by Stephen Whitehead as part of the 'heroic project' of modern, 'public man',[14] interlinking gender, men and paid employment with the social and legal reproduction of normative ideas about masculinity. In the case of law, and questioning why a much-heralded 'trickle up' effect should have been so slow in achieving results within the legal profession for example – why, notwithstanding the 'cat-flaps' in the glass ceiling, a glass ceiling remains – a range of men's practices have been singled out as problematic. In some feminist accounts of

---

[11] For a general discussion of some of the changes that have occurred in relation to 'women in law', see B. Hale and R. Hunter, 'A Conversation With Baroness Hale', *Feminist Legal Studies*, 2008, vol 16(2), p 237.

[12] R. W. Connell, 'The Big Picture: Masculinities in Recent World History', *Theory and Society*, 1993, vol 22, p 597.

[13] J. Hearn, *Men in The Public Eye*, London: Routledge, 1992; J. Hearn, *The Gender of Oppression: Men, Masculinity and the Critique of Marxism*, Brighton: Harvester Wheatsheaf, 1987.

[14] S. Whitehead, *Men and Masculinities: Key Themes and New Directions*, Cambridge: Polity, 2002, ch 4. See R. W. Connell, 'Men, Gender and State' in S. Ervo and T. Johansson (eds), *Among Men: Moulding Masculinities*, Aldershot: Ashgate, 2003.

the institutions of law, however, the problem lies in something at once more ephemeral yet more powerful than the question of what an individual man or group of men might do: it is the masculine culture of law itself. Men's practices, taken together and cumulatively, that is, have been understood to reproduce distinctive cultural forms and belief structures that have deleterious consequences for women in law (and, depending on the reading, some categories of subordinated men: see below).[15]

Seeking to engage with and challenge these gendered culture(s), a rich body of theoretical and empirical feminist scholarship has questioned how the resulting masculinity or masculinism[16] of law's institutions is linked to the reproduction of gendered, discriminatory beliefs and practices. This work has explored a wide range of organisations concerned with the practice and administration of law. In studies of solicitors (chapters 4 and 6), for example, and of legal academics within the setting of the university law school (chapters 2 and 3), we find some recurring themes in feminist interrogations of masculinity and legal practice, including the identification of, and an attempt to challenge:

- the marginalising effects for women of homosocial and homophobic cultures,[17] a sexualisation of women's bodies that, Margaret Thornton suggests, has accompanied the historical denial of women's corporeality within many legal workplaces;[18]
- the cultural dissociation of women, particularly evident in parts of the legal profession, from gendered ideas of authority and from the possession of the 'authoritative speaking voice'[19] – the voice or gravitas deemed essential to being a 'successful' lawyer;[20]

---

[15] Note, for example, S. Hall, 'Daubing the Drudges of Fury: Men, Violence and the Piety of the "Hegemonic Masculinity" Thesis', *Theoretical Criminology*, 2002, vol 6, p 35.

[16] 'Masculinism is the ideology that justifies and naturalises male domination ... [It] takes it for granted that there is a fundamental difference between men and women, it assumes that heterosexuality is normal, it accepts without question the sexual division of labour, and it sanctions the political and dominant role of men in the public and private spheres': A. Brittan, *Masculinity and Power*, Oxford: Blackwell, 1989, p 4.

[17] S. Law, 'Homosexuality and the Social Meaning of Gender', *Wisconsin Law Review*, 1988, vol 2, p 187; S. Bird, 'Welcome to the Men's Club: Homosociality and the Maintenance of Hegemonic Masculinity', *Gender and Society*, 1996, vol 10, p 120; C. M. Bell, 'All I Really Need to Know I Learned in Kindergarten (Playing Soccer): A Feminist Parable of Legal Academia', *Yale Journal of Law and Feminism*, 1995, vol 7, p 133; M. Thornton, 'Hegemonic Masculinity and the Academy', *International Journal of the Sociology of Law*, 1989, vol 17, p 115; R. Collier, 'Masculinism, Law and Law Teaching', *International Journal of the Sociology of Law*, 1991, vol 19, p 427.

[18] M. Thornton, 'Authority and Corporeality: The Conundrum for Women in Law', *Feminist Legal Studies*, 1998, vol 6, p 147.

[19] This male jurisprudential tradition has been described as 'a professionally constituted and legitimated vision of the male as an authority': J. Grbich, 'The Body in Legal Theory' in M. Fineman and N. Thomadsen (eds), *At the Boundaries of Law*, London: Routledge, 1991, p 75.

[20] Thornton, op cit, 1998.

- the association of women, in ways that contrast markedly to men, with normative gendered ideals that impact on women's opportunities for advancement; and, at the same time, the identification of a 'personal dimension'[21] that has historically privileged a distinctive 'male persona' and model of (legal) professional masculinity[22] (chapter 6) premised on an elaborate silencing of the contingency and structurally grounded nature of men's (but most certainly not women's) 'private' lives (although see further chapter 5);[23] and finally, in a sense encapsulating each of the above; and
- the persistent benchmarking[24] and assessment of women against a normative ideal figure, the 'man of law'. This is an individual understood simultaneously (somewhat paradoxically) to be both *gendered* in particular ways (as male/masculine: assertive, rational, competent, unemotional and so on) and, equally, *gender-neutral*, notably in relation to commitments and 'inevitable' dependencies[25] associated with caring practices that fall outside of the field of paid employment (chapters 5 and 6).

Thus, as culture, practice and institution merge, masculinity has been extensively deployed in such a way as to depict and explain something of the gendered character of law's practices and institutions.

Legal methods and reasoning

Underscoring this model of the benchmark 'man of law', if we look more closely, has been a particular *kind* of masculinity, one culturally associated, broadly, with white, middle- and upper-middle-class and able-bodied men. This social group,

---

[21] Thornton, op cit, 1998.

[22] S. Whitehead, 'Identifying the Professional "Man"ager: Masculinity, Professionalism and the Search for Legitimacy' in J. Barry, M. Dent and M. O'Neill (eds), *Gender, Professionalism and Managerial Change: An International Perspective*, London; Macmillan, 2003; M. Dent and S. Whitehead (eds) *Managing Professional Identities: Knowledge, Performativity and the 'New' Professional*, London: Routledge 2001. See further ch 6.

[23] S. Whitehead, 'Masculinity: Shutting Out the Nasty Bits', *Gender, Work and Organisation*, 2000, vol 7(2), p 133; S. Whitehead, 'Man – The Invisible Gendered Subject' in S. Whitehead and F. Barrett (eds), *The Masculinities Reader*, Cambridge: Polity, 2001. A persona interlinked with the 'psycho-sexual power flowing from the maintenance of women in subordinate roles': Thornton, op cit, 1989, p 118.

[24] The idea of the masculine 'benchmark', linked with the depiction of the 'man of law' (Naffine, op cit, 1990) has been a recurring theme within legal feminism and links to the critical study of masculinity (below) with regard to the tendency for men to claim (their) reason as final authority and arbiter of social Truth: see further discussion in V. Seidler, *Unreasonable Men: Masculinity and Social Theory*, London: Routledge, 1994; V. Seidler, *Rediscovering Masculinity: Reason, Language and Sexuality*, London: Routledge, 1989; V. Seidler, 'Men, Heterosexualities and Emotional Life' in S. Pile and N. Thrift (eds), *Mapping the Subject: Geographies of Cultural Transformation*, London: Routledge, 1995, p 171.

[25] M. Fineman, *The Neutered Mother, The Sexual Family and Other Twentieth Century Tragedies*, New York: Routledge, 1995.

in the UK as elsewhere, has historically dominated the upper echelons of law, government and business. This kind of association between masculinity and the realm of law was a particular feature of first phase liberal-progressive feminist scholarship.[26] That is, in work linked to what Harding[27] has influentially termed the perspective of feminist empiricism,[28] the very maleness or masculinity of law appeared as something that served to distort the gaze of an otherwise neutral observer. Law's 'sexism' and 'sexist' bias interlinked to the way it embodied particular masculine ideals and a male 'world-view', a dominant masculinity bound up with the empirical dominance by men of law's institutions. Such an approach informs, in different ways, a number of key and influential texts of the 1970s and 1980s such as Susan Atkins and Brenda Hoggett's (1984) *Women and the Law* and Albie Sachs and Joan Hoff-Wilson's *Sexism and the Law: A Study of Male Beliefs and Judicial Bias* (1978).[29] In contrast to such work, however, the development of later standpoint or 'second phase' feminist scholarship sought to draw on a forceful critique of the political and conceptual limits of this earlier liberal-progressive position.[30] In so doing, it brought about a subtle shift of focus in how masculinity was then seen to connect to law. This point requires clarification, as it relates to a theme that will run through each of the chapters to follow – the question of how the relationship between masculinity and law interlinks, at different moments, to understandings of the power of men.

By 1984, writing in the field of Family Law, Carol Smart had already begun to question, in her book *The Ties That Bind*, whether the fact that particular legal agents may be understood as 'subscribing to sexist attitudes to protect their material interests' necessarily rendered law itself, and as a whole, 'sexist or somehow masculine in nature'.[31] For those writers working within what Ngaire Naffine subsequently termed a 'second phase' feminist tradition, in contrast, what was at issue in engaging with law and gender was precisely the inherent masculinity or maleness of law and global patriarchal legal systems.[32] Within this strand of work, a link was made explicit between law's

---

[26] Naffine, op cit, 1990, pp 3–6.

[27] S. Harding (ed), *Feminism and Methodology*, Milton Keynes: Open University Press, 1987; S. Harding, *The Science Question in Feminism*, Milton Keynes: Open University Press, 1986.

[28] On feminist empiricism generally, in particular in relation to crime, N. Naffine, *Feminism and Criminology*, Cambridge: Polity, 1997, pp 30–37.

[29] S. Atkins and B. Hoggett, *Women in the Law*, Oxford: Blackwell, 1984; A. Sachs and J. H. Wilson, *Sexism and the Law: A Study of Male Beliefs and Judicial Bias*, Oxford: Martin Robertson, 1978.

[30] See further C. Smart, 'Feminist Approaches to Criminology or Postmodern Woman meets Atavistic Man' in L. Gelsthorpe and A. Morris (eds), *Feminist Perspectives in Criminology*, Buckingham: Open University Press, 1990; B. Brown, 'Reassessing the Critique of Biologism' in Gelsthorpe and Morris, op cit; B. Brown, 'Women and Crime: The Dark Figures of Criminology', *Economy and Society*, 1986, vol 15, p 355.

[31] C. Smart, *The Ties that Bind: Law, Marriage and the Reproduction of Patriarchal Relations*, London: Routledge & Kegan Paul, 1984, p 17.

[32] Naffine, op cit, 1990.

status as an androcentric, positivist discipline and the gendered (that is, masculine) nature of law's governance, institutions and jurisprudence. Law, implicated with other phallocentric, totalising and oppressive knowledge formations, was seen to have historically effaced the specificities of women's distinctive experiences in its embodiment of a particular masculine worldview, as above.[33] Thus at the very moment that classic tenets of liberal legalism such as individualism, reason, autonomy and freedom were refigured within legal feminism as somehow quintessentially 'masculine' values,[34] and a powerful critique of the limits of formal equality and gender neutrality was increasingly beginning to inform legal feminist thought,[35] law was not seen as simply equating to the power of men. Law constituted, in some accounts at least, that power in its purest form. Oft quoted, but summarising neatly, 'the state is male in the feminist sense. The law sees and treats women the way men see and treat women'.[36] Law's purported neutrality is simply a mask for the 'masculinity of its judgements'.[37]

Challenging what later came to be seen as the essentialism and reductionism of the above approach, and aligned to a rejection of 'categorical thinking' in relation to gender that was under way in sociological studies of men and masculinity (see below),[38] third phase feminist legal scholarship questioned the limits of each of the above two perspectives. In part, this shift reflected the growing impact of postmodernism and post-structuralism across the social sciences, arts and humanities by the mid to late 1980s.[39] Once again, however, on closer examination, a

[33] Whereby, within one strand of feminist thought, the social values, ethics and aesthetics of distinctively masculine or masculinist bodies of law have been contrasted with an alternative, progressive, ethics and politics seen as deriving from feminism and women's experiences.

[34] For discussion see Smart, op cit, 1989. Contrast R. West, 'Jurisprudence and Gender', *University of Chicago Law Review*, 1988, vol 55, p 1.

[35] On the unintended consequences of law reform, for example, see in particular M. Fineman, *The Illusion of Equality: The Rhetoric and Reality of Divorce Reform*, London: University of Chicago Press, 1991.

[36] C. Mackinnon, 'Feminism, Marxism, Method and the State: An Agenda for Theory', *Signs*, 1983, vol 8, p 635 at p 644. See further C. Mackinnon, *Feminism Unmodified: Discourses on Life and Law*, Cambridge, MA: Harvard University Press, 1987. For critique D. Cornell, *Beyond Accommodation: Ethical Feminism, Deconstruction and the Law*, New York: Routledge, 1991, esp ch 3; D. Cornell, 'Sexual Difference, the Feminine and Equivalency: A Critique of Mackinnon's "Toward a Feminist Theory of the State"', *Yale Law Journal*, vol 100, 1991, p 2247.

[37] 'Once masculinity appears as a specific position, not just the way things are, its judgements will be revealed in process and procedure, as well as adjudication and legislation': Mackinnon, op cit, 1983, p 658. Male dominance 'is perhaps the most pervasive and tenacious system of power in history … it is metaphysically nearly perfect. Its point of view is the standard for point-of-viewlessness, its particularity the means of universality': Mackinnon, op cit, 1983, pp 638–39.

[38] Connell, op cit, 1987.

[39] As in the reading, for example, of Smart, op cit, 1989. Although a work of synthesis, a useful summary of the debates at this time is provided by C. Weedon, *Feminist Practice and Post-structuralist Theory*, Oxford: Blackwell, 1987.

particular conceptualisation of masculinity remained central, if implicit, in how the relationship between law and the power of men was understood.

The second phase work, above, was criticised in part for its tendency to conceive of all men as a homogenous group, and of law as somehow akin to an embodiment of the power of all men. The problem with such an approach lay, critics suggested, in how this association between law, masculinity and male power served to efface the diversity, not just of women's lives, but also of men's, a theme of particular significance within the explosion of writings on the critical study of masculinity during the 1980s and early 1990s. Within this work, and notably following the publication of Connell's book *Gender and Power* in 1987, explicitly pro-feminist engagement with questions of power and social structure was meshed, increasingly, to an interrogation, not of a singular 'masculinity', but of the plural masculini*ties*. And in legal studies, similarly, drawing on related concerns about anti-essentialism[40] and intersectionality,[41] feminist work began to focus on the question of whether, whilst groups of men might not have equal access to cultural, symbolic or economic capital, all men, albeit in different ways, might still be seen as the beneficiaries of patriarchal social systems.

Taking up the question asked by Smart in 1984, feminist legal scholarship had begun by the late 1980s and early 1990s to engage in a growing critique of earlier approaches to law and the power of men. In ascribing to the category 'Woman' an essentialist ontological status,[42] such accounts, it was argued, not only negated the discursive construction of the (feminist) subject 'Woman' (the 'Woman' of law),[43] but also side-stepped the diverse positionality of, and differences within, men's lives. Seen ultimately as just as andocentric as the theories it purported to supersede,[44] a body of feminist legal work informed by

---

[40] N. Dowd and M. Jacobs (eds), *Feminist Legal Theory: An Anti-Essentialist Reader*, New York: New York University Press, 2003; E. Spelman, *Inessential Woman: Problems of Exclusion in Feminist Thought*, London, The Women's Press, 1988; bell hooks, *Aint I A Woman: Black Women and Feminism* London: Pluto, 1983; bell hooks, *Feminist Theory: From Margin to Center*, Cambridge, MA: South End Press, 1984.

[41] Work interrogating the interconnections of class, race, gender, age and sexual orientation, for example, questioning the hierarchies that can exist between women as well as between women and men; note bell hooks, op cit, 1984; bell hooks, op cit, 1983; A. Harris, 'Race and Essentialism in Feminist Legal Theory', *Stanford Law Review*, 1990, vol 42, p 581; K. Crenshaw, 'Mapping the Margins: Intersectionality, Identity Politics and Violence Against Women of Color', *Stanford Law Review*, 1991, vol 43(6), p 1241; J. Siltanen and A. Doucet, *Gender Relations in Canada: Intersectionality and Beyond*, Oxford: OUP, 2008; E. Grabham, D. Cooper, J. Krishnadas and D. Herman, *Intersectionality and Beyond: Law, Power and the Politics of Location*, London: Routledge-Cavendish, 2008. See also P. H. Collins and M. Andersen (eds), *Race, Class and Gender: An Anthology* New York: Wadsworth, 2003, 5th edn.

[42] M. Daly, *Beyond God the Father: A Philosophy of Women's Liberation* London: The Women's Press, 1985; M. Daly, *Pure Lust: Elemental Feminist Philosophy*, London: The Women's Press, 1984.

[43] Smart, op cit, 1989.

[44] Smart, op cit, 1989.

postmodernism and post-structuralism questioned an approach to masculinity which had embraced, not least in a depiction of seemingly omnipotent male sexuality[45] and disavowal of heterosexuality,[46] a profound essentialism, 'a paradoxical mix of debilitating pessimism and unfathomable optimism'.[47] In raising questions echoed in sociological studies of men at the time, it was difficult to see what a progressive politics of masculinity might then be, and, importantly, what such an approach might mean for the future of feminism (and, indeed, for the relationship between women and men).[48]

These historical debates are of significance for the readings that follow in this book as it has been from within a body of feminist scholarship building on the critique of these earlier approaches to men, gender and the power of law that the now dominant frame of analysis for the study of men and masculinities within legal studies has emerged. This perspective, now commonplace within contemporary work on gender, law and sexuality, has focused on what has been variously termed the 'social construction' of the 'man', 'men' or 'masculinities' within, or of, law and legal discourse.

Textual analysis: masculinity and the 'man' of legal discourse

Carol Smart's important and highly influential book *Feminism and the Power of Law*,[49] published in 1989, in many respects exemplifies in its approach

---

[45] For example, the reading of A. Dworkin, *Pornography: Men Possessing Women*, London: The Women's Press, 1981; E. Reynaud, *Holy Virility: The Social Construction of Masculinity*, London: Pluto, 1983.

[46] The relation between feminism and heterosexuality became, during the 1990s, the subject of some debate. Note L. Segal, *Straight Sex: Rethinking the Politics of Pleasure*, London: Virago, 1994, p 46, for whom 'The prescription that women should suppress heterosexual desire to further the cause of feminism is one I believe to be strategically and morally wrong'; W. Hollway, 'Recognition and Heterosexual Desire' in D. Richardson (ed), *Theorising Heterosexuality: Telling it Straight*, Buckingham: Open University Press, 1996; W. Hollway, 'Feminist Discourses and Women's Heterosexual Desire' in S. Wilkinson and C. Kitzinger (eds), *Feminism and Discourse*, London: Sage, 1995; W. Hollway, 'Theorising Heterosexuality: A Response', *Feminism and Psychology*, 1993, vol 3, p 412; C. Kitzinger and S. Wilkinson, 'Re-viewing Heterosexuality', *Feminism and Psychology*, 1994, vol 4, p 330; M. Maynard and J. Purvis *(Hetero) Sexual Politics*, London: Taylor and Francis, 1995; L. Segal, 'Feminist Sexual Politics and the Heterosexual Predicament' in L. Segal (ed), *New Sexual Agendas*, New York: New York University Press, 1997; C. Smart, 'Collusion, Collaboration and Confession on Moving Beyond the Heterosexuality Debate' in Richardson (ed), op cit, 1996; C. Smart, 'Desperately Seeking Post-Heterosexual Woman' in J. Holland and L. Adkins (eds), *Sex, Sensibility and the Gendered Body*, London: St Martins Press, 1996.

[47] E. Jackson, 'Catherine Mackinnon and Feminist Jurisprudence: A Critical Reappraisal', *Journal of Law and Society*, 1993, vol 19, p 195 at p 211.

[48] For example, debates in L. Segal, *Is the Future Female? Troubled Thoughts On Contemporary Feminism*, London: Virago, 1994. Contrast R. Coward, *Sacred Cows*, London: Harper Collins, 1999.

[49] Smart, op cit, 1989. For commentary see R. Sandland, 'Between "Truth" and "Difference": Post-structuralism, Law and the Power of Feminism', *Feminist Legal Studies*, 1995, vol 3(1), p 3.

themes that were taken up in the study of masculinity and law during the 1990s.[50] In this work Smart sought to re-address her earlier (1984) questioning of whether there might, in fact, be a distinction between 'legal regulation' and 'male control'; that is, the way in which:

> although it may be that it is men as biological entities who exercise most legally constituted forms of power, and indeed men as individuals who benefit most from the oppression of women, the law is not simply a conglomeration of individual, biological men. Neither is it a collection of individuals in this way, even though individuals have a responsibility for how they interpret or enforce the law.[51]

In part, the work drew on the broadly Foucauldian understanding of the relation between law and power that was becoming increasingly resonant across the social sciences at the time, prefiguring in some respects later studies concerned with law and governance.[52] Smart's analysis begins from a belief that, although law may be constituted as masculine on both empirical and cultural grounds (that, at the very least, 'doing law' and being identified as 'masculine' can be congruous),[53] this is not because of any straightforward biological imperative. Rather, she suggests, what is at issue is the 'significant overlaps' or 'mutual resonances' between how 'both law and masculinity are constituted in discourse'.[54] Thus, she argues:

> Law is not rational because men are rational ... law is constituted as rational as are men, *and men as the subjects of a discourse of masculinity* come to experience themselves as rational – hence suited to a career in law. In attempting to transform law, feminists are not simply challenging legal discourse *but also naturalistic assumptions about masculinity.*[55]

As within the earlier feminist studies discussed above, a challenge to a dominant notion of masculinity and a feminist critique of law are here fused. What is significant about the above passage, however, is the notion of men 'as the subjects of a discourse of masculinity'. This theme draws both on the discourse theory increasingly influential in feminist legal thought at the time, and the engagements with rhetoric, interpretation and hermeneutics that

---

[50] For example, R. Collier, *Masculinity, Law and the Family*, London: Routledge, 1995.

[51] Smart, op cit, 1984, p 18. This problem, Smart suggests, may itself be indicative of just 'how difficult it is to talk of structures of power and mechanisms of regulation *without* attributing these to biological agents who then become personifications of power and control': Smart, op cit, 1984, p 17.

[52] See below.

[53] This idea is discussed further in chapters 2, 3, 4 and 6.

[54] Smart, op cit, 1989, p 86.

[55] Smart, op cit, 1989, pp 86–87, my emphasis.

were informing legal theory more generally, and critical legal scholarship in particular, by the late 1980s and early 1990s.[56] It is an approach, importantly, that opens out to analysis the very questions noted above regarding the plurality and contingency of those discourses which speak of masculinity across diverse institutional and cultural contexts (including, but not confined to, law); the very issues, that is, effaced in the second phase feminist work discussed above.

Smart's argument thus built on a growing scepticism about the nature of a 'quest for a feminist jurisprudence'[57] within an emerging 'postmodern legal feminism',[58] whilst also being attuned to what was happening in sociological engagements with masculinity. It embraced a recognition that law, far from unproblematically oppressing women, could in certain instances be 'open ended' and contradictory in how it reproduced (or challenged) patriarchal relations.[59] Turning attention to the construction of the 'Woman' of legal discourse,[60] moreover, what was brought into question, inescapably, was the nature of the 'Man' of legal – and, indeed, of feminist – discourse.[61] If the fixity of law and feminism's subject Woman was displaced, revealing (her)self to be a sexed, classed and raced subject, an important question fell to be asked: what did this mean for feminism's – or law's – 'Man'? This may not, we shall see, have been a primary concern for legal feminism – but it was, at least, on the agenda in legal scholarship.

These questions were taken up by those scholars who, during the 1990s and to the present day,[62] have developed an engagement with masculinities and the 'man question'[63] within legal study. Much of the work since produced has been undertaken by writers who, albeit in different areas, and with different approaches, have sought to contribute to the development of a pro-feminist project in law. Some have addressed the challenges laid down by earlier feminists regarding those male academics who, across disciplines (including law) had hitherto focused so much of their attention on the 'woman problem',

---

[56] For example, of particular influence at this time, P. Goodrich, *Reading the Law: A Critical Introduction to Legal Methods and Techniques*, Oxford: Blackwell, 1986; P. Goodrich, *Legal Discourse*, Oxford: Blackwell, 1987.

[57] Smart, op cit, 1989, p 66.

[58] M. J. Frug, *Postmodern Legal Feminism*, New York: Routledge, 1993; D. Cornell, op cit, 1991.

[59] C. Smart, 'Feminism and Law: Some Problems of Analysis and Strategy', *International Journal of the Sociology of Law*, 1986, vol 14, p 109.

[60] Smart, op cit, 1992. See also discussion in K. O'Donovan, *Family Law Matters*, London: Pluto, 1993.

[61] Contrast K. E. Ferguson, *The Man Question: Visions of Subjectivity in Feminist Theory*, Berkeley: University of California Press, 1993.

[62] For example, N. Dowd, 'Masculinities and Feminist Legal Theory: An Anti-Essentialist Project', *University of Florida Legal Studies Research Paper No 2008–05*, Florida: University of Florida, 2008. Also available at *Wisconsin Women's Law Journal*, vol 13, 2009, <http://papers.ssrn.com/sol3/papers.cfm?abstract_id=1238070>, accessed 17 December 2008.

[63] N. Dowd, *The Man Question: Feminist Jurisprudence, Masculinities and Law*, New York: New York University Press, forthcoming; A. Howe, *Sex, Violence and Crime: Foucault and the 'Man' Question*, London: Routledge-Cavendish, 2009.

whilst leaving men, all too often, as the unexplained, taken for granted, norm.[64] Developments in law here mirror debates within sociology and other disciplines around the question of how, and by whom, a critical and reflexive interrogation of men and masculinities should take place.[65] Feminist legal work, we have seen, has made considerable analytic use of masculinity in seeking to address the power of law. Yet it has been less concerned, for understandable political reasons, to interrogate the gendered experiences of men *as men*.[66] As Katherine O'Donovan put it in 1993, 'it is for other men to make us see masculinities and to bring these into question'.[67] Within the work that emerged on masculinities and law during the 1990s, in contrast, and in Elizabeth Grosz's oft cited words, 'it is no longer women who are judged by the norms of masculinity and found to be "the problem". Now it is men, and not humanity, who are openly acknowledged as the objects and subjects of investigation.'[68]

It is necessary at this stage to turn away from the field of law. Work produced over this period within the area of men and masculinities scholarship, alluded to above, provides, alongside these feminist writings on law and gender, the second important backdrop against which the study of law, men and gender to follow in this book must be located. It is a literature on masculinity that, for all the insights it has provided into the relationship between law and gender, can also, I shall suggest, be questioned in terms of how it has engaged with the 'man of law'.

The critical study of men, masculinities and law

The term 'new sociology' or 'critical study' of men and masculinities has been widely used to refer to a now voluminous body of theoretical and empirical research concerned, in different ways, and from a variety of perspectives, to explore the gender of men in an explicitly pro-feminist

---

[64] A. Jardine, 'Men in Feminism' in A. Jardine and P. Smith (eds), *Men in Feminism*, London: Methuen, 1987, p 56.

[65] See for example P. Halewood, 'White Men Can't Jump: Critical Epistemologies, Embodiment, and the Praxis of Legal Scholarship', *Yale Journal of Law and Feminism*, 1995, vol 7, p 1; R. Braidotti, 'Envy: Or With My Brains and Your Looks' in Jardine and Smith, op cit, 1987; F. Ashe, *The New Politics of Masculinity: Men, Power and Resistance* (Routledge Innovations in Political Theory), London, Routledge, 2007, pp 76–91; T. Digby, (ed), *Men Doing Feminism*, New York: Routledge, 1998; R. W. Connell, 'Men, Masculinities and Feminism', *Social Alternatives*, 1997, vol 16(3), p 7; D. Porter (ed), *Between Men and Feminism*, London: Routledge, 1992; B. Lithgard and P. Douglas, *Men Engaging Feminisms*, Buckingham: Open University Press, 1999; J. E. Canaan and C. Griffin, 'The New Men's Studies: Part of the Problem, or Part of the Solution?' in J. Hearn and D. Morgan (eds), *Men, Masculinities and Social Theory*, London: Routledge, 1990; M. Kimmel, 'Integrating Men into the Curriculum', *Duke Journal of Gender, Law and Policy*, 1997, vol 4, p 181.

[66] D. Morgan, *Discovering Men: Sociology and Masculinities*, London: Routledge, 1992.

[67] O'Donovan, op cit, 1993, p 88.

[68] E. Grosz, quoted in S. Walklate, *Gender and Crime: An Introduction*, Hemel Hempstead: Prentice Hall/Harvester Wheatsheaf, 1995, p 69.

manner.[69] This literature is vast, a depth of work testified to by the sheer volume of books, articles and research reports on the topic. The scale of this research is evident in the existence of dedicated encyclopaedias on the subject[70] and the presence of extensive bibliographic databases. *The Men's Bibliography*, for example, a free-for-public-use source of research citations, contains at the time of writing over 17,000 references.[71] In providing a framework for the studies to follow in this book, it is important, therefore, to recognise the scope and depth of this interdisciplinary work on men and masculinities, the enormously wide range of issues and concerns that have been addressed and the complex relation this work has to a broader politics of masculinity and other social movements.[72] At this point, building on the above discussion of how masculinity has been conceptualised within feminist legal study, I wish to look more closely at certain features of this work in relation to law. In particular, I will explore how a rather different political trajectory has marked this masculinities literature, and has led it to a rather different kind of engagement with law and legal regulation from the feminist studies discussed above.

This work on men and gender, we have seen, has been informed in part by an attempt to take up the challenges of feminism and address masculinity – and with it, the power of men – in an explicitly pro-feminist manner. Whilst this can be seen as a politically and conceptually problematic endeavour in itself,[73] much of the research produced can be broadly aligned with the observation of Connell in 1987 that it is a 'politics of masculinity' that should be the business of the heterosexual men who have 'bared the brunt of the feminist critiques of

[69] This literature is, as noted below, voluminous. An excellent introduction is provided by N. Edley and M. Wetherell, *Men in Perspective: Practice, Power and Identity*, London: Prentice Hall, 1995; R. W. Connell, *Masculinities*, Cambridge: Polity, 1995; R. W. Connell, *The Men and the Boys*, Cambridge: Polity, 2000. See, in addition to work cited above, R. Connell, J. Hearn and M. Kimmel (eds), *The Handbook of Masculinity Studies*, London: Sage, 2004; R. Adams and D. Savran (eds), *The Masculinity Studies Reader*, Oxford: Wiley Blackwell 2002; Whitehead, op cit, 2002 esp ch 1; B. Pease, *Recreating Men: Postmodern Masculinity Politics*, London: Sage, 2000; B. Pease and K. Pringle (eds), *A Man's World: Changing Men's Practices in a Globalized World*, London: Zed Books, 2002; A. McMahon, *Taking Care of Men: Sexual Politics in the Public Mind*, Cambridge: Cambridge University Press, 1999; J. S. Kahn, *An Introduction to Masculinities*, Oxford: Wiley-Blackwell, 2009; L. Segal, *Slow Motion: Changing Masculinities, Changing Men*, London: Virago, 1990; S. Whitehead and F. Barrett (eds), *The Masculinities Reader*, Cambridge: Polity, 2001; H. Brod and M. Kaufman (eds), *Theorizing Masculinity*, Thousand Oaks, CA: Sage, 1994; K. Clatterbaugh, *Contemporary Perspectives on Masculinity: Men, Women and Politics in Modern Society*, Boulder, CO: Westview Press, 1990; M. Kimmel, *The Gendered Society*, Oxford: OUP, 2000; M. Kimmel and M. Messner, *Men's Lives*, 1997, Boston, MA: Allyn and Bacon; A. Petersen, *Unmasking the Masculine: Men and Identity in a Sceptical Age*, London: Sage, 1999.

[70] M. Flood, J. Gardiner, K. Pease and K. Pringle (eds), *The International Encyclopaedia of Men and Masculinities*, 1 Vol, London: Routledge, 2007.

[71] M. Flood (compiler), *The Men's Bibliography: A comprehensive bibliography of writing on men, masculinities, gender, and sexualities*, 19th edition, 2008. <http://www.xyonline.net/links.shtml> and <http://mensbiblio.xyonline.net> accessed 1 October 2008.

[72] See further Ashe, op cit, 2007.

[73] See p16, above.

masculinity'.[74] In contrast to the essentialism identified within a strand of feminist thought, for example, work that depicted law, we have seen, as the seeming embodiment *of* the power of men, a starting point here is a recognition that men 'are not excluded from the basic human capacity to share experiences, feelings and hopes'. For Jeff Hearn, a writer who has engaged in particularly insightful and reflective ways on the relationship between men, feminism and power (see further below), men who are concerned to 'oppose sexism' and who want to study gender should focus primarily on the critical study of men.[75] Similarly, in an early and influential article, the sociologist David Morgan noted how 'taking men into account' entailed a critical engagement with issues of masculinity, not treating men, by ignoring questions of gender, as the taken for granted 'normal' subject of research.[76]

Early pro-feminist studies of men and masculinities, including some key texts produced during the 1980s and early 1990s, tended to be informed by concerns about power and social structure that had shaped the politics of the men's anti-sexist movements in the 1970s, very much as response to 'second wave' feminism.[77] This approach can be seen, for example, in various accounts of men's violence and male sexuality, and around the question of whether a political project of 'changing men', as an integral part of pro-feminist activism, necessarily entailed rejecting or resisting dominant forms of masculinity.[78] In contrast to the broadly materialist and structural based accounts of the 1970s and 1980s,[79] however, research produced during the 1990s tended increasingly to be marked by engagements with post-structuralism and postmodernism, in ways that map to the developments that were taking place around masculinity within feminist legal studies, as above.[80] Thus, we find during this period an increasing focus on the discursive production of masculinities within specific institutional and cultural contexts, a growing concern with questions of performativity, representation and identity.[81] Elsewhere, linking to work at the

---

[74] Connell, op cit, 1987, p xiii.

[75] Hearn, op cit, 1987, p 21.

[76] D. Morgan 'Men, Masculinity and the Process of Sociological Enquiry' in H. Roberts, *Doing Feminist Research*, London: Routledge & Kegan Paul, 1981.

[77] Note A. Tolson, *The Limits of Masculinity*, London: Tavistock, 1977; A. Metcalf and M. Humphries (eds), *The Sexuality of Men*, London: Pluto 1985; V. Seidler (ed), *The Achilles Heel Reader: Men, Sexual Politics and Socialism*, London: Routledge, 1991. See further H. Christian, *The Making of Anti-Sexist Men*, London: Routledge, 1994.

[78] J. Stoltenberg, *The End of Manhood: A Book for Men of Conscience*, New York: Dutton, 2000; J. Stoltenberg, *Refusing to Be a Man: Essays on Sex and Justice*, London: UCL Press (revised edition), 1990.

[79] For example, Tolson, op cit, 1977. Compare Hearn, op cit, 1987; McMahon, op cit, 1999.

[80] See for example the approaches of Pease, op cit, 2000; Petersen, op cit, 1999; D. Gutterman, 'Postmodernism and the Interrogation of Masculinity' in S. Whitehead and F. Barrett (eds), *The Masculinities Reader*, Cambridge: Cambridge University Press, 2001.

[81] These issues are considered throughout this book. For a useful discussion of the development of this literature see Ashe, op cit, 2007, esp ch 11.

interface of feminism and psychology, there was a refocusing on the relationship between masculinity and the idea of the (gendered) male subject.[82] In more recent years, a further shift can be traced as, albeit still, I would suggest, to a rather limited degree, insights derived from critical race theory and queer theory have began to impact on the study of men and masculinities. Work in the area of sexuality studies and feminist philosophical engagements with the body and identity, for example, has charted a 'queering' of heterosexuality that has reframed traditional understandings of masculinity, not least around ideas of embodiment and its grounding within an overarching epistemic frame of sex/gender[83] (I shall return to this issue below).

One further point needs to be addressed by way of introduction, before I proceed to focus on how this work on masculinities has informed research on men and gender in legal studies. Whatever the lineage of the scholarship on men and masculinities and the distinctive political, intellectual and institutional influences that have shaped it, the development of the study of masculinities in law is reflective of what Margaret Thornton has termed a broader 'discursive attempt to stop the depiction of women as 'the problem'.[84] What we have here, rather, is an explicit:

> Deflection of the objectifying gaze from women and Indigenous people to benchmark masculinity and heterosexuality, as well as 'whiteness' ... an attempt to disrupt the conventional orderings of modernity within legal texts.[85]

This theme is important, and it will inform each of the chapters to follow. With regard to the political economy framing the production of research into men and gender in universities, an issue I consider in relation to contemporary

[82] See, for example, M. Wetherell and N. Edley, 'Negotiating Hegemonic Masculinity: Imaginary Positions and Psycho-Discursive Practices', *Feminism and Psychology*, 1999, vol 9(3), p 335. See further below.

[83] See for example J. Butler, *Gender Trouble: Feminism and the Subversion of Identity*, London: Routledge, 1990; J. Butler, *Bodies That Matter: On the Discursive Limits of Sex*, London: Routledge, 1993; J. Butler, 'Contingent Foundations: Feminism and the Question of "Postmodernism"' in J. Butler and J. W. Scott (eds), *Feminists Theorize the Political*, New York: Routledge, 1992. In law, D. Herman, *Rights of Passage: Struggles for Lesbian and Gay Equality*, Toronto: University of Toronto Press, 1994; D. Herman and C. Stychin (eds), *Legal Inversions: Lesbians, Gay Men and the Politics of Law*, Philadelphia, PA: Temple University Press, 1995; C. Stychin, *Law's Desire*, London: Routledge, 1996; W. Eskridge, *Gaylaw: Challenging the Apartheid of the Closet*, Cambridge, MA: Harvard University Press, 1999; R. Robson, *Sappho Goes to Law School*, New York: Columbia University Press, 1998; C. Stychin and D. Herman (eds), *Sexuality in the Legal Arena*, London: Athlone Press, 2000. See further E. Sedgwick, *Epistemology of the Closet*, New York: Penguin, 1990.

[84] M. Thornton 'Neoliberal Melancholia: The Case of Feminist Legal Scholarship', *Australian Feminist Law Journal*, 2004, vol 20, p 7, at p 12.

[85] Thornton, op cit, 2004, p 15. See also P. Middleton, *The Inward Gaze: Masculinity and Subjectivity in Modern Culture*, London: Routledge, 1992.

legal studies in chapter 2, it is necessary to see this work on masculinities as the product of a distinctive economic, political and cultural context. The emergence of an engagement with the politics of masculinity in the legal arena that I chart in this book has been marked, I shall suggest, by a particular conceptualisation of a 'problem of men',[86] a theme that cuts across political and policy debates bearing on law. In each of the areas discussed, whether the legal profession (chapters 4 and 6), men's rights and responsibilities in law (chapter 5) or parenthood and the politics of law (chapter 7), contemporary legal policy debates raise significant questions about men's practices and the implications, for women, men and children, of the embedding of formal equality and gender neutrality within law.

With regard to the critical study of men and masculinities, and tracking the implications of this work for studies in law, it is also important to recognise how the scholarship on men and masculinities has itself been made up of different strands and concerns, shaped by a particular generational 'episteme' of feminist thought (see below). Some of the research on men has focused directly on the questions of power central to feminist engagements with masculinity, as above. The work of Connell, in particular, can be associated with this political perspective.[87] Other research, in particular that aligned to a 'men's studies' approach, more developed in the United States perhaps than in the UK, has tended, in contrast, to engage in descriptive accounts of aspects of men's lives, interrogating what it means, whether in social or psychological terms, to be 'a man'.[88] The study of masculinity generally has had, and continues to have, an uncertain and contested status within parts of the academy, remaining, in the case of law at least, at the outer edges of mainstream legal scholarship.

Yet, I shall argue in this book, if we look more closely at developments that have coalesced in work on men and gender, what we are dealing with is a repositioning of masculinity that has had a direct bearing on a wide range of academic, political and policy agendas. What we are dealing with here is issues about what men 'do' and the ways in which gendered cultures and practices might, or might not, be changed via legal reform. At both national and cross-national levels,[89] I shall argue, an engagement with masculinity should therefore no longer be seen as marginal to debates about law but, rather, as

---

[86] J. Scourfield and M. Drakeford, 'New Labour and the "Problem of Men"', *Critical Social Policy*, 2002, vol 22, p 619.

[87] Ashe, op cit, 2007, ch 10.

[88] See for example H. Brod, *The Making of Masculinities: The New Men's Studies*, London: Allen and Unwin, 1987. For critique, see Canaan and Griffin, op cit, 1990.

[89] With regard to the influence of European Union agendas around diversity and the mainstreaming of gender equality note S. Mazey, *Gender Mainstreaming in the EU: Principles and Practice*, London: Kogan Page, 2001; F. Beveridge, S. Nott and K. Stephen (eds), *Making Women Count: Integrating Gender into Law and Policy-Making*, Aldershot: Ashgate, 2000; V. Schmidt, *Gender Mainstreaming: An Innovation in Europe? The Institutionalisation of Gender Mainstreaming in the European Commission*, Leverkusen Opladen: Barbara Burich, 2005.

something that has itself become a significant feature of research agendas, policy engagements and political contestations across a wide range of topics relevant to law.[90] To return to the kinds of engagements with masculinity considered above in the context of feminist legal studies, therefore, what has been argued and what has been said – and not said – about the 'man of law', the 'man question'?

Unpacking the 'man of law': text, practice, experience and policy

A rich picture has emerged within legal studies of the 'man' or, rather, we have seen, the 'men' of legal discourse. Across diverse areas of law, and involving the analysis of legal cases, statutes, utterances and representations, socio-legal research has unpacked the way in which ideas about men and their masculinities have been regulated and understood, constructed or otherwise depicted in law. This work has addressed both the legal regulation of the intimate, personal and (at least apparently) 'private parts' of life – of love and personal commitments, sexual desires and activities – as well as the world of 'public man' as a subject of political and legal theory.[91] It has encompassed ideas of responsibility and rights, community and citizenship, sociality and autonomy. By way of introduction, and to give no more than a flavour of the considerable body of work produced, masculinity has been utilised in engagements with law and the legal system in relation to topics as diverse as:

- the formation of the nation-state and law,[92] studies of male sexuality and marriage law,[93] the dynamics of policing cultures and the development of strategies aimed at challenging sex discrimination within both the legal profession and criminal justice systems;[94]

[90] Note, for example, the work of the 'Critical Research on Men in Europe' Network (CROME), an umbrella research network bringing together researchers from European countries and established with funding from the EU Framework 5 project 'The Social Problem of Men': <http://www.cromenet.org/>, accessed 1 October 2008. See further J. Hearn and K. Pringle, *European Perspectives on Men and Masculinities*, Basingstoke: Palgrave Macmillan, 2006; J. Hearn and K. Pringle, 'Men, Masculinities and Children: Some European Perspectives', *Critical Social Policy*, 2006, vol 26(2), p 365; B. Featherstone, *Contemporary Fathering: Theory, Policy and Practice*, Bristol: Policy Press, 2009, pp 151–52.

[91] T. Carver, '"Public Man" and the Critique of Masculinities', *Political Theory*, 1996, vol 24, p 673.

[92] M. Liddle, 'State, Masculinity and Law: Some Comments on English Gender and English State Formation', *British Journal of Criminology*, 1996, vol 36, p 361.

[93] L. Moran, 'A Study of the History of Male Sexuality in Law: Non-Consummation', *Law and Critique*, 1990, vol 1, p 155; R. Collier, '"The Art of Living the Married Life": Representations of Male Heterosexuality in Law', *Social and Legal Studies*, 1992, vol 1, p 543; O'Donovan, op cit, 1993, pp 65–73. See also M. Thomson, 'Viagra Nation: Sex and the Prescribing of Familial Masculinity', *Law, Culture, Humanities*, 2006, vol 2, p 259.

[94] For example N. Fielding, 'Cop Cantine Culture' in T. Newburn and E.A. Stanko (eds), *Just Boys Doing Business*, London: Routledge, 1994; R. Ryder, 'The Cult of Machismo', *Criminal Justice*, 1991, vol 9, p 12.

- in studies of offending by male youth, the dynamics of urban disorder and the relationship between multiple deprivation, law and family breakdown;[95]
- in work on legal education, legal academics and the university law school as a gendered institution as well as, more recently, the changing nature of Higher Education;[96]
- in numerous accounts of men, families and parenting,[97] in research on youth, schooling and the educational underachievement of boys;[98]
- in research on men's experiences of crime,[99] whether as offenders or victims,[100] in studies of men in the prison system,[101] child protection,[102] the work of probation officers[103] and the interconnections of class, race, ethnicity and law;[104]

[95] B. Campbell, *Goliath: Britain's Dangerous Places*, London: Methuen, 1993. Contrast C. Murray, *The Emerging British Underclass*, London: IEA, 1990; also I. Taylor, 'The Political Economy of Crime' in M. Maguire, R. Morgan and R. Reiner (eds), *The Oxford Handbook of Criminology*, Oxford: OUP, 1994.

[96] See further chapter 2.

[97] See chapters 5, 6 and 7.

[98] D. Epstein, J. Elwood, V. Hey and J. Maw (eds), *Failing Boys: Issues in Gender and Achievement*, Buckingham: Open University Press, 1999;: M. O'Donnell and S. Sharpe, *Uncertain Masculinities: Youth, Ethnicity and Class in Contemporary Britain*, London: Routledge, 2000, ch 1; R. Collier, 'Masculinities', *Sociology*, 2002, vol 36, p 737.

[99] J. Goodey, 'Boys Don't Cry: Masculinities, Fear of Crime and Fearlessness', *British Journal of Criminology*, 1997, vol 37, p 401.

[100] T. Jefferson and P. Carlen (eds), *British Journal of Criminology*, 1996, vol 36; R. Collier, *Masculinities, Crime and Criminology: Men, Heterosexuality and the Criminal(ised) Other*, London: Sage, 1998; T. Jefferson, 'Masculinities and Crimes' in M. Maguire et al (eds), *The Oxford Handboook of Criminology*, 2nd edn, Oxford: Clarendon, 1997; J. W. Messerschmidt, *Masculinities and Crime: Critique, and Reconceptualization of Theory*, Lanham, MD: Rowman and Littlefield, 1993; Newburn and Stanko, op cit, 1994.

[101] Y. Jewkes, 'Men Behind Bars: Doing Masculinity as an Adaptation to Imprisonment', *Men and Masculinities*, 2005, vol 8(1), p 44; D. Sabo, T. Kupers and W. London (eds), *Prison Masculinities*, Philadelphia, PA: Temple University Press, 2001; C. Newton, 'Gender Theory and Prison Sociology: Using Theories of Masculinities to Interpret the Sociology of Prisons for Men', *Howard Journal of Criminal Justice*, 1994, vol 33, p 193; J. Sim, '"Tougher Than the Rest?" Men in Prison' in Newburn and Stanko op cit, 1994; R. Thurston, 'Are You Sitting Comfortably? Men's Storytellings, Masculinities, Prison Culture and Violence' in M. Mac an Ghaill (ed), *Understanding Masculinities*, Buckingham: Open University Press, 1996.

[102] J. Scourfield, *Gender and Child Protection*, London: Palgrave Macmillan, 2003.

[103] S. Holland and J. Scourfield, 'Managing Marginalized Masculinities: Men and Probation', *Journal of Gender Studies*, 2000, vol 9, p 199.

[104] In addition to work cited above, see P. Williams, 'Meditations on Masculinity' in M. Berger, B. Wallis and S. Watson (eds), *Constructing Masculinity*, New York: Routledge, 1995; J.T. Gibbs and J.R. Merighi, 'Young Black Males: Marginality, Masculinity and Criminality' in T. Newburn and E.A. Stanko, op cit, 1994; J. Goodey, 'Understanding Racism and Masculinity: Drawing on Research with Boys aged Eight to Sixteen', *International Journal of the Sociology of Law*, 1998, vol 26, p 393; D. Carbado (ed), *Black Men on Race, Gender and Sexuality*, New York: New York University Press, 1999.

- in studies of globalisation, international law, war and peace,[105] of men's apparently random violence towards others,[106] environmental crime,[107] drug use[108] and men's bodies and men's health,[109] health care law and reproduction.[110]
- in relation to law and censorship,[111] the legal regulation, and historical censure, of (homo)sexuality,[112] the heterosexuality of law,[113] sex offending and the legal construction of the 'paedophile',[114] the rule of law[115] and the political relationship between men and legal feminism;[116]
- and, finally, perhaps with more resonance and in greater volume than any other topic, in relation to the seemingly intractable problem of men's violence(s) against women, children, and other men, and the development of legal responses to such violence.[117]

[105] R.W. Connell, 'Globalization, Imperialism and Masculinities' in M. Kimmel, J. Hearn and R. W. Connell (eds), *Handbook of Men and Masculinities*, London: Sage, 2005; R.W. Connell, '"Arms and the Man": Using the New Research on Masculinity to Understand Violence and Promote Peace in the Contemporary World', paper for UNESCO expert group meeting on Male Roles and Masculinities in the Perspectives of a Culture of Peace, Oslo, 1997; Connell, op cit, 2002, ch 12.

[106] S. Jones, *Understanding Violent Crime*, Buckingham: Open University Press, 2000, pp 96–101; R. Collier, 'After Dunblane: Crime, Corporeality and the (Hetero)Sexing of the Bodies of Men', *Journal of Law and Society*, 1997, vol 24, p 177.

[107] N. Groombridge, 'Masculinities and Crimes Against the Environment', *Theoretical Criminology*, 1998, vol 2, p 248.

[108] M. Collinson, 'In Search of the High Life: Drugs, Crime, Masculinities and Consumption', *British Journal of Criminology*, 1996, vol 36 p 428.

[109] S. Robertson, *Understanding Men's Health: Masculinity, Identity and Well-being*, Buckingham: Open University Press, 2007; B. Featherstone, M. Rivett and J. Scourfield, *Working With Men in Health and Social Care*, London: Sage, 2007; J.E. Canaan, '"One Thing Leads to Another": Drinking, Fighting and Working Class Masculinities' in Mac an Ghaill (ed), op cit, 1996.

[110] S. Sheldon, '*Re*Conceiving Masculinity: Imagining Men's Reproductive Bodies in Law', *Journal of Law and Society*, 1999, vol 26(2), p 129; M. Thomson, *Endowed: Regulating the Male Sexed Body*, New York: Routledge, 2007.

[111] M. Heins, 'Masculinity, Sexism and Censorship Law' in Berger et al, op cit, 1995.

[112] L. Moran, *The Homosexual(ity) of Law*, London: Routledge, 1996.

[113] R.Collier, 'Straight Families, Queer Lives' in Stychin and Herman (eds), op cit, 2000.

[114] R. Collier, 'The Paedophile, the Dangerous Individual and the Criminal Law: Reconfigurations of the Public/Private Divide' in C. Brants and P. Alldridge (eds), *Personal Autonomy, the Private Sphere and the Criminal Law: A Comparative Study*, Oxford: Hart, 2001.

[115] K. Thomas, '"Masculinity", "The Rule of Law" and Other Legal Fictions' in Berger et al, op cit, 1995.

[116] Halewood, op cit, 2005; N. Levit, 'Feminism for Men: Legal Ideology and the Construction of Maleness', *UCLA Law Review*, 1996, vol 43(4), p 1073.

[117] For example, J. Hearn, *The Violences of Men*, London: Sage 1998; J. Kersten, 'Culture, Masculinities and Violence Against Women', *British Journal of Criminology*, 1996, vol 36, p 381. See, generally J. Archer (ed), *Male Violence*, London: Routledge, 1994; S.E. Hatty, *Masculinity, Violence and Culture*, Thousand Oaks, CA: Sage, 2000; L. H. Bowker (ed), *Masculinities and Violence*, Thousand Oaks, CA: Sage, 1998.

It is impossible to summarise all of the themes contained within such a varied literature. It is necessary, however, by way of indicating the kinds of arguments deployed, and the overarching theoretical frameworks adopted, to look more closely at the ways in which ideas about masculinity have been seen as 'constructed' or otherwise constituted within law. Three main themes are of particular importance in delineating the contours of the engagement with the 'man of law' in this work. Each theme tracks to questions about masculinity contained within feminist legal scholarship, and will be explored in more detail, challenged and further unpacked across the specific legal contexts and areas discussed in the following chapters.

Law, autonomy and the masculine subject

First, an individualised notion of autonomy, central to liberal conceptions of the self,[118] has been associated with a set of beliefs and assumptions about the nature of masculinity. This can be seen in both feminist legal scholarship and the critical study of masculinities in the depiction of a model of autonomy based upon a historical separation of men from areas of social life connected to the affective domain, to relations of vulnerability, care, dependency and personal life (on which see below). The autonomous subject has been marked, Martha Fineman has argued in the area of Family Law,[119] by gendered ideas of self-sufficiency and moral independence, self-governance and liberty, each theme central to Western political culture and embodying culturally encoded (as masculine) ideas about the nature of this 'self-fashioning individual', a figure 'in control' of their lives. As we shall see in this book, however, such an ideal of gendered autonomy may, in some important respects, and increasingly, ill-fit aspects of dominant political and cultural ideas about, and the realities of, men's practices. This is an issue of particular significance in relation to policy interventions around men in the areas of work, parenting and families considered in chapters 5, 6 and 7. If a gendered dualism has been a key part of the 'sexual contract',[120] and the historical entrenching of sexual divisions[121] in law, developments around gender neutrality, gender convergence and equality are, I shall suggest in this book, playing a role in the creation of a new set of ideas around men and masculinities. This is a move with significant implications for understandings of men's role in relation to diverse social practices pertaining to law.[122]

Studies of law and masculinities have also questioned the ideas about male subjectivity (what it means to 'be' a man) enmeshed with this model of the autonomous subject. In accounts of heterosexuality, parenthood and family

---

[118] J. Raz, *The Morality of Freedom*, Oxford, OUP, 1986: R. Dworkin, *Life's Dominion*, London: Harper Collins, 1993.

[119] M. Fineman, *The Autonomy Myth*, New York: The New Press, 2004.

[120] C. Pateman, *The Sexual Contract*, Stanford, CA: Stanford University Press, 1988.

[121] O'Donovan, op cit, 1985.

[122] Fineman, op cit, 2004, p 195.

practices,[123] for example, socio-legal scholars have unpacked and challenged the political, practical consequences of a set of assumptions about men's physical and emotional distance from children, child care and associated ideas of dependency and vulnerability.[124] The 'flip-side' of an individualised autonomy has been an effacing of men's (but not women's) situated[125] and interconnected lives. This theme is particularly evident in recent debates around the development of a feminist ethic of care, work that has sought to question, and expose the contingency of, the public/private divide and challenge the political consequences of a historical erasure of men from understandings of the dependencies of social life.[126] In chapter 7 I will explore how these debates have played out within a highly polarised legal policy debate about men's 'rights talk' and 'care talk' in the area of post-separation parenting.

Embodiment

Second, and interlinked to this model of the gendered autonomous subject, studies in law have sought to explore the embodied nature of masculinity.[127] Work has drawn on sociological studies of the body and, in particular, the feminist philosophical engagements with corporeality that emerged in the wake of postmodernism and queer theory.[128] In relation to both Family and Criminal Law, for example, it has been argued that the penis has frequently appeared in law as somehow subject to a man's rational thought and control. The vagina, in contrast, has tended to be presented as a space, as an always-searchable absence.[129] Related assumptions have been made around the idea of there being a natural sexual 'fit' between the (sexed) bodies of women and

---

[123] On the latter, D. Morgan, *Family Connections: An Introduction to Family Studies*, Oxford: Polity, 1996.

[124] See for example R. Collier and S. Sheldon, *Fragmenting Fatherhood: A Socio-Legal Study*, Oxford: Hart, 2008; R. Collier, 'Male Bodies, Family Practices' in A. Bainham, S. Day Sclater and M. Richards (eds), *Body Lore and Laws*, Oxford: Hart, 2002; R. Collier, 'A Hard Time to be a Father?: Law, Policy and Family Practices', *Journal of Law and Society*, 2001, vol 28, p 520; R. Collier, 'In Search of the "Good Father": Law, Family Practices and the Normative Reconstruction of Parenthood', *Studies in Law, Politics and Society*, 2001, vol 22 (A. Sarat and P. Ewick (eds)), p 133; cf S. Coltrane, *Family Man: Fatherhood, Housework and Gender Equity*, New York: Oxford University Press, 1996.

[125] W. Marsiglio, K. Roy and G. Litton Fox (eds), *Situated Fathering: A Focus on Physical and Social Spaces*, Lanham, MD: Rowman & Littlefield, 2005.

[126] Fineman, op cit, 1995.

[127] Thomson, op cit, 2007; A. Hyde, *Bodies of Law*, Princeton, NJ: Princeton University Press, 1997; also J. Bridgeman and S. Millns (eds), *Law and Body Politics: Regulating the Female Body*, Aldershot: Ashgate 1995.

[128] E. Grosz, *Volatile Bodies: Towards a Corporeal Feminism*, Allen & Unwin, St Leonards, NSW, 1994; E. Grosz and E. Probyn (eds), *Sexy Bodies: Strange Carnalities of Feminism*, London: Routledge, 1995; M. Gatens, *Imaginary Bodies; Ethics, Power and Corporeality*, London: Routledge, 1996.

[129] Hyde, op cit, 1997, p 172.

men, with notions of male sexual activity and female passivity informing the determination of what does, and does not, constitute a legal marriage.[130] In accounts from the field of Criminal Law, the liberal, rational individual has been depicted not simply as a sexed, autonomous and masculine subject, as above. This is also a peculiarly *dis*embodied being; a figure bounded, constituted *as* male, in ways which are dependant on a separation from other men and also, crucially, on the establishment of (hierarchical) differences from women.[131]

Such arguments exemplify a more general theme in the literature regarding how, whilst women's bodies often appear in law as incomprehensible, fluid, *un*bounded and defined by 'openings and absences', the bodies of men, Sally Sheldon[132] has suggested, more often appear marked by ideas of bodily absence and physical disengagement than any sense of corporeal presence.[133] For Sheldon, like Michael Thomson, men's safe, stable and bounded bodies signify a far more tangential and contingent relation to gestation, fertility and reproduction.[134] In work by Lois Bibbings, similarly, the bodies of men have been positioned in particular ways in relation to culturally contingent ideas about masculinity and, more specifically, a condoning of intra-male violence within the criminal law and much of popular culture.[135] Other work has questioned the encoding of men's bodies as (hetero)sexual across diverse legal contexts;[136] the associations these bodies bring with them in terms of normative beliefs about parenting, employment, 'family life', authority, rationality, emotion and so forth.

Masculinities, policy and practice

Third, finally, and alongside these engagements with the gendered nature of autonomy and embodiment, the study of the relationship between masculinity and law has transcended the analysis of legal texts, be they cases or statutes. A questioning of masculinity has also occurred at the level of legal policy and practice, with a growing body of work exploring how lawyers and

---

[130] As in work cited above n 93.

[131] N. Naffine, 'Possession: Erotic Love in the Law of Rape', *Modern Law Review*, 1994, vol 57, p 10. See also Thomson, op cit, 2007.

[132] Sheldon, op cit, 1999. Note also S. Sheldon, 'Sperm Bandits: Birth Control Fraud and the Battle of the Sexes', *Legal Studies*, 2001, vol 21, p 460.

[133] Feminism, Sheldon, op cit, 1999 suggests, has produced a rich scholarship representing the female body as leaky, volatile, permeable and so forth. What it has not done, however, is pay the same kind of attention to the (implicit) contrasted construction of the male body as bounded, stable and (it is assumed) non-permeable; C.Waldby, 'Destruction: Boundary Erotics and Refigurations of the Heterosexual Male Body' in Grosz and Probyn (eds), op cit, 1995; Thomson, op cit, 2007.

[134] See Collier and Sheldon, op cit, 2008, ch 3.

[135] L. Bibbings, 'Boys Will be Boys: Masculinity and Offences Against the Person' in J. Bridgman and D. Monk (eds), *Feminist Perspectives on Criminal Law*, London: Cavendish, 2000.

[136] Thomson, op cit, 2007; Collier, op cit, 1998.

other legal actors 'talk about men' across diverse areas of legal regulation.[137] What metaphors, similes and other verbal constructions, for example, cumulatively form a 'discourse of masculinity' within the legal field (let us say, the solicitor's office or the prison, the courtroom or the classroom)?[138] What are the social effects of such a discourse? In the deployment of masculinity within some feminist accounts of legal practices and institutions, we have seen above, work has questioned how legal cultures become gendered in such a way as to exclude or marginalise individuals and social groups. How, for example, have men been systematically *de*sexed, evacuated from a distinctively gendered (as well as classed, raced) presence in law in particular settings?[139] How do legal workplaces, such as the firms of solicitors discussed in chapters 4 and 6 of this book, come to be perceived as masculine, and what are the implications for the women, and men, who work in or otherwise encounter them?[140]

The study of law and masculinity cannot be confined, in other words, to the analysis of legal texts and/or discourse, and socio-legal research has increasingly engaged with questions about gender and social policy, work that will inform discussion in chapters 5 and 7 of men and parenting. Sociological debates, in particular, have explored policy issues in the context of an idea of masculine crisis or crisis of masculinity,[141] a theme that has become emblematic of wider concerns and anxieties about the meaning of social, economic, cultural and technological change, and an issue that will run throughout this book. Masculinity has had a powerful, symbolic significance within these debates about law reform, we shall see, serving as a cipher for social tensions, not least around shifting relations between men and women (as well as, I would add, children). The result is a cultural and political questioning of masculinity that, in terms of diverse legal policy debates, it would seem at times, has left no aspect of social life unaffected.[142]

Where does this leave us? The studies of law and masculinity discussed above suggest that there are multiple constructions of the gender of men available to legal and other speakers in ways that are neither 'natural' nor limited by biology. What we are dealing with is, rather, a set of conversations about men and

---

[137] This issue is discussed further in chapters 2, 3, 4 and 6 in the context of legal education and the legal profession.

[138] Compare Hyde, op cit, 1997.

[139] Collier, op cit, 1998; Thornton, op cit, 1993; Thomson, op cit, 2007.

[140] See further L. McDowell, *Capital Culture: Gender at Work in the City*, Oxford: Blackwell, 1997.

[141] A. Clare, *On Men: Masculinity in Crisis*, London: Chatto & Windus, 2000; contrast S. Faludi, *Stiffed: The Betrayal of the Modern Man*, London: Chatto & Windus, 1999; Brittan, op cit, 1989, pp 25–36; Hearn, op cit, 1987, pp 16–31; Connell, op cit, 1987, pp 183–86; Carrigan et al, op cit, 1985, p 598.

[142] Capturing a nature of these debates in the UK media, 'Men Uncovered: The State They're In', 'Lovers and Fighters, fathers and sons, prophets and liars and more confused than ever', and 'The British male examined – what is he good for?', *The Observer*, 27 June 2004.

masculinity understood as discursive creations approached in legal studies from within an overarching project of denaturalisation or deconstruction. Much legal work has sought to 'defetishise' the law and engage in analyses whereby the given is shown not to be natural but a 'socially and historically constituted, and thus changeable reality'.[143] Allied (albeit somewhat contentiously) to the field of critical legal scholarship, this work on masculinities and law has built on, and added another dimension to, the well-documented socio-legal critiques of the 'intellectual strait-jacket' of traditional doctrinal positivism.[144] The explicit interdisciplinarity of this scholarship, meanwhile, has been 'aimed ... at breaking down the closure of legal discourse and at critically articulating the internal relationships it constructs with other discourses'.[145]

To summarise my argument at this stage: readings of the masculinities of legal cases, statutes, utterances and representations have informed discussion of law and gender across a now wide range of books, journal articles and research reports. An engagement with masculinity has been part of an attempt to disturb traditional legal categories and focus on the 'hidden gender' of law.[146] For some writers, drawing on analytic techniques from postmodernism, this has been aligned with a questioning of the 'phallogocentrism' of legal discourse itself, the fusing of a masculine and, at times, heterosexual imperative with the fixing of a sign/signifier in a patriarchal structure of power/knowledge.[147] Across diverse legal contexts, signifying practices in the legal field have then been seen to function in such a way as to promote certain discursive and political ends. For others, meanwhile, an attempt has been made to challenge how ideas of sex difference come to signify hierarchically within particular legal policy settings. The result is a collection of readings, drawing on different approaches and methods, that has explored the ways in which men – their masculinities, bodies, subjectivities, rights, responsibilities and duties – have been constructed within legal discourse.

I have conveyed thus far something of the way in which masculinity has been approached in law, the kinds of areas in which the concept has been utilised and the arguments that have been made. A question remains unanswered, however, one that I wish to address in the second part of this introductory chapter – precisely *how* has 'masculinity' been conceptualised in this work? Each of the readings of masculinity and law discussed above tells us something about how law constructs, sees or otherwise produces notions of men's

[143] S. Benhabib, *Critique, Norm and Utopia: A Study of the Foundations of Critical Theory*, New York: Columbia University Press, 1986, p 47; S. Benhabib, *Situating the Self*, London: Routledge, 1997.

[144] Collier, op cit, 1995.

[145] Goodrich, op cit, 1986, p 212.

[146] R. Graycar and J. Morgan, *The Hidden Gender of Law*, Sydney: Federation Press, 2nd edn, 2002.

[147] Smart, op cit, 1989, p 86. Phallocentric culture has been taken as referring to 'the needs of the masculine imperative which receive a cultural response': O'Donovan, op cit, 1993, p 5.

gender. What this work has tended not to do, however, is provide us with an account of lived practices and the everyday experiences of women and men themselves (and, importantly, we shall see, children). In addressing this question, it is necessary to look more closely at the conceptual underpinning of this scholarship and, in particular, at how a reading of, say, the 'masculinities of legal discourse' might relate or connect to the 'real lives' of men and women. It is here – in relation to this question of what men *do* – that, I wish to argue, engagements with masculinity in legal study have rested upon a number of questionable assumptions. Developments taking place in other disciplines, alluded to above, have interrogated the concept of masculinity more closely and critically than in law and, in the remainder of this chapter, I will explore the implications of this work for developing the study of law, men and gender.

Rethinking men, law and gender: beyond the limits of masculinity

Two main sociological or social-psychological perspectives have shaped the engagement with masculinity within Anglophone jurisprudence. What marks out each as different from the functionalist, positivist frameworks that informed the earlier sociological studies discussed above is a two-fold rejection of the once influential sex role theory and an attempt to take seriously the insights of feminism and engage with the social power of men. The first perspective, informing both feminist work and the critical study of men and masculinities, has tended to focus on one key, recurring, and at times seemingly ubiquitous concept – hegemonic masculinity, an idea associated with a structured model of gender power.[148]

Hegemonic masculinity: law and structured action

The origins of hegemonic masculinity can be traced to the publication of the Australian sociologist R. W. Connell's book *Gender and Power*.[149] This work, a systematic sociological theory of gender, in a sense 'kick-started' the engagement with masculinity in legal study, just as it did in other disciplines. Connell's thesis has been subject to extensive discussion and analysis and the significance of his work for the study of masculinity, including pro-feminist activism, cannot be underestimated. Importantly, Connell, writing either alone or with others, has recently modified his earlier depiction of hegemonic masculinity in a number of ways, responding to critics whilst elaborating the idea in relation to new emerging issues, including an engagement with the global politics of men and masculinities.[150] In this section, I will trace how the idea of

---

148 Whitehead, op cit, 2002, pp 84–99, p 103.
149 Connell, op cit, 1987. Also Connell, 1995, Connell, 2000.
150 R. W. Connell and J. W. Messerschmidt, 'Hegemonic Masculinity: Rethinking the Concept', *Gender and Society*, 2005, vol 19(6), p 829; R. W. Connell, 'Globalization, Imperialism and Masculinities' in M. Kimmel, J. Hearn and R. W. Connell (eds), *Handbook of Men and Masculinities*, London: Sage, 2005; R. W. Connell, 'On Hegemonic Masculinity and Violence: Response to Jefferson and Hall', *Theoretical Criminology*, 2002, vol 6(1), p 89. See further below.

hegemonic masculinity has informed the study of law discussed above, focusing in particular on the strengths, and weaknesses, of the concept in this area.

Hegemonic masculinity has been used by Connell and those who have followed this analysis of gender and power to address what by 1987 had become a pressing issue both within legal studies and across the social sciences and humanities. That is, in ways similar to the question posed by Carol Smart in 1984 about the relationship between men, law and gender (above, p 14), how might it be possible to 'conceptualise relations among men, especially when class and ethnic and generational relations are included?'[151] How, in other words, can the diversity of men's lives be addressed whilst at the same time recognising the existence of a culturally exalted form of (heterosexual) masculinity and the structural nature of men's power? For Connell the answer lay in hegemonic masculinity, a 'configuration of gender practice ... which guarantees (or is taken to guarantee) the dominant position of men',[152] something 'always constructed in relation to various subordinated masculinities as well as in relation to women'.[153] Masculinities are defined by Connell as configurations of practice structured by gender relations, inherently historical in 'their making and remaking ... a potential process affecting the balance of interests in society and the direction of change'.[154]

Central to hegemonic masculinity is the idea that masculinities can be ordered hierarchically and that gender relations are constituted through three inter-related structures: what Connell terms 'labour', 'power' and 'cathexis'.[155] What orderliness exists between them is not that of a fixed system but a 'unity of historical composition'. What is produced is a gender order, 'a historically constructed pattern of power relations between men and women and definitions of femininity and masculinity'.[156] The development of a progressive politics of masculinity, Connell suggests, is a project that cannot be confined to the level of the personal (be it matters of choice, conditioning, human nature and so forth). Masculinities are, rather, relational, embedded in the gender regime or social structure of a society at particular historical moments, always, in marked contrast to essentialist accounts, in a dynamic process of constitution: 'structures identified by analysis ... exist only in solution, they are not absolutely prior to the subject but themselves are always in process of formation. Social and personal life are practices.'[157] As Lynne Segal concisely noted, masculinity is here understood:

---

[151] T. Jefferson, 'Theorizing Masculine Subjectivity' in Newburn and Stanko (eds), op cit, 1994, p 15.
[152] Connell, 1995, p 77.
[153] Connell, op cit, 1987, p 183.
[154] Connell, op cit, 1995, p 44.
[155] Connell, op cit, 1987.
[156] Connell, op cit, 1987, at pp 98–99.
[157] Middleton, op cit, 1992, p 153.

as transcending the personal, as a heterogeneous set of ideas, constructed around assumptions of social power which are lived out and reinforced, or perhaps denied and challenged, in multiple and diverse ways within a whole social system in which relations of authority, work and domestic life are organised, in the main, along hierarchical gender lines.[158]

Following Gramsci,[159] any resulting hegemony, importantly, is always incomplete.[160] The politics of gender (and, in this case, of gender and law), Connell argues, arise from the always-contested nature of men's power and the ever-present possibility of resistance and contestation. It is a key feature of this argument, in short, that hegemonic masculinity is never finally closed, fixed or resolved.

It is not difficult to see how law and legal regulation is of central importance in the reproduction of any such gender regime or organisation of gender. Challenging patriarchy entails, as part of contesting men's dominance (in the State, the family, the professions, the military, in relation to men's violence and so forth) an engagement with law.[161] Equally, within sociological analyses of 'the gendered society',[162] law has had a pivotal role in the reproduction of structural, systemic inequality. Nor is it difficult, bearing in mind the open-ended nature of law of increasing concern to feminist legal scholars by the late 1980s,[163] to see the potential usefulness of the concept of hegemonic masculinity for a discipline struggling to make sense of its own contestations around gender, power and resistance. In the analyses of law discussed above, we find numerous references to how law might 'reproduce', 'assert' or 'privilege' a distinctive hegemonic masculine form interlinked, in Connell's schema, with the interests of all men. In much of this work,[164] an association is made, we have seen, between aspects of 'doing law' and 'doing masculinity'.[165] Similarly, to take the example from Criminology whereby men have been seen as 'accomplishing' masculinity by engaging in crime,[166] a particularly fruitful area of study over the past decade, hegemonic masculinity has been enmeshed with the workings of the legal system in complex ways. At a conceptual level, meanwhile, each of the ideas of autonomy, rationality and embodiment discussed above, culturally associated with the 'man question' in feminist legal scholarship, can be read as further manifestations of a dominant form of hegemonic masculinity in law, a particular feature of the benchmark 'man of law'.

---

[158] Segal, op cit, 1999, p 288.
[159] A. Gramsci, *Selection From the Prison Notebooks*, London: Lawrence and Wishart, 1971.
[160] Connell, op cit, 1987, p 184.
[161] Connell, op cit, 2005, p 229.
[162] Kimmel, op cit, 2000.
[163] Smart, op cit, 1989.
[164] I certainly do not wish to exclude much of my own previous work in this area from this critique: see below.
[165] Smart, op cit, 1989, p 18.
[166] Messerschmidt, op cit, 1993. For discussion Collier, op cit, 1998; Howe, op cit, 2009, esp ch 4.

The structured action model from within which the idea of hegemonic masculinity has been most commonly articulated has been rightly heralded as an 'extremely important'[167] 'significant advance'[168] in theorising masculinity. Hegemonic masculinity is, in a sense, at the very heart of contemporary masculinity theory.[169] As an attempt to integrate the complexities of race, class, gender and sexuality, and to take structural patterns of inequality seriously, Connell's work paved the way for numerous studies adopting a broadly social constructionist approach to gender[170] across disciplines, including law. Drawing on diverse traditions in sociological thought,[171] Connell's work highlights the notion of a multiply structured field of gender relations, a terrain marked by hegemonic and subordinated masculinities.[172] If we look more closely, however, it leaves a number of important questions unanswered, and the concept has itself been subjected to extensive critique.[173]

What we do not find here, for example, is an attempt to engage with or theorise the subjectivity of individual men, or explore why some men 'turn to' certain kinds of behaviour, or invest in particular (masculine) subject positions, whilst others do not. In the case of those men who transgress the law and accomplish masculinity in the form of crime, for example, it is now 'widely recognized most crime is committed by highly specific sub-groups of the category "men",'[174] men who are often also the principal victims of crime.[175] What tends not to be asked in this account, however, is why it is 'only particular men from a given class or race background (usually only a minority)' who come to identify with the crime option, whilst others identify with other

---

[167] Hood-Williams, op cit, 2001, p 53.

[168] Jefferson, op cit, 1996, p 340.

[169] Evidenced by the sheer volume of work that has been produced on hegemonic masculinity; for a useful discussion and overview see Ashe, op cit, 2007, pp 143–57.

[170] Kahn, op cit, 2009, ch 11.

[171] Informed, for example, by the work of Giddens: A. Giddens, *Modernity and Self-Identity*, Cambridge: Polity, 1991; A. Giddens, *New Rules of Sociological Method*, London: Harper Collins, 1976, p 121 (see Messerschmidt, op cit, 1993, p 77) also J. Acker, 'The Problem with Patriarchy' *Sociology*, 1989, vol 23, p 235, and C. West and D. H. Zimmerman, 'Doing Gender', *Gender and Society*, 1987, vol 1, p 125; S. Fenstermaker, C. West and D. Zimmerman, 'Gender Inequality: New Conceptual Terrain' in R. L. Blumberg (ed), *Gender, Family and Economy*, Newbury Park, CA: Sage, 1991; E. Goffman, *Gender Advertisements*, New York: St Martin's Press, 1979.

[172] Jefferson, op cit, 2002; Jefferson, op cit, 1997.

[173] See further, for analysis of this concept, R. Howson, *Challenging Hegemonic Masculinity*, London: Routledge, 2005; C. Beasley, 'Rethinking Hegemonic Masculinity in a Globalising World' *Men and Masculinities*, 2008, vol 11(1), p 86; M. Donaldson, 'What is Hegemonic Masculinity?', *Theory and Society*, 1993, vol 22, p 643; S. Whitehead, 'Hegemonic Masculinity Revisited', *Gender, Work and Organization*, 1999, vol 6(1), p 58; T. Jefferson, 'Subordinating Hegemonic Masculinity', *Theoretical Criminology*, 2002, vol 6(1), p 63; D. Demetrious, 'Connell's Concept of Hegemonic Masculinity: A Critique', *Theory and Society*, 2001, vol 30, p 337; A. Petersen, 'Research on Men and Masculinities: Some Implications of Recent Theory for Future Work', *Men and Masculinities*, 2003, vol 6(1), p 54.

[174] Hood-Williams, op cit, 2001, p 43.

[175] Hall, op cit, 2002; Collier, op cit, 1998.

resources to accomplish masculinity.[176] This raises a broader question. If masculinities are 'offered up' for all men within a specific socio-cultural, structural location, why do men choose one, and not another, masculine identity? To turn to an example that will be considered in depth later in this book, why might one separated father, let us say, identify with a strand of fathers' rights activism and a commitment to values associated with hegemonic masculinity, whilst another man does not (chapter 7)? How adequate is hegemonic masculinity in explaining the complexity of men's diverse engagements with law? How, in short, does individual life history and personal biography impact on any such 'choice'? (See below.)

It can be argued that, in the terms of Connell's thesis, most men regardless of their socio-economic group 'do' a masculine gender without resorting to certain kinds of behaviour (they just 'do' it in different ways). Equally, that all men derive a 'patriarchal dividend' from the 'shock-troops' of those who most clearly relate to, embody and reproduce hegemonic masculine values.[177] Yet it is difficult to see within structured action theory any account of why this should be the case,[178] and whether hegemonic masculinity, necessarily, does benefit men. What happens, as it were, to the 'costs' of 'being a man', perceptions of which have, I shall suggest in this book, been significantly reshaped by the rise of gender neutrality, ideals of egalitarianism and complex social, legal and cultural shifts?[179] In the reproduction of the normative hegemonic masculine ideal there is, rather, a certain degree of rigidity in how men are seen to accomplish or aspire to the attributes of the dominant masculinity. At times structure would seem to constrain social practice to such a degree that it is difficult to see where the contestation and resistance, the 'historically mobile'[180] nature of masculinity central to Connell's original thesis, fits in.

This relates to a more general question about how the (gendered) social subject has been theorised in this approach. For all the declarations within much socio-legal scholarship that law and legal discourse are implicated in how distinctive masculinities are constituted or constructed, it is extremely difficult to grasp the process by which this takes place. At least, beyond the making of generalised statements that law somehow 'shapes our lives' or is part of a 'discursive context' of 'gendered subjectivication'. What tends to be deployed, rather, on closer examination, is a model of men as somehow inherently reflexively rational, self-interested beings; men the social action of whom then relates, in a distinctly deterministic way, to the cultural norms associated with hegemonic masculinity, as above. Yet what remains unclear is precisely what these cultural norms are, and how they are understood within grounded contexts.[181] Can it be assumed

---

[176] Jefferson, op cit, 1997, p 341.
[177] Connell, op cit, 1995, pp 79–80.
[178] See further discussion in Jefferson, op cit, 2002; Jefferson and Carlen, op cit, 1996.
[179] Although this has been addressed: Connell and Messerschmidt, op cit, 2005; see further below.
[180] Connell, op cit, 1995, p 77.
[181] See, for example, the argument of Collier, op cit, 1998.

(if it ever could) that a form of masculinity is somehow unproblematically 'inherited' by individuals? It could be argued that the processes involved in 'being masculine' are, in many respects, profoundly contingent and problematic, defined by a range of consumer practices (see, for example, the discussion of male lawyers and corporate lifestyle in chapters 4 and 6), created within a social context marked by a multiplicity and diversity of choice.[182] Further, if 'masculinity' floats free from the sexed bodies of women and men, as suggested in some accounts informed by postmodernism and queer theory, what are the implications for feminism of dislocating masculinity from the (sexed) bodies of men?

Certainly, an overarching matrix of, say, compulsory heterosexuality,[183] or allegiance to specific gender(ed) cultural norms, may be experienced by individuals within some social contexts as framing choice to the degree that, for some, it could be seen as no choice at all. Yet it does not follow that the values associated with hegemonic masculinity are then seen as unambiguously positive attributes for men, values that, for a host of (unexplored) psychological imperatives, are to be desired, achieved or accomplished. Nor, as noted, can it be assumed that all men are beneficiaries of such a model of masculinity and gender relations.[184] Autobiographical, empirical and theoretical work on men in the fields of sociology, psychology, history and literature would suggest that the relationships and investments individual men have to, and in, gendered categories are far more complex.[185]

In reflecting on the above arguments, some critics have suggested that hegemonic masculinity entails a kind of structural determinism,[186] an idea that Connell (writing with Messerschmidt) has 'flatly rejected'.[187] Nonetheless, the structured model of gendered power, it has been argued, does appear to hold in place a normative masculine gender (hegemonic masculinity, to which is then assigned a range of usually undesirable/negative characteristics) whilst, at the same time, imposing 'an a priori theoretical/conceptual frame on the psychological complexity of men's behaviour'.[188] What continues to be evaded in such an account, however, is 'the ways in which each act of aggression or kindness, sensitivity or independence, self-sacrifice or selfishness is encoded at particular moments and locations as a "masculine" or "feminine" attribute' (see below).[189]

---

[182] That is, the material conditions of advanced capitalism have themselves given rise to new channels of communication, knowledge and experience, new and diverse gendered identities and subjects – new ways of 'doing' gender, doing masculinity, of being masculine, an issue discussed in more detail in chapter 4 in the context of the legal profession: Giddens, op cit, 1991, p 80.

[183] A. Rich, *Compulsory Heterosexuality and Lesbian Existence*, London: Onlywomen Press, 1981.

[184] Hall, op cit, 2002; Dowd, op cit, 2008.

[185] Note for example Wetherell and Edley, op cit, 1999. Also D. Jackson, *Unmasking Masculinity: A Critical Autobiography*, London: Routledge, 1990.

[186] Whitehead, op cit, 2002.

[187] Connell and Messerschmidt, op cit, 1993, p 843.

[188] Collier, op cit, 1998, p 22.

[189] Collier, op cit, 1998, p 22.

This means that masculinity can very easily appear, at once, as a primary and underlying cause or source of a social effect (masculinity *causes* men to act in a certain way); and, simultaneously, as something which results from certain social actions (masculinity is produced *by* men acting in a certain way). This is, as has been observed in the context of debates about crime, something of a tautologous proposition.[190] What, ultimately, is it in hegemonic masculinity that causes certain kinds of behaviour? In an attempt to address these problems an alternative perspective towards theorising masculinity has emerged in recent years. A concern of this work has been to engage precisely with the complexity and multi-layered nature of this masculine social subject.

Law, discourse and the (masculine) psychosocial subject

Whilst a theme that has marked debates within Criminology, in particular, over the past decade, there has also emerged within legal studies, as in the sociology of men and masculinities, a growing move to explore the relationship between the social and psychological processes that inform men's experience of masculinity.[191] It is an approach, building on the critique of the structured action model, as above, that has been presented as an explicit attempt to take the psychic dimensions of (masculine) subjectivity seriously. Whilst it is not possible to do justice here to the complexity of the many substantive analyses that have been produced in the area, nor the complex groundings of one strand of this work within contemporary psychoanalysis,[192] it is possible to trace some of the key characteristics of this development as they relate to readings of masculinities in legal studies. It is my aim in what follows to outline the implications of this work for developing understanding of how masculinity might be approached within law, and to consider questions arising about the 'man of law' that will run throughout each of the following chapters.

---

[190] As the criminologist Sandra Walklate has observed, 'not only does this reflect a failure to resolve fully the tendency towards universalism, it can also be read as tautological': Walklate, op cit, 1995, p 181.

[191] Wetherell and Edley, op cit, 1999; Kahn, op cit, 2009, ch 10. In the area of crime, and in addition to work cited above, note for example, the work of T. Jefferson, 'For a Psychosocial Criminology' in K. Carrington and R Hogg (eds), *Critical Criminologies: An Introduction*, Cullompton, Devon: Willan, 2002; T. Jefferson, 'The Tyson Rape Trial: The Law, Feminism and Emotional Truth', *Social and Legal Studies*, 1997, vol 6, p 281; T. Jefferson, '"Muscle", "Hard Men" and "Iron" Mike Tyson: Reflections on Desire, Anxiety and the Embodiment of Masculinity', *Body and Society*, 1998, vol 4, p 103. See also D. Gadd, 'Masculinities and Violence Against Female Partners', *Social and Legal Studies*, 2002, p 61; D. Gadd, 'Masculinities, Violence and Defended Psycho-Social Subjects', *Theoretical Criminology*, 2000, vol 4, p 429. For critique of this work see Howe, op cit, 2009.

[192] P. Adams, *The Emptiness of the Image: Psychoanalysis and Sexual Differences*, London: Routledge, 1995; N. Chodorow, *Femininities, Masculinities, Sexualities: Freud and Beyond*, Lexington, KY: Free Association, 1994; A. Elliot, *Psychoanalytic Theory: An Introduction*, Oxford: Blackwell, 1994.

This is a perspective that tends to draw on the concept of discourse rather than that of social structure.[193] It places centre-stage, that is, an engagement with the presentational forms of various 'masculine' performances, identities, corporeal enactments and so forth,[194] rejecting, in suitably postmodern fashion, the idea of there being a unitary rational male subject.[195] The aim is, rather, to develop a *social* understanding of the masculine *psyche*; one that might then, it is argued, shed light on men's behaviour across diverse contexts, including in relation to law and legal practice. For advocates of this approach there are clear advantages over structured action theory. It 'prises open' the possibility of making sense of the contradictions and difficulties that men may experience in the process of 'becoming masculine'.[196] Integrating questions of individual biography and life history, addressing the contingency and conflicted dimensions of lived experience and the contradictory aspects of masculinity within particular social settings, a handle is then given on the important question, noted above, of why some men do, and others do not, invest or engage in certain kinds of behaviour or subject positions.[197] Importantly, questions of social power remain. The focus of analysis shifts, however, to how a (non-unitary) 'inherently contradictory' subject comes (himself) to invest, whether consciously or unconsciously, in what are seen at particular historical moments and contexts as socially empowering discourses around masculinity.[198]

[193] Compare here the reading of Gutterman, op cit, 2001; Pease, op cit, 2000.

[194] Connecting in this respect to developments at the interface of feminist philosophical work and queer theory: Butler, op cit, 1993, Butler, op cit, 1990. For a useful overview, see D. Bell and G. Valentine, 'The Sexed Self: Strategies of Performance, Sites of Resistance' in S. Pile and N. Thrift (eds), *Mapping the Subject: Geographies of Cultural Transformation*, London: Routledge, 1995.

[195] Weedon, op cit, 1987; Middleton, op cit, 1992, pp 131–45; E. Grosz, 'A Note on Essentialism and Difference' in S. Unew (ed), *Feminist Knowledge: Critique and Construct*, London: Routledge, 1990, p 332; Grosz, op cit, 1994; Grosz and Probyn (eds), op cit, 1995.

[196] T. Jefferson, 'Crime, Criminology, Masculinity and Young Men' in A. Coote (ed), *Families, Children and Crime*, London: IPPR, 1994, pp 28–29.

[197] Whitehead, op cit, 2002, ch 7. See further, on issues of methodology, W. Hollway and T. Jefferson, *Doing Qualitative Research Differently: Free Association, Narrative and the Interview Method*, London: Sage, 2000. Contrast M. Andrews, S. Day Sclater, C. Squire and A. Treacher (eds), *Lines of Narrative: Psychosocial Perspectives*, London: Routledge, 2000; M. Andrews, S. Day Sclater, C. Squire and A. Treacher (eds), *The Uses of Narrative: Explorations in Sociology, Psychology and Cultural Studies*, London: Transaction, 2004.

[198] Whitehead, op cit, 2002. Jefferson's work in the area of crime and law, cited above, thus seeks to locate individuals within an array of 'discursive positionings'. Breaking with the traditionally asocial subject of psychology, and following on from the earlier work of Henriques et al (J. Henriques, W. Hollway, C. Urwin, C. Venn and V. Walkerdine, *Changing the Subject: Psychology, Social Regulation and Subjectivity*, London: Methuen, 1984; W. Hollway, *Subjectivity and Method in Psychology: Gender, Meaning and Science*, London: Sage, 1989), this draws on a psychoanalytic model which sees the emergence of masculine subjectivities as constituted through reference to a range of relational defence mechanisms (such as splitting, projection and introjection) interlinked to the contingent processes of early life 'object relating'. For a critique of this approach, contrast the reading of Howe, op cit, 2009, pp 136–42.

In contrast to those approaches that posit a seemingly omnipotent sense of the power of men, a power that correlates with a dominant form of (hegemonic) masculinity (a masculinity, ironically, that 'no man can ever embody'),[199] this perspective appears different. In some accounts, addressing the biography of an individual is seen as a way of facilitating a more complex recognition of 'the *reality*, and not simply the theoretical *rhetoric*, of relative power and powerlessness [as] experienced by different men throughout their lives'.[200] An overarching social structure or gender norm is no longer seen as accounting for what men do. It is, rather, in the complex interaction between this social realm and the individual psyche that the disposition or motivation towards particular action is located.[201] The result, advocates of the approach suggest, is a great advance politically on the (always, already) empowered masculine subject implicit within the structured model of gender power. At issue becomes the discursive strategies whereby men position themselves (or do not) in relation to gendered categories, the process whereby ideas about masculinities are then constituted, not pre-defined.[202] This perspective speaks to the possibility of developing a progressive politics of change by engaging with the complexity of men's experiences and social practices. Nonetheless, and notwithstanding these advantages over structured action theory, this work has itself not escaped criticism.

The charge that this is an approach which (to put it mildly) sits uneasily with the sociological moorings of much traditional law and society scholarship is one which can be easily dismissed. The very point is that much of the work on masculinity and law, like sociology, has failed to engage with the 'lived reality' and 'inner life' of the complex male subject in any meaningful way.[203] The well-established broader critique of psychoanalysis remains pertinent in this context, however, and the relation of some of these accounts to other psychoanalytic traditions, non-psychoanalytic psychology or, indeed, the idea that there might be multiple psychological mechanisms of subjective positioning is, at best, uncertain. We may choose to leave aside here the question of whether the more explicitly psychoanalytically informed strand of this work on masculinity has itself been informed by an unduly mechanistic model of personality formation.[204]

---

[199] Wetherell and Edley, op cit, 1999, p 337.

[200] J. Goodey, 'Biographical Lessons for Criminology', *Theoretical Criminology*, 2000, vol 4, p 489, my emphasis.

[201] Social action depicted, in effect, as the product of biographically contingent anxieties and desires: V. Walkerdine, 'Subject to Change Without Notice: Psychology, Postmodernity and the Popular' in S. Pile and N. Thrift (eds), *Mapping the Subject: Geographies of Cultural Transformation*, London: Routledge, 1995, p 327; V. Walkerdine (ed), *Challenging Subjects: Critical Psychology for a New Millenium*, London: Palgrave, 2002.

[202] Wetherell and Edley, op cit, 1999.

[203] C. Smart, *Personal Life*, Cambridge: Polity, 2007.

[204] R. W. Connell, 'Psychoanalysis on Masculinity' in H. Brod and M. Kaufman (eds), *Theorizing Masculinities*, Thousand Oaks, CA: Sage, 1994; cf I. Craib, 'Masculinity and Male Dominance', *The Sociological Review*, 1987, vol 35, p 721.

The argument remains, however, that although this approach offers a rich story for describing the effects of 'discourses of masculinity' in particular contexts, these remain, ultimately, just that: stories. It is difficult to see how the kinds of readings produced about the taking up of masculine subjectivity can ever be tested or proven in any meaningful way.[205] Are we reduced, effectively, to an 'all is discourse' position which, disavowing any outer reality, embraces a wholly semiotic account of the subject? One in which, as Connell has put it, 'so much emphasis on the signifier, the signified tends to vanish'?[206] What is lost is precisely the focus of Connell's attempt to engage with the concrete, grounded institutional spaces of masculinities, the social sites in which ideas take on meaning (such as a location in law). As John Hood-Williams has observed,[207] is it also not difficult to maintain simultaneously that there are many 'discourses of subjectivication' whereby masculine identities become attached to individuals; and, at the same time, maintain that the claims this approach is making are grounded in real, historically specific and irreducible psychological processes?[208]

The implications of this work on masculinity in terms of politics, policy and practice in relation to law are similarly uncertain. It is unclear, for example, how theorising subjectivity at the level of the individual can ever be an effective strategy in facilitating social change in a broader sense. Unpacking the heterogeneity of gendered identifications within and between categories of men, for example, has no clear relationship to developing concrete strategies that might engage with gender politics in terms of the 'social, economic, legal and political inequities' that exist 'between pluralist communities of men and women'.[209] As Connell has argued, reducing an analysis of masculine identities to psychological processes leads, rather, to individualistic therapeutic approaches that afford little grasp on these broader gender inequalities.[210]

In a recent feminist critique of one strand of this work on masculinity, as it has developed in the area of crime and criminology, Adrian Howe has powerfully argued that the psychosocial approach does more than simply misread feminism and the nature of feminist work informed by postmodernism, including work on law and crime. She identifies a troubling, profoundly regressive development here, one that is as politically problematic as it is methodologically suspect.[211]

---

[205] Or are we dealing here with little more than a reflection of the researcher's own projections (no more, or less, plausible than any other reading)? S. Frosh, *Sexual Difference: Masculinity and Psychoanalysis*, London: Routledge, 1994; S. Frosh, *For and Against Psychoanalysis*, London: Routledge, 2006. Contrast, again, the feminist critique of Howe, op cit, 2009.

[206] Connell, op cit, 1995, pp 50–51.

[207] Hood-Williams, op cit, 2001.

[208] A particular criticism levelled at the work of Jefferson. See Howe, op cit, 2009. Also Collier, op cit, 1998.

[209] Ashe, op cit, 2007, p 159.

[210] Connell, op cit, 2000, Connell, op cit, 1995.

[211] Howe, op cit, 2009, pp 136–42.

Noting the 'irony' of how, after decades of feminist work, it has been left to men to make us 'see men *as men*', Howe argues that the psychosocial approach in criminology has been informed by 'an extraordinary anti-feminist animus'.[212] This has resulted in the silencing of the violence(s) of men, the harms that men do, the materiality of men's practices (see further below). In contrast to the work of Connell and Hearn, where questions of social structure and, importantly, power have remained central to their analyses of masculinities, Howe identifies in much of this psychosocial work a profound lack of empathy with women and an individualistic focus of attention on the 'insecure, vulnerable, anxious' man.[213]

In noting that there is, as Connell has argued, no such thing as *the* hegemonic masculinity thesis,[214] both the structural model of gender power and the psychosocial approaches, I have suggested, engage, in different ways, with the question of how ideas of masculinity become problem*atised* at particular historical moments and contexts. Both can be seen, in the light of the above discussion, to have strengths and weaknesses. Each, importantly, stands in an uneasy relation to essentialist conceptualisations of and presuppositions about masculinity and it is therein, in the concept of masculinity itself, that I wish to argue in the concluding section, the problem in this area may ultimately be seen to lie. This is an issue with significant implications for the study of law and gender.

Concluding remarks

I have traced in this chapter the development of an engagement with the gender of men in legal studies, a body of literature that will shape the discussion throughout this book. Both feminist legal scholarship and the critical study of men and masculinities, I argued, have deployed the concept of masculinity in different ways in seeking to explain and understand diverse aspects of the relationship between law, men and gender. Focusing on two approaches that have dominated socio-legal accounts, the idea of hegemonic masculinity and the psychosocial study of masculinity, this work, I suggested, has a number of strengths and weaknesses. There is a tendency in relation to hegemonic masculinity, for example, to assume the existence of culturally dominant values that individual men are, for a host of (unexplored) psychological imperatives, assumed to desire, achieve or accomplish. Turning to psychosocial accounts of masculinities, we see that the formation of personal commitments to cultural norms is a more psychologically complex process than the model of structured action would allow. Yet what it is often difficult to see in the readings of masculinity then produced is how questions of social structure and, importantly, power 'fit in' – and, with it, how law might relate to concerns about men that, as Howe notes, have been central to feminist work

---

[212] Howe, ibid op cit, 2009, p 139, original emphasis.

[213] Howe, op cit, 2009, p 140.

[214] Connell, op cit, 2002.

around law.[215] At issue here, I shall suggest in these concluding remarks, is the problematic nature, if not inadequacy, of the concept of masculinity itself in approaching the idea of the gendered legal subject.

Turning personal[216]

In the readings to follow in this book, I will consider aspects of what has *not* been said in these debates about law, men and gender. Recent sociological scholarship has identified a tendency, in approaching this social subject, to 'miss out' on whole swathes of human experience. Located as part of an attempt to progress a cultural turn in sociology, Carol Smart has recently written of the need for a more complete account of human behaviour than that provided by the 'big narratives' of social theory. Smart's account is focused primarily on the discipline of sociology and, more specifically, the study of families. It is, however, of considerable relevance for legal study and this engagement with law and masculinity.

In her 2007 book *Personal Life*,[217] Smart questions a number of influential ideas about the interrelationship between gender, families and social change, highlighting the deficiencies of these approaches (for example, individualisation theory).[218] Seeking to move beyond the conceptual frameworks that, she suggests, have hitherto limited understanding in this area, *Personal Life* represents an important attempt to reappraise ideas about affect and emotion, memory, love and commitment, as well as to promote a renewed engagement with the significance of social class, race, ethnicity, intimacy and ideas of relationality and kinship. In so doing, she draws on work that has sought to question the long-standing neglect of feelings in the social sciences, the gendered conceptions of human nature and intellectual divisions of labour in which this approach has had its roots.

Each of these concerns bears upon the relationship between law, men and gender in the chapters to follow. Approaching the gendered dimensions of social experience in ways that do not lose track of the issues of power raised by feminism entails, I shall suggest, integrating an appreciation, at both a theoretical and political level, of the complexity and often contradictory nature of 'personal life'.[219] In

---

[215] Howe, op cit, 2009.

[216] This term is taken from a conference held in September 2009 in the UK: *Turning Personal: An Interdisciplinary Conference*, 16–17 September 2009, University of Manchester, an event seeking to explore 'how social research can incorporate more complex and multi-layered accounts of personal lives into academic writings and analyses' (issues considered further below): <http://www.socialsciences.manchester.ac.uk/morgancentre/events/2009/turning-personal>, accessed 2 May 2009.

[217] Smart, op cit, 2007.

[218] U. Beck and E. Beck-Gernsheim, *Individualization*, London: Sage, 2002.

[219] Contrast can be made with work by the legal academic John Eekelaar, where personal life has been used to denote a reframing of the terrain of 'Family Law': J. Eekelaar, *Family Law and Personal Life*, Oxford: OUP, 2006.

seeking to reframe gendered associations that have attached to the male subject, disrupt codes of practice and refigure how the relation between law, men and gender can then be understood, in the remainder of this chapter I outline some of the implications of this work as they inform the studies to follow in this book.

It is possible to see an engagement with personal life, in its refocusing on issues of affect, emotion and 'interior life', as in some respects broadly aligned to the accounts of the social and psychological processes that inform men's experiences of masculinity discussed above. It differs, however, in not losing sight of the sociological grounding of these processes and, with it, an engagement with the questions about law discussed in this chapter, building, that is, on earlier feminist work on the masculinity of law.[220] We are concerned with the reality, and not simply the rhetoric, of the experiences of men's power and powerlessness referred to above. As studies by Hearn and Connell each, in different ways, show, emotions and experiences can themselves be seen as effects of power, which may have the potential not just to reinforce dominant masculinities but also, importantly (and possibly at the same time), to generate oppositional practices and resistances (see further chapter 7). What comes into view is the potentially contradictory nature of aspects of men's social experience, a theme that will run through each of the following chapters. These psychodynamic dimensions of social experience 'as a man' can be marked, I have suggested above, as much by emotional ambivalence and contradiction as by any notion of straightforward hegemonic masculine identification. The complexities and nuances of emotion, intimacy and the effects of memory, and their interplay with an individual's behaviour, aspirations and motivations, are not necessarily, as we shall see, exercised or experienced rationally or logically. This does not mean that questions of power and social structure, and the insights that can be derived from sociological work, then fade from view. Rather, that discursive positionings and gender categories are themselves the product of a particular matrix of social relations shaped by ideas about power and entitlement, subjectivities that are not necessarily 'held out' or available to all individuals in the same way.

In light of the above, and to conclude this scene setting for the readings of law, men and gender to follow, two related issues emerge as of particular significance. The first entails a return to the question of the sex/gender distinction, an issue that, I suggested at the beginning of this chapter, has framed the dominant approach to masculinity in legal study. The second, building on the above discussion, concerns the conceptual limits of masculinity itself.

---

[220] Including arguments raised within a frequently misrepresented body of 'radical' feminist work that must itself be grounded in a particular political, economic and cultural context, an episteme (below) and stage of feminism without the legacy of which these contemporary debates about masculinity and law would not be happening. This raises the issue of how the development of masculinity in legal thought links to ideas of generational change and feminist 'time-lines'.

Gender and the 'sexual divisions' of law and society

Central to a growing questioning of the concept of masculinity in recent years has been an attempt to engage with, and challenge, the analytic utility and coherence of concepts premised on the epistemic frame of sex/gender, as outlined earlier. Within scholarship termed a new corporeal[221] or 'sexed bodies' approach to gender, for example, we find a forceful critique of the dualism between sex and gender.[222] The idea of the sexed body has been seen in this work as neither inherently (masculine) brute/active, rational, reasonable and so forth, nor (feminine) passive/vulnerable, irrational, unreasonable, and so on. It is, rather, positioned as an object interwoven with and constitutive of a heterogeneity of systems of meaning, signification and representation that varies across social contexts. This approach rejects the idea that there exists a natural (naturally given) pre-social body, a body which exists, as it were, 'before discourse'. Far from presuming such a pre-discursive body, a body that is then the passive recipient of gender 'roles' or 'messages' (for example, the messages conveyed by the media, peer groups or law), this perspective seeks to integrate an appreciation of the specificity of the bodies of women and men in determining consciousness. Equally, rather than see the body as a *tabula rasa* upon which social lessons are inscribed (the approach which, we have seen in this chapter, underscores much gender and law scholarship), what is at issue, rather, is the materiality of gender in/of bodies, the significance of embodiment and the contingent, socially grounded nature of these processes.

This work raises a number of questions relevant to the discussions of law, men and gender to follow in this book, including the limits of legal policies based on assumptions about gender convergence.[223] Far from negating the complexity of men's subjectivity, as in the social constructionist approach discussed above, an attempt is made here to 'see sex' (difference), like gender, as something constituted in discourse. This does not occur, however, via an essentialist fixing of meaning about what constitutes a male/female, masculine/feminine body, experience, identity, culture and so forth in the first place. Rather, it is via reference to cultural and historically specific discourses and practices that women and men come to have differential relationships to, say, reproduction and gestation, parenting and employment, caring, crime and so forth. This approach thus questions the view that bodies can be understood as simply and inescapably categorised into two, mutually exclusive groups, male

---

[221] Grosz, op cit, 1995.

[222] M. Gatens, 'A Critique of the Sex/Gender Distinction' in J. Allen and P. Patton (eds), *Beyond Marxism? Interventions After Marx*, Sydney: Intervention Publications, 1983; M. Gatens, *Imaginary Bodies: Ethics, Power and Corporeality*, London: Routledge, 1996; Cealey Harrison and Hood Williams, op cit, 2002; K. Daly, 'Different Ways of Conceptualising Sex/Gender in Feminist Theory and Their Implications for Criminology', *Theoretical Criminology*, 1997, vol 1, p 25.

[223] See W. Hollway, *The Capacity to Care: Gender and Ethical Subjectivity*, London: Routledge, 2006, suggesting limitations to this idea as it has been deployed in the field of policy.

and female, at once biologically fixed and separate from the cultural contexts in which they exist, marked by heterosexist, gendered frameworks of sexual difference.[224] At the same time, ideas about what constitute supposedly quintessentially masculine qualities are seen as grounded in specific social and cultural contexts, gendered in distinctive ways via reference to how individuals are socially situated or embodied within particular locations.

A charge that can be levelled against such an engagement is, of course, that it is no less essentialist and/or reductionist in the way gender difference is conceptualised than the approaches outlined earlier in this chapter. To accept that active processes are involved in becoming a particular (gendered) subject, however, involves a recognition that there may be some bodily experiences and life events (childbirth, let us say) which, though they may lack any fixed significance within particular cultural contexts, are nonetheless likely to be seen as privileged sites of social significance. Anthropological and historical evidence has been used to show that the body can, and does, intervene to confirm or to deny social significances, albeit that some technological developments (for example around assisted reproduction) have transformed, and are transforming, the contours of 'what is possible' in this regard.[225] The problem with the sex/gender dualism, however, is that it polarises accounts in such a way that the human subject is then characterised as being either predominantly (or wholly) determined by the influence of, on the one hand, social relations (be they environment/society/gender/law); or, on the other, biological forces (be they heredity/the body/sex).

The critique of the division between (biological) sex and (socially constructed) gender can be located as part of a broader attempt within sociological theory and socio-legal work to transcend binary oppositions that have historically informed, and served to constrain, the development of understanding around gender and law. Other significant dualisms singled out for attention have been nature/nurture, the public/private and, in particular within a body of queer legal theoretical work, the binary between hetero and homosexuality. An interrogation of the latter, I intimated above, is of particular significance to the study of law, men and gender, raising important questions regarding the way that assumptions about the normative nature of heterosexuality have encoded and structured many aspects of everyday life.[226] For some critical and

---

[224] Cealey Harrison and Hood Williams, op cit, 2002; see also Petersen, op cit, 2003; Sharpe, op cit, 2002.

[225] Sharpe, op cit, 2002; note, for example, the insights of anthropological work: D. Gilmore *Manhood in the Making: Cultural Concepts of Masculinity*, New Haven, CT: Yale University Press, 1991; A. Cornwall and N. Lindisfarne (eds), *Dislocating Masculinity*, London: Routledge 1994.

[226] D. Richardson (ed), *Theorising Heterosexuality: Telling it Straight*, Buckingham: Open University Press, 1996; M. Wittig, *The Straight Mind*, Boston: Beacon Press, 1992; R. Johnson, 'Contested Borders, Contingent Lives' in D. L. Steinberg, D. Epstein and R. Johnson (eds), *Border Patrols: Policing the Boundaries of Heterosexuality*, London: Continuum, 1997.

socio-legal scholars developing this approach, gender is seen as something naturalised through repetition, something that is contingent, unstable and nothing more (or less) than a temporary association with a particular desire and/or social identity. Within such work, any masculine subject is understood more as a fluid performative practice, being 'masculine' just one manifestation of a gendered self conceptualised in terms of a series of constantly shifting practices and techniques. Thus, the having, obtaining or taking up of a masculine identity becomes 'a public process of power relations in which everyday interactions [are seen to] take place between actors with sexual identities in sexualized locations'.[227] These locations encompass, we shall see in this book, such diverse legal arenas as family law courts (chapter 7), solicitor's offices (chapters 4 and 6) and the university law school (chapters 2 and 3). Challenging masculinity is, from this perspective, intimately related to broader attempts to question these binary divisions and to 'turn personal' in an engagement with social life.

On the limits of 'masculinity'

Finally, as we commence this study of the 'man of law', it is important to reconsider what is meant by masculinity. Both the psychosocial and structured action accounts, I suggested, engage in different ways with social practice, politics and power. Yet whether understood as embedded within and reproduced through the interaction of social structure and practice, or discursively constituted via the contingencies of psyche and society, a concept of masculinity has been deployed in some essentialist ways. Masculinity, it is important to remember, remains a primary 'reference point' for the study of law and gender, a 'symbolic icon' for broader questions about men, gender and social change.[228] What remains unclear, however, is what masculinity is ultimately being used to denote here. As Peter Middleton questioned in his book *The Inward Gaze: Masculinity and Subjectivity in Modern Culture*, 'is it a discourse, a power structure, a psychic economy, a history, an ideology, an identity, a behaviour, a value system, an aesthetic even?'[229] Or is it 'all these and also their mutual separation, the magnetic force of repulsion which keeps them apart ... a centrifugal dispersal of what are maintained as discrete fields of psychic and social structure?'[230] Within the work on law and gender considered above, masculinity has embraced such diverse attributes as the psychological characteristics of men, gendered experiences and identities as well as an array of cultural practices, values and rationalities. Masculinity has been central to both psychoanalytic and power-based readings of gendered

---

[227] Bell and Valentine, op cit, 1995, p 146.

[228] J. Hearn, 'Is Masculinity Dead? A Critique of the Concept of Masculinity' in Mac an Ghaill (ed), op cit, 1996, p 203.

[229] Middleton, op cit, 1992, p 152. See also Pease, op cit, 2000.

[230] Middleton, op cit, 1992.

practice, as well as numerous analyses of men's gendered behaviour within specific institutional settings involving law. Yet, all too often, masculinity appears to 'float free' from what men *do*, diverting attention from the content and consequences of men's actions, evacuating questions of responsibility and agency whilst critical attention (and, we shall see in chapter 5, public policy) continue to focus on this abstract gender category.[231]

The problem is, Whitehead has suggested, that the individual then becomes lost when what is privileged is an 'ideological apparatus' of masculinity,[232] a reification of a particular gender category that results in the further erasure of men's practices and the very questions about social power raised by feminism. Put simply, it is masculinity, existing prior to its production through social agency,[233] that would appear to be 'the problem', not the actual practices of men. To speak legitimately in such a diverse body of work on law and gender of there having been a coherent discourse *of* masculinity in the first place, it would be necessary to show that 'a particular set of usages was located structurally within a clearly defined institution with its own methods, objects and practices'.[234] It is certainly possible that one could argue this in relation to law, although the heterogeneity of the legal contexts discussed in this chapter, as well as throughout this book, strongly suggests otherwise. In which case, references to discourses of 'hegemonic masculinity in law' are really simply references to 'repeated patterns of linguistic usage'.[235] It is far from clear that, in talking about masculinity, legal scholars have been talking about the same thing.

For a growing number of writers, reflecting on these issues, therefore, it is the concept of masculinity itself that has become increasingly problematic. Work arising at the interface of the cultural turn in sociology, sociological studies of personal life and anti-essentialist and materialist feminist scholarship[236] has sought to reappraise what it means to speak of, perform or 'do' a masculine gender. This move can be located as part of a wider shift within the social sciences to develop a self-reflective science of the subject and focus on how social experiences are 'offered to thought in the form of a problem requiring attention' in ways involving law.[237] How, for example, have ideas about men and masculinity been constituted as a problem for law and legal

---

[231] An argument made, in different ways, by Hearn, op cit, 1996; McMahon, op cit, 1993, p 690; Howe, op cit, 2009.

[232] Whitehead, op cit, 2002, p 94.

[233] Ashe, op cit, 2007, p 155.

[234] Middleton, op cit, 1992, p 142.

[235] Middleton, op cit, 1992, p 142.

[236] R. Hennessy and C. Ingraham (eds), *Materialist Feminism: A Reader in Class, Difference and Women's Lives*, London: Routledge, 1997: R. Hennessy, *Materialist Feminism*, London: Routledge 1993.

[237] N. Rose and M. Valverde, 'Governed by Law?', *Social and Legal Studies*, 1998, vol 7(4), p 541. See also J. I. Kitsuse and M. Spector, 'The Definition of Social Problems', *Social Problems*, 1973, vol 20(4), p 407.

systems at certain historical moments? Such questioning chimes with the broadly Foucauldian-inspired engagement in socio-legal studies with the role of legal mechanisms, legal arenas, functionaries and forms of reasoning in late modern forms of governance.[238] It also sheds light on how legal study might 'take masculinity seriously' without falling into essentialist notions of masculine identity and men's power and, as such, is an approach that will inform, if not without qualification, the readings to follow in this book.

Masculinity has been charged with being more than analytically imprecise, however. In Jeff Hearn's words, 'it is as if [it] ... exemplifies [a] field of concern and even, possibly, distils the aggregation of activity of men in the social world into one neat word'.[239] More recently, Hearn has sought to move from 'masculinities' and 'back to men', to distinguish between hegemonic masculinity and what he terms 'the hegemony of men', a subtle but potentially important difference in rethinking the place of power in analyses of law and gender.[240] For Hearn, what is at issue is not so much masculinity but *men*, and he calls for an interrogation of how 'men are both a social category formed by the gender system and dominant collective and individual agents of social practices'.[241] The general use of the term masculinity, in contrast, has, across disciplines, all too often been premised on questionable 'heterosexist' assumptions, with masculinity 'an ethnocentric or even a Eurocentric notion', mediated by ideas about class and disadvantage,[242] a product of a particular historical moment that is, in some cultural contexts at least, at best 'irrelevant or misleading'.[243]

---

[238] See further, on the 'governmentality' approach with which this argument is aligned, N. Rose, 'Expertise and the Government of Conduct', *Studies in Law, Politics and Society*, 1994, vol 14, p 359; M. Valverde, *Law's Dream of a Common Knowledge*, Princeton, NJ: Princeton University Press, 2003; P. O'Malley, *Risk, Uncertainty and Government*, London: The Glasshouse Press, 2004. See also M. Foucault, 'Governmentality' in G. Burchell, C. Gordon and P. Miller (eds), *The Foucault Effect: Studies in Governmentality*, London: Harvester Wheatsheaf, 1991; N. Rose, *Governing the Soul*, London: Routledge, 1995. Note here, in the context of legal studies, the influence of Rose, building on feminist critiques of the public/private divide: N. Rose, 'Transcending the Public/Private', *Journal of Law and Society*, 1987, vol 14, p 61; cf F. Olsen, 'The Myth of State Intervention in the Family', *University of Michigan Journal of Law Reform*, 1985, vol 18, p 835.

[239] Hearn, op cit, 1996, p 202. See further J. Hearn, 'The Implications of Critical Studies on Men', *Nora*, 1997, vol 3(1), p 48.

[240] See further J. Hearn, 'From Hegemonic Masculinity to the Hegemony of Men', *Feminist Theory*, 2004, vol 5(1), p 49; J. Hearn, 'Theorizing Men and Men's Theorizing: Varieties of Discursive Practices in Men Theorizing of Men', *Theory and Society*, 1998, vol 27, p 781; J. Hearn 'Research in Men and Masculinities: Some Sociological Issues and Possibilities', *The Australian and New Zealand Journal of Sociology*, 1994, vol 30, p 47.

[241] Hearn, op cit, 1994, p 59.

[242] Hall, op cit, 2002.

[243] Hearn, op cit, 1996, p 209. Compare Connell, op cit, 1995, pp 30–34; G. Spector-Mersel, 'Never-Aging Stories; Western Hegemonic Masculinity Scripts', *Journal of Gender Studies*, 2006, vol 15(1), p 67.

To conclude this introductory chapter. Masculinity, we have seen, has been viewed within much socio-legal scholarship as potentially yielding high explanatory returns for legal study.[244] Yet, as outlined above, some problematic binary oppositions remain inextricably bound up with a particular *form of thinking* about men and masculinity, involving ideas about men and women that may themselves be increasingly obsolete, at least in certain respects, in late modern political, economic and cultural contexts. Both the structured action and psychosocial perspectives seek to give 'primacy to one form of explanation rather than another', in so doing categorising 'a vast range of activities' by 'treat[ing] ... them as if they were all subject to the same laws'.[245] Yet such a form of thinking about law, men and gender, based around the divisions of masculinity/femininity, can itself be located as part of a particular episteme of legal theory the time for which may well have now passed.[246] What is required is a re-theorising 'of men's identities beyond the term "masculinities" to produce a more multi-conceptual framework for examining men's subjectivities, bodies and practices'.[247]

In the remainder of this book, I will attempt to chart a way through these debates. Masculinity is not, I have argued elsewhere,[248] a fixed, homogenous or unchanging concept. Far from taking for granted what is meant by the term, locating its meaning in a grand narrative or 'big debate' of sociology (or, indeed, of any other discipline),[249] it is more helpful to look at how it has been deployed in different contexts, in different ways and at different moments, as a particular kind of (inter)discursive construction. In the chapters to follow I explore the multiple meanings of masculinity, unpacking how ideas about men, and the 'man of law', have been produced and reproduced in the legal field.

Law, we shall see, has been marked by a range of binaries that have constructed ideas about gender in particular ways. Whilst continuing to engage with the idea of masculinity and use the term,[250] I will consider how its deployment in debates about law relates to ideas of the public/private dualism, of hetero/homosexuality, of sex/gender and the interconnections of a multiplicity of parallel worlds – of the workplace, family, friendships, body regimes, sexual practices and social relationships. In questioning 'gender' as contingent, discursive and of variable significance, it remains possible to locate ideologies, and beliefs about men and masculinity, that are socially

---

[244] Gatens, op cit, 1996, p 3.
[245] Smart, op cit, 1990, p 77.
[246] Hood Williams, op cit, 2001, p 53.
[247] Ashe, op cit, 2007, p 158.
[248] Collier, op cit, 1998.
[249] Smart, op cit, 2007.
[250] Recognising that the term does, for example, have meaning(s) in contemporary society, is used, albeit in the diverse and often contradictory ways outlined above: see further Connell, op cit, 2002; Connell and Messerschmidt, op cit, 2005.

powerful and experientially significant.[251] This includes beliefs circulating in the legal domain where, in Connell's terms, crisis tendencies within the gender order become visible in a particularly stark form. Law is the terrain for a series of contestations around the 'historical collapse of the legitimacy of patriarchal power'.[252] Masculinity, as a marker of social identity (connected in some way to feeling oneself to be, or to be seen by others, as 'a Man'), has, we shall see, been produced and sustained by discourses of sexuality and gender that are interwoven and rooted within the dualistic configurations which pervade liberal legal thought. In seeking to take up Margaret Thornton's challenge, and progress 'a conversation ... so that we might discursively constitute a new episteme of feminist legal theory that is linked to the political',[253] the time is propitious to reassess what it means to speak of a relationship between law, men and gender. That is what this book seeks to do.

[251] Masculinity, that is, can be seen as both essentially contested and a significant praxis of 'everyday' social relations: Connell, op cit, 2000.

[252] Connell, op cit, 1995, p 85.

[253] Thornton, op cit, 2004, p 22.

Chapter 2

The restructured university

Rethinking the gendered law school

Introduction

> The state of academia must reflect broader social processes: since globalization ultimately affects everything, it stands to reason that the knowledge economy will also be altered. The reduction of state funding to universities and the general move to a corporate profit culture are other relevant forces. Surprisingly there has been little attempt to document systematically either the extent or the shape of these changes in the way universities work, or to consider what kinds of impact they might be having on staff, students or knowledge – one of the things universities supposedly exist for.[1]

This chapter begins from a paradox. Notwithstanding the well-established nature of gender and law scholarship within legal studies, considered in relation to ideas about men and masculinity in chapter 1, relatively little is known about the connections between gender and what has been termed, in the context of recent discussion of women legal academics in the UK, the 'private life' of the university law school.[2] Internationally, a rich theoretical and empirical body of research has been concerned with social relations between men and women inside diverse organisations involved in the teaching and study of law.[3] It is understandable, perhaps, given the relatively high status, and the cultural

---

[1] A. Oakley, 'Foreword' in A. Brooks and A. Mackinnon (eds), *Gender and the Restructured University*, Buckingham: SRHE/Open University Press, 2001, p xii.

[2] F. Cownie, 'Women Legal Academics – A New Research Agenda?', *Journal of Law and Society*, 1998, vol 25(1), p 102, citing M. Trow, 'The Public and Private Lives of Higher Education' *Daedelus*, vol 104, p 113. See further F. Cownie, *Legal Academics: Culture and Identities*, Oxford: Hart, 2004.

[3] For a flavour of this work see C. Wells, 'Working Out Women in Law Schools', *Legal Studies*, 2001, vol 21(1), p 116; Cownie, op cit, 2004; C. Wells, 'Women Law Professors – Negotiating and Transcending Gender Identity at Work', *Feminist Legal Studies*, 2002, vol 10(1), p 1; F. Cownie, 'Women in the Law School – Shoals of Fish, Starfish or Fish Out of Water?' in P. Thomas (ed), *Discriminating Lawyers*, London: Cavendish, 2000. There is also a vast international literature on this issue: for example, M. Thornton, *Dissonance and Distrust: Women in the Legal Profession*, Oxford: OUP, 1996; L. Bender, 'For Mary Joe Frug: Empowering Women Law Professors', *Wisconsin Women's Law Journal*, 1991, vol 6, p 1.

and political profile of the legal profession, that particular attention has focused on issues of gender inequality and discrimination as they relate to the work of solicitors and barristers (see chapters 4 and 6). It is intriguing, therefore, in such a context, how it has become increasingly common in recent years within legal scholarship to state not simply that there have been few studies of legal academics and law teachers,[4] but also that there has been little research into the relationship between gender, the law school and what has been termed the 'changing or restructured university'.

The claim that there is 'very little research examining the position of British women academics', and almost none into 'the everyday experience of male legal academics',[5] has led to calls from legal scholars that this is an absence which needs to be addressed by the undertaking of small-scale qualitative and/or ethnographic research into the contemporary university law school. Developing this research agenda, Fiona Cownie's 2006 book *Legal Academics* presents a sustained account of these issues, suggesting a powerful connection between the cultures and practices of the legal academy and the development of the legal discipline.[6] Emphasising the analytic potential of 'an anthropological approach to legal education', developing 'an ethnography of the disciplines',[7] Cownie argues that 'the behaviour, values and attitudes of legal academics have implications for the future development of the discipline of law'.[8] The 'ways in which particular groups of academics organise their professional lives are intimately related to the academic tasks on which they are engaged'.[9] Linking this 'cultural approach to studying law'[10] to the questions of identity discussed in chapter 1, and presented as a device 'for analysing the culture of academic law', Cownie notes that, with regard to earlier empirical surveys of the legal academy,[11] 'although we can glean much information, both about the tribe of academic lawyers and their territory' from such work, it 'belongs to the "public life" of academic law. What is required, in contrast, is a 'venture ... into *the more private aspects* of legal academia'.[12]

---

[4] Although see, for example: P. Leighton, T. Mortimer and N. Whatley, *Today's Law Teachers: Lawyers or Academics?* London: Cavendish, 1995.

[5] Cownie, op cit, 1998, pp 102 and 104.

[6] Cownie, op cit, 2004.

[7] Cownie, op cit, 2004, p 9. See further T. Becher, *Academic Tribes and Territories: Intellectual Enquiry and the Culture of Disciplines*, Buckingham: Open University Press, 1989; T. Becher and M. Kogan, *Process and Structure in Higher Education*, London: Routledge, 1992, 2nd edn; P. Trowler, *Academics Responding to Change: New Higher Education Frameworks and Academic Cultures*, Buckingham: Open University Press/SRHE, 1998.

[8] Cownie, op cit, 1998, p 103.

[9] T. Becher, quoted in Cownie, op cit, 1998, p 109.

[10] Cownie, op cit, 2004, p 9.

[11] For discussion, Cownie, op cit, 2004, pp 41–42.

[12] Cownie, op cit, 2004, p 42, my emphasis.

This and the following chapter have two, interrelated, objectives. First, I will explore what is meant by 'the private aspects' or 'private life' of legal academia in the context of significant shifts that have taken place in understandings about the structure, place and purpose of universities in society. These changes, I suggest, interlinked with the rise of what has been termed a neo-liberal university model, have impacted profoundly on (legal) academic life. Second, developing the engagement with men, law and gender central to this book, the 'man of law' of my title, I will approach these questions via a closer look at how a particular kind of gendered subject has been theorised within discussions of the private life of the law school. I do so, in chapter 3, by exploring issues of gender and social class.[13] Class, I shall suggest, has been overlooked in much of this work on legal academics, in ways that have served to side-step important questions about the nature of the academic subject. Building on research that has taken the form of an attempt to 'work out' women in the law school,[14] I will in this chapter focus, in contrast, on how ideas about men and masculinity have been deployed in various accounts of the restructured university and legal academic practice.

Building on the discussion in chapter 1, and connecting to themes that will be explored in relation to the work of solicitors in chapters 4 and 6, what follows interrogates the local and micro-levels of gender power, how ideas about men and masculinities operate within one specific area (in this case, universities and their law schools). Distinctive masculinities, I suggest, are produced at a nexus of ideologies and practices that involve, in this context, government, universities, the cultures and discourses of institutions, departments and disciplines as well as the activities of individuals. At this local level, masculinities are constituted through diverse cultural, economic, discursive, social and political forces, embracing, we shall see in this and in the following chapter, disciplinary regimes of the body (see also chapter 4, p 113). Unpacking the problematic nature of the 'man of law' in this area, and taken together, chapters 2 and 3 explore not just what has been said about women and men within studies of the gendered law school, but also what has *not* been said, what has remained silent and what has, all too often, been effaced.

The argument is structured as follows. I begin in the first section by outlining themes and concerns within the growing literature on the restructured university, contextualising the law school in relation to wider debates about Higher Education. I proceed, in the second section, to look more closely at university law schools, legal education and research, paying particular attention to the study of law and gender therein. Do developments in law support, or undermine, the 'corporatisation thesis', as it has been termed (see below)?

---

[13] Issues of class are also considered in chapters 4, 5 and 7.

[14] Wells, op cit, 2002; Wells, op cit, 2001; Cownie, op cit, 1998; Cownie, op cit, 2000.

Or is it the case, as I shall suggest, that social changes impacting on universities are more contradictory and ambiguous than they may at first seem? I will proceed, in the third section, to review the debate in this area by exploring how ideas about the academic subject and the law school as a masculine institution have been reshaped in this process. In chapter 3, without negating the intersectional nature of social categories, I use social class as a way of unpacking further some methodological and conceptual limitations of this debate about gender and the private life of the law school. Chapters 2 and 3, therefore, seek to develop a deeper appreciation of the interconnections between the everyday practices of individuals and the contingency of the 'man of law' idea, as well as – pursuing a theme introduced in chapter 1 – exploring further the limits of masculinity as a way of explaining these complex social relations.

The changing university, the law school and the 'global knowledge economy'

> Somebody told *you*, and you hold it as an article of faith, that higher education is an unassailable good. This notion is so dear to you that when I question it you become angry. Good. Good, I say. Are those not the very things which we should question? I say college education, since the war, has become so a matter of course, and such a fashionable necessity, for those either of or aspiring *to* the new vast middle class, that we *espouse* it, as a matter of right, and have ceased to ask, 'What is it good for?'[15]

A debate has been taking place for some time within the legal academic community about the implications for legal research and teaching of developments in the field of Higher Education,[16] changes within the political economy in which academic research is produced.[17] There exists, in the vast body of scholarship on the changing nature of universities, a general consensus that we are, internationally, living in a 'new era'.[18] This is a time when

---

[15] D. Mamet, *Oleanna*, London: Methuen Royal Court Writers Series, 1993, p 33, emphasis in original.

[16] Reflected, for example, in the pages of the *Socio-Legal Newsletter* (*SLN*): S. Tombs and D. Whyte, 'Shining a Light on Power? Reflections on British Criminology and the Future of Critical Social Science', *SLN*, 2003, vol 41, p 1; L. Bibbings, 'The Future of Higher Education: "Sustainable Research Businesses" and "Exploitable Knowledge"', *SLN*, 2003, vol 40, p 1; R. Collier, '"Useful Knowledge" and the "New Economy": An Uncertain Future for (Critical) Socio-Legal Studies', *SLN*, 2003, vol 39, p 3.

[17] P. Hillyard and J. Sim, 'The Political Economy of Socio-Legal Research' in P. Thomas (ed), *Socio-Legal Studies*, Aldershot: Dartmouth, 1997.

[18] This literature is voluminous. See, for example: M. Henkel, *Academic Identities and Policy Change in Higher Education*, London: Jessica Kingsley, 2000; M. Kogan and S. Hanney, *Reforming Higher Education*, London: Jessica Kingsley, 2000; R. Barnett, *Realizing the University in an Age of Supercomplexity*, Buckingham: Open University Press, 2000; B. Clark, *Creating Entrepreneurial Universities: Organizational Pathways of Transformation*, Oxford: Pergamon Press, 1998; F. Coffield and D. Williamson (eds), *Repositioning Higher Education,*

traditional understanding of what universities are 'for' has been questioned. The debate in legal studies around these issues is perhaps less developed than it has been in some other fields of scholarship.[19] Nonetheless, different interpretations have emerged as to what these developments mean for universities[20] and their law schools.[21] In providing a context for the discussion to follow, and introducing themes that will be taken up in the analysis of social class and legal academics in chapter 3, this section outlines the main contours of this debate.

Buckingham: Open University Press, 1997; G. Williams (ed), *The Enterprising University: Reform, Excellence and Equity*, Buckingham: Open University Press, 2003; A. Smith and F. Webster (eds), *The Postmodern University? Contested Visions of Higher Education in Society*, Buckingham: SRHE/Open University Press, 1998; H. Miller, *Management of Change in Universities: Universities, State and Economy in Australia, Canada and the United Kingdom*, Buckingham: SRHE/Open University Press, 1995; M. Walker, *Higher Education Pedagogies*, Buckingham: Open University Press, 2006; T. Coady (ed), *Why Universities Matter: A Conversation about Values, Means and Directions*, Sydney: Allen and Unwin, 2000. Work critical of these changes in universities is discussed below.

[19] Contrast P. Hillyard et al, 'Leaving a 'Stain upon the Silence': Contemporary Criminology and the Politics of Dissent', *British Journal of Criminology*, 2004, vol 44, p 369; R. Walters, 'New Modes of Governance and the Commodification of Criminological Knowledge', *Social and Legal Studies*, 2003, vol 12(1), p 5. It is important to note that developments in the UK, discussed in this chapter, do not necessarily map to what has happened elsewhere in Europe: see R. Middlehurst, 'The International Context For UK Higher Education' in S. Ketteridge, S. Marshall and H. Fry (eds), *The Effective Academic*, London, Kogan Page/THES, 2002.

[20] J. Currie, B. Thiele and P. Harris, *Gendered Universities in Globalized Economies: Power, Careers and Sacrifices*, Lexington, MD: Lexington Books, 2002; J. Currie and J. Newson (eds), *Universities and Globalization*, London: Sage, 1998; A. Brooks and A. Mackinnon (eds), *Gender and the Restructured University*, Buckingham: SRHE/Open University Press, 2001; V. Gillies and H. Lucey (eds), *Power, Knowledge and the Academy: The Institutional is Political*, London: Palgrave Macmillan, 2007; A. Brooks, 'Restructuring Bodies of Knowledge', in Brooks and MacKinnon, op cit, 2001; S. Slaughter and L. Leslie, *Academic Capitalism: Politics, Policies and the Entrepreneurial University*, Baltimore: Johns Hopkins University Press, 1997; S. Cooper, J. Hinkson and G. Sharp (eds), *Scholars and Entrepreneurs: The Universities in Crisis*, Melbourne: Arena Publications, 1992; S. Marginson and M. Considine, *The Enterprise University: Power, Governance and Reinvention in Australia*, Cambridge: Cambridge University Press, 2000; J. Kelsey, 'Academic Freedom Needed More Than Ever' in R. Crozier (ed), *Troubled Times, Academic Freedom in New Zealand*, Palmerston North: Dunmore Press, 1999.

[21] See, for example, the contrasting interpretations of A. Bradney, *Conversations, Choices and Chances: The Liberal Law School in the Twenty-First Century*, Oxford: Hart, 2003; Cownie, op. cit, 2004; P. Hillyard, 'Invoking Indignation: Reflection on Future Directions of Socio-Legal Studies', *Journal of Law and Society*, 2002, vol 29(4), p 645; M. Thornton, 'The Demise of Diversity in Legal Education: Globalisation and the New Knowledge Economy', *International Journal of the Legal Profession*, 2001, vol 8(1), p 37; M. Thornton, 'Among the Ruins: Law in the Neo-Liberal Academy', *Windsor Yearbook of Access to Justice*, 2001, vol 20, p 3; M. Thornton, 'Technocentrism and the Law School', *Osgoode Hall Law Journal*, 1998, vol 36(2), p 369; A. Goldsmith, 'Standing at the Crossroads: Law Schools, Universities, Markets and the Future of Legal scholarship' in F. Cownie (ed.), *The Law School – Global Issues, Local Questions*, Ashgate: Aldershot, 1999; R. Collier, 'The Changing University and the (Legal) Academic Career – Rethinking the "Private Life" of the Law School', *Legal Studies*, 2002, vol 22(1), p 1.

What is meant by the term 'restructured' university? The relationship between British universities and the wider political economy, Paddy Hillyard and Joe Sim suggested in their 1997 account of socio-legal studies, had at that time 'not appear[ed] to have been studied systematically'.[22] A decade on, there is a rich literature concerned with the restructured, corporatised or entrepreneurial university. The themes of commodification, privatisation, managerialism, credentialism and bureaucratisation have become commonplace within this literature, key ideas through reference to which the reform of universities in the UK, as elsewhere, has been approached. At the centre of the debate has been one central and recurring notion; that of the global knowledge economy.[23] Globalisation has been understood here, in part, as a phenomenon associated with the borderless world economy,[24] the flow and instantaneous sharing of information, whether ideas/knowledge, capital and/or financial services, and the compression of time and space arising at the interface of technological advance and political, economic and cultural change.[25] It is an idea that has informed, in a number of ways, the evolving debate about legal academics and the restructured university.

Privatisation and the restructured university: the (legal) academic as 'knowledge worker'

> Perpetuating the life of scholarship for its own sake is no longer an acceptable mission statement, nor is the delivery of inaccessible knowledge from the secret garden of academic seclusion to a grateful public (Sir Howard Newby, then Chief Executive of the Higher Education Funding Council [HEFCE], March 2002).[26]

[22] Hillyard and Sim, op cit, 1997, p 52. Similar observations have been made by others, for example Oakley, op cit, 2001. Although note B. Readings, *The University in Ruins*, Cambridge, MA: Harvard University Press, 1996; A. H. Halsey, *Decline of Donnish Dominion: The British Academic Professions in the Twentieth Century*, Oxford: OUP, 1995.

[23] H. Etzkowitz and L. Leydesdorff (eds), *Universities and the Global Knowledge Economy: A Triple Helix of University-Industry-Government Relations*, London: Pinter Press, 1997; J. Kenway and D. Langmead, 'Governmentality, the "Now" University and the Future of Knowledge Work', *Australian Universities Review*, 1998, vol 41(2), p 28; M. Castells, 'The University System: Engine of Development in the New World Economy' in J. Salmi and A. Verspoor (eds), *Revitalizing Higher Education*, London: Pergamon, 1994. See also S. Slaughter, 'National Higher Education Policy in a Global Economy' in Currie and Newson (eds), op cit, 1998; W. Morrison, 'Legal Education and Globalisation' (2002) *Academic Reporter* (Summer), 4–5, London: Cavendish, 2002.

[24] R. Robertson, *Globalization*, London: Sage, 1992; S. Sassen, *Globalisation and Its Discontents: Essays on the New Mobility of People and Money*, New York: The New Press, 1998; M. Waters, *Globalization*, London: Routledge, 1995; J. Jenson and B. de Sousa Santos (eds), *Globalizing Institutions: Case Studies in Social Regulation and Innovation*, Dartmouth: Ashgate, 2000.

[25] Brooks, op cit, 2001, identifies three 'fundamental principles of operation' in the way in which universities now operate – *corporatisation*, *commodification* and *privatisation*. A concern with these themes can also be found in the work of Margaret Thornton, see n 21.

[26] Quoted in D. Macleod, 'A Higher Vision', *The Guardian*, 19 March 2002.

What marks the rise of the entrepreneurial university, it has been argued, is an explicit redirection, experienced at all levels of the institution, towards an intensified emphasis on the capitalisation and exploitation of learning and knowledge practices. Slaughter and Leslie[27] characterise this development as having 'far-reaching implications' for the 'academic capitalists'[28] who work in such a university.[29] The term corporatisation has been used, at a general level, to capture the idea that there has been a heightened interconnection between the objectives, goals and practices of the business and traditionally academic worlds. Thus, we find an apparent consensus amongst politicians, policy-makers and senior university managers in the UK that the economic, political and social transformation of the knowledge base of society is an increasingly important source of value within advanced capitalist economies.

Developing an understanding of the dynamics of corporatisation on social practices within universities, however, Polster has suggested, cannot be seen simply in terms of an 'add-on' to the university, 'such that after their establishment one has the old university plus these links'. Corporate links, rather, should be seen as an 'add-into' the university, producing qualitative changes in the institution and in the practices of academics themselves; changes in a university's overarching culture, operating practices, funding systems, staff development practices, reward structures and so forth.[30] In England and Wales, therefore, this process of privatisation should not be confined to the move towards a 'user-pays' system of Higher Education (notably via the introduction of fees, albeit, at the time of writing, capped at a maximum figure). Rather, it has informed the way in which faculties, schools and individual academics have been charged with redirecting their energies towards the capitalisation and exploitation of learning, readjusting the focus of their work (towards, for example, the maximising of external income).[31] At an institutional level,

---

[27] Slaughter and Leslie, op cit, 1997.

[28] Slaughter and Leslie, op cit, 1997. Thornton similarly notes the links between the movement in favour of academic capitalism and neo-liberalism: Thornton, op cit, 2001, 'The Demise of Diversity in Legal Education', p 47.

[29] Slaughter and Leslie, op cit, 1997, pp 36–37; Brooks and Mackinnon, op cit, 2001, p 3.

[30] C. Polster, 'The Advantages and Disadvantages of Corporate/University Links: What's Wrong with this Question?', D. Doherty-Delorme and E. Shaker (eds.), *Missing Pieces II: An Alternative Guide to Canadian Post-Secondary Education*, Ottawa: Canadian Centre for Policy Alternatives, 2000, at p 183.

[31] This has taken different forms. For some disciplines, it has involved the creation of 'spin-off companies', patents and innovation development, partnering with industries and applying 'knowledge products' to the business community. In the case of many law schools, increasing importance has been attached to securing further income streams, whether from Continuing Professional Development (CPD) or 'third-strand' 'outreach' income-generating activity. Such work, not least the obtaining of Research Council funding, is no longer considered marginal to what university legal academics 'do' within a changed funding context. It is a core academic activity with promotion and appointment criteria adjusted accordingly to reflect the institutional importance of income generation and business development.

Margaret Thornton has suggested, 'university managers have accepted that they must enter the market'[32] and 'must have a product packaged under a brand name that is going to be attractive to consumers.'[33]

It is against this backdrop that performance-driven tables, hierarchies and an array of rankings of achievement have become pervasive in Higher Education as universities – and their law schools – compete for resources, students and income streams. For critics of these developments, however, one consequence has been to undermine well-established intellectual traditions and practices, not least in relation to 'disinterested inquiry'[34] and the maintenance of academic standards.[35] The repositioning of academics as individuals for whom knowledge is no longer primarily valuable 'in and of itself' – it is, rather, a commodity, a resource to help create wealth and competitive advantage – has become a common theme and object of concern within critical debates around the restructuring of universities.[36] Via the citation of Newman, Halsey, Readings and others,[37] questions have been raised about whether operating universities like businesses involves a fundamental change in the epistemological foundations of the traditional, Westernised, humanistic university ideal.[38] A rather different issue, however, one that bears upon the argument I wish to make about gender and law schools, concerns *how* such change has been instituted in the first place.

The structural reform of Higher Education has involved, Cuthbert[39] has suggested, 'High' and 'Low' frequency interventions aimed at transforming the form and content of individual academic and management practices, producing

---

[32] Thornton, op cit, 2001, 'The Demise of Diversity in Legal Education', p 47.

[33] 'If not, the consumers will exercise their prerogative of market choice and go elsewhere': Thornton, op cit, 2001, 'The Demise of Diversity in Legal Education', p 47; P. Curtis, 'Competition Time', *The Guardian*, 9 March 2004.

[34] Hillyard and Sim, op cit, 1997.

[35] '"Dumbing Down" Fear as Leading Universities Award More Firsts', *Daily Telegraph*, 16 March 2004; 'Conflicting Forces Result in Falling Standards', *The Guardian*, 3 September 2001; 'Universities are having to make intellectual compromises … but many lecturers are reluctant to speak out for fear of losing their jobs or ruining reputations': M. Garner and P. Leon, 'Dumbing Down has Become a Fact of Life!', *THES*, 3 May 2002, p 22.

[36] Note, for example, C. Clarke, quoted in *THES*, 16 May 2003, p 1; G. Day, 'No Thinking Please, We're New Labour', *THES*, 23 May 2003, p 13; Letters, *THES*, 23 May 2003, p 15; C. Bassnett, 'Opinion', *The Guardian*, 27 May 2003, p 10; S. Cooper, 'Post-Intellectuality? Universities and the Knowledge Economy' in Cooper et al, op cit, 1992.

[37] J. H. Newman, *The Idea of a University*, New York: Holt, Rinehart and Winston, 1960; Halsey, op. cit, 1995; Readings, op cit, 1996; Bradney, op cit, 2003, esp ch 2, 'Holistic Education: What is a Liberal Education?'; C. Kerr, *The Uses of the University*, Cambridge, MA: Harvard University Press, 1995.

[38] C. Polster, 'Dismantling the Liberal University: The State's New Approach to Academic Research' in R. Brecher, O. Fleischman and J. Halliday (eds), *Universities in a Liberal State*, Aldershot: Avebury, 1996.

[39] R. Cuthbert, 'The Impact of National Developments on Institutional Practice' in Ketteridge et al (eds), op cit, 2002.

a 'leaner', more flexible, cost-efficient and accountable sector.[40] The term 'corporate managerialism' has denoted a significant shift in the content, style, structure and nomenclature of management practice,[41] with the drive towards standardisation of practice across teaching, assessment and research manage- ment described by Parker and Jary as part of a 'McDonaldisation' of the con- temporary university.[42] Yeatman, meanwhile, has identified a form of 'new contractualism' in universities, whereby social relationships are understood, increasingly, to be based on the demands of the market and 'top-down' man- agerial imperatives.[43] It has been via the idea of performativity, in particular, that the imperatives of the new knowledge economy have been most clearly linked to the institution of change in the behaviour of academics themselves. Drawing on Lyotard's use of the term, a logic of performativity[44] has been used to describe the way both individual academics and universities are now judged, across a range of areas, on the basis of their performance, measured against an input/output equation in such a way as to determine efficiency (and inefficiency) against pre-determined criteria (for example, research quality and income, number of research students and so forth).[45]

[40] Although such government-sourced reform should be seen, Cuthbert suggests, as the outcome of shifting alliances between the State, the private sector and international bodies.

[41] For example, J. Dearlove, 'The Academic Labour Process: From Collegiality and Professional- ism to Managerialism and Proletarianisation?', *Higher Education Review*, 1997, vol 30(1), p 56; I. McNay, 'From the Collegial Academy to Corporate Enterprise: The Changing Culture of Universities' in T. Schuller (ed), *The Changing University?* Buckingham: Open University Press/ SRHE, 1995; J. Newson, 'The Decline of Faculty Influence: Confronting the Effects of the Corporate Agenda' in W. Carroll, L. Christiansen-Rufman, R. Currie and D. Harrison (eds), *Fragile Truths: 25 Years of Sociology and Anthropology in Canada*, Ottawa: Carleton Uni- versity Press, 1992; H. Willmott, 'Managing the Academics: Commodification and Control in the Development of University Education', *Human Relations*, 1995, vol 48(9), p 993; A. Utley, 'Outbreak of "New Managerialism" Infects Faculties', *THES*, 20 July 2001.

[42] M. Parker and D. Jary, 'The McUniversity: Organization, Management and Academic Sub- jectivity', *Organization*, 1995, vol 2(2), p 319.

[43] A. Yeatman, 'Corporate Managerialism and the Shift from the Welfare to the Competitive State', 1993, *Discourse*, vol 13(2), p 3; A. Yeatman, 'The New Contractualism and the Politics of Quality Management', *Women, Culture and Universities: A Chilly Climate? National Conference on the Effects of Organizational Culture on Women in Universities. Conference Proceedings*, 19–20 April, Sydney: University of Technology, 1995, cited in Brooks, op cit, 1997, p 33.

[44] J. F. Lyotard, *The Postmodern Condition*, Manchester: Manchester University Press, 1984, p 51: 'The question asked by universities is no longer "Is it true?" but "What use is it?" – which also can mean "Is it saleable?" or "Is it efficient?"' See further R. P. Mourad, *Postmodern Philoso- phical Critique and the Pursuit of Knowledge in Higher Education*, Westport, CT: Bergin and Garvey, 1997.

[45] Of particular significance has been the assessment of the performance of academics in terms of research productivity in the form of various Research Assessment Exercises (RAE) since 1986. At the time of writing, with the future of research assessment subject to consultation, the results of the most recent RAE round (2008) have been published: <http://www.rae.ac.uk>, accessed 18 December 2008. The RAE has been widely seen to have transformed the cultures of universities and to have embodied, in a particularly clear way, the spirit and ethos of individual and col- lective performativity. Earlier accounts of the effects of the RAE in law can be found in

How is all this relevant to legal academics and the questions around men, law and gender central to this book? In the next section, I will look more closely at university law schools in the UK and the idea of the 'private life' of legal academia. Does the case of law support, or undermine, the corporatisation thesis set out above and, more specifically, what have these developments meant for understandings of the law school as a 'masculine' institution, in terms of the framework outlined in chapter 1? I wish to suggest that, far from reproducing a model of the gendered law school as masculine (and with it, an evocation of certain ideas of the 'man of law') gender relations have been reconfigured in ways that are, for both women and men, contradictory and double-edged.

The law school, gender and the limits of the corporatisation thesis

A note on UK university law schools

There is, of course, no 'one' type of university law school and UK law teachers are diverse, although, it has been suggested, legal academics do tend to be a relatively homogeneous employment grouping in terms of ethnicity and socio-economic background (although see further chapter 3).[46] The 'everyday' experience of legal academic employment is mediated by (amongst other things) the contingencies of personal biography, professional status and stage of life course, as well as the cultures of the specific law school and university in which an individual works. Legal education and research into law also take place, it is important to note, in locations other than universities and their law schools.[47] Recognising such diversity, the university law school can be seen as a creature of two domains. It is part of the legal profession, a component within a wider legal community in relation to

J. Barnard, 'Reflections on Britain's Research Assessment Exercise', *Journal of Legal Education*, 1998, vol 48(4), p 467; D. Vick, A. Murray, G. Little and K. Campbell, 'The Perceptions of Academic Lawyers Concerning the Effects of the United Kingdom's Research Assessment Exercise', *Journal of Law and Society*, 1998, vol 24(4), p 536; K. Campbell, D. Vick, A. Murray and G. Little, 'Journal Publishing, Journal Reputations and the United Kingdom Research Assessment Exercise', *Journal of Law and Society*, 1999, vol 25(4), p 470; S. Court, 'Negotiating the Research Imperative: The Views of UK Academics on their Career Opportunities', *Higher Education Quarterly*, 1999, vol 53(1), p 65.

[46] As Celia Wells has put it, 'Readers of this journal [*Legal Studies*] most likely work in a law school. Readers of this journal most likely are male, pale, middle-class and able-bodied. True, there is more chance that they are female than there would have been 20 years ago, but those women will almost invariably be fit and white': Wells, op cit, 2001, p 116.

[47] For example, teaching in schools and further education colleges. Private, profit-making organisations, government departments and charitable foundations each produce 'in house' research into law.

which it plays a key role in the production of future generations of lawyers (as a gatekeeper, transmitter of foundational knowledge, inculcator of appropriate values and so forth). And it is part of the university itself, having historically evolved, for some, in an uncertain intellectual and political relationship to other disciplines concerned with the 'disinterested pursuit of knowledge'.

As such, university law schools and legal academics have not been immune from the changes associated with the restructuring of universities discussed in the first section of this chapter. These developments, indeed, have been acutely felt, although by no means in the same way as in other disciplines, across all university law schools. The history of legal education and scholarship is, of course, the subject of a now vast body of work[48] and I do not want to repeat here the arguments that have been made for 'taking the law school seriously'.[49] With regard to the corporatisation of universities, however, the proposition has been advanced by scholars working both in law and in legally related subjects (such as criminology), in the UK and internationally, that the developments outlined above have resulted in particular problems for those in university law schools who are engaged in 'unprofitable ... political ... or theoretical' research,[50] scholarship that would include, of course, much work on gender, law and sexuality. What has occurred, it has been suggested, is an increasing marginalisation of the space to engage in critical social science scholarship.[51] Yet how valid are these arguments and, if this view is correct, what has this meant for understandings of the law school as a masculine institution?

---

[48] For simply a flavour of this work: Bradney, op cit, 2003; W. L. Twining, *Blackstone's Tower: The English Law School*, London: Sweet & Maxwell, 1994; Cownie, op cit, 2004; W. Twining, *Law in Context: Enlarging a Discipline*, Oxford, Clarendon Press, 1997; A. Bradney, 'Law as a Parasitic Discipline', *Journal of Law and Society*, 1998, vol 25, p 71; F. Cownie (ed), *The Law School: Global Issues, Local Questions*, Aldershot: Ashgate, 1999; A. Bradney and F. Cownie, 'Transformative Visions of Legal Education', *Journal of Law and Society*, 1998, vol 25, p 1; W. L. Twining, 'Thinking About Law Schools: Rutland Reviewed', *Journal of Law and Society*, 1998, vol 25, p 1; A. Bradney and F. Cownie, 'British University Law Schools in the 21st Century' in D. Hayton (ed), *Law's Futures*, Oxford: Hart, 2000; P. Goodrich, 'Of Blackstone's Tower: Metaphors of Distance and Histories of the English Law School' in P. Birks (ed), *Pressing Problems in the Law: What Are Law Schools For?* Oxford: OUP, 1996. Note also in this context the work of the UK Centre for Legal Education (UKCLE). <http://www.ukcle.ac.uk>, accessed 15 October 2008; also A. Sherr and J. Webb, 'Law Students, the External Market and Socialization: Do We Make Them Turn to the City?', *Journal of Law and Society*, 1989, vol 16(2), p 225.

[49] A point well made in work concerned with women legal academics. See also J. Finch, 'Foreword: Why Be Interested in Women's Position in Academe?', *Gender, Work and Organisation*, 2003, vol 10(2), p 133.

[50] Bibbings, op cit, 2003.

[51] In addition to work cited above, n 20, Hillyard and Sim, op cit, 1997; Hillyard, op cit, 2002; A. Hunt 'Governing the Socio-Legal Project: Or what Do Research Councils Do?', *Journal of Law and Society*, 1994, vol 21, p 522; cf R. Cotterrell, 'Subverting Orthodoxy, Making Law Central: A View of Socio-Legal studies', *Journal of Law and Society*, 2002, vol 29(4), p 632.

A story: the rise of liberal legal education

It is possible to present a rather different interpretation of these changes. There exists a central narrative about legal education and university law schools in the UK in the period from the 1960s to the present day which questions the picture of research and teaching presented within the corporatisation thesis. This story suggests, far from any marginalisation of critical socio-legal research, including the study of law and gender, that there has been a 'breaking out' of law from 'the sterile technocratic straitjacket' that accompanied the post-war expansion of universities.[52] Tony Bradney and Fiona Cownie have argued, writing together and separately, that within contemporary legal studies the majority of, if not all, university law schools can be characterised as embracing a broadly 'liberal', pluralistic approach to legal education and scholarship. In Cownie's book *Legal Academics* we find an account that, in its discussion of how audit, equity and anti-discrimination agendas have impacted on legal academics, would appear to run 'against the grain' of much recent work on the corporatisation of Higher Education.[53] Far from seeing a re-visioning of the commitments and aspirations of the legal academic subject in ways aligned to the imperatives of the new economy,[54] Cownie presents 'considerable evidence' in UK law schools of:

> the enduring nature of certain core aspects of the culture of academic law, which suggest that the professional identities of legal academics may be more resistant to pressure than some commentators have acknowledged. Their prime objective as teachers was to teach students to think; despite benchmarks, audit and other forms of quality assessment they did not talk in terms of 'transferable skills' or increasing the employability of their students.[55]

Bradney, reviewing the recent literature in the field, makes a similar point.[56] Whilst 'academic lawyers are subject to the changes taking place in higher education just as much as members of other "academic tribes"', the 'culture of academic law and the professional identities constructed within it display a great deal of resilience, retaining, importantly, a fundamentally academic orientation'.[57]

---

[52] Thornton, op cit, 2001,'The Demise of Diversity in Legal Education'. See further W. Twining, 'Remember 1972: The Oxford Centre in the Context of Developments in Higher Education and the Discipline of Law' in D. Galligan (ed), *Socio-Legal Studies in Context: The Oxford Centre Past and Future*, Oxford: Blackwell, 1995; B. Hepple, 'The Renewal of the Liberal Law Degree', *Cambridge Law Review*, 1996, vol 55, p 471.

[53] Cownie, op cit, 2004. See also Bradney, op cit, 2003.

[54] Slaughter and Leslie, op cit, 1997.

[55] Cownie, op cit, 2004, p 206.

[56] Bradney, op cit, 2003.

[57] Cownie, op cit, 2004, p 206. Also A. Bradney, 'Elite Values in Twenty-First Century United Kingdom Law Schools', *Law Teacher*, 2008, vol 42, p 291; R. Brownsword, 'Where Are All The Law Schools Going?', *Law Teacher*, 1996, vol 30, p 6.

What the majority of university law students thus study in, and what legal scholars teach and research in, is a 'liberal law school'.[58] This is an institution marked by methodological and epistemological diversity; by a commitment to a distinctive academic (as opposed to vocational) stage of legal education; by a less deferential relation to the legal profession and legal hierarchy compared to what had existed in the past; and, importantly, by an institutional acceptance of original, often interdisciplinary, legal research, including the study of gender.[59] Whilst socio-legal studies may for some simply 'stand alongside'[60] the 'still dominant' approach of black-letter law, for Bradney and Cownie, in contrast, it is socio-legal studies that now constitutes the 'dominant approach' to scholarship in UK law schools.[61] Their work can be broadly aligned to other defences of progressive liberal education, work which has explicitly sought to embrace, rather than confine, the links between law and the insights of other disciplines.[62]

Such a picture of contemporary legal scholarship would, therefore, appear to not fit well with many aspects of the story of the rise of the restructured, entrepreneurial university and the corporatisation thesis. Two further arguments can be made to support such an interpretation and, in pursuing this theme, I will focus more closely on questions of gender and how these developments may have reshaped gender relations within the law school.

Gender, equality and the changing nature of work: socio-legal studies and the legal academy

There is, of course, considerable historical continuity in seeing links between universities and commercial interests and the idea of a conflict between alternative images of universities as, variously, businesses and repositories of disinterested scholarship, has a long history. It was a matter of debate even at the purported high point of social liberalism in the 1960s,[63] a point of significance in

---

[58] Bradney, op. cit, 2003. A. Bradney, 'Liberalising Legal Education' in Cownie (ed), op cit, 1999; Hepple, op cit, 1996; R. Burridge and J. Webb, 'The Values of Common Law Legal Education: Rethinking Rules, Responsibilities, Relationships and Roles in the Law School', *Legal Ethics*, 2007, vol 10, p 74; R. Burridge and J. Webb, 'The Values of Common Law Legal Education Reprised', *Law Teacher*, 2008, vol 42(3), p 265.

[59] A view supported, on one reading at least, by the work of the Law Panel reflected in the results of 2001 and 2008 RAE (see n 45).

[60] R. Card, Presidential Address, 11 September 2002, Society of Legal Scholars Annual Conference, De Montfort University.

[61] Bradney, op cit, 2003; Cownie, op cit, 2004.

[62] Note in particular M. Nussbaum, *Cultivating Humanity: A Classical Defense of Reform in Legal Education*, Cambridge, MA: Harvard University Press, 1997.

[63] E. P. Thompson, *Warwick University Ltd: Industry, Management and the Universities*, Harmondsworth: Penguin, 1970: on 'the species Academicus Superciliosus' who is 'inflated with self-esteem and perpetually self-congratulatory as to the high vocation of the university teacher' pp 153–55. Also E. P. Thompson, 'The Business University', *New Society*, 19 February 1970. In law, from this period, note O. Kahn-Freund, 'Reflections on Legal Education', *Modern Law Review*, 1966, vol 29, p 121.

considering issues of gender and equality. To clarify, Halsey and Trow's typical 'British Academic'[64] in 1971 was, in all likelihood, white, male and middle class; the form of community in which he participated marked by what Jeff Hearn has characterised as a white, middle-class, male colleginality.[65] It is this ostensibly liberal autonomous regime of the old universities, of a 'managerial control, largely by men, and largely of men', that has, on one view of the rise of liberal legal education, been disrupted by new managerial controls from government and the equity agendas with which they have been associated.[66] Such changes can be read as having opened out a university system (and with it, their law schools) hitherto based on patronage, elitism and unaccountability to what are, for all their limitations (below), more egalitarian processes and cultures in relation to areas such as recruitment and promotion.[67]

At the same time, privatisation measures and associated drivers of internal and external competition have, of course, been introduced across diverse organisational and employment contexts. A range of institutions and professions, to an arguably far greater degree than British universities, have been encouraged to behave in 'market-like' ways.[68] Processes of downsizing, audit and concerns about deprofessionalisation, for example, are not confined to the legal academy and, within the 'new economy', work at all levels has become characterised by a lack of conceptual clarity and growing inequality.[69] At the time of writing, amidst a period of severe economic downturn, an issue I consider in later chapters in relation to the legal profession and gender

[64] A. H. Halsey and M. A. Trow, *The British Academics*, London: Faber and Faber, 1971.

[65] J. Hearn, 'Men, Managers and Management: The Case of Higher Education' in S. Whitehead and R. Moodley (eds), *Transforming Managers: Engendering Change in the Public Sector*, London: UCL Press, 1999. Also J. Hearn, 'Academia, Management and Men: Making the Connections' in Brooks and Mackinnon (eds), op. cit, 2001; C. Pritchard, 'Managing Universities: Is It Men's Work?' in D. Collinson and J. Hearn, *Men as Managers, Managers as Men*, London: Sage, 1996; Wells, op cit, 2001, p 129. Note also D. Howell, 'The Clubbable Chaps', *AUTLook*, 22 October 1992, pp 19–20.

[66] S. Whitehead, 'Men, Managers and the Shifting Discourses of Post-Compulsory Education', *Research in Post-Compulsory Education*, 1996, vol 1(2), p 151; D. Kerfoot and S. Whitehead, 'Boys' Own Stuff: Masculinity and the Management of Further Education', *Sociological Review*, 1998, p 436.

[67] There is, Oakley has suggested in the context of the restructured university, something attractive to the marginalised about cultures that stress the need for open procedures and that question potentially inefficient and unfair concepts as tenure: 'But when the culture of bureaucracy and commodification is combined with a disregard – flagrant in its explicitness – for the way power operates, the result is bound to be discriminatory': Oakley, op cit, 2001, p xiii.

[68] C. Pollitt, *Managerialism and the Public Services: The Anglo-American Experience*, Oxford: Blackwell, 1990; M. Burrage, 'From a Gentleman's to a Public Profession: Status and Politics in the History of English Solicitors', *International Journal of the Legal Profession*, 1996, vol 3, p 45.

[69] For discussion R. Sennett, *The Corrosion of Character: The Personal Consequences of Work in the New Capitalism*, New York: W. W. Norton, 1998; U. Beck, *The Brave New World of Work*, Cambridge: Polity, 2000.

identity, job security and salary levels in universities can be viewed as relatively secure and advantageous (although see below).

If we look more closely, moreover, many of these changes in universities appear more double-edged in their effects than might at first appear to be the case. For example, far from witnessing an undermining or negation of collegiality within law, it is possible to interpret new technologies as having opened up opportunities for legal academics, new intellectual communities forming as a result of the national and global networks developed through the use of the Internet, including in relation to the study of gender and sexuality in law. Equally, whilst the evidence that academic life in the UK is more demanding than in the past is compelling, any suggestion that the law school is, per se, a more oppressive and difficult environment in which to work must be treated with caution. For both women and men, Bradney has argued, academia remains a field of employment unlike many others in the way it facilitates a potential management of 'balance' between home and work.[70] This can be seen, in the light of social shifts to be detailed in chapter 5, as an issue of significance for women and men who may wish, for example, to seek relative flexibility in their work and address work and child care commitments, even if this is an autonomy that has diminished compared with other historical periods. In terms of the model of the 'committed academic' emerging from this process, meanwhile, for those women and men, straight or gay, who are willing or able to adapt to the temporal and spatial demands of contemporary legal academic life, and who culturally 'fit' within a particular law school (chapter 3), the opportunities and rewards are arguably similar, at least at lower levels of university hierarchies, for both sexes. Both men and women negotiate, albeit in ways mediated by stage of career, social background and personal ambition, the consequences of collective and individual judgements of research success or failure in terms of their everyday experiences of legal academic life.

These points can be taken further. As has been noted in other disciplines, 'once outsiders' can, over time, 'become insiders'.[71] Across many UK universities, therefore, individuals engaged in socio-legal research, including critical work around gender, sexuality and feminism, are now in senior managerial positions within their institutions: key figures, either within central university administrations (as Deans, Faculty Directors of Research, Pro-Vice Chancellors, Vice Chancellors and so forth) or else Heads of Law Schools, Chairs of Professional Associations or RAE panel members. As such, they are in positions to influence, at least to a degree, the future strategic direction of

[70] 'Working in a liberal law school and seeking to combine avocation and vocation offers the possibility of a way of life that is beyond the reach of most in modern society': Bradney, op cit, 2003, p 203. 'The environment of the liberal law school thus seems to be best placed to give academics an opportunity to satisfactorily manage their lives': Bradney, op cit, 2003, p 202.

[71] On the field of criminology, see R. Collier, *Masculinities, Crime and Criminology*, London: Sage, 1998, pp 36–67. Note also D. Subotnik and G. Lazar, 'Deconstructing the Rejection Letter: A Look at Elitism in Article Selection', *Journal of Legal Education*, 1999, vol 49, p 601.

law, both in the university in which they work and in the field of legal education more generally. A case can be made that the rise of the performative university may have served well, at least in certain respects, socio-legal research, including feminist scholarship, a view supported by one interpretation of past research assessments and Cownie's study.[72] In support of Bradney and Cownie's thesis, therefore, far from seeing a constraining of the scope of legal study over the past twenty years, there has occurred a proliferation of new socio-legal journals open to work on gender and law, the revitalisation of professional associations (such as the Socio-Legal Studies Association [SLSA]) and a shifting of the staff profile in institutions, with the result that there is now a critical mass of socio-legal scholars in many, if by no means all, UK university law schools. As Margaret Thornton has observed, law generally is still perceived across many universities (internally at least) as falling on the 'applied' side of the research equation, with empirical socio-legal studies lending itself well to the demands of the new university (although see further below).[73]

Resistance, contestation and diversity

Finally, corporatising imperatives should not be understood as achieved ends.[74] There has been a tendency in some of the literature on the restructured university to engage with macro-processes, paint in 'broad brush strokes' in such a way as to overplay the impact of a dominant neo-liberal ideology on disciplines and the individual practices therein (such as, in this case, what legal academics do). One result, Bradney has argued, has been to underplay individual and collective resistance to such changes. Practices and cultures associated with traditional models of the university may be more structurally embedded and resistant to top-down reforms than advocates of the corporatisation thesis allow.[75] Equally, there can be marked differences between what politicians, policy-makers and senior university management such as Vice-Chancellors say law schools should do, and what the academics who work in them actually do.[76] Bradney cites in this regard successful resistance in the past on the part of the legal academic community to audit reforms and initiatives from the profession. This points to the importance of engaging with the complexity of power and resistance within specific institutional and disciplinary contexts, questioning how dialogue, debate and struggle[77] play out in negotiating the competing imperatives of a range of stakeholders in

---

[72] On the former see Hillyard, op cit, 2002.

[73] Thornton, op cit, 2001, 'The Demise of Diversity in Legal Education'. See also W. Pue, 'Legal Education's Mission', *Law Teacher*, 2008, vol 42, p 275.

[74] A central argument in Bradney, op cit, 2003.

[75] See further J. Newson 'Conclusion: Repositioning the Local Through Alternative Responses to Globalization' in Currie and Newson (eds), op cit 1998.

[76] Note also the argument of Cownie, op cit, 2004; A. Bradney, 'Academic Duty', 2004, *The Reporter*, No. 28, Spring, pp 1–2.

[77] Bradney, op cit, 2003, ch 7.

the law school.[78] Studies of women managers in universities, for example, reveal a complex picture of strategies of resistance and coping, as gendered subjectivities adapt in the process of becoming a manager in universities.[79] This is not, in short, a picture of neo-liberalism being imposed on otherwise passive universities and their law schools.

Three further points can be made. First, there has been, and remains, a degree of consensus in the legal academic community about the desirability of defending the liberal model of education and research outlined above.[80] Second, there is little evidence to support the view that the research agendas and curriculum of UK law schools have become significantly more techno-cratic and corporatised, at least not in the way that advocates of the restructuring thesis suggest. Far from being directed to the needs of, for example, the legal profession, 'research users' or the economy, contemporary legal research, Bradney argues, reflects a diverse set of research agendas. These, ultimately, Cownie suggests, derive from the interests and personal beliefs of individual academics themselves.[81] Thus, for all the continued dominance of the 'core' and private law subjects, the contemporary law school curriculum is one in which contextual, socio-legal, critical, 'essentially academic' subjects abound and prove popular with students, including the study of law and gender. Law schools are, compared with the past, more open to diverse perspectives and intellectual debates, including work on gender and sexuality (including studies of masculinities such as this).[82]

Set against this backdrop the changing academy can be seen to have facilitated a complex transformation, therefore, in the form, content and scope of legal scholarship and, with it, significant changes in understandings of gender, equal-ity and opportunity in the context of the prevailing culture of law schools.

And yet ... gender and the reshaping of the academic subject

> Newman ... would not have recognized the government's concept of glorified fur-ther education colleges with a sideline in helping local business. There may be a managerial logic in taking this route, but such institutions will find it hard to recruit high-calibre staff or students.[83]

---

[78] Cownie, op cit, 2009.

[79] R. Deem, 'Power and Resistance in the Academy: The Case of Women Academic Managers' in Whitehead and Moodley (eds), op cit, 1999.

[80] Bradney, op cit, 2003, pp 64–171. Equally, developments around the promotion of university links with industry suggest a picture of resistance and compromise: HM Treasury, *Lambert Review of Business-University Collaboration: Final Report*, London: HMSO, 2003. Available at: <http://www.hm-treasury.gov.uk/media/EA556/lambert_review_final_450.pdf>, accessed 14 July 2008.

[81] Cownie, op cit, 2004.

[82] See, for example, and generally, the arguments contained in Thomas (ed) op cit, 1997.

[83] Editorial, 'Would Newman See His Idea in Labour's vision?', *THES*, 24 January 2003, p 18.

Counter-tendencies

Notwithstanding the above, however, I shall argue in this section that there is considerable cause to be concerned about the reshaping of the (legal) academic subject that has accompanied this process. I will begin by considering some counter-tendencies that suggest the future of critical scholarship in law, including the study of law and gender,[84] may indeed be uncertain. I then proceed to look more closely at the conceptualisation of gender, masculinity and ideas about the 'man of law' in these debates, suggesting that what has occurred is not so much an unproblematic, progressive embrace of egalitarianism and gender neutrality but a complex refiguring of gender relations, a re-gendering, of the law school that has resulted, for women and men, in new opportunities, new uncertainties and new questions about what it means to be a legal academic.

With regard to the logic of performativity discussed above, a case can be made, we have seen, that the various Research Assessment Exercises (RAE) have served (some) socio-legal scholars and, in certain respects, the study of law and gender well. There is no guarantee, of course, that the framing of assessment criteria adopted in the future will have the same result.[85] For many legal academics in UK university law schools powerful organisational imperatives exist internally to engage with business and industry, maximise external income and embrace applied research agendas. The messages conveyed within the political and cultural economy in which universities now operate point towards a clear expectation that '[research] results should [have] clear and direct policy implications'.[86] Further, notwithstanding the robust defence of liberal legal education made by writers such as Bradney and Cownie, the influence of the legal profession on law schools, and of the large City and corporate provincial firms in particular (see chapter 6), remains significant and may be increasing. This influence cannot be confined, I shall argue in chapter 4, to issues about the control and regulation of the curriculum via accreditation requirements.[87] The cultural relationship between the university law school and the legal profession is, rather, in the context of an increasingly privatised and marketised Higher Education sector, shifting in more subtle ways.[88] The wider processes of corporatisation, meanwhile,

---

[84] See further D. E. Chunn, S. Boyd and H. Lessard (eds), *Reaction and Resistance: Feminism, Law and Social Change*, Vancouver: UBC Press, 2007.

[85] In relation to the forthcoming Research Excellence Framework (REF), for example, much will depend on what are considered to be the appropriate indicators for each discipline: <http://www.hefce.ac.uk/Research/ref>, accessed 15 January 2008.

[86] Hillyard and Sim, op cit, 1997, p 56.

[87] See B. Puchalska, 'Legal Education: Professional, Academic or Vocational?' *European Journal of Legal Education*, 2004, vol 4, p 19; also R. Collier, 'Peter's Choice: Issues of Identity, Lifestyle and Consumption in Changing Representations of Corporate Lawyers and Legal Academics' in S. Greenfield and G. Osborn (eds), *Readings in Law and Popular Culture: Routledge Research Monographs*, London: Routledge, 2007.

[88] R. Collier, 'The Liberal Law School, The Restructured University and the Paradox of Socio-Legal Studies', *Modern Law Review*, 2005, vol 68(3), p 475.

Thornton has suggested, have helped shift 'the orientation and purpose of universities generally from intellectual inquiry to instrumentalism and vocationalism'.[89] This has resulted in the added impetus within many law schools towards a more practice-centred and market-oriented model of legal education.[90]

In such a context the positioning of the 'purely academic' as less attuned to the dominant economic, cultural and political climate interlinks with 'the populist message of neo-liberalism ... that one should not waste time on knowledge lacking use value'.[91] The argument that universities, and their law schools, remain relatively advantaged within the context of an economic recession must also be treated with considerable caution at a time of further polarisation[92] in the sector and when, as Jane Kelsey has predicted, there are signs across many law schools of a withering away of non-market-friendly sectors of curricula.[93] At the time of writing, amidst significant cuts in public finances, there is growing concern about job losses across universities, with expansion plans in student numbers curbed and warnings made about the financial sustainability of some universities[94] and the possible closure of departments.[95] For many scholars working outside the 'elite' institutions, organisational pressures and demands are such that everyday academic life is, for many, far removed from the model of a unity of 'vocation and avocation' underscoring Bradney's analysis of the liberal law school.

Questions can also be raised about future research capacity in law. Within the technocentric, research-user-focused legal academy it might be expected that empirical policy- and practice-orientated socio-legal research would fare well. Yet a 'crisis in waiting' has been identified in research capacity in the field of socio-legal studies,[96] prompting a major inquiry into the issue.[97] Law is one of a

89 Thornton, op cit, 2001, 'The Demise of Diversity in Legal Education', p 43.
90 It is Thornton's argument that 'law schools, too, [appear] magnetically drawn to the wealthy firms and their perceived needs in design of their curricula': Thornton, op cit, 2001, 'The Demise of Diversity in Legal Education', p 40.
91 Thornton, op cit, 2001, 'The Demise of Diversity in Legal Education', p 44. Compare C. Symes and J. McIntryre (eds), *Working Knowledge: The New Vocationalism and Higher Education*, Buckingham: Open University Press, 2000; T. Tysome, 'Sector Caught in Parent Trap', *THES*, 30 July 2004, p 1.
92 H. Fearn, 'Funding Focus on Research Elite Set to Split Sector', *Times Higher Education*, 27 November 2008; C. Johnston and A. Thomson, 'Golden Diamond Outshines the Rest' *THES*, 23 July 2004, pp 10–11; 'Fears of Elite Split', *The Guardian*, 10 September 2002.
93 J. Kelsey, 'Academic Freedom Needed More Than Ever' in R. Crozier (ed), *Troubled Times, Academic Freedom in New Zealand*, Palmerston North: Dunmore Press, 1999.
94 H. Richardson, 'Universities "May Face Deficit"', *BBC News*, 10 December 2008.
95 D. Turner, 'Warning on Student Numbers in England', *Financial Times*, 9 May 2009; D. Turner, 'Extra £120m education savings sought', *Financial Times*, 8 May 2009; J. Sherman and A. Frean, 'Thousands of jobs to go at universities as budgets slashed', *The Times*, 7 May 2009.
96 S. Witherspoon, 'Research Capacity: A Crisis in Waiting?', 2002, *SLN*, No 37, p 1. Also T. Varnava, 'Building Research Capacity in Legal Education', 2002, *SLN*, No 38, p 4.
97 H. Genn, M. Partington and S. Wheeler, *Law in the Real World: Improving Our Understanding of How Law Works: Final Report and Recommendations* (The Nuffield Enquiry on Empirical Legal Research), London: Nuffield, 2006.

number of disciplines that has experienced well-documented difficulties in recruit-ment, especially at senior levels and in certain subject areas.[98] If the 'proletar-ianisation' of university academics is a long-standing theme in the Higher Education literature, therefore, these questions about research capacity may have, notwithstanding the impact of economic recession, a particular salience for law. It is with regard to the issue of gender, however, that the contradictory nature of these developments can be seen in a particularly clear way.

Re-masculinising the academy?

> Gender is far more than an individual trait somehow connected with bodily dif-ference, like red hair or left-handedness. With gender, we are dealing with a com-plex, and powerfully effective, domain of social practice.[99]

I have suggested above that social changes opened out university law schools to more egalitarian processes and cultures in relation to areas such as recruitment and promotion. I positioned this as part of broader cultural, economic and poli-tical developments around ideas of equality, diversity and gender convergence, themes discussed in different legal contexts throughout this book. It is important, however, in considering the gendered law school, not to overstate such claims.

Emerging work, including scholarship on women legal academics,[100] suggests that this transformation of universities has produced new configurations around gender and new ideas about what it now means to speak of the law school as a 'gendered' institution. At the same time, a wealth of research on the restructured university indicates that gender remains highly pertinent to understandings of contemporary academic life.[101] Across institutions and disciplines, for example, campaigns and networks have been established to support women academics[102] and challenge still pervasive disparities around pay and promotion. In the field of law, there remain few women heads of department and, relative to men, few women law professors.[103] Notwithstanding the transformation in the gender

---

[98] For example, J. Hurstfield and F. Neathy, *Recruitment and Retention of Academic Staff in UK Higher Education 2001*, London: IRS Research, 2002.

[99] R. W. Connell, *The Men and the Boys*, Cambridge: Polity, 2000, p 18.

[100] Such as that cited above, n 3.

[101] See Brooks and Mackinnon (eds), op cit, 2001; Currie et al, op cit, 2002; Currie and Newson (eds), op cit, 1998.

[102] The discipline of law in the UK, for example, has seen the formation of groups and networks designed to support, encourage and bring together women legal academics. The establishment of the Women Law Professors Network in 1998 was followed by conferences supported by the leading professional associations: 'Working With Women Workshop: The Cat-Flap in the Glass Ceiling' (June 1999: ALT/SPTL sponsored); 'Strategic Thinking for the Millennium: Women and Law Conference' University of Westminster, London, 2000. Note also the Socio-Legal Studies Association Women's Network and National Network of Women in Legal Education.

[103] C. McGlynn, *The Woman Lawyer: Making the Difference*, London: Butterworths, 1998; Cownie, op. cit, 2004.

ratio of the intake into university legal education over the past thirty years, that is, law schools, like the legal profession, remain dominated by men at senior levels. Further, many aspects of academic work, and the nature of management practices and cultures, continue to be perceived as profoundly gendered and, in the terms set out in chapter 1, masculine in nature.[104]

For some writers the restructuring of Higher Education detailed in this chapter has served not so much to diminish men's power or the significance of gender in universities but to *re-masculinise* the academy. Thus, the model of the academic as new knowledge worker, a figure committed to visible achievements that are quantifiable, and a model of performance that negates content in the name of productivity,[105] has itself been characterised as masculine in nature, embodying a gendered notion of labour in its 'relentless promotion of the self' at the expense of good citizenship.[106] With regard to the temporal and spatial parameters of academic work,[107] meanwhile, the 'freedom' to 'choose' the high levels of commitment necessary to secure career success in the contemporary university entails the presence of material and psychological networks of support that are arguably not dissimilar from those associated with the 'commitment question' in the careers of practising lawyers (see further chapter 4, p 119, chapter 6, p 177). Far from allowing for flexibility and autonomy, the very indeterminacy of academic labour in terms of time and commitment can prove a double-edged sword within the work-intensive emotional economy fostered by the corporatised university, one in which new subjective attachments and ways of 'being' a legal academic appear to be emerging. This latter point requires clarification.

Studies of the restructured academy suggest that significant changes have occurred in relation to organisational identity (what it means to be, to identify *as* an academic).[108] New modes of self-management, in particular, have been identified within universities, a process that has had physical, emotional and intellectual

---

[104] See M. David and D. Woodward (eds), *Negotiating the Glass Ceiling: Careers of Senior Women in the Academic World*, London: Falmer Press, 1998; A. Brooks, *Academic Women*, Milton Keynes: SRHE and Open University Press, 1997; L. H. Collins, J. C. Chrisler, and K. Quina (eds), *Career Strategies for Women in Academe*, London: Sage, 1998; D. Malina and S. Maslin-Prothers (eds), *Surviving the Academy: Feminist Perspectives*, London: Falmer Press, 1998; L. Morley and V. Walsh (eds), *Breaking Boundaries: Women in Higher Education*, London: Taylor and Francis, 1996; L. Morley, *Organising Feminisms: The Micro politics of the Academy*, London: Macmillan Press, 1999; J. West and K. Lyon 'The Trouble with Equal Opportunities: The Case of Women Academics', *Gender and Education*, 1995, vol 7, p 51.

[105] Although, for some 'We would all be better off if academics wrote fewer but better books': L. Segal, 'Opinion', *The Guardian*, 13 February 2001.

[106] Thornton op cit, 2001, 'The Demise of Diversity in Legal Education'.

[107] See further M. Glucksmann, *Cottons and Casuals: The Gendered Organisation of Time and Space*, York: Sociologypress, 2000.

[108] E. McWilliam 'Changing the Academic Subject' in R. Hunter and M. Keys (eds.), *Changing Law: Rights, Regulation, Reconciliation*, Aldershot: Ashgate, 2005.

consequences for women and men, although not necessarily, in keeping with themes developed in chapter 1, in the same way.[109] It is in this context that, McWilliam[110] has argued, as an assessment of the performativity of academics comes to pervade numerous aspects of university life, new organisational cultures and forms of governance have sought to remodel and refashion the academic subject in ways in keeping with the new world in which universities operate.[111] This has involved, she suggests, in a prevailing culture of risk minimisation and audit, of individuals, institutions, departments and organisations, a process that has sought to engage 'all individuals within the university (managers and non-managers) in doing particular sorts of *work on themselves*, the work of turning themselves into "professional experts"'.[112]

The emergence of this subjectivity, however, may have itself favoured some individuals rather than others.[113] At more senior levels, the new management practices required by the restructured university have been characterised as 'overly rational, disembodied and instrumental pursuits' which 'make modern management particularly important sites for the reproduction of masculine discourses and practices'.[114] The discourses of the new corporate management styles, Deborah Kerfoot and David Knights suggest, are thus well suited to the patterns of a form of 'compulsive masculinity' which can, in turn, lead to a sense of disembodiment in the continuous pursuit of the new targets and challenges within an overarching ethos of performativity. Whilst this is something that can, of course, be experienced by both men and women, studies of academics and university managers suggest that 'men are more likely to (and/ or more likely to be perceived to) match the (embodied) requirements of bureaucratic organization far more closely than women do'.[115]

---

[109] Brooks op cit, 2001, pp 32–38; McWilliam, op cit, 2005; C. Pritchard, 'The Body Topographies of Education Management' in J. Hassard, R. Holliday and H. Willmott (eds), *Organization and the Body*, London: Sage, 2000; C. Pritchard, 'Know, Learn and Share! The Knowledge Phenomena and the Construction of a Consumptive-Communicative Body' in C. Pritchard, R. Hull, M. Chumer and H. Willmott (eds), *Managing Knowledge: Critical Investigations of Work and Learning*, Basingstoke: Macmillan, 2000; A. Talib, 'The Continuing Behavioural Modification of Academics Since the 1992 RAE', *Higher Education Review*, 2001, vol 33, p 30; C. Casey, 'Corporate Transformation: Designer Culture, Designer Employees and "Post-Occupational" Solidarity', *Organization*, 1996, vol 3(3), p 317.

[110] McWilliam, op cit, 2005.

[111] Thornton, op cit, 2001, 'Among the Ruins: Law in the Neo-Liberal Academy'; C. Polster and J. Newson, 'Don't Count Your Blessings: The Social Accomplishments of Performance Indicators' in Currie and Newson (eds), op cit, 1998.

[112] McWilliam, op cit, 2005, p 107, my emphasis.

[113] D. L. Collinson and M. Collinson, 'Delayering Managers: Time-Space Surveillance and its Gendered Effects', *Organization*, 1997, vol 4(3), p 375, at p 399.

[114] McWilliam, op cit, 2005, p 97.

[115] A. Witz, S. Halford and M. Savage, 'Organized Bodies: Gender, Sexuality and Embodiment in Contemporary Organizations' in L. Adkins and V. Merchant (eds), *Sexualising the Social: Power and the Organization of Sexuality*, Basingstoke: Macmillan, 1996, p 175, cited in Brooks, op cit, 2001, p 36; D. Kerfoot and D. Knights, 'The Best is Yet to Come? The Quest for Embodiment in

At issue here, however, is more than a matter of developing a culture of 'in early, out late'. What we are dealing with are broader understandings of what it means to speak of universities and their law schools as gendered institutions in the first place (chapter 1, pp 10–13). For some critics, the restructured university has been marked by the emergence of distinctive 'Entrepreneurial Masculinities'.[116] Recognising differences between universities and other sectors of education, such an argument aligns itself with the notion of structural backlash identified in work on schooling whereby a restructuring of educational systems is seen to have resulted in the emergence of new forms of entrepreneurial, rather than older-style paternalistic, masculinities at the core of policy-making. Thus, the form of paternalistic masculinity associated with the dominant culture of universities of, say, thirty years ago, has increasingly been seen as incompatible with formal gender equality, the product of a historical moment marked by clearer gender divisions of labour.[117] It is a form of masculinity that frames the comments cited by Celia Wells in her 2001 discussion of women legal academics in the UK, who characterise these men variously as kindly, paternalistic, protective or else (at the same time) sexist in their diverse 'demonstrations of masculinity'.[118] The 'entrepreneurial' man, in contrast, is highly attuned to discourses of gender equity and diversity, and knows the 'rules of the game'. We have moved, that is, away from the 'fairly liberal', autonomous regime of the old universities – of the 'managerial control, largely by men, and largely of men' discussed above[119] – towards a new hegemonic bureaucratic managerialism – one that can still be characterised as largely male dominated, fratriarchal in

Managerial Work' in D. Collinson and J. Hearn (eds), *Men as Managers, Managers as Men: Critical Perspectives on Men, Masculinities and Management*, London: Sage, 1996; P. Redman and M. Mac an Ghaill 'Educating Peter: The Making of a History Man' in D. Steinberg et al (eds), *Border Patrols: Policing the Boundaries of Heterosexuality*, London: Cassell, 1997; D. Knights and W. Richards, 'Sex Discrimination in UK Academia', *Gender, Work and Organisation*, 2003, vol 10 (2), p 213; J. Currie, 'Restructuring Employment: The Case of Female Academics', *Australian Universities Review*, 1995, vol 2, p 49; C. Davies and P. Holloway, 'Troubling Transformations: Gender Regimes and Organizational Culture in the Academy' in Morley and Walsh (eds), op cit, 1995; Y. Benschop and M. Brouns, 'Crumbling Ivory Towers: Academic Organising and its Gender Effects', *Gender, Work and Organisation*, 2003, vol 10(2), p 194. On gender differences in intrinsic, altruistic and social rewards see M. Mooney Marini, P. Fan, E. Finley and A. M. Beutel, 'Gender and Job Values', *Sociology of Education*, 1996, vol 69, p 49.

[116] Hearn, op cit, 1999, Hearn, op cit, 1996; Collinson and Hearn, op cit, 1996; C. Itzin and J. Newman (eds), *Gender, Culture and Organisational Change*, London: Routledge, 1995; J. Wajcman *Managing Like A Man: Women and Men in Corporate Management*, Cambridge: Polity Press, 1998; A. Sinclair, *Doing Leadership Differently: Gender, Power and Sexuality in a Changing Business Culture*, Melbourne: Melbourne University Press, 1998.

[117] At one time personified in many institutions, for example, by the presence of a 'University Wives Club'.

[118] Wells, op cit, 2001.

[119] Wells op cit, 2001, p 129.

nature[120] and, frequently, marginalising of women and those who do not 'fit' the dominant cultural codes, an issue I return to, in relation to social class, in chapter 3. These new cultural norms may themselves be, we have seen above, double-edged in their effects and, on closer examination, still gendered in distinctive ways, not least in relation to regimes of target-setting and control.[121]

I have suggested in this chapter that understandings of the legal academic as a gendered subject have been reconstituted, remade in a process whereby new academic subjectivities have emerged to which both individual men and women might aspire or identify. This chapter has traced some of the features of the legal academic as new knowledge worker, noting the complexity of resistance and contestation in the discipline of law and the contradictory nature of many of the changes that have impacted on universities and their law schools.[122] Far from erasing questions of gender, I have argued that a reframing of gender relations marks the contemporary university. At this stage, and to pursue this theme further in terms of reconceptualising the male subject in law, it is necessary to ask some different questions about methodology, gender and the private life of the law school.

[120] Thornton, op cit, 2001, 'The Demise of Diversity in Legal Education', observes the way in which these senior managers, who are almost invariably male, surround themselves with men who possess similar characteristics to themselves. R. Collier, 'Masculinism, Law and Law Teaching', *International Journal of the Sociology of Law*, 1991, vol 19, p 427; M. Thornton, 'Hegemonic Masculinity and the Academy', *International Journal of the Sociology of Law*, 1989, vol 17, p 115.

[121] S. Whitehead, 'From Paternalism to Entrepreneurialism: the Experience of Men Managers in UK Post Compulsory Education', *Discourse: Studies in the Cultural Politics of Education*, 1999, vol 20(1), p 57; Redman and Mac an Ghaill, op cit, 1997; R. Collier, '"Nutty Professors", "Men in Suits" and "New Entrepreneurs": Corporeality, Subjectivity and Change in the Law School and Legal Practice', *Social and Legal Studies*, 1998, vol 7, p 27.

[122] Curiously, it has been suggested that 'men are being deterred by a decline in the perceived status of higher education fuelled by low pay and increased regulation', and that 'men leave the lower status academy to women': Editorial 'The Future's Female', *THES*, 25 June 2004, p 12.

Chapter 3

Beyond the 'private life' of the law school

Class and the (legal) academic subject

Academic careers share many characteristics with other employment careers. They are lived within organizational and social networks which have particular rules, hierarchies, culture and politics. The academic world, like other areas of employment, is highly competitive ... It requires, among other things, a similar range of administrative, organizational and personal skills to many other professional careers. Being an academic is a job, with core tasks, *as well as a way of life.*[1]

Introduction

In this chapter, following on from the discussion of gender and the changing university in chapter 2, I explore in more detail how the legal academic has been approached within the literature on the 'private life' of the law school. I do so via an interrogation of the relationship between social class and the legal academy. Fiona Cownie has observed, in her 2004 book *Legal Academics*:

> In considering the lived experience of legal academia [class] is a factor which is too important to be overlooked.[2]

Further:

> The 'identity matters' of gender, class, race and sexuality include some of the least explored areas of legal academia, yet this study provides evidence that *they have significant effects*, not only upon the professional identities of legal academics, but also on key aspects of the culture of academic law.[3]

What does it mean, however, in the context of the changes in Higher Education outlined in chapter 2, to speak of 'significant effects' of class upon the

---

[1] L. Blaxter, C. Hughes and M. Tight, *The Academic Career Handbook*, Buckingham: Open University Press, 1998, p 3, my emphasis.

[2] F. Cownie, *Legal Academics: Culture and Identities*, Oxford: Hart, 2004, p 203.

[3] Cownie, op cit, 2004, p 203, my emphasis.

'professional identities of legal academics and the culture of academic law', how being a legal academic might involve a 'way of life'? In focusing on class, I do not wish to efface the intersectional nature of social categories, the multiple dimensions of discrimination and diversity in relation to experience. I do not wish, at all, to downplay the importance and interconnected nature of gender, race and sexuality and how these issues cannot, in fact, be disaggregated.[4] Rather, in unpacking the idea of the 'man of law' in the context of a re-gendering of the corporatised university, it is important to look more closely, I shall suggest, at how legal academics have been conceptualised in recent studies of legal education as a particular kind of *classed* individual. In so doing, I wish to question how useful the idea of the private life of the law school is in seeking to progress understanding of the relationship between gender, law and the university.

The argument is structured as follows. First, I will explore how class has been deployed within recent research on the legal academy, including studies discussed in chapter 2. Second, I proceed to look more closely at a theme central to this work, the idea that working-class experience can be understood in terms of a 'social mobility project'. Third, I consider methodological questions around social experience and the gendered subject underscoring this work, doing so in the light of the conceptual discussion of men and masculinity in chapter 1. There is, I argue, a pressing need to reassess theoretically and in terms of methodology the idea of the classed subject in accounts of legal academics and the private life of the law school. Finally, I conclude this analysis of gender, class and the restructured university by summarising key themes of my argument thus far.

Class, legal academics and the private life of the law school

I noted above how Cownie's book *Legal Academics* connects the cultures and practices of the legal academy and the development of the discipline of law. In this work, she emphasises the analytic potential of an anthropological approach to legal education, locating her study of law as part of a developing 'ethnography of the disciplines'. Importantly, against the backdrop of the changes in Higher Education outlined in chapter 2, *Legal Academics* engages explicitly, as part of a study of 'identity matters' in legal education, not only with questions of gender, race, ethnicity and sexual orientation, but also with how social class relates to the working lives of legal scholars. If we look more closely, what does it tell us about legal academics and class?[5]

---

[4] See further the readings in K. P. Sveinsson (ed), *Who Cares About the White Working Class?* London: Runnymede Trust, 2009. Issues of intersectionality are discussed in chapter 1.
[5] Cownie, op cit, 2004, p 10.

Social class and legal academics

Drawing on the views of the respondents in her study,[6] Cownie suggests that class background had 'little effect upon their professional identities', although 'half of them immediately qualified this by saying that in fact it had affected their research interests, or their desire to be involved in education'. Additionally, a 'significant minority of respondents *did not feel at ease* in the middle-class milieu of the legal academy'.[7] While:

> rejecting the notion that class had any particular effects upon the culture, the reality appears to be that it is a significant factor for many academics working in law schools ... Being a legal academic was unequivocally regarded as being a middle-class occupation.[8]

Unpacking the apparent tension between these comments, it is revealing to look more closely at this relationship between class and the legal academy.

Class, of course, is a deeply contested concept.[9] It has been addressed within earlier studies of universities[10] and features, at least to a degree, in recent accounts of women legal academics.[11] Socio-economic background, meanwhile, is an issue central to the policies of the present British government around the expansion of Higher Education,[12] whilst class has become a key question in debates about access to the legal profession.[13] Class concerns are, in addition, a prominent theme within diverse cultural representations of universities and academic life generally (for example, in novels, plays, films and television programmes).[14] Cownie's study presents, however, a focused discussion of how class can impact in the contemporary legal academy, one that has been reshaped in the ways discussed in chapter 2. Drawing primarily on a sociological and occupation-based framework informed by the concepts of social and cultural capital derived from

---

[6] Cownie's study is based on interviews with fifty-four legal academics working in University law schools in England. For discussion of methods and access questions, see Cownie, op cit, 2004, pp 14–15.

[7] Cownie, op cit, 2004, p 203, my emphasis.

[8] Cownie, op cit, 2004, p 203.

[9] S. Edgell, *Class*, London: Routledge, 1993; A. Milner, *Core Cultural Concepts: Class*, London: Sage, 1999; D. Cannadine, *Class in Britain*, London: Yale University Press, 1998.

[10] A. H. Halsey, *Decline of Donnish Dominion: The British Academic Professions in the Twentieth Century*, Oxford: OUP, 1995; A. H. Halsey and M. A. Trow, *The British Academics*, London: Faber and Faber, 1971.

[11] Chapter 2, p 53.

[12] See, in relation to law for example, L. Bibbings, 'Widening Participation in Higher Education', *Journal of Law and Society*, 2006, vol 33, p 74.

[13] S. Vignaendra, *Social Class and Entry into the Solicitor's Profession: Research Study 41*, London: The Law Society, 2001. See further chapter 4.

[14] As Cownie observes, 'stereotypically, academia has a very middle-class image. The pages of academic novels, from *Lucky Jim* to *Changing Places* are littered with images of the middle-class milieu of the academic life': Cownie, op cit, 2004, p 176.

the work of Pierre Bordieu,[15] Cownie's study reveals that a number of contradictions inform perceptions of class on the part of her interviewees.

Class is described as having 'little effect' upon the professional identity of legal academics, whilst, at the same time, for 'half of them', it had affected their chosen research interests and personal experience of Higher Education.[16] Intriguingly, this group 'contained almost no one with a middle class background' suggesting a correlation, for this 'significant minority',[17] between aspects of having a working-class background and an experience of 'not feeling at ease' within the legal academy:

> About a fifth of the respondents did not feel that they wholly identified with the middle classes. This group was a mixture of people from working class and lower middle class backgrounds *who still felt distanced from the middle class milieu of the legal academy*.[18]

'Being' a legal academic was unequivocally seen by 'all the respondents' in Cownie's study as 'a middle class job'[19] (with, presumably, a middle-class 'way of life'). If legal academics 'unquestionably perceive their current status as inherently middle class', however, the reading suggests that 'they do not all come to that position with the same cultural capital'; they are drawn 'from a slightly wider class background than the students they teach'.[20] These observations broadly mirror those of scholars from other disciplines. They map to the picture emerging, for example, within sociology and cultural studies, where research has been concerned to explore what it means to speak of distinctive working-class subjectivities or experiences, both in general terms[21] and in the specific context of

---

[15] P. Bordieu, *Outline of a Theory of Practice*, Cambridge: Cambridge University Press, 1977; P. Bordieu, *Homo Academicus*, Paris: Editions de Minuit, 1984; P. Bourdieu, *Distinctions: A Social Critique of the Judgement of Taste*, London: Routledge, 1989. Note also in this context P. Bordieu, 'Symbolic Power', *Critique of Anthropology*, 1979, vol 4, p 77; P. Bordieu, 'What Makes a Social Class? On the Theoretical and Practical Existence of Groups', *Berkeley Journal of Sociology*, 1987, vol 32, p 1. For critical discussion see L. Adkins and B. Skeggs (eds), *Feminism After Bordieu*, Oxford: Blackwell, 2004.

[16] Cownie, op cit, 2004, p 203. It is suggested, for example, that those from a working-class background took 'a particular interest in subjects such as welfare law, criminal law or labour law'.

[17] Cownie, op cit, 2004, p 203.

[18] Cownie, op cit, 2004, p 180, my emphasis.

[19] Cownie, op cit, 2004, 176. Note also observations by C. Wells, 'Working Out Women in Law Schools', *Legal Studies*, 2001, vol 21(1), p 116. In one 2006 study, 79% of university teachers described themselves as middle class, 4% as working class: 'Who do you think you are?', *The Times*, 5 May 2006. The corresponding figures for solicitors, in contrast, are 65% and 18% respectively.

[20] Cownie, op cit, 2004, p 180. The Law Society's longitudinal study, cited by Cownie, suggests that only about 18% of law students' parents were engaged in 'working class occupations': D. Halpern, *Entry into the Legal Professions: The Law Student Cohort Study Years 1 and 2*, London: The Law Society, 1994, p 21. See further chapter 4.

[21] See, for a useful summary of themes in this work, F. Devine, M. Savage, J. Scott and R. Crompton (eds), *Rethinking Class: Cultures, Identity and Lifestyle*, London: Palgrave Macmillan, 2005. In particular, F. Devine and M. Savage, 'The Cultural Turn in Sociology and Class Analysis' in Devine et al, op cit, 2005.

universities.[22] In the next section I look more closely at this work, and explore how it can help to 'flesh out' the observations of the legal academics in Cownie's study, helping to make sense of some of these apparent contradictions.

On 'becoming' middle class[23]

Where Does Memory End and Imagination Begin?[24]

Within my working environment, it's middle class. *But in my home life, it's more of a mix.* I know I'm middle class in terms of career, but *I feel different – I don't have the same background as my middle class friends* so their families, and what they do when they go and visit them for the weekend and so on is very different. Their parents are well-educated, and mine are not, *so it makes a difference.* But not within my job.

(lecturer, early career, female, new university)[25]

A number of recent discussions of working-class academics[26] have been driven, in part,[27] by a desire to question the gap within earlier qualitative work on class in terms of its failure to adequately theorise the social subject and engage with the complex, and frequently contradictory, nature of social experience.[28] That is, as Carol Smart[29] argued, and as we have already seen in this book, many traditional sociological engagements, whether in relation to families or employment, have tended to ignore the significant affective dimensions of social relations, effacing the interconnectedness of the lives of women, children and men.[30]

---

[22] See further below.

[23] Such a term is problematic and in what follows I wish to resist a reifying of class in recognising the multi-dimensional and (temporal, spatial, cultural) contingent nature of class identification. Class itself is internally stratified along race, gender and ethnic lines and, on one level, it thus makes little sense to speak of a 'middle-class' or 'working-class experience'. See further discussion in S. Munt (ed), *Cultural Studies and the Working Class: Subject to Change*, London: Cassell, 2000: especially A. Medhurst, 'If Anywhere: Class Identifications and Cultural Studies Academics,' in Munt (ed), op cit, 2000.

[24] T. Davies, cited in P. Farley, *Distant Voices, Still Lives: BFI Modern Classics*, London: BFI Publishing, 2006, p 7.

[25] Cited in Cownie, op cit, 2004, p 180, my emphasis.

[26] For example, Munt, op cit, 2000.

[27] It is also important to note how questions of social class have been central to political and policy debates about schooling and the expansion of Higher Education (see below), with intersections of gender, race and education providing further impetus to this work: e.g. L. Archer and B. Francis, *Understanding Minority Ethnic Achievement: Race, Gender, Class and 'Success'*, London: Routledge, 2006.

[28] On the background to the theoretical/political trajectories of this work see further B. Skeggs, 'Haunted by the Spectre of Judgement: Respectability, Value and Affect in Class Relations' in Sveinsson (ed), op cit, 2009, pp 36–37.

[29] C. Smart, *Personal Life: New Directions in Sociological Thinking*, Oxford: Polity, 2007.

[30] There has been a growing interest, curiously, in questions of affect and emotion across disciplines: J. Halley and P. Clough, *The Affective Turn: Theorizing the Social*, Durham, NC: Duke University Press, 2007; E. Sedgwick and A. Frank, *Touching Feeling: Affect, Pedagogy, Performativity*, Durham, NC: Duke, 2003; L. Berlant, *Intimacy*, Chicago: Chicago University Press, 2000. At the time of writing, there are signs that this work is also beginning to impact in the field of law and this chapter therefore presents a contribution to this development.

This point has particular bearing on attempts to engage with the experiences of legal academics via reference to the idea of the private life of the law school. 'Real lives', I argued in chapter 1, are mediated (inevitably) by a range of factors (such as age, ethnicity, sexuality, health, disability, class, geographical location, religion and so forth). In this context, beyond differences that exist between social groups, what it subjectively means for a particular individual to 'be' a legal academic will vary enormously, depending not just on the institution in which one is employed but also on the specificities of life history and biography, as well as on the social contexts that situate specific practices. One challenge in approaching the private life of the legal academy, therefore, is to avoid a form of analysis that side-steps this complexity, the richness of the social subject and the potentially contradictory nature of social experience (chapter 1, pp 44–45).

In exploring these issues, and seeking to draw attention to the affective domain in social relations,[31] a number of studies have sought to re-engage with issues of class and, in some accounts, explore the potential of autobiography and use of cultural memory in seeking to account for the emotional politics of class identity.[32] These questions of emotion, as Cownie's interviewees illustrate, and as Smart has indicated in her account of personal life,[33] are rarely far below the surface in discussion of the effects of class. As Beverley Skeggs has observed, issues of respectability and affect inform the making of value judgements, a 'moral boundary drawing', in ways encoded by ideas of class.[34] They are evident, for example, in the comments of several respondents in *Legal Academics* who report a sense of loss, dislocation and 'not belonging' in the process of 'becoming' middle class. These feelings of being 'out of place' have been reported within sociological and cultural studies accounts of class mobility, denoting the sense of a 'half-and-half existence' marked by dislocation with parental and wider family experience. In ways mediated by generation, gender and race, such narratives of class mobility through education are,

---

[31] Note, in addition to the work cited above, from the field of geography, N. Thrift, *Non-Representational Theory: Space, Politics, Affect*, London: Routledge, 2007.

[32] See further, and generally, B. Skeggs, *Formations of Class and Gender: Becoming Respectable*, London: Sage, 1997; B. Skeggs, 'Haunted by the Spectre of Judgement: Respectability, Value and Affect in Class Relations' in Sveinsson (ed), op cit, 2009; B. Skeggs, 'The Rebranding of Class: Propertising Culture' in Devine et al, op cit, 2005; B. Skeggs, *Class, Self, Culture*, London: Routledge, 2003; B. Skeggs, 'The Making of Class and Gender Through Visualising Moral Subject Formation', *Sociology*, 2005, vol 39(5), p 965; M. Savage, *Class Analysis and Social Transformation*, Buckingham: Open University Press, 2000; S. Charlesworth, *A Phenomenology of Working Class Experience*, Cambridge: Cambridge University Press, 2000; Munt, op cit, 2000; T. Edensor 'A Welcome Back to the Working Class', *Sociology*, 2000, vol 34, p 805.

[33] See chapter 1.

[34] Skeggs, op cit, 2009, pp 37–39.

on one level, not dissimilar from those charted by Richard Hoggart over fifty years ago in his book *The Uses of Literacy*.[35] Thus, what we see here is a process of status mobility fraught with experientially powerful feelings of being uprooted, anxious, ever watchful and vigilant, of being 'neither here nor there', subject to judgements of taste than can have spatial consequences.[36] It is a sense of distance and rupture evocatively captured in poetry (for example, in Tony Harrison's poem *Bookends*)[37] as well as in cinema and sociological writings.[38]

Cownie's study suggests, however, that it is also part of the lives of some legal scholars, who present a complex picture of the tensions involved in acceptable self-presentation in what for some is experienced as an indeterminate class position. And, of particular importance in considering the effects of class and capital on the legal academy in the context of the changing university, this is a process that appears to have social consequences. As one of Cownie's respondents notes:

> Most of the students are from the same [middle class] background as me, so *it's no problem at all.*
>
> (reader, experienced, male, old university)[39]

What is really happening here, however, with working-class experience or background somehow depicted as a potential 'problem' for an individual?

Cownie, in her adaptation of ideas of social and cultural capital deriving from Bordieu, sees social confidence and familiarity with cultural codes around, for example, ways of speaking, dress, modes of participation and interaction, as associated with educational background in ways that inform perceptions of success and status.[40] Experiences of discrimination and disadvantage in career progression, meanwhile, are linked to a sense of institutional belonging (or not belonging), an ability to 'play the game' and to ideas of cultural capital that privilege those from more established middle-class backgrounds who are familiar with dominant cultural codes. At the same time, sociological research suggests classed cultures of consumption and

---

[35] R. Hoggart, *The Uses of Literacy: Aspects of Working-Class Life with Special Reference to Publications and Entertainments*, London: Penguin, 1966. Note also B. Jackson and D. Marsden, *Education and the Working Class: Some General Themes Raised by A Study of 88 Working-Class Children in a Northern Industrial City*, London: Routledge and Kegan Paul, 1962.

[36] Skeggs, op cit, 2009, p 37.

[37] 'Back in our silences and sullen looks, for all the Scotch we drink, what's still between's not the thirty or so years, but books, books, books': T. Harrison, 'Bookends' in *Collected Poems*, London: Viking, 2007.

[38] Note J. Seabrook, *A World Still to Win: Reconstruction of the PostWar Working Class*, London: Faber and Faber, 1985; M. Pickering, *History, Experience and Cultural Studies*, London: MacMillan, 1997; J. Bourke (ed), *Working Class Cultures in Britain 1890–1960: Gender, Class and Ethnicity*, London: Routledge, 1994.

[39] Cited in Cownie, op cit, 2004, p 179, my emphasis.

[40] Whether of the self or of the standing of the institution in which one studies or is employed. Note, on anxieties mediated by age, R. Attwood, 'Young Academics Striving to Fit in Reveal Anxiety', *THE*, 7 August 2008, p 6.

lifestyle powerfully inform perceptions of commodity desire,[41] judgement, taste and value at a more general level,[42] with a working-class background commonly associated with distinctive personal characteristics (including, for example, being driven or over-conscientious, of feeling a 'need to prove' oneself).[43] Interlinked to the above, social class mediates access to the cultural and material resources of generations gone before in the form, notably, of the advantages potentially provided by inheritance in terms of wealth transmission and life-course planning. Each can be seen as an important part of the material basis of these 'private lives', although, intriguingly, rarely addressed in these terms.

Class also, however, importantly, informs the structures of feeling referred to in the above comments by Cownie's respondents, the emotional dimensions of a cultural assessment of value and distinction that informs the sense of belonging or being seen as 'other'.[44] Feeling distanced from the middle-class milieu of the legal academy comes, it would seem, with certain psychosocial consequences. 'Passing' as middle class, however, can involve far more than subjugating or amending accent and modes of expression, monitoring dress and deportment (or, as it once was put to me, 'holding the right cutlery at the formal dinner'). In a telling observation, the sociologist Beverley Skeggs, who has been at the forefront of studies of class and gender, has observed how, ultimately, 'class passing' may be fraught with dangers[45] in a context in which judgements of 'respectability [have become] the trope by which class relations [come] into view'.[46] Reflecting the extent to which assumptions about class have been embedded within institutional practices and cultures, as well as ingrained in lived experiences, structures of feeling and cultural memory, the working-class man or woman, it has been suggested, will eventually make themselves known as such, just as the middle-class subject can rarely get away with 'slumming it' (a point on which I defer to the astute observations of Pulp's 'Common People').[47]

---

[41] See further chapter 4, pp 111–114.

[42] For an excellent overview of this issue see Skeggs, op cit, 2009.

[43] A correlation, remarked on in personal correspondence, between perceived lack of social and cultural capital and feelings of needing to work ever harder, being over-conscientious for fear of being 'found out'. A 'relaxed', 'laid back' persona, in contrast, has been associated with high educational status, whereby established paper credentials (and in particular any association with Oxbridge) are seen to 'speak for themselves'. It has been suggested that, for some from particularly wealthy backgrounds, there may be less 'at stake'.

[44] R. Williams, *Marxism and Literature*, Oxford: Oxford University Press, 1997, p 132: 'The term is difficult, but "feeling" is chosen to emphasise a distinction from more formal concepts of "world-view" or "ideology" ... we are concerned with meanings and values as they are actively lived and felt ... not feeling against thought, but thought as felt and feeling as thought'.

[45] B. Skeggs, 'The Appearance of Class: Challenges in Gay Space' in Munt (ed), op cit, 2000, p 142.

[46] Skeggs, op cit, 2009, p 37.

[47] Pulp, 'Common People' from *Different Class* (Island Records, 1999): 'But still you'll never get it right, cos when you're laid in bed at night, watching roaches climb the wall, if you call your Dad he could stop it all.'

Recent sociological work provides further insights into what Andrew Sayer has evocatively termed the 'moral significance of class' in British society.[48] Sayer suggests that emotions are subject to moral judgements in ways informed by assumptions about class. Thus, following Sayer, the interlinking of social class, emotion and normative judgement would appear present in a number of aspects in the discussion of everyday academic life under consideration by Cownie, although it is not addressed in these terms. As Smart has noted, drawing on Sayer's work, everyday experiences of emotions such as anxiety, disappointment and shame can be deeply informed by judgements of class.[49] These classed dimensions of experience may shape, for example, how individual women and men negotiate the organisational cultures and forms of governance discussed in chapter 2 that, I have suggested, are seeking to remodel or refashion the academic subject. To refer back to the work of McWilliam,[50] individual academics doing work on themselves, turning themselves into professional experts, academic capitalists or, indeed, respected figures in their disciplinary field, do not work on a *tabula rasa*, but in a manner mediated by their situated negotiations of social formations and boundaries shaped by (amongst other things) social class:

> If class position, like gender and race, fundamentally affects people's lives, disadvantaging and even injuring some while advantaging and empowering others, *then it affects the kind of people individuals become.*[51]

It becomes clearer in such a context to see how, for one individual in Cownie's study, class was not perceived as a 'problem'. A cursory look at the cultural norms and modes of interaction within different university law schools reveals how deeply rooted these classed codes and assumptions can be, informing, as Cownie suggests, dominant organisational cultures, the practices of staff and students alike and the intersubjective policing of acceptable social boundaries:

> I've seen these academics, impeccable 'liberal' credentials all of them, freeze, look askance, in the prolonged company of someone from what is quite clearly (but never named as) a working-class background. They're happy with their own, for sure, and they are so polite to the face. But listen carefully to the way and where judgements are expressed, to opinions about clothing, an accent, body presentation and, especially for

---

[48] A. Sayer, *The Moral Significance of Class*, Cambridge: Cambridge University Press, 2005.

[49] Smart, op cit, 2007, p 140. On the effects of 'shame', see S. Munt, *Queer Attachments: The Cultural Politics of Shame*, Aldershot: Ashgate, 2007.

[50] E. McWilliam 'Changing the Academic Subject' in R. Hunter and M. Keys, *Changing Law: Rights, Regulation, Reconciliation*, Aldershot: Ashgate, 2005.

[51] Sayer, op cit, 2005, p 206, my emphasis.

women, anything at all related to being 'too' sexual. Don't tell me class doesn't inform that.

(reader, experienced, male, old university: personal correspondence)[52]

The above discussion reflects on aspects of the mobility narrative observed by some of Cownie's respondents, a sense of being 'cut' from the resources of generations gone before. This is just one example, however, of how class can be understood as an identity with significant effects in law schools, informing ways of feeling, judgement, value and so forth. Building on the discussion of the intersectional nature of social relations discussed in chapter 1 and in the specific context of the changing university law school considered in chapter 2, a rather different question can be asked. How, in the restructured university and expansion of Higher Education noted above, may these effects of class be now changing and playing out in rather different ways?

Changing universities: new formations[53] of class in the law school?

In considering the significant effects of class referred to by Cownie, it is important to note how social change has differential impacts depending on the embodied, situated location of individuals.[54] Gender, we have already seen, is but one part of this, as are race and ethnicity (see further, in the context of the legal profession, chapters 4 and 6). In relation to class, it is intriguing how a grammar school girl/ boy mobility narrative has become, for example, a distinctive feature of the literature on legal academics ('I'm the first in my family to attend university ... '),[55] as well as in broader accounts of academic life such as novels. Such narratives, however, must be socially and historically contextualised as the product of a particular cultural moment. Within a very different political and economic infrastructure, such as that of the corporatised university discussed in chapter 2, it would appear that class identities and experiences of mobility may be playing out in rather different ways. In particular, in the context of the re-gendering of the university detailed above,[56] research suggests rather different structures of feeling and cultural encoding may now be informing the effects of class with regard to the law school and differential access to economic, social and cultural capital therein.

To clarify. I have argued above that the remodelling of the academic as new knowledge worker involved, within an increasingly corporatised environment, a complex, and in many ways contradictory, shift in the dominant configurations of legal education and research (in relation, for example, to the gendered

---

[52] Personal correspondence; copy with author.

[53] Skeggs, op cit, 1997.

[54] Medhurst, op cit, 2000, p 25.

[55] Note, for example, interviews in C. McGlynn, *The Woman Lawyer: Making the Difference*, London: Butterworths, 1998.

[56] A. Brooks and A. Mackinnon (eds), *Gender and the Restructured University*, Buckingham: SRHE/Open University Press, 2001.

cultures of law schools and the shifting status of contextual/socio-legal study). There is reason to believe, however, that this model of performativity may have had 'special consequences for the class-mobile person in the academy'.[57] The reality of access to Higher Education for many working-class and ethnic-minority adults reveals paradoxes and inconsistencies within national policy and institutional practice on widening participation.[58] Far from increasing, research suggests that social mobility has in fact decreased over the past two decades, a point which sheds interesting light on the observations about mobility in Cownie's study discussed above.[59] A considerable evidence base, meanwhile, suggests working-class and ethnic-minority groups not only historically have been, but continue to be, excluded from participation in Higher Education, notwithstanding the expansion of the system and policy drives towards greater inclusion.[60] Working-class 'drop out' from university tends to be portrayed in both policy and the media as a symptom of working-class 'failure' (see below) rather than the result of complex processes of inclusion and exclusion.[61] Further, research is emerging, drawing on both qualitative and quantitative data, concerned with the intersectional nature of social class, ethnicity and gender in the process whereby individuals choose which university to attend[62] and their experiences once they are there.[63] In the case of law schools, much is known about how class can inform perceptions of career options, the status of institutions and experience of subsequent professional legal practice (see further chapters 4 and 6).[64]

[57] Cownie, op cit, 2004, p 213, citing J. Ryan and C. Sackrey, *Strangers in Paradise: Academics from the Working-Class*, Boston, MA: South End Press, 1984, p 18.

[58] M. Bowl, *Non-Traditional Entrants to Higher Education: 'They Talk About People Like ME'*, Stoke: Trentham Books, 2003.

[59] J. Blanden, P. Gregg and S. Machin, *Intergenerational Mobility in Europe and North America*, London: Sutton Trust, 2005; J. Goldthorpe, 'The Myth of Education-Based Meritocracy', *New Economy*, 2003, vol 10(4), p 234.

[60] Note for example, L. Archer, M. Hutchings and A. Ross, *Higher Education and Social Class: Issues of Exclusion and Inclusion*, London: RoutledgeFalmer, 2002; Archer and Francis, op cit, 2006; D. Gillborn, *Racism and Education: Coincidence or Conspiracy?* London: Routledge, 2008; G. Paton, 'Number of Working Class Students Has Barely Increased', *Daily Telegraph*, 25 June 2008; National Audit Office 2008, reporting that 'white working-class boys' are more likely to 'miss out' on Higher Education than any other group; G. Paton, 'Fewer Poor Students Attend University in England', *Daily Telegraph*, 4 December 2008. Further, students from poor families who receive 'preferential places' at top universities are more likely to drop out of their courses than their counterparts: R. Garner, 'Top Schools monopolise elite university places', *The Independent*, 20 September 2007.

[61] J. Quinn et al, *From Life Crisis to Lifelong Learning: Rethinking Working-Class 'Drop-Out'-From Higher Education*, York: Joseph Rowntree Foundation, 2005.

[62] T. Greenhalgh, K. Seyan and P. Boynton, '"Not a University Type": Focus Group Study of Social Class, Ethnic and Sex Differences in School Pupils' Perceptions about Medical School', *British Medical Journal*, 2004, vol 328, p 1541.

[63] J. Shepherd, 'Poor Students forced to stay close to home', *The Guardian*, 25 November 2008.

[64] Note M. Shiner 'Young, Gifted and Blocked! Entry to the Solicitor's Profession' in P. Thomas (ed), *Discriminating Lawyers*, London: Cavendish, 2000, pp 87–120; P. Thomas and A. Rees 'Law Students – Getting in and getting on' in P. Thomas (ed) *Discriminating Lawyers*, London:

If the shift from an elite to a mass system[65] of Higher Education has been accompanied by much political rhetoric about widening access and meritocratic equalisation, therefore, research suggests that universities have been slow to widen their social mix[66] and this expansion is at best partial and may, in some respects, have deepened social stratification and generated new and different inequalities.[67] It is most important, in such a context, to reflect further on what it means to state that university law schools are marked by 'significant effects' of class in terms of their operational codes and cultures. What, precisely, is meant by this? It remains possible, for example, if not without qualification, to broadly map the hierarchy of UK law schools and the career progression of their graduates to profiles of class and ethnicity, with higher concentrations of working-class and black and ethnic-minority staff and students in the 'new' universities and those outside the research-intensive 'elite'. Participation in Higher Education among people from working-class groups remains, more generally, stubbornly low, with lower social classes and ethnic minorities seen by the present government as either not going into Higher Education in sufficient, politically acceptable, numbers or, where they are attending Higher Education, not attending the higher-status institutions.[68] This lends accounts of not (fully) 'fitting in' a particular salience in the present political and economic context. Moreover, legal academics generally, as members of a distinctive, segmented socio-spatial consumption group,[69] stand in an uneasy relation to 'private/corporate capital, knowledge-based activities' and new ideas of 'middle-class consumption'[70] in ways that suggest that what it means to be and to identify *as* middle class is also shifting considerably, a point I consider further in the context of gender and the legal profession in chapter 4.

Cavendish, 2000; see further E. Duff, M. Shiner and A. Boon, *Entry into the Legal Profession: The Law Student Cohort Study Year 6*, London: Law Society, 2000; D. Halpern, *Entry into the Legal Professions – The Law Student Cohort Study Years 1 and 2*, London: Law Society, 1994.

[65] Ministers have set a target to get 50% of young people into Higher Education. At the time of writing, and in the context of economic recession, there is growing reason to believe that this target will be missed.

[66] J. Shepherd, 'White, middle class families dominate university places', *The Guardian*, 3 February 2009; D. Turner, 'Universities Slow to Widen Social Mix', *Financial Times*, 26 February 2009.

[67] D. Reay, M. David and S. Ball, *Degrees of Choice: Social Class, Race and Gender in Higher Education*, Stoke: Trentham Books, 2005.

[68] Reay, David and Ball, op cit, 2005; Bibbings, op cit, 2006.

[69] P. Chatterton and R. Hollands, 'Theorising Urban Playscapes: Producing, Regulating and Consuming Youthful Nightlife City Spaces', *Urban Studies*, 2002, vol 39(1), p 95, at p 109.

[70] Chatterton and Hollands, op cit, 2002, p 97. See further on reformations of middle-class identity, M. Savage, P. Dickens and T. Fielding, *Property, Bureaucracy and Culture: Middle Class Formation in Contemporary Britain*, London, Routledge, 1992; F. Devine, 'Middle Class Identities in the United States' in Devine et al, op cit, 2005; M. Savage and T. Butler (eds), *Social Change and the Middle Classes*, London, UCL Press, 1995; T. Butler, *Gentrification and the Middle-Classes*, Aldershot: Ashgate, 1997.

In the light of the above, it may be more accurate to suggest that, far from fading away, the significance of class, as of gender (chapter 2), has been reshaped and remodelled, and is playing out in rather different ways in the context of the changing university and the shifting narratives of social mobility discussed above. Economic and cultural changes, that is, are producing different *kinds* of engagements with the processes of aestheticisation and emotionalisation that have become key features of (self-) management within the performance cultures and consumption practices that mark the 'everyday' within late modernity.[71] Set in this context, it may be that, for both women and men, ideas about academic vocation continue to be marked by classed distinctions between *having* a paid job (traditionally, a working-class identification) and *being* or embodying the job one does, divisions that, in some contexts, are becoming increasingly blurred. It is difficult to see, however, I shall argue in the following section, how the gendered subject central to the idea of the private life of the law school can engage with these structures of feeling in any meaningful way, nor with the many nuances, and contradictions, of personal life.

Method: class and the limits of the private life of the law school

Where does this leave us? The developments around class outlined above can be located as part of a broader engagement with, if not a return to, the material in sociology, a move that has opened up new questions about the way class gives shape to and forms social norms, identities and communities.[72] This is an issue I shall return to later in this book. In this context there exists, notwithstanding institutional commitments to formal equality and diversity in universities, a certain sense of awkwardness around class, including within parts of the legal academic community, interlinked to the questions of emotion and feeling, self-identity and cultural positioning discussed above. In developing strategies to conserve collective and individual identities, not least around what it means to be a 'critical' scholar of law perhaps,[73] if not an institutional 'outsider', issues of class and a reflexive awareness of one's own cultural and economic capital and advantage may be, for some, understandably disquieting. The mantle of outsider may sit uneasily in a social context where, if Cownie is right, the dominant cultural

---

[71] See, for example, Z. Bauman, *Consuming Life*, Oxford: Polity, 2007; Z. Bauman, *Liquid Times: Living in an Age of Uncertainty*, Oxford: Polity, 2006; S. M. Lash and J. Urry, *Economies of Signs and Space*, London: Sage, 1993.

[72] For example, see K. Plummer, *Intimate Citizenship: Personal Decisions and Public Dialogues*, Washington: University of Washington Press, 2003; K. Plummer, 'Intimate Inequalities' in M. Romero and J. Howard (eds), *The Blackwell Companion to Social Inequalities*, Oxford: Blackwell, 2005.

[73] Note the reading of P. Goodrich, 'The Critic's Love of the Law: Intimate Observations on an Insular Jurisdiction', *Law and Critique*, 1999, vol 10(3), p 343.

codes of the institution are themselves profoundly marked by class-based assumptions. What, after all, as mentioned, is the potential problem alluded to by one of Cownie's respondents in his observation that 'most of the students are from the same [middle-class] background as me' so '*it's no problem at all*'?[74] As Skeggs has noted, in a context where the working class have not historically had access to the 'legal, aesthetic or moral authority' which gives legitimacy to social positions, what processes of '(dis)identification' and moral boundary drawing are at play here?[75] Gender, sexuality, race, ethnicity, age, physical ability, each, of course, mediates the effects of class in complex ways.[76] There is no *one* classed individual, just as there is no 'one' experience of gender or race. This does not negate the fact, however, that class has relevance for understanding the everyday that is often effaced in discussions of the law school and legal academics. This issue, I shall now suggest, relates in part to the methodology that has been deployed and, more specifically, to the limits of the idea of the private life of the law school and legal academics.

We can begin this discussion of method by asking a question. If class has been 'the ghost at the feast' of much critical legal scholarship, how far is one to go in a 'venture … into the more private aspects of legal academia'?[77] In his 1999 account of a 'flight to the elite' institutions amongst UK critical legal scholars, Peter Goodrich looked to the potential of an engagement with psychoanalysis that, he suggested, might have analytic and political purchase for legal studies.[78] It is difficult to see how the interlinking of social class and the complexity of the material and emotional structures in which career 'choice' is exercised play out, however, in this reading of career progression and personal advancement. Equally, in the accounts of the effects of class reported by Cownie in *Legal Academics*, seeing class as a 'significant factor for many academics working in law schools'[79] it is unclear what happens to the *experience* of, say, loss and pain, pleasure and achievement discussed above, what it means to be one person in 'my working environment', another 'in my home life'. What we miss is precisely the richness, depth and emotional resonances of social experiences that are central to recent sociological engagements with personal life. The affective domain, that is, appears to fade away *at the very moment* it is evoked as being of some (unspecified) political and intellectual significance.

This raises the question of methodology, the limits of ethnography and how the private life has been theorised in this work. With regard to method, alternative explorations are emerging which point to new ways of engaging with

---

[74] Cited in Cownie, op cit, 2004, p 179, my emphasis.
[75] B. Skeggs, op cit, 1997, p 76. See also Sayer, op cit, 2005.
[76] See chapter 1, p 16, n 41.
[77] Cownie, op cit, 2004, p 42.
[78] Goodrich, op cit, 1999.
[79] Cownie, op cit, 2004, p 203.

questions of emotion and class in relation to academic cultures and experiences. In seeking to 'make the familiar strange',[80] Cownie's 'meso-qualitative'[81] study of legal academics explores 'how the social world is experienced by legal academics'. Deriving from the anthropological tradition of studying the 'other' ethnographically, it adopts the recognised qualitative research method whereby the researcher uses participant observation and/or interviews in order to gain a deeper understanding of a group's culture (in this case, legal scholars). The aim is to help understand and theorise modes of human behaviour within the group across different contexts (here, different law schools across various universities in the sector and a diverse body of legal academics).

Emotion, however, we have seen, is rarely far below the surface in such readings of the effects of class. Identity matters, that is, are to the fore; identity seen as multiple and never unified, marked by a 'fragmentation of the self'.[82] Ethnographical work has well-documented limits, however, in taking forward our understanding of the intersubjective effects of class discussed above, and the precise nature of this fragmentation of the self (chapter 1, pp 44–45). Engaging with the question of the authenticity of voice, for example, where the researcher is her/himself a member of the group in question, we face the important problem of shared processes of self-inscription between the researcher and the researched. To refer back to the moral significance of class discussed by Andrew Sayer, above, this raises the question of how recognition and the multiple dimensions of interaction underscore the way features of social life are 'made visible' to the researcher in contexts where 'actions, looks or expressions rather than words [can] convey the significant meaning'.[83]

It is in contrast to such an approach that recent work in the area of biographical genre and auto-ethnography has sought to engage with the meanings and uses of personal narrative in developing knowledge of how self-identity and social forms can be culturally constituted.[84] Whilst certainly open to critique, this approach has informed a number of accounts seeking to explore precisely the intersectional nature of social class, offering some potential advantages over traditional ethnography in exploring the significant effects of class in the university law school. In particular, it opens up the emotional and affective realm as a way of understanding the links between the

---

[80] S. Delamont, 'Just like the Novels? Researching the Occupational Culture(s) of Higher Education' in R. Cuthbert (ed), *Working in Higher Education*, Buckingham: SRHE and Open University Press, 1996, quoted in Cownie, op cit, 2004, p 14.

[81] Cownie, op cit, 2004, p 14.

[82] Cownie, op cit, 2004, p 12.

[83] Smart, op cit, 2007, p 152.

[84] See, for example, D. Reed-Danahay (ed), *Auto-Ethnography: Rewriting the Self and the Social*, London: Berg, 1997; A. Meneley and D. J. Young (eds), *Auto-Ethnographies: The Anthropology of Academic Practices*, Peterborough, Ont: Broadview Press, 2005; S. Denshire, 'In Praise of Auto-Ethnography', *Australian Occupational Therapy Journal*, 2006, vol 53(4), p 346.

specific social context under study (in this case, the university law school) and the processes whereby emotion is, or is not, then made 'visible'. As developed by academics within cultural studies, at times used interchangeably with personal narrative and autobiography, in some accounts life history has been used as a way of providing important insights into various dimensions of class experience.[85] These auto-ethnographies, far from being work that can simply be dismissed as introspective, subjective, 'unscientific' testimony, can themselves be seen as political in nature, engaging readers to revalue the place of cultural memory and structures of feeling and requiring us to reconsider issues hitherto 'off the radar' – not least, I suggest, the often contradictory nature of structural developments presently reshaping gender and class. The film director Terence Davies's question 'where does memory end, and imagination begin?'[86] thus captures how 'the past' can be present and active within cultural memory, a key element of autobiographical discourse, denoting something that is not 'left behind' but that which continues to inform the commitments of the present;[87] part of who 'we' are.

I wish to conclude this section with a question therefore. What might an auto-ethnography of the *middle-class* legal academic – assuming that there is such a thing, given the conceptual identifications at play here – actually look like? Far from routinely pathologising working-class experience, constituting it again and again as the actual or potential analytic problem, what would it mean to turn attention to the nature of middle-class cultures and norms in university law schools (for, implicitly, it is being claimed that there is such a thing) in a discursive attempt to stop the depiction of the working class as Other? Of what would we speak? To return to the work of Sayer, in considering how researchers seek to account for the actions of others, and to 'offer explanations for things that "other" people do' (other stakeholders in the law school?), this raises the 'question of whether sociologists regard themselves as the exceptions when they speak or write about the lives of ordinary people'. [88] What, after all, is 'ordinary' about being middle class? As Skeggs has written, here drawing on Sayer's work:

---

[85] Note, for example, V. Walkerdine, *Schoolgirl Fictions*, London: Verso, 1991; A. Kuhn, *Family Secrets: Acts of Memory and Imagination*, London: Verso, 1995; Medhurst, op cit, 2000. See further the reading of V. Walkerdine, 'Reclassifying Upward Mobility: Femininity and the Neo-Liberal Subject', *Gender and Education*, 2003, vol 15(3) p 237.

[86] Farley, op cit, 2006.

[87] Evoking, for example, the fragmented nature of memory in focusing on how class has shaped the stories individuals tell about their lives and their relations with others, an engagement with writing as a way of understanding self in a explorations of feeling. See further discussion in Smart, op cit, 2007. The work of the film maker Terence Davies in many ways exemplifies this point: see *Of Time and the City: A Love Song and A Eulogy*, HanWay/BBC films, 2008. See further R. Crompton and J. Scott 'Class Analysis: Beyond the Cultural Turn' in Devine et al, op cit, 2005.

[88] Smart, op cit, 2007, p 65.

The middle-class rarely want to acknowledge the privileged social and economic position from which they speak, displaying embarrassment and evasion, often denying the significance of class, or individualizing differ- ence, responses which ... indicate an awareness that class differences lack moral justification.[89]

Perhaps here we find a powerful insight into why class has been, for many men and women in the contemporary legal academy, that which is often not spoken of but which, if Cownie's reading is correct, might indeed have 'sig- nificant effects' for some individuals. If discussion of policy change in Higher Education has paid insufficient attention to the complexity of agency, what might emerge from the stories of those who have been positioned as the subjects of the structural changes detailed above? If an ethnography of the disciplines is to seriously engage with the effects of class, it will miss much, I suggest, if it fails to address the processes that 'constitute the subjectivity, defences and coping practices of most of the population ... not taking apart, this fiction which functions in truth [it seems] ... not to see the ways in which subjects cope, produce defences against ... conditions'.[90] How, for women and men, does that which falls beyond the conventional categories of academic identity (but undoubtedly, as Smart has shown, within the 'perso- nal' domain) – questions of intimacy and sexuality, desire and friendship, of health, sickness and ageing, of love, care and dependency, of jealously, dis- like and, indeed, fear, ambition and inevitable disappointment – connect to the cultures of academic law, and how are these situated experiences articu- lated and made sense of?[91]

In a telling passage, Cownie notes how:

> awareness of gender issues is not very deeply embedded into the culture of academic law, and that most academic lawyers *have to be specifically directing their attention to the subject* before they readily identify gender as problematic.[92]

In writing this chapter, and in thinking of the recent debates about legal aca- demics and the changing university discussed in chapter 2, I have frequently asked myself whether many academic lawyers have to be specifically directing their attention to the subject of class before they identify it as in any way

---

[89] Skeggs, op cit, 2009, p 38.
[90] V. Walkerdine, 'Subject to Change Without Notice: Psychology, Post-Modernity and the Pop- ular' in S. Pile and N. Thrift (eds), *Mapping the Subject: Geographies of Cultural Transfor- mation*, London, Routledge, 1995, p 329.
[91] Cownie's study suggests that work-life balance, for example, 'is an issue which is intimately connected with the culture of academic law, and the ways in which legal academics construct their professional identities': Cownie, op cit, 2004, p 118.
[92] Cownie, op cit, 2004, p 118, my emphasis.

problematic. Class, as Valerie Walkerdine and others have argued, is not something consigned to the past, that which is left behind in the narrative of an individual mobility project, a journey of 'progress' to somehow 'become' middle class (and thus to become 'better', to be respectable?).[93] It is always present and active to varying degrees, part of our life histories, our cultural memories, that which is shared (with some) and, all too often, unsaid, seen as intensely personal. Yet 'naming class', it has been argued, can be seen not as an act of essentialism, but as an assertion of belonging (whether in family, education, community and/or regional culture), of the value of memory and history, not a form of alienation and loss in the move to another class, but 'part of a narrative which allows me a place from which to struggle, a sense of belonging'.[94] As Sayer notes:

> Through both subtle and unsubtle differences in recognition of others, people are in varying degrees included or excluded, and allowed access to different opportunities.[95]

This chapter has traced some ways forward in thinking about class in developing understanding of the legal academics and university law schools. We live in a time when discourses of social mobility, classlessness and gender neutrality have become culturally powerful. To what extent, however, do myths about class still operate to ensure the perpetuation of existing inequalities? To what extent has class 'become an awkward part of the social jigsaw', the focus of heightened social stereotyping, political containment and marginalisation?[96] What new identifications are thrown up if, as some suggest, speaking of class is no longer seen as legitimate, if 'we're all middle class now'?[97] What would it mean, in developing further the study of legal academics, and the idea of the 'man of law', to rethink the concepts and methods through which class has been discussed, to reclaim class as a 'lost identity'? What new insights and hitherto silent voices might be revealed, and of what stories of pain, and joy, might they speak?

---

[93] Skeggs, op cit, 1997.

[94] Walkerdine, op cit, 1991, p 158.

[95] Sayer, op cit, p 55.

[96] I. Jack, 'Working class has come to mean beer guts and white vans', *The Guardian*, 1 December 2007, p 36. See further B. Byrne, *White Lives: The Interplay of 'Race', Class and Gender in Everyday Lives*, London: Routledge, 2006.

[97] A particular theme within recent debates around working-class cultures and questions of race and ethnicity. See, for example, Byrne, op cit, 2006; M. Collins, *The Likes of Us: A Biography of the White Working Class*, London: Granta, 2004; G. Dench, K. Gavron and M. Young, *The New East End: Kinship, Race and Conflict*, London: Profile Books, 2006; A. Nayak, 'Displaced Masculinities: Chavs, Youth and Class in the Post-Industrial City', *Sociology*, 2006, vol 40(5), p 813.

Chapter 4

'Read what the law firms say'

Gender and the representation of career success in the contemporary legal profession

Introduction

Entering the City law firm means that you enter the business world ... You are embarking on a career in business. Your knowledge of the commercial world is an expectation. *Read what the law firms say.*[1]

Social worlds are organised, structured and imbued with meaning by reference to what sort of people the protagonists are, that is their sense of their own social identity ... lifestyles are reflexive projects: we (and relevant others) can see (however dimly) who we want to be seen to be through how we use the resources of who we are.[2]

The relationship between law and popular culture has been the subject of a considerable and growing literature and socio-legal research in this field has explored diverse aspects of law, legal regulation and legal practice.[3] Within this work, particular attention has been paid to images of legal professionals in films, literature and television shows, as well as within the print media,

---

[1] R. Lee, 'A Finger on the Pulse', *Legal Week*, Student Special, Spring 2004, p 16, my emphasis.

[2] D. Chaney, *Lifestyles*, London: Routledge, 1996, p 37.

[3] See, for example, S. Greenfield and S. Osborn (eds), *Readings in Law and Popular Culture*, London: Routledge, 2005; M. Thornton (ed), *Romancing the Tomes: Popular Culture, Law and Feminism*, London: Routledge-Cavendish, 2002; R. K. Sherwin (ed), *Popular Culture and Law*, Aldershot: Ashgate, 2006; R. K. Sherwin, 'Law in Popular Culture' in A. Sarat (ed), *Blackwell Companion to Law and Society*, Oxford: OUP, 2004; W. P. MacNeil, *Lex Populi: The Jurisprudence of Popular Culture*, Stanford: Stanford University Press, 2007; M. Freeman (ed), *Law and Popular Culture*, Oxford: OUP, 2005; R. K. Sherwin *When Law Goes Pop: The Vanishing Line Between Law and Popular Culture*, Chicago: Chicago University Press, 2000; A. Sarat and J. Simon (eds), *Cultural Analysis, Cultural Studies and the Law*, Durham: Duke University Press, 2003; P. W. Kahn, *The Cultural Study of Law: Reconstructing Legal Scholarship*, Chicago: University of Chicago Press, 1999; A. Sarat and T. Kearns (eds), *Law in the Domains of Culture*, Michigan: University of Michigan Press, 2000; L. C. Bower, T. Goldberg and M. Musheno (eds), *Between Law and Culture: Relocating Legal Studies*, Minneapolis: University of Minnesota Press, 2001.

advertising, radio and, more recently, websites.[4] There has to date, however, been little analysis of the depiction of women and men within a range of advertising and publicity materials aimed at encouraging undergraduate and graduate university students to apply for a training contract with law firms. In developing my analysis of law, men and gender across different legal contexts, and building on the discussion of gender and the university law school in chapters 2 and 3, what follows explores the representation of gender in the legal profession in relation to the work of solicitors. The focus, in particular, is on how ideas about men and masculinities have informed images of the 'everyday' nature of lawyers' work within one distinctive area of legal practice, that of the large corporate commercial 'City' law firm.

What are these texts, and what is their place in relation to the contemporary legal profession? Produced by and circulating largely within the legal community, and directed to a fairly well-defined target market, these materials sell a specific product – the training contract. They are concerned, that is, to attract new recruits into the profession, the 'lawyers of tomorrow'. Notwithstanding the high profile within the contemporary profession of issues of diversity and equality, however, these materials have seldom been subject to critical analysis in their own right within legal scholarship. It is the aim of this chapter to address this absence. What follows presents an analysis of the way in which, through words and pictures, a career in law is 'sold' to prospective trainee solicitors within large commercial law firms based in the City of London and other regional financial centres in the UK. The reading draws on a small-scale qualitative study of text and visual images contained within a range of materials depicting the nature of corporate legal employment. Three principal themes will be addressed, each of which bears, to a different degree, on questions of gender, men and law.

First, this chapter unpacks connections between images of the (generally) young, would-be lawyer and assumptions about gendered identity and the nature of commitment to a successful legal career. Second, it explores how ideas about consumption and personal lifestyle are communicated to the 'new recruit' via these materials. Finally, I question the messages these images radiate about gender, race/ethnicity and social class more generally, developing further the discussion in chapters 1–3. Interrogating how these images come to 'work' involves, I suggest, engaging with a complex interplay of ideas. It entails an interrogation of contemporary youth cultures, beliefs about lifestyle and the shifting spatiality of lawyers' work. Distinctive dynamics of consumption, social capital and identity formation, I argue, have become central to the selling of the training contract by the large commercial or 'big City' law firm. I am not concerned in what follows to engage with an image of legality in the sense of unpacking legal

---

[4] S. Greenfield, G. Osborn and P. Robson, *Film and the Law*, London: Cavendish, 2001; S. Machura and P. Robson, *Law and Film: Representing Law in Movies*, Oxford: Wiley Blackwell, 2001; O. Kamir, *Framed: Women in Law and Film*, Durham: Duke University Press, 2006.

doctrines or the substance of law,[5] nor with tracing how representations of law are understood in the legal consciousness of 'ordinary people'.[6] Bringing together insights derived from fields of literature usually considered outwith the study of the legal profession, rather, this chapter is concerned with the socio-cultural significance of promotional and recruiting materials used by large law firms. In so doing it develops an understanding of the training contract as a distinctive – and relatively under-explored – stage of socialisation within the legal profession.[7] The questions the chapter raises, however, go beyond the field of legal practice and speak to a reconfiguration of gender relations that, I suggest in this book, is reshaping understandings of the interconnections between law and masculinity in some far-reaching ways.

Method: reading images and texts

When you're applying to the big law firms, at first glance it's difficult to differentiate them. They all have massive reputations, they all do amazing work and they all have well-known clients. Luckily, I had done a vacation placement here, so I got to appreciate what sets Allen & Overy apart – *its culture.*[8]

I approached Weil Gotshal's stand at the Manchester Law Fair because they were giving away freebies! Feeling that it would be a little rude not to take a brochure I picked one up and put it on top of my huge pile of other brochures.[9]

The following analysis is based on a reading of brochures and advertisements produced by City of London and large regional firms in the UK,[10] drawn from over a period of seven years and targeted at men and women considering a career in (broadly) corporate commercial, 'blue-chip' City work. The brochures vary in size and content but they convey, taken together, a central core of information to the would-be lawyer. This covers the nature of the firm's work, detail on what the experience of the trainee

---

[5] B. Carlsson and M. Baier, 'A Visual Self-Image of Legal Authority: "The Temple of Law"', *Social and Legal Studies*, 2002, vol 11(2), p 185; D. Curtis and J. Resnik, 'Images of Justice', *Yale Law Journal*, 1987, vol 96, p 1726.

[6] P. Ewick and S. Silbey, *The Common Place of Law: Stories From Everyday Life*, Chicago: Chicago University Press, 1998.

[7] See further M. Shiner 'Young, Gifted and Blocked! Entry to the Solicitor's Profession' in P. Thomas (ed), *Discriminating Lawyers*, London: Cavendish, 2000, pp 87–120.

[8] Allen and Overy, 2000, my emphasis. Specific examples drawn from the materials will be cited henceforth via reference to the firm name and year.

[9] Kevin Cook, Trainee: Weil, Gotshal and Manges, 2003, quoted in *Target*, 7th edn, London: GTI Specialist Publishers, 2003.

[10] The materials collected over this period, and on which this reading is based, contain over 150 examples of brochures and related advertising. The majority of these derive from the 'Top 20' firms, as listed in *Chambers Guide to the Legal Profession*, London: Chambers, 2005–6. This analysis is based on materials from this larger collection, a smaller sample of 45 brochures and 50 advertisements.

solicitor will be during the traineeship and/or vacation placement (the opportunities that will be offered, the demands that will be made and, on occasion, the salary). They also address aspects of life after qualification as a solicitor, such as the future promotion prospects, available areas of employment and so forth. The related advertisements cover more limited information and focus on branding the firm within a competitive market-place, communicating the nature of the work and providing contact details (how, for example, to obtain the information contained within the recruit-ment brochures). The latter are distributed at regular 'milk round' recruit-ment events at UK universities, often alongside an increasingly diverse array of 'freebies'.[11] They are also obtainable directly from the firms and many university careers offices.

Recognising the differences between these two sets of texts, the firm bro-chures and the advertisements, together they constitute a discrete body of information focused, in essence, around two key stages of professional recruitment and socialisation into the legal profession in England and Wales. These are, first, the obtaining of the vacation placement and, second, the sub-sequent securing of a training contract with the firm. Before beginning to unpack these materials, however, it is important to consider the limitations, and possibilities, of a study such as this. How might we make sense of these representations of lawyers work?

Methodological limitations

Three limitations suggest themselves. First, we are dealing with texts concerned with the development of a legal career in one – albeit professionally powerful, prestigious and potentially highly lucrative – field of legal employment: that of the 'mega-lawyer'.[12] They do not necessarily (although they might) tell us about other areas of legal practice or about the work of other private com-mercial enterprises, which also tend to recruit, predominantly, from a number of elite UK universities. The worlds of the corporate commercial multinational, the high street firm and the legal aid practitioner have become so different that

---

[11] For example, pens, notepaper, pocket FM radios, 'shot' glasses for spirits, luxury carrier bags, postcards, wall calendars and stationery products embossed with the name of the firm (see, for example, Wragge & Co, 2005). Interestingly, there has been an observable reduction in the distribution of such freebies following the economic downturn of 2008.

[12] M. Galanter and T. Palay, *Tournament of Lawyers: Growth and Transformation of the Big Law Firm*, Chicago: Chicago University Press, 1991; J. Flood, 'Globalization and Large Law Firms' in P. Cane and J. Conaghan (eds), *The New Oxford Companion to Law*, Oxford: OUP, 2008; R. G. Lee, 'From Profession to Business: The Rise and Rise of the City Law Firm', *Journal of Law and Society*, 1992, vol 19, p 31; R. G. Lee '"Up or Out" – Means or Ends? Staff Retention in Large Law Firms' in Thomas (ed), op cit, 2000; R. G. Lee, *Firm Views: Work of and Work in the Largest Law Firms: Research Study No 35*, London: Law Society, 1999.

they belie any notion of the contemporary legal profession as a unified, homo-genous entity.[13] These texts circulate largely, if not exclusively, within dis-tinctive legal and/or law-related communities; amongst, for example, law students, their peer groups and families, within law schools (workrooms and staff offices) and university careers advisers, as well as within the profession itself. They do not necessarily inform popular consciousness of law in any more general sense.[14] It is, in addition, difficult to gauge from a reading such as this how images compare with materials produced within other jurisdictions.

Second, there are many other sources of information about legal careers to be found within the public domain, beyond the marketing material produced by law firms (or, more accurately, by the public relations firms they employ). These sources may be seen by prospective trainees to be more or less reliable indicators of what the reality of legal employment as a solicitor will involve. They include the knowledge derived from the work placement, the vacation visit, the open day, work shadowing and voluntary work (or internships); knowledge from family and friends; and, increasingly, knowledge obtained via the Internet (where much of this information also appears). Information can be obtained via gossip and received knowledge handed down from earlier law school cohorts. The brochures and advertisements do not stand alone therefore. They are part of a package of information derived by the prospective solicitor from a variety of sources and aimed at informing their decision to enter, or not to enter, the legal profession.

Third, the reading that follows cannot tell us about how an individual woman or man (let us say, a particular law student) reads, receives, responds (or does not respond). Their effects, as it were, cannot be known from textual analysis. Did someone proceed to apply? Did the materials influence their decision?[15] I will utilise interpretative categories derived from sociology and social theory around ideas of social class (see chapter 3), gender, race/ethnicity and sexuality (see chapter 1). These categories, however, are defined, constructed and rendered experientially significant in multifarious ways, not just by institutional structures and practices but through 'everyday' talk and behaviour.[16] Thus, we are dealing with concepts problematic in and of themselves, not least in their relationship with social experience. The words and images discussed below are artifice, cultural representations using certain devices in order to convince.[17] We cannot

[13] Flood, op cit, 2008; H. Sommerlad, 'Women Solicitors in a Fractured Profession', *International Journal of the Legal Profession*, 2002, vol 9(3), p 213.

[14] Compare M. Galanter, 'The Faces of Mistrust: The Image of Lawyers in Public Opinion and Political Discourse', *Cincinnati University Law Review*, 1998, vol 66, p 905.

[15] D. Schleef, 'That's a Good Question! Exploring Motivations for Law and Business School Choice', *Sociology of Education*, 2000, vol 73 (July), p 155.

[16] In keeping with the frameworks outlined in chapter 1, ideas of gender are constructed via the interaction of institutions and individuals, bound up with social structures and inequalities that have historically reproduced ideas of differences between men and women; see further M. Kimmel, *The Gendered Society*, Oxford: OUP, 2000.

[17] E. Chaplin, *Sociology and Visual Representation*, London: Routledge, 1994.

ascertain, from representations of trainee lawyers, knowledge of the cultural, economic and psychological investments individual women and men make in adapting to or resisting working practices, cultural codes or value systems within the legal profession.

Possibilities: why these materials are important

> Professions are not things 'out there' to be found ... Rather they are dynamic and complex social constructions loaded with normative meanings.[18]

Notwithstanding the above, these materials have considerable social significance. Again, three reasons present themselves for suggesting that, in developing analysis of gender and the legal profession, and looking to the interconnections between men, law and gender, they are revealing and politically significant cultural artefacts. First, they communicate something, if not about how one part of the legal profession 'sees itself' (which may be a different issue),[19] then at least about how it wishes to depict a legal career to new recruits. These texts are approved, licensed and used by the law firms to clear and instrumental ends (recruiting solicitors). They tell us something about how a career in law *appears* to those who are at the very least curious about entering the profession. If it is 'not like in the brochure' then there is a potential disjuncture between image and reality.

This question is important in a social context where the process by which individuals become lawyers is a matter of 'considerable practical and ideological importance'.[20] Solicitors are widely recognised as 'an elite professional group with high status, substantial earning potential and a key role in applying and administering the law'.[21] The training contract is a key stage, not just in establishing 'who gets in' but also in playing a 'pivotal role in relation to the early stages of solicitors' careers once they have qualified'.[22] The elite status within the solicitor's profession[23] of the City and large provincial firms under discussion here and in chapter 6, therefore, is such that their recruitment

---

[18] H. Sommerlad, 'Women Solicitors in a Fractured Profession', *International Journal of the Legal Profession*, 2002, vol 9(3), p 213, at p 214, original citation removed.

[19] In relation to which see further <http://www.rollonfriday.com/index_freetime.htm>, accessed 10 November 2008.

[20] Shiner, op cit, 2000, p 87; L. Norman, *Career Choices in Law: A Survey of Law Students (Research Study 50)*, London: The Law Society, 2004; H. Rolfe and T. Anderson, *A Firm Decision: The Recruitment of Trainee Solicitors*, London: The Law Society, 2002. Important though information about the background to obtaining a position as a trainee solicitor is, 'it is less important than *what happens* during the process of training itself. It is at this stage that we would expect the most intense period of acculturation to take place as the law student becomes absorbed into the community of solicitors. However, it is precisely at this point that we know least': A. Bradney and F. Cownie *The English Legal System in Context*, London: Butterworths, 1998, p 142, my emphasis.

[21] Shiner, op cit, 2000, p 87.

[22] Shiner, op cit, 2000, p 99.

[23] Shiner, op cit, 2000, p 117.

process is a matter of considerable importance in understanding the internal dynamics of professional socialisation and reproduction. These firms exert, Lee has observed, an almost 'magnetic quality in attracting new recruits'.[24] They pay high salaries and, Shiner has suggested, 'are able to cream off the best qualified candidates' as a result of their greater ability to finance trainees through the Legal Practice Course (LPC) and, where relevant, the Common Professional Examination (CPE).[25] They recruit the 'most highly qualified candidates from the most prestigious institutions'.[26] This being the case, it is revealing to ask what the connections might be between the trainee profile presented by the firms and the way in which these firms maintain their elite status[27] in the context of a rapidly changing profession.[28]

Second, the importance of these materials is not confined to the precise time when they are deemed of interest to an individual. They have a wider socio-cultural significance within the legal community. The process by which people enter the profession 'has implications which go beyond the "rights" of individual applicants'[29] and these texts contribute to a knowledge base about what corporate legal employment entails. The economic and cultural allure of these firms transcends, therefore, their specific appeal to law students.[30] Recognising that 'the power and prestige of the large firms is out of proportion to their number',[31] this social significance reaches beyond the human resource concerns of a particular law firm.

---

[24] Calculated from *The Lawyer, Student Special* (2000), quoted in Lee, op cit, 2000, p 183.

[25] According to Shiner, op cit, 2000, p 117, while 75% of City trainees in the Law Society cohort studies (below) received professional sponsorship to pay their fees and/or maintenance costs, this compares with less than 5% of high street trainees.

[26] Shiner, op cit, 2000, p 117.

[27] These firms have been seen as organisations going from strength to strength, outstripping the growth in other areas of the profession.

[28] In addition to work cited above, see further R. L. Abel, *English Lawyers Between Market and State: The Politics of Professionalism*, Oxford: OUP, 2003; R. L. Abel, *The Legal Profession in England and Wales*, Oxford: Basil Blackwell, 1988; J. Flood 'Megalawyering in the Global Order: The Cultural, Social and Economic Transformation of Global Legal Practice', *International Journal of the Legal Profession*, vol 3, p 169; A. Sherr, 'Superheroes and Slaves: Images and Work of the Legal Professional', *Current Legal Problems*, 1995, vol 48(2), p 327; A. Boon and J. Levin, *The Ethics and Conduct of Lawyers in England and Wales*, Oxford: Hart, 1999; M. Burrage 'From a Gentleman's to a Public Profession: Status and Politics in the History of English Solicitors', *International Journal of the Legal Profession*, 1996, vol 3, p 45; B. Cole, *Solicitors in Private Practice – Their Work and Expectations. Research Study No. 26*, London: Law Society (Research and Policy Planning Unit), 1997.

[29] Shiner, op cit, 2000, p 87.

[30] M. Thornton, 'The Demise of Diversity in Legal Education: Globalisation and the New Knowledge Economy', *International Journal of the Legal Profession*, 2001, vol 8(1), p 37 at p 43.

[31] Shiner op cit, 2000, p 87. See further A. Smith, 'Vicious (Magic) Circle', *Legal Ethics*, 2006, vol 9(2), p 152; A. T. Kronman, *The Lost Lawyer: Failing Ideals of the Legal Profession*, Cambridge, MA: Belknap, 1993; A. Freeman, 'A Critical Look at Corporate Practice', *Journal of Legal Education*, 1987, vol 37, p 315, cited in Thornton op cit, 2001, 'Demise … '.

Finally, the relevance of these materials is heightened when consideration is given to how gender, race, ethnicity and socio-economic background interact with the development of a career as a lawyer. Shiner has noted that, 'if certain communities face discrimination in the process by which the legal profession recruits its members, then how legitimate are any claims that the profession may make in terms of *representing* these communities?'[32] It is beyond dispute that the Law Society and Bar Council take equal opportunities and diversity with increasing seriousness,[33] including in relation to recruitment. What is also clear, however, as the Law Society Law Student Cohort Research Studies illustrate,[34] is that, for all their elite status within the profession, the City firms and, to a lesser degree, the large provincial firms have been a '*driving force* behind ... [these] institutional and social class biases'. The applicants who enjoy particularly high levels of success tend to be, research suggests, young, white and not disabled. They are more likely to have been educated at an independent school and to be from a privileged social class background;[35] to have a professionally qualified parent and to have attended an 'old' university as a law undergraduate, or the College of Law as a CPE (Common Professional Examination) student.[36] City firms have a 'strong bias in favour of Oxbridge graduates and trainees from privileged class backgrounds'.[37] In relation to gender, meanwhile, set against a rich interdisciplinary literature on women in the legal profession,[38] the

---

[32] Shiner op cit, 2000, p 87, my emphasis.

[33] This is the case whether in relation to gender, race, class, sexual orientation or disability: Law Society, *Law Society's Model Anti-Discrimination Policy* (policy issued under Rules 3 and 4 of the Solicitors Anti-Discrimination Rules 2004), London: Law Society, 2005; Law Society, *The Law Society Equality and Diversity Policy and Strategy*, London: Law Society, 2005. For an excellent discussion see H. Sommerlad, 'That Obscure Object of Desire, Sex Equality and the Legal Profession' in R. Hunter (ed), *Rethinking Equality*, Oxford: Hart, 2008.

[34] See work cited in Chapter 3, p 80, n 20.

[35] M. Shiner, *Entry into the Legal Profession: Law Student Cohort Study Year 5*, 1999, Table 4, London: Law Society, 1999; Shiner, op. cit 2000, p 99. See further E. Duff, M. Shiner and A. Boon, *Entry into the Legal Profession: The Law Student Cohort Study Year 6*, London: Law Society, 2000.

[36] Shiner, op cit, 2000, p 115. Research suggests that CPE students appear more likely to be white, male, well qualified and from an independent school background: Shiner, op cit, 2000, p 93.

[37] Shiner, op cit, 2000, p 118.

[38] Sommerlad, op cit, 2008; H. Sommerlad and P. Sanderson, *Gender Choice and Commitment: Women Solicitors in England and Wales and the Struggle for Equal Status*, Aldershot: Ashgate, 1998; J. Brockman, *Gender in the Legal Profession: Fitting or Breaking the Mould?* British Columbia: UBC Press, 2001; H. Sommerlad and P. Sanderson, 'The Legal Labour Market and the Training Needs of Women Returners in the United Kingdom', *Journal of Vocational Education and Training*, 1997, vol 29(1), p 45; M. J. Mossman, *The First Women Lawyers: A Comparative Study of Gender, Law and the Legal Professions*, Oxford: Hart, 2006; H. Sommerlad, 'Becoming a Lawyer: Gender and the Processes of Professional Socialization' in S. McIntyre and E. Sheehy (eds), *Calling for Change: Women, Law and the Legal Profession*, Ottawa: University of Ottawa Press, 2006; J. Hagan and F. Kay, *Gender in*

conclusions of the Law Society data are striking. Women still find it more difficult than men to make progress through the profession to Partner level, are less well paid than men, under-represented in the upper echelons of law firms, more likely than men to remain at assistant solicitor level and to 'drift' from the profession at an earlier age.[39]

What, therefore, given that the training contract serves as a key barrier to entry into the legal profession, are the messages conveyed *prior* to entry to the profession? They provide representations of lawyer's work that draw on, and reproduce, a knowledge base about legal practice that operates through a differentiation of the field of representation – at its simplest, a question of what is seen, and what is not seen.[40] Far from being neutral statements of an empirical reality of legal practice, however, discursive regimes within these texts position individual lawyers as – or as not – the bearers of historically specific subject positions. What is held out, I shall argue, is a disembodied individual, absented from questions of gender, race and class.[41] In developing understanding of the contingency of the 'man of law' idea, however, these are subject positions that, on examination, communicate ideas about conditions for future agency and individual and collective identity within the context of contemporary legal employment. If we look more closely, what emerges in these materials are attributes, characteristics and positionalities that rank women and men as social subjects in revealing and, at times contradictory, ways.

Practice: A Study of Lawyers' Lives, New York: Oxford University Press, 1995; U. Schultz and G. Shaw (eds), *Women in the World's Legal Professions*, Oxford: Hart, 2003; D. Podmore and A. Spencer 'Gender in the Labour Process – The Case of Women and Men Lawyers' in D. Knights and H. Wilmott (eds), *Gender and Labour Process*, Aldershot: Gower, 1986; E. Skordaki, 'Glass Slippers and Glass Ceilings: Women in the Legal Profession', *International Journal of the Legal Profession*, 1996, vol 3, p 7; H. Sommerlad, 'The Myth of Feminisation: Women and Cultural Change in the Legal Profession', *International Journal of the Legal Profession*, 1994, vol 1, p 31.

[39] L. Duff and L. Webley, *Equality and Diversity: Women Solicitors, Research Study 48, Vol II: Qualitative Findings and Literature Review*, London: Law Society, 2004.

[40] See further S. Nixon, *Hard Looks: Masculinities, Spectatorship and Contemporary Consumption*, London: UCL Press, 1996, p 11; F. Mort, *Cultures of Consumption*, London: Routledge, 1996. In what follows I am not so much concerned with the construction of meaning through rules of signification internal to representations. Rather, the focus will be the wider cultural forms and discourses on which these materials draw. See further A. Tudor, 'Culture, Mass Communication and Social Agency', *Theory, Culture and Society*, 1995, vol 12, p 81; M. Emmison and P. Smith, *Researching the Visual*, London: Sage, 2000; G. Rose, *Visual Methodologies*, London: Sage, 2000. See generally, S. Hall (ed), *Representation: Cultural Representation and Signifying Practices*, London: Sage, 1997.

[41] H. Sommerlad, 'Researching and Theorizing the Processes of Professional Identity Formation', *Journal of Law and Society*, 2007, vol 34, p 190.

Representing the lawyer: first impressions

Let us begin with first impressions. Within these images of legal professionalism, appearance is central. As Beverley Skeggs[42] has observed, appearance *matters*. It is the means by which others are recognised, and part of the way we want ourselves to be recognised.[43] Appearance is, of course, just one mechanism within an evaluative classification that frames gate-keeping entry into a legal career. I will here discuss three features of the texts in terms of appearance. I will proceed to present a more multi-layered account of corporate legal employment than any focus on first impressions alone would allow.

Age and seniority

Two main groups appear: the younger lawyer, men and women (the student on vacation placement and/or graduate trainee solicitor) and the more senior figure within the firm (the qualified lawyer, the Partner and, to a lesser degree, the corporate client). Recognising the presence of a relatively small but significant number of trainee solicitors who are 'late starters'[44] to the profession, the brochures focus, primarily, on images of youth and young adulthood. Accompanying text is routinely framed by a concern with the move away from late adolescence/university life into the independent adult life during the training contract.[45] The decision to apply is repeatedly presented as a key life stage, the law firm an organisation sensitive to the importance of helping an individual 'bridge the gap' between university and work.[46] Older lawyers, almost invariably men,[47] are regularly positioned as observers, watchers, teachers; figures who will assess and guide their young charges. They frequently appear in close physical proximity to the trainee, sometimes touching, observing a task in hand, although usually from a vantage point suggesting seniority. On occasion, firm Partners partake in cultural activities around life in the firm (for example, the office party).[48] Most often,

---

[42] B. Skeggs, *Formations of Class and Gender: Becoming Respectable*, London: Sage, 1997.

[43] As central markers of identity, class, gender and race appear bound up with the ability of an individual to make use of cultural capital in matters of economic and symbolic exchange within particular employment contexts. See further chapter 3.

[44] G. Walker, 'Born Again Lawyers', *The Lawyer*, 5 March 2001, p 35. See further Shiner, op cit, 2000, p 91. In the discussion that follows, it is important to recognise that in England and Wales the contrast between the relative youth of assistant solicitors and the demands of the job may appear more marked because law is, in contrast to some other jurisdictions, a first-degree subject.

[45] F. K. Goldscheider and C. Goldscheider, *The Changing Transition to Adulthood: Leaving and Returning Home*, London: Sage, 1999.

[46] 'From university to the profession is a big step. At Berwin Leighton we try that bit harder to ensure the transition is a smooth one.' The issue of the 'gap year' (what to do? is it desirable?) has become a common theme within both the student legal press and the material produced by the firms: see, for example, 'To Gap or Not To Gap: The Pros and Cons', *Plum*, 5th edn, SJ Berwin, 2003, p 22.

[47] See further D. L. Collinson and J. Hearn (eds) *Men as Managers, Managers as Men: Critical Perspectives on Men, Masculinities and Managements*, London: Sage, 1996.

[48] *Plum*, 4th edn, SJ Berwin, 2002, p 9.

however, when not directing their attention to the trainee, they are the object of the trainee's gaze, the latter looking up from what would be characterised within film studies as a classic feminine subject position.[49]

Women and men: convergence and equality

To continue at the level of what appears most immediate and obvious, a dominant and recurring image in these materials is of women and men, regardless of race or ethnic background (see below), working together happily and harmoniously. The gender balance of the trainee solicitors is such that it is common to find more women than men in these representations of trainee solicitors. On one level, this reflects gender shifts at point of entry and women have for some time constituted the majority of those studying law and entering the profession.[50] A rich body of data suggests that the traditional character-isation of the legal profession as being made up of public school, Oxbridge-educated, white and middle-aged men is, increasingly, simplistic. I will return to the issue of gender and how it connects to youth transitions later in this chapter, where I consider the lifestyle of the successful lawyer.

Dressing the lawyer: sex and suits

Finally, still at the level of these first impressions of age and gender, it is difficult to underestimate the centrality of dress. The legal profession shares with other workplace contexts the primary cultural norm of the post-war business and corporate sphere within Western capitalist economies as well as throughout the world.[51] That is, the wearing of the business suit as a visible marker of social respectability. As Ann Hollander puts it in her study of men's business clothes *Sex and Suits*,[52] tailored jackets, trousers, waistcoats, over-coats, shirts and neckties make up the 'standard masculine civil costume'.[53] Studies of the legal workplace[54] have sought to explore the relation between the wearing of this business suit and the idea of the sexed body in

[49] L. Mulvey, *The Visual and Other Pleasures*, London: Macmillan, 1989.

[50] Shiner, op cit, 2000, p 91. See further Law Society, *Trends in the Solicitor's Profession: Law Society Annual Statistical Report 2007*, London: Law Society, Strategic Research Unit, 2007; Law Society, *Factsheet 2006: Women Solicitors*, London: Law Society, 2006.

[51] See M. Roper, *Masculinity and the British Organization Man Since 1945*, Oxford: OUP, 1994; M. Roper and J. Tosh (eds), *Manful Assertions: Masculinity in Britain Since 1800*, London: Routledge, 1991; Mort, op cit, 1996.

[52] A. Hollander, *Sex and Suits: The Evolution of Modern Dress*, New York: Alfred A.Knopf, 1994; also F. Davies, *Fashion, Culture and Identity*, Chicago: University of Chicago Press, 1992.

[53] Hollander, op cit, 1994, p 3.

[54] M. Thornton, *Dissonance and Distrust: Women in the Legal Profession*, Oxford: OUP, 1996; R. Collier, '"Nutty Professors", "Men in Suits" and "New Entrepreneurs": Corporeality, Sub-jectivity and Change in the Law School and Legal Practice', *Social and Legal Studies*, 1998, vol 7 (1), p 27.

law,[55] the gendered embodiment of ideals of authority, the benchmarking of a 'knowing (legal) subject'.[56] Intriguingly, the few occasions in the materials where women and men are not dressed in formal business attire tend to relate to activities outside the legal workplace (for example, leisure pursuits). Or, more usually, some feature of life beyond or before the training contract, denoting the student deep in thought and, implicitly, considering their career options at the point of application.[57]

Age, gender and dress constitute immediate first impressions. In unpacking the socio-cultural significance of these texts, however, outlined above, it is necessary to shift the gaze, and turn towards a literature concerned with the sociologies of consumption, lifestyle and youth culture. It is via this work that it becomes possible to cast a rather different and more nuanced light on these representations of the trainee City solicitor.

Living 'the lifestyle': spatialities of lawyer's work and pleasure

> Herbert Smith London is based in stunning offices above Liverpool Street Station, in the heart of the Broadgate complex. Surrounded by City banks and other institutions, this area was built in the 1980s to cater for *the City worker's lifestyle*.[58]

The idea of developing a distinctive lifestyle has been understood within sociology to be a project invested with both ethical and aesthetic significance. It has been described as a way of denoting the 'creative use of consumer facilities'[59] and, importantly, as an element within the formation of individual and collective social identity – part of how we identify ourselves as similar to and, simultaneously, different from, others. Lifestyles have been understood as 'patterns of action that differentiate people' and in everyday interaction, we 'employ a notion of lifestyle without needing to explain what

---

[55] Whereas women lawyers, like other business and professional women, 'are expected to look like women – that is, *sexed* – although the code requires that they do not look "*sexual*" men do not look "sexed" for what is here considered to be "sexual" would deflect from the establishment of neutral authority': Thornton, op cit, 2006, pp 226–27, emphasis in original; also Collier, op cit, 1998.

[56] Thornton, op cit, 2006, p 223, has identified the man in the dark suit, plain shirt and unostentatious tie as one 'most commonly equated with the image of impersonal authority': the epitome of the disembodied, rational worker. This has been entwined with a historically constituted form of masculinity: 'emotionally flat, centred on a specialist skill, insistent on professional esteem and technically based dominance over other workers, and requiring for its highest (specialist) development the complete freedom from child care and domestic work': R. Connell, *Gender and Power*, Sydney: Allen and Unwin, 1987, p 181.

[57] On this 'diversity of choices' see A. Giddens, *Modernity and Self-Identity: Self and Society in the Late Modern Age*, Cambridge: Polity, 1991, p 80.

[58] Herbert Smith, 2002. Contrast 'Bishops Square represents a genuine revolution in the way we work. This move is ... *an investment in the community* where we will be based': Allen and Overy 2006, my emphasis.

[59] Chaney, op cit, 1996, p 37.

we mean'.[60] In the context of developing an identity as a particular kind of successful lawyer, this involves having an embedded sense of how we do, and should, feel about other 'places and people'.[61] The notion of lifestyle, interestingly, has itself become a central feature of how the career progression of the (successful) City solicitor is presented in these texts. Quite explicitly, an appeal is made to ideas about lawyer's work mobilised in both ethical and aesthetic terms and in such a way as to position the City lawyer via reference to two key or recurring concerns. First, ideas about youth culture and related consumption practices and, second, a concern with urbanism and, more specifically, what I shall term the shifting spatiality of corporate legal work.

In this section, I will explore these twin themes of consumption and urbanism. I will then proceed to reconsider what developing a workplace performance as a successful City solicitor is seen to involve in this context – and what all this might mean for those men and women who do not 'fit'. What is produced in these materials is, I shall suggest, a figure already encoded as a gendered, raced and classed subject in some subtle and frequently contradictory ways.

Youth culture and consumption: how to obtain the 'complete lifestyle'

Within representations of the articled clerk/trainee solicitor drawn from the 1980s and early 1990s (outside the sample used for the bulk of this analysis), although a theme that continues to appear, to a degree, in brochures and advertisements, there is one dominant and recurring image of the trainee lawyer. It is of the young solicitor – male or female – facing direct to camera, looking (usually) thoughtful or smiling and, repeatedly, holding an open book. Frequently, these figures appear against the backdrop of the bookshelves of a library, depicting a thoughtfulness and studiousness associated with university study (the 'bookish' world of the academic lawyer perhaps). Although legal research is just one (and by no means the most important) feature of the training experience, these earlier images accord such work a misleadingly high priority in their depiction of what lawyers 'do'. Over the past fifteen years, however, there has occurred a marked shift away from this once ubiquitous image of the young man or woman 'holding the book'. This has involved a more sophisticated and multi-layered representation of the training contract, focused instead around an engagement with the 'Complete lifestyle' of the City lawyer; the question, that is, of how, by working for a particular organisation, the trainee will 'Get a Life' within 'The Complete Law Firm'.[62] This point requires clarification.

---

[60] Chaney, op cit, 1996, p 4.
[61] N. Thrift, '"Us" and "Them": Re-imagining Identities' in H. Mackay (ed), *Consumption and Everyday Life*, London: Sage, 1997.
[62] Pannone and Partners, 2002.

The brochures now outline as a matter of routine a one-shop package of employment and leisure activities, a theme noted elsewhere in the literature on the corporate employer as 'total institution'. It is commonplace, for example, to find reference to the extensive range of benefits provided by the firm. These include facilities such as the travel season ticket loan, private medical scheme and annual health screening. Trainees are offered free membership of a gym and sports club (some on-site and with professional instruction), a subsidised food bar and ticket schemes for selected theatres, in-house consultation and treatment with a doctor and dentist, dry cleaning collection and delivery service and the provision, when required, of serviced apartments. Such facilities aimed at body servicing the lawyer should not be seen as fringe benefits. They are essential elements that facilitate and make possible the demanding physical and psychological investments and practices required by the corporate legal employer.

On closer examination, however, something else is also happening here, beyond the all-inclusive corporate world in which 'work' and 'life' seamlessly seem to come together (on the tensions around which for male lawyers see chapter 6). For the young solicitor, mapping to ideas of gender convergence and the commodification of masculinities discussed in chapter 1, this process entails a reworking of gender relations in the making of a legal career. The following is taken from a relatively recent brochure and is presented as a text illustrative of a traditional and now somewhat dated imaging of firm life in how leisure pursuits associated with legal employment are understood:

> Working in a city law firm is often hard, but it's not all long hours. The quality and frequency of Ashurst's sporting and social events are well known. Apart from the annual party for the whole firm and a variety of departmental functions, there are also periodic quiz evenings, wine tastings and many other one-off events ... Roger Finnow ... hosts a garden party each summer for all trainees, and all members of the firm are invited to attend the annual tennis evening, and barbecue and cricket event. We also have groups of musicians who play at suitable firm occasions.[63]

In contrast to this depiction of social and sporting events, however, representations produced during the past five years or so are marked by something very different. Not simply a heightened emphasis on the package of body care (above) offered by firms,[64] but also a far more vigorous, knowing and sophisticated attempt to connect the trainee experience to wider trends around youth consumption and popular culture. The legal press aimed at the undergraduate student market[65] has for some time engaged in an appropriation of the visual

---

[63] Ashurst Morris Crisp, 2002, p 22.
[64] On the body of the lawyer, see below.
[65] For example, *Lex: For the Lawyer of the Future*, London: Legalese; *Target Law*, London: GTI Specialist Publishers; *The Trainee*, the magazine of the Trainee Solicitors Group, Harrogate: Barker Brooks Media Ltd; *LegalWeek Magazine* (Student Specials), London: Global Professional Media Ltd; and *The Hobson's Law Guide*, Cambridge: CRAC Publications/Hobsons PLC.

styles, images and products associated with youth in their representation of diverse aspects of a legal career.[66] The law firms are increasingly connecting the trainee experience to cultural reference points which, it is assumed, will be familiar to the readers of their publicity material: 'This Life is about Friends', declare the firm DJ Freeman, above an image of ten trainees (six women, four men), a play on the titles of two popular television programmes.[67] One brands its brochure 'Unplugged and Uncovered'.[68] Others have utilised the work of modern artists to denote the distinctive cutting-edge character of the firm, often via use of an increasingly diverse array of fonts and formats.[69] Such examples are illustrative of the growing number of references to contemporary popular cultural artefacts that occur within these brochures.

In one of the most interesting examples of this trend, law firms have turned to the style and content of contemporary youth magazines.[70] The following is from a piece entitled 'Beer and Bonding in the Boardroom', taken from the 4th edition of *Plum*, published by SJ Berwin as an adjunct to the core information about the training contracts offered by the firm:

> Although the phrase 'the Boardroom' conjures up images of pinstriped old goats smoking cigars and congratulating themselves on being masters of the universe, this is not the case at SJB. Well, at least not on the last Friday of every month, for that is the firm drinks evening. The Boardroom's exotic flower arrangements are booted out to make way for much more interesting items – namely glasses and alcohol. As the noise level increases the Boardroom is

---

[66] Note, for example, from 1998 (considered in popular culture to be the high point of 'Brit Pop' and 'new laddism') the image of two men, without trousers and sitting on washing machines: 'Suits You Sir', *Lex*, Summer Term 1998 Issue 1, p 1. The playful nature of much of the student legal press has cross-referred to other texts, including television programmes and magazines such as *Viz Comic*, London: John Brown Publishing.

[67] DJ Freeman, 2001/2, a reference to *This Life* (BBC TV) and *Friends* (Channel 4), both popular television dramas concerned with youth friendships in transition, and the former a well-received drama set in a legal practice.

[68] Wragge and Co., 2001, utilising a texture and style similar to the work of the designer Peter Saville for Factory Records, Manchester, during the 1980s and 1990s: P. Saville, *Designed by Peter Saville*, Princeton: Princeton Arch, 2003.

[69] For example, Laurence Graham, 'Car Tyres, Containers and Career Opportunities', 2002/3, a series of postcards of modern art works, with information on the back covering aspects of training offered by the firm; 'Be Involved', Hammonds, 2008, involved a boxed set of cards.

[70] N. Stevenson, P. Jackson and K. Brooks, *Making Sense of Men's Magazines*, Cambridge: Polity, 2001; B. Benwell (ed), *Masculinity and Men's Lifestyle Magazines: Sociological Review Monographs*, Oxford: Blackwell, 2003; B. Crewe, *Representing Men: Cultural Production and Producers in the Men's Magazine Market*, London: Berg, 2005. Some firms have used the comic book format to depict the 'tale of two trainees' journey into the world of law': Reynolds Porter Chamberlin, *Decision Impossible*, 2008 edn.

transformed into the Gray's Inn Road branch of *All-Bar-One* (well, almost) ... For trainees the evenings are a perfect opportunity to ... indulge in some alcohol fuelled bonding with people from all over the firm – though it has to be said that it is not the right time to test whether your new boss has a good sense of humour! It is a popular and highly recommended start to the weekend.[71]

This illustrates three recurring themes within the depiction of youth and consumption in these representations of the training contract. First, the 'pleasures of leisure' are policed within the legal workplace and any notion of transgression is set within the parameters of formal codes of acceptability. Notwithstanding the attempt to regularise social relations, a relationship of power/deference with Senior Partners frames an ostensibly informal social event such as the 'Friday drinks evening'. Hierarchy is ever-present, excessive informality to be guarded against (although, as we shall see, conformity and individuality make uneasy bedfellows). The office party represents, Holliday and Thompson have noted, an 'in-between', liminal space that 'mixes together and confuses spaces and codes of conduct'.[72] Second, this passage reveals the centrality of alcohol and alcohol consumption in the depiction of the life of the firm across many of these texts.[73] Intriguingly, there is (albeit understandably) no mention of other recreational drugs, notwithstanding what is known about the range and prevalence of drug use amongst the student community, the youth population and within the City.[74] At times, references to alcohol are light-hearted and playful, hinting at the existence of a life beyond the hard work in the firm.[75] Alcohol is, nonetheless, seen as a key feature of the lifestyle of the City lawyer, a depiction in keeping with research indicating that mainstream youth culture in the UK is itself now 'awash on a sea of alcohol'.[76] How such images might be read by trainees whose social

[71] *Plum*, 4th edn, SJ Berwin, London, 2002, p 16.

[72] R. Holliday and G. Thomson, 'A Body of Work' in R. Holliday and J. Hassard (eds), *Contested Bodies*, London: Routledge 2001.

[73] The consumption of alcohol is a recurring theme in trainee profiles: 'After dinner (which itself included an unlimited supply of wine) ... the alcohol had already robbed me of all sense of sight and sound ... This is when it gets hazy': Kevin Cook, Trainee, op cit, see n 9 above. Alcohol also features in lifestyle articles in the general legal press: see, for example, 'London Barfly', *The Trainee*, Spring, 2001, p 14; 'Wild Wild East: Never Ones to Turn Down a (Drinking) Challenge, We Accepted An Invite ... ', *Lex*, Spring Term 2006, p 86.

[74] T. Newburn and M. Shiner, *Teenage Kicks? Young People and Alcohol – A Review of the Literature*. York: Joseph Rowntree Foundation, 2001; K. Brain, *Youth, Alcohol and the Emergence of the Post-Modern Alcohol Order*, London: Institute of Alcohol Studies, Occasional Paper, 2000.

[75] 'We Often Go out Drinking', Wragge and Co., 2000. On which see further M. Adler, 'From Symbolic Exchange to Commodity Consumption: Anthropological Notes on Drinking as a Symbolic Practice' in S. Barrows and R. Room (eds), *Drinking Behaviour and Belief in Modern History*, Berkeley: University of California Press.

[76] D. Hobbs, S. Lister, P. Hadfield and S. Hall, 'Receiving Shadows: Governance, Liminality in the Night-Time Economy', *British Journal of Sociology*, 2000, vol 53(1), p 89, cited in P. Chatterton and R. Hollands, 'Theorising Urban Playscapes: Producing, Regulating and Consuming Youthful Nightlife City Spaces', *Urban Studies*, 2002, vol 39(1), p 95 at p 102.

backgrounds mean alcohol will not be a part of their 'firm life' (for example, because of religious or other beliefs) is, of course, a different question.

Third, and building on the above, this text illustrates what the sociologists Paul Chatterton and Robert Hollands have termed the corporatisation of youth experience within contemporary Western societies. This point is of importance in considering how these images work in selling a lifestyle and requires clarification. It raises issues about the way shifts within corporate and youth cultures have, together, impacted on the image of the trainee lawyer in ways that have reshaped understandings of what it means to speak of the masculine nature of legal practice.

Corporate youth: consumption, leisure and hard work

Spend, spend spend ... It's a Lifestyle Thing![77]

'Every girl's crazy 'bout a sharp dressed man'; 'I'm gonna get dressed for success'; 'All your suits are custom-made in London'. Matt, Lisa and Sarah advise on 'office essentials' and, most importantly, how not to get caught out.
(On the 'Magic Wardrobe' for the 'Ambitious Trainee')[78]

As traditional sites of identity for young adults have weakened within late-modern societies, the focal concerns of consumption, leisure and popular culture, especially in urban centres, have been seen within sociology as central elements in the formation and experience of youth identities.[79] The shifting cultural and political economy around youth, Chatterton and Hollands have argued, can be characterised over the past decade or so by a process involving:

- the increasingly mainstream production of youth leisure, notably through the corporatisation and branding of the ownership of the spaces in which young people tend to socialise (clubs, bars, pubs, venues and so forth);
- the heightened regulation of the emerging 'urban playscapes'[80] in major UK cities (a process which has resulted in the marginalisation of radical/non-conformist youth cultures, an issue outside the scope of this chapter); and

---

[77] *Lex*, Spring Term 2002, p 42, exemplifying themes in R. Shields (ed), *Lifestyle Shopping: The Subject of Consumption*, London: Routledge, 1992; D. Wynne, 'Leisure, Lifestyle and the Construction of Social Position', *Leisure Studies*, 1990, vol 9, p 21.

[78] *Lex*, Spring Term 2002, p 42.

[79] Chatterton and Hollands, op cit, 2002, p 96. This argument is explored in more depth in P. Chatterton and R. Hollands, *Urban Nightscapes: Youth Cultures, Pleasure Spaces and Corporate Power*, London: Routledge, 2003. See also D. Slater, *Consumer Culture*, Oxford: Polity Press, 1997; R. Bocock, *Consumption*, London: Routledge, 1993; T. Edwards, *Contradictions of Consumption: Concepts, Practices and Politics in Consumer Society*, Buckingham: Open University Press, 2000.

[80] Chatterton and Hollands, op cit, 2003; also P. Chatterton, 'Governing Nightlife: Profit, Fun and (Dis)Order in the Contemporary City', *Entertainment and Sports Law Journal*, 2005, vol 1(2), p 23.

• a shift in the location and patterns of youth consumption practices 'through new forms of segmented nightlife activity based around more "exclusive" and "upmarket" identities amongst young adults'.[81]

These themes of production, regulation and consumption bear upon the social context in which the experience of the trainee corporate lawyer is lived out in these images;[82] and, importantly, each of these themes pervades the representation of corporate youth within texts aimed at the trainee City lawyer.

In what way? Understanding consumption as a 'symbolically meaningful and active relationship', one which '*produce[s]* experiences and identities',[83] in these materials the young adult as would-be lawyer is viewed in two ways. First, as recipients of economically produced and regulated activities (such as drinking in a branded, mainstream theme bar like *All Bar One*, as above);[84] and, second, as active participants within a distinctive cultural realm (as purchaser/consumer of a particular lifestyle).[85] The idea that the trainee solicitor will be both a recipient of commercially produced activities and a participant within popular culture has become a key leitmotif of these documents aimed at selling the training contract. What is presented is, in effect, a 'work hard, play hard' discourse framed by an overarching ethic of *playful responsibility*. This theme resonates with the wider literature concerned with changing identifications amongst young adults in the UK[86] (the term 'work hard, play hard' is, revealingly, used by several of the large firms in their recruitment brochures: see chapter 6, p 178). If ideas of (mainstream, conformist) production and regulation frame the lifestyle of the young City solicitor, however, it is a particular focus on patterns of consumption associated with 'exclusive' and 'upmarket'

---

[81] Chatterton and Hollands, op cit, 2003. See also F. Trentmann (ed), *The Making of the Consumer: Knowledge, Power and Identity in the Modern World*, London: Berg, 2005. The literature on contemporary youth lifestyles and cultures is voluminous. See, by way of illustration: S. Miles, *Youth Lifestyles in a Changing World*, Buckingham: Open University Press, 2000.

[82] A context that, as the economic and cultural shifts associated with the 'credit crunch' of 2008 play out, is shifting in complex ways, and can now itself be seen as distinct in some respects from the period largely under review (2002–8).

[83] Chatterton and Hollands, op cit, 2002, pp 108–9, my emphasis.

[84] Chatterton and Hollands, op cit, 2002, pp 122, 156–57. 'All Bar One' has been marketed specifically (if not exclusively) at the young professional market and with a particular focus on attracting women.

[85] 'What to spend the "first glorious pay check" on? What do partners of the future dream of?' The answer: 'Rent an Aston Martin for the weekend; a visit to a country club; bachlorette pad in Regents Park; a surround sound stereo system; pool table; pale blue BMW 73 ... my own beautiful boat ... pay off the Peugeot 206 coupe': *Lex*, Spring Term 2002, p 43. Alternatively, see N. Klein, *No Logo*, London: Flamingo, 2000.

[86] Miles, op cit, 2000; G. Valentine, T. Skelton and D. Chambers, *Cool Places: An Introduction to Youth and Youth Cultures*, London: Routledge, 1998. 'Going out/drinking' has been identified as the third most important spending priority amongst 16–24 year olds in the UK: Mintel, *Nightclubs and Discotheques*, in Mintel, *Pre-Family Leisure Trends*, London: Leisure Intelligence, January 2000.

identities that is of especial interest here. Enmeshed with the appeal to developing a high-status identity, the selling of the corporate lifestyle is marked by the culture of the 'groomed', perfected (and perfectible) body, an interest in body culture that reflects what sociological work has suggested is a more general heightened reflexivity about the self within late modernity.[87]

Importantly, this move has transformed the representation of normative masculinity in the materials. The practices of grooming and dressing and the activity of shopping are each understood as important practices for both women and men, with ideas of masculinity, as well as femininity, commodified in complex ways.[88] It is unsurprising that, alongside the acquisition of positional goods (see chapter 6, p 177), the body of the lawyer, regardless of whether they are a man or a woman, should be seen as a site for specific consumption practices. We find in these materials a representation of the body addressed, simultaneously, in terms of, first, the maintenance of health and optimum functioning (in relation, for example, to the facilities of body servicing referred to above),[89] and, second, via a concern to regulate the 'appearance [and] the movement and control of the body within social space', marking out, that is, the selective times in which one is to be 'relaxed',[90] the parameters whereby the management of impressions will become a concern in 'getting on'.[91] From this perspective, becoming, presenting and experiencing oneself as a City solicitor is part of an ongoing process of subjectivisation involving complex techniques of care, consumption and self-policing. To follow Foucault, these practices of the self emerge as important elements in the acquisition of a distinctive subjectivity – that is, being, or potentially being, a successful corporate lawyer.

Whilst attaining the legal 'lifestyle thing' involves engaging in consumption practices constituted through the production of a particular aesthetic, however, an analysis of consumption and lifestyle only takes us so far in seeking to understand *why* this kind of imagery might be so appealing. To understand this question it is necessary to locate these processes in relation to the political, economic and cultural contexts within which the training contract with the

---

[87] Giddens, op cit, 1991; M. Featherstone, *Consumer Culture and Postmodernism*, London: Sage, 1991.

[88] Nixon, op cit, 1996; Mort, op cit, 1996. See also S. Bordo, *The Male Body: A New Look at Men in Public and in Private*, New York: Farrar, Straus and Giroux, 1994.

[89] Self-presentation within this context demands maintenance of the body, not simply in the face of the disease and deterioration that are part of the ageing process, but also in ways in keeping with the situated, local cultural norm of the law firm as to what does (and does not) constitute an 'acceptable' appearance.

[90] See M. Featherstone, 'The Body in Consumer Culture', in M. Featherstone, M. Epworth and B. S. Turner (eds), *The Body: Social Process and Cultural Theory*, London: Sage, 1991, where a useful distinction is made between the idea of an 'inner and the outer body [which] become conjoined: the prime purpose of the maintenance of the inner body becomes *the enhancement of the appearance of the outer body*' (p 171, original emphasis).

[91] E. Goffman, *The Presentation of Self in Everyday life*, London: Allen Lane, 1969; E. Goffman, *Relations in Public*, Harmondsworth: Penguin, 1976.

large firm is now experienced.[92] It is necessary to consider, that is, how the 'lawyer lifestyle', and related issues of consumption and identity, connect to infrastructural changes that have taken place within British society.

Reshaping the city: geographies of lawyers' work and pleasure

The economic downturn gathering apace at the time of writing is reshaping the geography of urban spaces, the very 'look' of British cities. Over the past two decades in the UK these city centres have been remodelled as part of wider socio-economic processes of restructuring 'as places in which to live, work and be entertained'.[93] Contemporary urban sociology, as well as film, has charted the erosion of the idea of the city strongly connected to a manu-facturing and industrial past[94] and a move to an idea of city space constituted as a locus for:

> private/corporate capital, knowledge-based activities, middle-class con-sumption and an entrepreneurial turn in urban governance aimed at attracting and satisfying the demands of highly mobile global capital.[95]

This cultural economy of cities[96] has been marked by a 'renewed emphasis on business service employment', a 'dematerialized and knowledge-based econ-omy' and a greater economic role for 'corporately organised leisure, retail and consumption-based rather than production-based activities'.[97] The large law firm exemplifies these shifts and the lifestyle of the City lawyer presented in the materials illustrates the way consumption practices have become entwined with the economic, aesthetic and ethical logic of private/corporate capital; and, more generally, with a commodification of workplace cultures associated, at least until the present recession, with a rapidly expanding urban

---

92   Chatterton and Hollands, op cit, 2002.

93   Chatterton and Hollands, op cit, 2002, p 95.

94   M. Featherstone and S. Lash (eds), *Spaces of Culture: City-Nation-World*, London: Sage, 1999; D. Ley, *The New Middle-Class and the Remaking of the Central City*, New York: OUP, 1996; *Of Time and the City: A Love Song and A Eulogy*, HanWay/BBC films, 2008.

95   Chatterton and Hollands, op cit, 2002, p 97. Although these developments around the mobility and status of global capital have, of course, taken on rather different meaning in the light of the economic global downturn: N. Cohen, 'Why I Blame the Left for Britain's Financial Ruin', *The Observer*, 25 January 2009, pp 8–9.

96   A. Scott, *The Cultural Economy of Cities*, London: Sage, 2000.

97   Chatterton and Hollands, op cit, 2002, p 97. See further B. Jessop, 'The Entrepreneurial City: Reimagining Localities, Redesigning Economic Governance or Restructuring Capital' in N. Jewson and S. McGregor (eds), *Transforming Cities*, London: Routledge, 1997; N. Blomley, 'The Properties of Space: History, Geography and Gentrification', *Urban Geographer*, 1997, vol 18(4), p 286; J. Hannigan, *Fantasy City: Pleasure and Profit in the Postmodern Metropolis*, London: Routledge, 1998.

service class.[98] The location of the trainee solicitor within the new urban environment is an important dimension of how self-identity as a successful lawyer is marked in the texts through territorial and geographical attachments, evoking a sense of belonging and ontological security: here is where you will 'fit in', belong, be 'part of the team'. In the context of over a decade of urban change 'directed towards mobile, non-local and corporate capital, property developers and high income urban-livers'[99] this involves positioning those employed in corporate legal employment as a social group well placed to benefit from the spoils of socio-economic restructuring:[100]

> The Broadgate complex ... contains a number of smart bars and restau-
> rants, summer seating areas, a croquet lawn, an ice rink, numerous cafes
> and access to shops, banks and boutiques ... Five minutes walk from the
> office [the subsidised leisure club] has a swimming pool, Jacuzzi, steam
> rooms and sauna, as well as free classes and large multi–gym facilities.[101]

The lifestyle associated with the new urbanism plays out in different ways, however, depending on the national, global and regional contexts the materials seek to address. The dominant representation of the urban within many texts is that of the City of London,[102] the historical landmarks of the 'Square Mile' combining with the architecture of the 'New London' and the skyscraper in such a way as to depict an appealing blend of tradition and modernity. Increasingly, however, other world centres of corporate activity feature heavily, reflecting the transnational nature of legal work and the increasing importance of the global market (and, indeed, the reach of transnational business masculinities: chapter 6, p 182). Seeking to convey what this will mean for the young lawyer, the depiction of space, place and status in the development of a successful legal career has moved on a long way therefore from the images of earlier years. In the past, the representation of the opportunity to travel involved little more than an image of an aeroplane taking off from an unknown airport, a passport sticking from a

---

[98] Although public service does appear in occasional references to pro bono work and, to a lesser degree, via reference to activities to be undertaken via the 'gap year': '[The work camp] shows Kay is willing to roll up her sleeves and get stuck in' (Graham Stoddart, Graduate Recruitment Officer, Macfarlanes, quoted in *Target*, 7th edn, 2003).

[99] Chatterton and Hollands, op cit, 2002, p 97.

[100] A factor in what has been perceived to be, as a result of the move towards economic recession, a cultural backlash towards these groups during much of 2008–9, ongoing at the time of writing: see further below.

[101] Herbert Smith, 2002. This text exemplifies the targeting of corporate leisure activities (commercially provided bars, gyms, pubs and so forth) at 'cash-rich groups such as professionals and high level service sector workers (the "suits")': Chatterton and Hollands, op cit, 2002, p 99. Note N. Wrigley and M. Lowe, *Retailing, Consumption and Capital: Towards the New Retail Geography*, Harlow: Longman, 1996.

[102] Understandably, given that London remains the base for the principal offices of many of these firms.

dark suit pocket (with the assumption that the lawyer would, usually, be male: see below). Now, however, the overseas location is associated explicitly more with the night-time economy, the possibilities of the city as a pleasure space, the city as a site of consumption, play and entertainment; a space 'saturated with signs and images to the extent that anything can be represented, thematized and made an object of interest'.[103] Globally, as well as nationally, that is, lifestyle, consumption and the acquisition of positional goods[104] mark the City lawyer as part of a distinct class faction within a particular social space. These themes illustrate how a global gender order has impacted on the 'private' arenas of men's personal lives, redistributing men's bodies (in this case, the lawyer who 'gets to travel') through migration and geographies of labour.

At the national level, reference is similarly made to the rebranding of UK cities associated with the new urbanism, as above. However, in the local context the idea of the city as a space for consumption plays out in rather different ways. This is evident in how large regional firms have sought to appeal to trainees who may wish to resist the allure of the City of London for reasons of personal lifestyle, quality of life and the maintenance of family ties and friendship networks: 'Most of my friends in larger firms seem exhausted. That doesn't mean you don't work hard here, but there's got to be a balance'[105] (see further chapter 6). The reasons for joining regional firms continue to be linked, however, to the possibilities for having 'fun': 'Newcastle has something of a reputation for enjoying itself. We should know. But the nightlife isn't all you'll enjoy at Dickinson Dees.'[106] Common to the representation of UK cities such as Leeds, Sheffield, Manchester, Birmingham and Newcastle, the cultural characteristics of the urban centre – as, say, lively, exciting, friendly – are drawn on so as to present the firm itself as similarly small but manageable.[107] What these regional city spaces share

---

[103] M. Featherstone, *Consumer Culture and Postmodernism*, London: Sage, 1991, p 101; J. Urry, *Consuming Places*, London: Routledge, 1995; K. Hetherington, *Expressions of Identity: Space, Performance, Politics*, London: Sage, 1998. The images of the city at night are often blurred in such a way as to depict the city 'on the go'; note, for example, the imaging of Hong Kong, Paris, London and Singapore: Herbert Smith, 2002; Allen and Overy, 2006.

[104] Featherstone, op cit, 1991.

[105] Bristows, 2002.

[106] Dickinson Dees, 2001. Also Dickinson Dees, 2003, 2006: 'A Life Worth Living: If Dickinson Dees provides big career opportunities, then Newcastle and the surrounding area provide equally big social opportunities'; Watson Burton, 2003. On the re-imaging of a particular 'cultural city': R. Hollands, 'From Shipyards to Nightclubs: Restructuring Young Adults' Employment, Household and Consumption Identities in the North-East of England', *Berkeley Journal of Sociology*, 1997, vol 41, p 41.

[107] 'Birmingham has a bit of a bad reputation, Spaghetti junction and all ... so what is it really like for the ... employees who live and work there? ... People who have been away for a few years are quite shocked at all the new bars, pubs and clubs that have sprung up': Wragge and Co., 2003. Contrast 'Second to None', *The Trainee*, Issue 14, 2003, pp 20–21; I. Taylor, K. Evans and P. Fraser, *A Tale of Two Cities: Global Change, Local Feeling and Everyday Life in the North of England: A Study in Manchester and Sheffield*, London: Routledge, 1996.

is an overarching depiction as places in which work and pleasure are entwined. And, importantly, they are locations in which a successful legal career will be dependent on a particular kind of acceptable workplace performance.

'Looking good': appearance and the (acceptable) workplace performance

Be Smart ... what sort of person thrives in a premier international law firm?

Be Successful ... [we offer] the ideal environment for realising your ambitions.

Be Yourself. ... we believe that people perform better *when being themselves*.[108]

Alongside the corporate lifestyle, these texts must communicate something about the nature of employment in the large firms. They contain essential information, that is, about the work and tasks that a trainee will undertake and the energy and commitment that obtaining career success will demand. In this respect, possessing certain personal characteristics and skills is seen as vital in the reproduction of an acceptable workplace performance.[109] What, therefore, do these materials tell us about what will be required of the (potentially) successful corporate lawyer?

Meeting the needs of and dealing with the business client is a dominant theme running through the brochures, although seldom made as explicit as in the following illustration of what is 'really' going on in an interview for the training contract:

Every interviewee wonders what's going through the interviewer's mind. Norton Rose can reveal that, in at least one Partner's case, it is: Am I enjoying this? Would I happily let this person go on a long-haul flight with one of our best clients? Could this person have a sensible conversation with someone we're trying to impress? Would they be prepared to mend a photocopier that breaks down at 3 a.m. on an all-nighter?[110]

Beyond the appeal to being a personable individual, however, on closer examination the nature of this commitment is more complex than it may seem at first. There is some recognition that both women and men might be addressed by identifications beyond that of 'lawyer', 'professional' or 'employee' and that cultural identities, as it were, may be plural and fluid. This is seen in the

---

[108] Allen & Overy, 2001, my emphasis.
[109] L. McDowell, 'Body Work: Heterosexual Gender Performances in City Workplaces' in D. Bell and G. Valentine (eds), *Mapping Desire*, London: Routledge, 1995.
[110] Norton Rose, 2002.

repeated construction of the desirable recruit as someone who will have a 'full life', who will be a 'rounded individual':

> Stephen Donnelly … Wine buff … Keen surfer … and trainee solicitor … At Watson, Farley and Williams we see individuality as an asset. We think it makes for more rounded and interesting lawyers.[111]

What is also clear, however, is that the construction of an identity *as* a successful lawyer will involve the organisation of a more or less coherent sense of self in which paid employment will and must have a central and primary significance. This means that tensions arise in the texts with regard to how the desirable recruit is then depicted in the attempt to sell the training contract. Thus, on one level, we find recurring appeals to ideas of camaraderie, friendship, community and mutual support within the trainee community. At the same time, there is a clear acceptance that competition, individualism and culturally legitimate self-promotion will be called for; the need to 'push oneself'; to be visible, to be seen to be there and to succeed over and above others. As one image puts it, depicting a smiling man, 'Partner at 32. It doesn't come much quicker than that.'[112]

These tensions assume a particular significance in an employment context marked by an 'up or out' culture,[113] in which competition for limited positions and promotion is structured into the way the firms operate (only some will, and can, succeed to Partner level: see chapter 6, p 171). As Lee has observed, following Galanter, the distinctive structure in the large law firm in the UK is one in which 'highly qualified law graduates … compete over an extended period (five to ten years) in a more or less meritocratic tournament in which only some are chosen to become partners; the others typically depart'.[114] The images, and the messages they communicate, thus reflect the reality of the stratified nature of the national and international law firm as a bureaucratised, top-down organisation. If the competitive edge ascribed to cultural practices is unsurprising, however, it stands in a complex relation to the tension elsewhere in the texts between ideals of individualism and conformity. The brochures are replete with references to 'Be Yourself',[115]

---

[111] Watson Farley Williams, 2000: 'At Watson Farley Williams we see individuality as an asset.' '[T]o the client, he's the top corporate lawyer … to you, he's Raj': Norton Rose, 2005.

[112] 'J. Fortnam, Partner, Age 33 (Law, Liverpool)': Pinsent Curtis Biddle, 2001. In fact, it does come sooner: Norton Rose, 2002: 'You [could] be a partner sooner than you imagine – our youngest partner is just 31.'

[113] Lee, op cit, 2000.

[114] M. Galanter 'Old and In the Way: The Coming Demographic Transformation of the Legal Profession and its Implications for the Provision of Legal Services', *Wisconsin Law Review*, 1999, p 1081, quoted in Lee, op cit, 2000, p 195. That progression will involve competition between trainees is itself, at times, explicit: 'Our work environment is competitive': Norton Rose, 2002.

[115] 'Just be yourself': Simmons and Simmons, 2003; 'Great minds think differently': Slaughter and May, 2008.

to 'Be an Individual'; to the fact 'One Person Can Make A Difference'.[116] Perhaps more than any other tag line, the call is for 'A Different kind of Lawyer', someone who 'does not fit into anyone's mould'.[117] The successful trainee will be 'one of a kind', 'not stuffy' and have 'character'. What is sought is an 'exceptional' individual. This discourse resonates with social processes of individualisation[118] but it also rests uneasily with the high degree of social conformity demanded by the firm, a conformity that involves the acceptance, not just of firm cultures and practices, but the dominant notions of commitment and social capital at play in getting on.

At this point, in consideration of these cultural resources, it is important to consider how a differentiation of the field of vision interplays with ideas of social acceptance within the corporate legal field. This raises the question, in particular, of how individuals are understood to have (or not to have) the ability to utilise resources, to draw on social, cultural and economic capital, as discussed in chapter 3 in the context of the 'private life' of the university law school. It leads us to question, that is, how ideas about a career as a lawyer, even at this early stage, have *already* been enmeshed with the making of assumptions about precisely who the would-be-successful lawyer will be – and who, importantly, they might be prepared, in later life, to become. On closer examination, I shall argue in the remainder of this chapter, this is a figure far removed in certain respects from the idea of the 'man of law' discussed in chapter 1.

Selling the long-hours culture: commitment and the gendered workplace

> My experience with the firm over the last year has shown that there is more to it than red braces and power breakfasts.[119]

> Reach ... Inspire ... Breathe ... Give ... Work is important, of course. But it's not everything.[120]

The gendered nature of what Hilary Sommerlad and Peter Sanderson have referred to as 'the commitment question', and the related career disadvantages for women of 'starting a family',[121] raise a potential problem for law firms seeking to sell the long hours culture as part of the package of corporate legal employment discussed above. What is interesting, therefore, is how the

---

[116] White and Case, 2000; Macfarlanes, 2002.
[117] Landwell (A Correspondent Law Firm of Price Waterhouse Coopers), 2001; 'Great Minds Think Differently': Slaughter and May, 2008; 'Out of the Ordinary': Simmons and Simmons, 1998.
[118] U. Beck and E. Beck-Gernsheim, *Individualization: Institutionalized Individualism and its Social and Political Consequences*, London: Sage, 2002.
[119] 'E. Shaw, Trainee Profile': SJ Berwin, 2002 in *The Trainee*, Autumn 2002, p 13.
[120] 'Start at the Top': Allen & Overy, 2008.
[121] P. Sanderson and H. Sommerlad, 'Professionalism, Discrimination, Difference and Choice in Women's Experience in Law Jobs' in Thomas, op cit, 2000, p 155.

materials do this. The need to work long hours is explicitly seen as part of the job: 'Work life balance: is this possible in law, or just an illusion? This is up to you. You know that long hours are likely, but the rewards will be great.'[122] Long hours are depicted, above all, as a pleasurable, rewarding challenge: 'Working through the night ... how teamwork and black coffee cracked one of the world's biggest debt purchases.'[123] The recognition that long hours will be called for is couched, that is, in terms of the positive value of the hours to the trainee her/himself. It is part of team-building, fostering a collegiate culture, bringing people together in a shared task. It is the 'working hard' allied to the 'playing hard' in the depiction of leisure and consumption discussed above. Above all, it is associated with youth, energy and, again, the sense of the need to 'have fun' at work:[124]

> There were a few all night sittings – it's the nature of Corporate work. It's not unusual to have a curry or KFC at 4am followed by a celebration champagne breakfast at 7. But deals like that are exciting; there's a sense of urgency; you feel you are doing something important.[125]

There is no recognition, in the texts explored for the purposes of this chapter, that long hours might constitute a problem for some (older?) individuals who may have other commitments or responsibilities in their lives. It is important to remember that the workplace performance of the City lawyer (as well as the life-style with which it is related) does not just 'happen'. It requires an emotional and material investment involving complex techniques of body care and consumption (not least, we have seen, around the maintenance of an acceptable appearance). These techniques are provided not only by the self but also through the work of others, notably in relation to the need for some individuals to meet (or, more accurately, to be freed from) the dependencies of child care. With regard to the deployment of social capital, moreover, this self-representation itself entails a gendered aspect, evocatively captured by Hollander as involving a desire to:

> look sincere and spontaneous ... Looking carefully in the mirror, so as to actually gain some understanding and possible control of the physical qualities that might give one away, smacks of caring too much ... It is much easier to rely on signs and forget real looks; to project the desire that you and your clothes be read and not really seen.[126]

---

[122] Allen & Overy, 2003; note, for example, the 'Lex-O-Matic Work Life Quiz', *Lex*, Spring Term 2006, pp 54–55; 'Yes, There Will Be the Occasional Late Night': DentonWildeSapte, 2008.

[123] C. Phillips, *Target Law*, 2002, p 88.

[124] Long hours, that is, become *part* of the lifestyle of the young lawyer, with associations around youth embedded in the depiction of the temporal and spatial demands placed on the trainee.

[125] Pinsent Curtis Biddle, 2001.

[126] Hollander, op cit, 1994, p 190.

Questions about gender and sexuality, therefore, pervade the depiction of the legal workplace in general and subtle ways. This is revealed by one, no means atypical, set of images seeking to address the temporal and spatial parameters of the typical working day of one trainee solicitor with the law firm. In detailing the expected working hours, a series of representations stage various moments during the day of the trainee. These are presented alongside text that reads as follows:

07.45 Starting Out. Piccadilly Line; 08.28 Lacon House (arrival);

09.14 Early Result; 09.43 Client Meeting; 10.52 Question; 11.50 Research:

12.31 Lunch; 12.37 Pause; 13.09 Listening; 15.23 Winning Strategies;

18.20 Early Evening; 18.45 Relaxing; 19.20 Late shopping. Tottenham Court Road.[127]

The images accompanying the final three stages, italics above, depict respectively the following. At 18.20, a man and woman are working together at a desk, the picture framed in such a way as to suggest they are alone in the office. It is dark outside and both are smiling, the demeanour and body language suggesting a private joke. At 18.45, the image shifts to a wine bar or public house, with two women and two men, all smiling. One woman, standing face to camera, is holding a wine glass, the slightly blurred bottle (it is suggested that it is alcohol) heightening the focus of the reader on the face of the central woman. At 19.20, we are in an apparently deserted supermarket, and the number of lawyers has reduced – a woman and a man are together in an aisle shopping; the man is pushing the trolley, the woman choosing items from the shelves. With these scenes of (possible) flirtation and pleasurable social contact culminating in a hint of domesticity, these images exemplify a feature of the materials; a recurring depiction of young women and men, across a range of workplace and leisure scenarios, in situations encoded by assumptions about sexuality and (hetero)sexual attraction.

A sense of normative heterosexuality frames both workplace and leisure time interaction within the texts. Indeed, they are replete with images of women and men in close eye contact, relaxed, smiling, socially engaged. Regardless of the permutations – a sole woman in a group of men, a man in a group of women – the overriding message is clear. Here is a job in which you will meet people and in which there are all kinds of social possibilities. Images

---

[127] Nabarro Nathanson, 2001/2. Such a breakdown of the day has been used by a number of firms: for example, D.J. Freeman, 2003 'A Day in the Life of … Joanne Smith (08.45–18.10).' As noted above, alcohol is integrated into this image of the desirable trainee day: 18.10: 'I finalise time … switch telephone to voicemail and head down to the local pub for a well-earned drink!'

of same-sex encounters, in particular those depicting two men alone, routinely appear more formal, encoded as distanced and professional. In publications aimed at the law student market, the references to sex and sexuality are more overt.[128] There is no suggestion that the reality of the corporate leisure package might at times involve more overtly exploitative social relationships (for example, in the form of the expense account visit to the lap dancing club), nor that sexuality might be complex or contested, a body 'at work' masking the transgression of subjects 'passing' as one thing but 'really' being another.[129] Importantly, as Chatterton and Hollands have observed, 'there appears to be little evidence to suggest that women in gentrified mainstream nightlife spaces are any less harassed or exposed to various forms of sexism'.[130] Far from any simplistic image of a 'man of law', we are dealing with complex and multi-layered representations of gender and sexuality that position women and men in some distinctive ways.

Race and ethnicity

Alongside these representations of gender, one of the most striking changes in the materials to have taken place over the past ten years is in the number of black and ethnic minority men and women appearing. The texts present an inclusive legal profession, a respecter of ability and intelligence oblivious to questions of race.[131] When read alongside Law Society statistics and other studies, this numerical figuring of black and ethnic minority trainees might appear disproportionate to what is known to be the actual representation of these groups within the large City firms. This is the case whether at the level of trainee solicitor or at more senior levels.[132] Shiner has suggested, drawing on Law Society data, that there exist 'particular social and institutional biases [within] City and large provincial firms' which impact on the securing of a training contract and, amongst those who do enter the profession, later issues of pay and concentration 'in less prestigious firms or in less prestigious positions' (see also chapter 3, p 88).[133] Yet, intriguingly, it is common to find the image of these trainees appearing alongside text referring to the very qualities of inclusiveness, diversity and opportunity the firms are seeking to

---

[128] 'Countdown to more opportunities ... Number 10: Sexy Deals', Cadwalder, 2001; SJ Berwin, *Plum*, 5th edn, front page.

[129] N. Duncan, *Bodyspace: Geographies of Gender and Sexuality*, London: Routledge, 1996.

[130] Chatterton and Hollands, op cit, 2003, p 157; 'Profitability is ensured by corporate expense accounts and a core audience drawn from the business community during the week and stag parties at the weekend': Chatterton and Hollands, op cit, 2003, p 160.

[131] 'It's not where you're from, it's where you're going': Haarmann Hemmelrath, 2002. Although see D. Wilkins, 'Fragmenting Professionalism: Racial Identity and the Ideology of Blacked Out Lawyering', *International Journal of the Legal Profession*, 1998, vol 5, p 141.

[132] S. Vignaendra, M. Williams and J. Gavey, 'Hearing Black and Asian Voices – An Exploration of Identity' in Thomas (ed.), op cit, 2000; Shiner, op cit, 2000, p 99.

[133] Shiner, op cit, 2000, p 118.

sell.[134] Such inclusivity is alluded to as a selling point, part of the attractiveness of the firm and its engagement with equality agendas.

This is not to charge firms with the accusation of tokenism. Undoubtedly, the images reflect real and well-documented changes within the profession, a shifting market reality. It is known, for example, that law is a particularly popular choice for ethnic minority candidates. Linking the complexity of this issue to a consideration of the socio-economic background of trainees, however, and the questions of class considered in chapter 3, it is important to remember that trainee recruits to City firms still tend to come, Law Society research shows, from a fairly selective number of prestigious 'old' universities.[135] Like the law students in such institutions, they are more likely to be predominantly white and middle class.[136] The profile of the student cohort, as well as the status of the law school,[137] remains of significance in assessing chances of obtaining a vacation placement and/or training contract. Social class remains a significant barrier to entry to the profession, a fact recognised in relation to the legal profession and the law school, as discussed in chapter 3.[138] What is revealing, therefore, is how particular assumptions about social class nonetheless inform aspects of this depiction of this City lawyer's lifestyle in some subtle ways.

Social class, culture and the body

Social class, as we have seen already in this book, is a fluid and contested idea. Drawing on sociological work, I argue that the lifestyle of the 'mega lawyer' embodies aspects of what Savage et al have termed a distinctively 'postmodern' kind of middle-class lifestyle; one that can be contrasted with an ascetic and undistinctive middle-class variant.[139] This lifestyle is marked by characteristics that feature prominently in the imaging of the City lawyer in these materials, interwoven with the specificities of gender, age, race, educational attainment and location.[140] For example, a lifestyle marked by the blurring of conventional stylistic distinctions between ideas of 'high' and 'low' culture, evident in the play of cultural artefacts in the representation of corporate (legal) youth. This is a world where an appeal to partaking in 'sexy' deals and 'alcohol-fuelled bonding' co-exists with the garden party, the opera and the

---

[134] For example Nicholson, Graham and Jones, 2003; Weil, Gotshal and Manges 2006: 'Multi-Jurisdictional, Multi-disciplined, Multi-talented'.

[135] P. Thomas and A. Rees, 'Law Students – Getting in and getting on' in Thomas (ed.), op cit, 2000.

[136] See further chapter 3, p 88.

[137] Shiner, op cit, 2000, p 93.

[138] S. Vignaendra, *Social Class and Entry into the Solicitor's Profession: Research Study 41*, London: The Law Society, 2001.

[139] M. Savage, P. Dickens and T. Fielding, *Property, Bureaucracy and Culture: Middle Class Formation in Contemporary Britain*, London: Routledge, 1992. See also M. Savage and T. Butler (eds), *Social Change and the Middle Classes*, London: UCL Press, 1995; T. Butler, *Gentrification and the Middle-Classes*, Aldershot: Ashgate, 1997.

[140] Savage et al, op cit, 1992, p 127.

wine-tasting evening. It is a world in which high cultural forms of art (opera, classical music) lie cheek by jowl with an employee lifestyle that verges on the carnivalesque in the way it appeals to hedonism, excess and an overarching appeal to 'having fun'. Each of the above, we have seen, is presented as part of the dominant and culturally sanctioned norms of the large law firm at the point of entry to the legal profession.

What is revealing, however, is how this register of objectification ruptures not just codes of class but also some traditional ideas of masculinity and femininity, further questioning the idea that the 'man of law' embodies a particular kind of gendered subjectivity. This can be seen in an increasingly explicit eroticism and turn to sexual imagery, albeit one reduced to a signifier of irony and 'playfulness'. Whilst a theme particularly clear in the student legal press,[141] it is also evident in the way in which the firm brochures depict women and men in the legal workplace via a representation of heterosexuality marked by a turn to the playful. This move can be seen as a corollary of the symbolic restructuring that has accompanied the entry of women in ever greater numbers into the legal workplace. The way the lawyer lifestyle combines, that is, a gendered body culture with many of the traditional characteristics of non-healthy living (heavy drinking, 'partying' hard) reflects how the development of the 'pastiched and eclectic lifestyle' has come to demonstrate 'the demise of certain traditions of taste and how ... cultural practices [can] be sampled and juxtaposed in novel and heterodox patterns'.[142]

In keeping with this tendency to mix and mesh cultural styles – and as an attempt also to evoke some sense of cultural 'authenticity' – corporate law firms have drawn on ideas traditionally associated with certain aspects of working-class cultures.[143] Notions of manliness, in particular, and an entwining of ideas about manual labour and the male body, feature in this context.[144] It is intriguing in these materials how there appears to be an almost nostalgic sense of loss (or mourning?) for what might be termed the 'dignity of manual labour', given how the shift from manufacturing to

---

[141] 'Lisa was really glad she hadn't worn a skirt that day', *Lex*, Issue 15, Spring Term 2003, p 1. 'Glittering Prizes', *Lex*, Issue 12, Spring Term 2002, front cover.

[142] Savage et al, op cit, 2000, p 214. 'While we certainly work hard, we play hard too ... ', Freshfields, Bruckhaus Deringer, 2003. Thrift observed, two decades ago, how the purchase of a substantial country house in the southern half of England itself became a 'reasonably common element' of lifestyle practices by private-sector young(ish) professionals: N. Thrift, 'Images of Social Change' in C. V. Hamnett, L. McDowell and P. Sarre (eds), *The Changing Social Structure*, London: Sage, 1989.

[143] Henley Centre, *Working Class Heroes*, Henley: The Henley Centre, Press Release No 5, April 2001. See Chapter 3.

[144] Put at its simplest, and to adapt Paul Willis's celebrated *Learning to Labour: How Working Class Kids Get Working Class Jobs*, Westmead: Saxon House, 1977, if white-collar, office-based, managerial and professional work was the destination for the 'Ear 'oles', the academically inclined 'swots and wimps', the 'lads' (originally in school with the 'Ear 'oles') moved in to work that was more 'truly' masculine.

predominantly service-based economies has withdrawn understandings of men's gender and labour across workplace contexts. We find here repeated references to lawyers' work in terms of the demands of physical labour and the corporeal, a world of 'getting your hands dirty', of 'mucking in', of 'pushing oneself to the limits'. These references play ironically alongside stark images of (male) bodies at physical labour.[145] Such depictions evoke a masculine notion of labour that sits uneasily, however, with the appeals to equality and gender convergence that appear in other contexts.[146] The need to 'push oneself' to the limits is allied to a need to establish (fraternal) collegiality and bonding, a 'willingness to roll up their shirtsleeves with the rest of the team'; to work hard, play hard and, above all, to economically and socially 'succeed' (and to be *seen to* succeed).[147]

Concluding remarks

> Though individualistic self-interest and consumer desires are core parts of who we are and nothing to be ashamed about, they are not all of who we are … We know that our values, capacities, aesthetics, and sense of meaning and justice are, in part, created and nurtured by communal attachments.[148]

> Venture. Myriad. Astute. Belong.[149]

Building on the discussion of gender, social class and the university law school in chapters 2 and 3, and developing our interrogation of what it means to speak of 'the man of law' introduced in chapter 1, what has emerged from this reading of texts of law hitherto, I suggested, 'off the radar' of legal analysis? What do we know that we did not before? Simply that large City firms work their assistant solicitors hard? (on which, see chapter 6.) That they seek to attract and retain them with high salaries and the lure of glamour? That the latter may well be, for some at least, mostly fictitious? In contrast to such observations, this chapter has engaged in a more complex, rich and multi-layered reading of these representations of legal practice.

I have presented an exploration of how, within a discrete set of texts and images, ideas about what it means to achieve professional success as a lawyer are operationalised in such a way as to produce a particular *kind* of social identity and understanding of a workplace performance.[150] This is an identity far removed from any simple association between a model of masculinity and an

---

[145] Rowe and Mawe, 2001. Linking, curiously, an appeal to 'bucking the trend' with ideas of 'breaking the law': Wragge & Co 2008.

[146] Sanderson and Somerland, op cit, 1998.

[147] See R. Pahl, *After Success*, Oxford: Blackwell, 1995.

[148] J. Bakan, *The Corporation*, Toronto: Viking Canada, 2004, p 166.

[149] Lovells, 2008, cover of hard-back brochure representing a 'snapshot' of the firm.

[150] H. Sommerlad, 'Researching and Theorizing the Processes of Professional Identity Formation', *Journal of Law and Society*, 2007, vol 34(2), p 190.

ideal of 'the man of law'. I have charted, rather, how a narrative of career development as a successful lawyer is marked by recurring features and focal concerns involving ideas about consumption, identity and youth; space, place and practice; of appearance, class and respectability. On closer examination, a workplace that appears ostensibly equitable and just, open and inclusive, is a site *already* constituted at the point of entry by reference to assumptions about social, economic and cultural capital that are mediated by ideas of class, gender, race and ethnicity.

Importantly, recognising the specificity of the discursive context and institutional sites within which these images circulate, the analysis presented in both this and the preceding two chapters points to a broader reading of why the training contract with the large City firm should have such an allure for so many law students. A great deal is now known about the realities of attrition rates in this area of the profession, concerns about quality of life issues (considered in chapter 6), the insecurity of employment and the contingencies of promotion to Partnership.[151] Yet in the social context discussed in chapters 2 and 3, and as cleavages within youth populations entrench,[152] it is perhaps unsurprising that these materials should have such powerful resonance, communicating persuasive and appealing messages about what social and economic success entails. The trainee City solicitor depicted, regardless of whether they are male or female, black or white, embodies aspects of a now dominant mode of young-adult consumption, exemplifying processes around the commodification of desire and pleasure within late modernity. Their focal concerns are 'characterised by smart attire ... pleasure seeking and hedonistic behaviour', framed within a largely corporately owned leisure context.[153] Individualistic[154] in nature, and viewing education as a dispassionate means to an end, they appear highly conformist in nature and circumscribed by the

---

[151] Issues themselves discussed in the student legal press: 'My City Hell: The Pain Barrier' (of the ex-'magic circle' trainee), *Lex*, Issue 15, Spring 2003, pp 86–88 ('When I resigned a number of senior staff members came up to me and told me that they wished they had [had] the courage to do the same when they were my age'); J. Currie, 'Walking Away', *Lawyer 2B*, December 2002, p 45 ('The pinstripes of the City may be more glamorous than a cagoule, but for Nicky Warden campaigning ... is more fun than Pensions Law ... [meet] the lawyer who just didn't want to earn those fees'); J. Currie, 'Dead End', *Lawyer 2B*, March 2003, pp 24–25. Lee notes there are 'serious quality of life issues facing such firms, and that staff retention is a major headache' (Lee, op cit, 2000, p 183). A rather different issue concerns the psychological ramifications of achieving success: Pahl, op. cit, 1995; M. E. P. Seligman, P. R. Verkuil and T. H. Kang, 'Why Lawyers Are Unhappy', *Cardozo Law Review*, 2002, vol 23(1), p 33.

[152] Between, for example, unemployed young people, those dependent on welfare benefits, university students and those in stable, well-paid and full-time employment: S. Ball, M. Maguire and S. Macrae, *Choice, Pathways and Transitions Post-16: New Youth, New Economies and the Global City*, London: Routledge, 2000.

[153] Chatterton and Hollands, op cit, 2002, p 109. Hollander has observed, op cit, 1994, p 187: 'With the new freedom of personal choice unfettered by strict social codes, the individual psyche can privately illustrate itself in some detail for its own satisfaction using the modern visual vocabulary of dress.' The imaging described above meshes with the kinds of representations of 'success' and 'fun' also found in many university law school student publications.

[154] Beck and Beck-Gensheim, op cit, 2002, esp ch 3, 'Beyond Status and Class?' pp 30–42.

imperatives of profit-making and maintaining their (individual, class) status, concerns alluded to as involving a sense of 'civic' identity, 'of belonging or community'.[155]

The global financial crisis of 2008, ongoing at the time of writing, has had a profound impact on broader public perceptions of the ethics of many aspects of financial markets, raising political questions about law's regulation of financial services. Notwithstanding recent events, however, it is testimony to the wider cultural and symbolic power of corporate culture over the past two decades that these knowledge professionals can seem 'implicated in a virtuous cycle of growth', positioned as 'denizens of the reimagined urban landscape'.[156] They are, at once, 'meritocratic yet exclusive, very highly paid yet powerfully convinced of the justice of [their] ... rewards, and increasingly divorced from the rest of society by wealth, education, residence and lifestyle'.[157] There is, ultimately, a rather instrumental calculative rationality informing this ethic, one neatly summed up in the imaging of a large destroyed building used by the law firm Norton Rose in advertising the training contract, the figures of fire-fighters concertedly putting out the flames: 'Do you see a problem,' the advertisement asks, 'or are you thinking about the opportunity?'[158]

What is held out to the trainee is an individual and collective identity that facilitates a differentiation of their self from others – those who do not 'make the grade', who do not 'have what it takes' to succeed in this most competitive but potentially rewarding area of legal work. Yet these images and texts, I have argued, address a complex set of economic, cultural and psychological investments in that social success. They provide the reader with a distinctive knowledge base about the sort of people these protagonists are, a knowledge of the social resources they have (or will soon obtain) and, crucially, of the social identity they will assume in their developing a career as a lawyer.

This chapter has argued that, far from falling back on simplistic associations between masculinity, gender, social class and a unitary model of the 'man of law', this is an identity benchmarked against a normative (ideal) professional employee in complex and contradictory ways. In the following chapter, I will develop further this engagement with law, men and gender, by turning to an issue that has been implicit within much of the discussion in this book thus far – the changing nature of men's responsibilities at the interface of work and 'family life'.

---

[155] Chatterton and Hollands, op cit, 2002, p 109.

[156] M. Featherstone, *Consumer Culture and Postmodernism*, London: Sage, 1991.

[157] Featherstone, op cit, 1991, p 67

[158] Norton Rose, 2001. Compare 'Make Money Not Love' – T-shirts worn by trainee solicitors at SJ Berwin (*Plum*, 4th edn, SJ Berwin, 2002) – with the depiction of 'pathological pursuit of profit and power' by Bakan, op cit, 2004, p 166: 'The corporation and its underlying ideology are animated by a narrow conception of human nature that is too distorted and [too] uninspiring to have lasting purchase on our political imagination.'

Chapter 5

Engaging fathers, changing men?

Law, gender and parenting cultures

Introduction

> What has been missing from policy and reform discussions thus far is a debate
> about the nature of fatherhood and the transformation of the role of the father in
> response to changing expectations, norms and practices. How does the desire for
> gender neutrality and the ideal of egalitarianism play a role in the creation of a
> new set of norms for fatherhood?[1]

I traced in chapter 1 the emergence of work that has brought into the socio-legal
gaze the plurality and contingency of discourses which speak of men and masculinities across diverse institutional and cultural contexts pertaining to law.
Building on this approach, I argued against an essentialist conceptualisation of
the 'masculinity of law', an idea that has served to erase much of the complexity
and heterogeneity of the personal lives of women and men. Related to this, I
questioned readings of men, law and gender that pass over the complex and
double-edged nature of legal regulation itself. In this chapter, and in chapter 7, I
consider in more detail a topic that has become a focal point for much contemporary political and policy debate around law and gender – fatherhood.

The question of how the gender of men is conceptualised has a particular
bearing on the relationship between law and men's parenting in two significant
respects. First, fatherhood is a topic central both to the interdisciplinary literature on men and masculinities discussed in chapter 1 and the study of masculinity as it has developed within the discipline of law. Fatherhood has become a
key site for interrogation of the conceptual basis of masculinity and with it,
following my argument in chapter 1, consideration of the place of law in relation to the reproduction of gender relations. Fatherhood has also become the
subject of a now voluminous literature in its own right.[2] Second, the theme of

---

[1] M. Fineman, *The Autonomy Myth*, New York: The New Press, 2004, p 195.

[2] B. Featherstone, *Contemporary Fathering: Theory, Policy and Practice*, Cambridge: Policy Press,
2009; E. Dermott, *Intimate Fatherhood: A Sociological Analysis*, London: Routledge, 2008;
D. Lupton and L. Barclay, *Constructing Fatherhood: Discourses and Experiences*, London: Sage,
1997; B. Hobson (ed), *Making Men into Fathers: Men, Masculinities and the Social Politics of*

fatherhood and law, which I explore in more detail in chapter 7, has been central to contemporary debates about the politics of law and gender. Law has had a particular significance in high-profile public and political conversations that have interlinked questions about men's rights and responsibilities to concerns about changing families, crime and social order.[3] What fathers *do* (and what they *don't* do) has been seen as a causal factor in a range of social problems and, for some, what is at stake in these contestations is no less than the future of the 'family' and, indeed, society.[4] What this literature has tended not to address, however, I have argued elsewhere,[5] with Sally Sheldon, is the representation of law itself within readings of men and gender, nor has it explained how a mutually constituted crisis around fatherhood and masculinities has drawn on problematic assumptions about the nature of law and legal regulation. I shall return to these issues below.

I argue in this chapter that the reframing of the relationship between law and gender resulting from the rise of formal equality agendas and gender neutrality, discussed in chapter 1, has been a key feature of a reconstruction of fatherhood as a social problem and object of intervention for law.[6] The emergence of a policy agenda around 'engaging fathers', detailed below, is set against the backdrop of an intensification of social concern about the scope of fathers' legal responsibilities and rights. How to promote ongoing, positive and 'healthy' relationships between men and children is, of course, a subject with a long and well-documented history.[7] In recent years, however, the question has become a ubiquitous feature of diverse cultural texts, raising issues about how law regulates family practices. In relation to married and

---

Fatherhood, Cambridge: Cambridge University Press, 2002; N. Dowd, *Redefining Fatherhood*, New York: New York University Press, 2000; R. LaRossa, *The Modernization of Fatherhood: A Social and Political History*, Chicago: University of Chicago Press, 1997; A. Burgess, *Fatherhood Reclaimed: The Making of the Modern Father*, London: Vermillion, 1997; A. Doucet, *Do Men Mother? Fatherhood, Care and Domestic Responsibility*, Toronto: University of Toronto Press, 2006; W. Marsiglio (ed), *Fatherhood: Contemporary Theory, Research and Social Policy*, London: Sage, 1995; C. Lewis and M. Lamb, *Understanding Fatherhood: A Review of Recent Research*, York: Joseph Rowntree Foundation, 2007; G. Barker et al, *Supporting Fathers: Contributions from the International Fatherhood Summit 2003*, The Hague: Early Childhood Development: Practice and Reflections Series, Bernard van Leer Foundation, 2004.

[3] R. Collier, *Masculinities, Crime and Criminology*, London: Sage, 1998, ch 5.

[4] Centre for Social Justice, *The Family Law Review Interim Report*, London: Centre for Social Justice, 2008. 'The Decline of Marriage Harms the whole nation', Editorial, *Daily Telegraph*, 18 November 2008. Contrast, in the United States, D. Blakenhorn, *Fatherless America: Confronting Our Most Urgent Social Problem*, New York: Basic Books, 1995. Cf R. R. Daniels (ed), *Lost Fathers: The Politics of Fatherlessness in America*, New York: St Martin's Press, 1998.

[5] R. Collier and S. Sheldon, *Fragmenting Fatherhood: A Socio-Legal Study*, Oxford: Hart, 2008.

[6] J. Scourfield and M. Drakeford, 'New Labour and the "Problem of Men"', *Critical Social Policy*, 2002, vol 22, p 619.

[7] As, indeed, has concern about 'fatherlessness': J. Gillis, 'Marginalization of Fatherhood in Western Countries', *Childhood*, 2000, vol 7(2), p 225.

unmarried, cohabiting and separated, biological and 'social' fathers, we shall see, law has a pivotal role in these discussions.[8] I have explored elsewhere how law serves as a focal point for political frustrations, playing a central role in mediating disputes and operating as a symbolic authorised discourse, providing an official account of what fathers' rights and responsibilities should be.[9] Yet law also, we shall see below, and in chapter 7, involves complex issues about the affirmation of fathering identity. Thus, at a time when a socio-legal and social policy scholarship is seeking to explore how fathers have been understood in law,[10] the time is propitious to reconsider the relationship between law, men and masculinity in an area where, I suggest, different ideas about 'the man of law' co-exist in a debate about engaging fathers, reflecting deep uncertainties about the changing nature of men's relationships to families and children.

The structure of the argument

In chapter 7, I focus this discussion of law, men and gender on the increased political and cultural prominence of legal debates about fathers' rights groups and an international 'fathers' rights movement'. This chapter, in contrast, concerns developments relating to men's responsibilities as fathers in a more general sense, in relation both to subsisting marital and cohabiting relationships and to men's post-separation parenting. I consider, more specifically, how a policy agenda around engaging fathers in families has involved a conceptualisation of law, men and masculinity. Bridging the discussion of the law school and the legal profession in chapters 2, 3 and 4 with the consideration of male lawyers and work-life balance in chapter 6, I unpack the contours of legal policy around men's responsibilities in relation to 'work' and 'family life'. Marriage has played a pivotal role in how law has historically attached men to their children.[11] However, a complex amalgam of demographic, economic, cultural, technological and political changes, as well as shifts in the nature of law's governance,[12] has challenged the possibility of relying on marriage as a way of grounding legal fatherhood and the rights and responsibilities that have traditionally accompanied it. Against this backdrop, shifts have occurred in how law has approached the responsibilities of men and, with it, ideas about men's parenting. These developments, I suggest in this chapter, have redrawn social and legal understandings of the relationship between men and gender.

---

[8] See discussion in Collier and Sheldon, op cit, 2008.

[9] Collier and Sheldon, op cit, 2008.

[10] Collier and Sheldon, op cit, 2008. Also Dowd, op cit, 2000.

[11] Collier and Sheldon, op cit, 2008, ch 4; C. Smart, *The Ties That Bind: Law, Marriage and the Reproduction of Patriarchal Relations*, London: Routledge & Kegan Paul, 1984.

[12] R. van Krieken, 'Legal Informalism, Power and Liberal Governance', *Social and Legal Studies*, 2001, vol 19(1), p 5.

The structure of the argument is as follows. In the first section I briefly trace the development of family law and policy from a position where men held exclusive rights over their children to one in which, by the mid-twentieth century, fathers had been reconstituted primarily as familial breadwinners. In the second section, I explore how the move from legal rights to responsibilities has taken a further turn in recent years, reconfiguring ideas about men and gender. Encapsulated in the idea of the 'new fatherhood', contemporary fathers are now widely expected to have, and to desire, a closer, more emotionally involved and nurturing relationship with their children. In this move from 'cash to care'[13] British fathers, it is argued, 'are now expected to be accessible and nurturing as well as economically supportive to their children'. They are, it has been suggested, increasingly self-conscious about juggling the conflict between looking after children and paid employment.[14]

In the final section, I look more closely at the conceptual assumptions underscoring this narrative of social change in relation to men and gender. Understandings of fathers' responsibilities, I suggest, are marked by contrasting beliefs about masculinity. In dealing with the different discourses that have shaped a 'problem of men'[15] within legal policy there has occurred, I argue, a politicisation of paternal responsibility. Unpacking these shifts reveals diverse beliefs about men bound up with assumptions about change and continuity in gendered divisions of labour, parenting cultures, the scope of men's rights and responsibilities in law, the normative nature of heterosexuality, social class and masculinities. At issue, however, is something more than the gap between cultures of change in fatherhood and ideas about fatherhood as a social practice. We are dealing with a political debate about what can, and cannot, be expected from law in seeking to change men's parenting practices.

Reconstructing fatherhood, reshaping masculinity

Married fathers were invested at common law with sole rights of custody and control over their legitimate children.[16] By the early nineteenth century inroads had been made into this model of paternal rights and a move away from the 'empire of the father' had begun.[17] Fathers' rights at the time were seen as largely symbolic, the embodiment of patriarchal authority, a man's control within, and

---

[13] Hobson (ed), op cit, 2002, particularly ch 1.

[14] M. O'Brien, *Shared Caring: Bringing Fathers into the Frame*, Manchester: Equal Opportunities Commission, 2005; M. O'Brien and I. Shemilt, *Working Fathers: Earning and Caring*, Manchester: Equal Opportunities Commission, 2003; C. Lewis, *A Man's Place in the Home: Fathers and Families in the UK*, York: Joseph Rowntree Foundation, 2000.

[15] Scourfield and Drakeford, op cit, 2002. See also J. Scourfield, *Gender and Child Protection*, London: Palgrave Macmillan, 2003.

[16] Blackstone's *Commentaries on the Law of England*, 1765 Vol. 1: 453; *Re Agar Ellis* (1883) 24 Ch D 317, per Bowen LJ at 338.

[17] See further A. Diduck and F. Kaganas, *Family Law, Gender and the State: Text, Cases and Materials*, 2nd edn, Oxford: Hart, 2006, p 305; S. Maidment, *Child Custody and Divorce: The Law in Social Context*, London: Croom Helm, 1984.

over, his family interlinked to the maintenance of social order and the orderly transmission of property.[18] Equitable doctrines developed by the Court of Chancery sought to lessen the harshness of common law rules. Divorce, however, remained severely restricted and permeated by double standards. This understanding of fathers' responsibilities reflected, in short, the dominant attitudes of the period towards family, parenting, gender and class.[19]

During the latter part of the nineteenth and the first half of the twentieth century, reforms were introduced to enable mothers to seek custody and access to their children, albeit in prescribed circumstances.[20] The Guardianship of Infants Act (1925) provided that the court, in deciding questions relating to the custody or upbringing of a child, should henceforth have regard to the welfare of the child as the 'first and paramount consideration'.[21] This paramountcy principle continues to inform child law to the present day, enshrined in the 1989 Children Act[22] as amended and further elaborated as a result of the Human Rights Act 1998.[23] For the purposes of this chapter, and noting the indeterminate nature of the welfare principle itself,[24] it is necessary to look more closely at how, throughout this period of an apparently egalitarian and progressive reform, ideas about men, gender and fatherhood were reconstructed.

Making the modern father

Legal constructions of the rights, obligations and responsibilities of men at particular moments must be historically,[25] economically and politically

---

[18] See further T. L. Broughton and H. Rogers (eds), *Gender and Fatherhood in the Nineteenth Century*, London: Palgrave Macmillan, 2007.

[19] L. Holcombe, *Wives and Property: Reform of the Married Women's Property Acts*, Toronto: University of Toronto Press, 1983; Collier and Sheldon, op cit, 2008.

[20] For example, Custody of Infants Act 1839; Divorce and Matrimonial Causes Act 1857; Custody of Infants Act 1873; Guardianship of Infants Act 1886.

[21] S. Cretney, '"What Will Women Want Next?" The Struggle for Power Within the Family 1925–75', *Law Quarterly Review*, 1996, vol 12, p 110. See further J. Eekelaar, *Family Law and Personal Life*, Oxford: OUP, 2006, pp 140–44.

[22] Section 1(1) of the Children Act 1989 provides that when a court determines any question with respect to a range of circumstances concerning children 'the child's welfare shall be the court's paramount consideration'.

[23] H. Fenwick, 'Clashing Rights, the Welfare of the Child and the Human Rights Act', *Modern Law Review*, 2004, vol 67(6), p 889.

[24] H. Reece, 'The Paramountcy Principle: Consensus or Construct?', *Current Legal Problems*, 1996, vol 49, p 267.

[25] M. Richards, 'Fatherhood, Marriage and Sexuality: Some Speculations on the English Middle-class Family', in C. Lewis and M. O'Brien (eds), *Reassessing Fatherhood: New Observations on Fathers and the Modern Family*, London: Sage, 1987, p 27; J. Mangan and J. Walvin (eds), *Manliness and Morality: Middle Class Masculinity in Britain and America 1800–1940*, Manchester: Manchester University Press, 1987; J. Tosh, *A Man's Place: Masculinity and the Middle-class Home in Victorian England*, London: Yale University Press, 1999, p 195; J. R. Gillis, *A World of Their Own Making: Myth, Ritual and the Quest for Family Values*, Cambridge, MA: Harvard University Press, 1996.

grounded within the context of longer-term changes in family structures, adult/child relations, gender configurations and forms of law's governance. The legal changes that have occurred around fatherhood, for example, I have argued elsewhere,[26] are the product of a complex interweaving and inter-discursive nexus of law, medicine, psychology, religion and science, all of which (in different ways) have been implicated in the production of norma-tive beliefs about 'family life', children, childhood and child welfare, health and illness, sexuality, social class and ideas about the nature of 'good' par-enting. Importantly, during the shift that occurred within the twentieth cen-tury from a focus on rights towards one of parental responsibilities in law there emerged a new way of talking about gender and parenthood. In this process, well documented in feminist work, mothers were subject to levels of surveillance, scrutiny and regulation by law in significant ways that fathers were not, judged against a range of (gendered) assumptions.[27] Reflecting the relational nature of gender categories discussed in chapter 1, however, ideas about what constitutes a 'good father' and 'family man'[28] were also transformed. It is to this reconstruction of paternal responsibility that I now turn.

By the mid-twentieth century the central assumption that households would be organised on a sexual division of labour between (male) primary breadwinner and (female) child-rearer was entrenched across many areas of law and policy.[29] At the macro-level, beliefs about fathers as breadwinners were embedded in the model of the male wage and the idea that a man should provide for his family, binding men to an economic system which had structured household economies via the allocation to one family member (usually the man) the role of primary wage earner.[30] Fineman has observed how:

> Men's role as economic providers [has served] an essential function in an ideological system in which dependency is privatised and will not readily be displaced until there is some greater public responsibility for the pro-vision of essential goods.[31]

---

[26] Collier and Sheldon, op cit, 2008.

[27] For detailed discussion see S. Boyd, *Child Custody, Law and Women's Work*, Oxford: OUP, 2003; M. Fineman, *The Neutered Mother, The Sexual Family, and Other Twentieth Century Tragedies*, New York: Routledge, 1995; A. Diduck, 'Legislating Ideologies of Motherhood', *Social and Legal Studies*, 1993, vol 2, p 461; M. Fineman and I. Karpin (eds), *Mothers in Law: Feminist Theory and the Legal Regulation of Motherhood*, New York: Columbia University Press, 1995; E. Silva (ed), *Good Enough Mothering? Feminist Perspectives on Lone Motherhood*, London: Routledge, 1996.

[28] S. Coltrane, *Family Man: Fatherhood, Housework and Gender Equity*, Oxford: OUP, 1997.

[29] K. O'Donovan, *Sexual Divisions in Law*, London: Weidenfeld & Nicolson, 1985.

[30] H. Land, 'The Family Wage', *Feminist Review*, 1980, vol 6, p 55.

[31] Fineman, op cit, 2004, p 199.

In the post-war period debates about wages, taxes and welfare benefits reflected this idea that men and women had differential primary commitments towards their families, sociological research showing how these gendered divisions had become embedded within household economies and cultural norms.[32] The assumption that a father's primary family responsibilities lay as breadwinner was reproduced extensively within the domains of leisure, advertising and the media during the 1950s and 1960s,[33] as well as within the texts of law of the period. Case law is replete with assumptions about the natural familial roles and responsibilities of men and women, in relation to child care, (pre-1989) child custody,[34] domestic labour[35] and paid employment.[36] Developments in sociological and social theory embodied, and legitimated, normative ideas about the role of men in relation to the functional family life, fusing fatherhood with beliefs about heterosexual masculinity.[37] It is against this context that, we have seen in chapter 1, the bodies, identities and emotional lives of fathers have been understood within much feminist and pro-feminist legal scholarship largely in terms of ideas about men's primary location within the public, rather than the domestic or private, sphere.[38]

During much of the twentieth century, therefore, a dominant understanding of a man's familial responsibilities was mobilised primarily, if not exclusively, in terms of a model of masculinity as an economic resource,[39] a theme reflected across law and notably in the legal history of the obligation to maintain.[40] Judges sought to introduce notions of fairness into a legal recognition of domestic labour and child care as work of equal significance to paid employment, through the development of principles of equity.[41] However, fathers' primary commitments to work were widely seen within law as largely, if not

---

[32] M. Young and P. Wilmott, *Family and Kinship in East London*, Harmondsworth: Pelican, 1957; M. Young and P. Wilmott, *The Symmetrical Family*, Harmondsworth: Penguin, 1973.

[33] L. Segal, *Slow Motion: Changing Masculinities, Changing Men*, London: Virago, 1990, ch 1.

[34] For an excellent discussion see further Boyd, op cit, 2003; also C. Smart and S. Sevenhujsen (eds), *Child Custody and the Politics of Gender*, London: Routledge, 1989; Smart, op cit, 1984.

[35] R. Auchmuty, 'Unfair Shares for Women: The Rhetoric of Equality and the Reality of Inequality' in A. Bottomley and H. Lim (eds), *Feminist Perspectives on Land Law*, London: Routledge-Cavendish, 2007; O'Donovan, op cit, 1985.

[36] S. Atkins and B. Hoggett, *Women and the Law*, Oxford: Blackwell, 1984; O'Donovan, op cit, 1985.

[37] T. Parsons and F. Bales, *Family Socialization and Interaction Process*, Glencoe, IL: Free Press, 1955.

[38] J. Hearn, *Men in the Public Eye*, London: Routledge, 1992, p 96; note also S. Whitehead, *Men and Masculinities*, Cambridge: Polity, 2002, pp 113–24.

[39] Connell, op cit, 1987, p 106.

[40] M. Finer and O. R. McGregor, 'History of the Obligation to Maintain' in Department of Health and Social Security, *One-Parent Families: Report of the Committee on One-parent Families*, Cmnd 5629-I, 1974, Appendix 5. For detailed discussion of child support see N. Wikeley, *Child Support: Law and Policy*, Oxford: Hart, 2006.

[41] A. Diduck, 'Fairness and Justice for All? The House of Lords in *White v White*', *Feminist Legal Studies*, 2001, vol 9, p 173; Diduck and Kaganas, op cit, 2006, pp 258–71; Eekelaar, op cit, 2006, pp 144–45.

entirely, precluding their extensive participation within child care and domestic labour.[42] At the same time, social policy was premised on 'the need to compensate for the risks of unemployment, sickness or the absence of the male breadwinner'.[43] It was this kind of framework that informed the readings of my 1995 book *Masculinity, Law and the Family*.[44] It is, however, to significant changes in this idea of the father as the embodiment of a particular kind of masculinity that I now turn.

Law, masculinities and men's responsibility

Fathers have been reconstituted in law as a desirable presence within families, Sally Sheldon and I argued in the book *Fragmenting Fatherhood*, via reference to three key themes, each of which draws on ideas about men and gender that, I want to suggest, have been challenged and undermined, to varying degrees, in recent years.[45] These are beliefs about, first, fathers as heterosexual (the sexual father); second, fathers as family breadwinners (the worker father, as above); and, third, fathers as the embodiment of a particular kind of masculinity associated with paternal authority and prerogative within the household (the father as patriarch). Taken together, each can be positioned as key elements of hegemonic masculinity, as discussed in chapter 1. Each, importantly, has been subject to challenge as a result of political, social, economic, cultural and technological shifts that have occurred in the context of a legal framework marked by commitments to formal equality and gender neutrality.[46] At the same time, a rethinking of the place of the father in child welfare and development[47] has reshaped understandings of the relationship between men and children.[48] The result has been a 'ratcheting up' of the importance of the father across diverse legal policy contexts, a move that, I shall suggest below, has shifted the parameters within which ideas about men and gender are now understood. This development, the

[42] R. Collier, 'A Hard Time to be a Father? Law, Policy and Family Practices', *Journal of Law & Society*, 2001, vol 28(4), p 520; R. Collier, 'In Search of the "Good Father": Law, Family Practices and the Normative Reconstruction of Parenthood', *Studies in Law, Politics and Society*, 2001, vol 22, p 133.

[43] Featherstone, op cit, 2009, p 128.

[44] R. Collier, *Masculinity, Law and the Family*, London: Routledge, 1995.

[45] Collier and Sheldon, op cit, 2008, esp ch 4.

[46] M. Fineman, *The Illusion of Equality: The Rhetoric and Reality of Divorce Reform*, London: University of Chicago Press, 1991; Fineman, op cit, 1995; Boyd, op cit, 2003; S. Boyd, 'From Gender Specificity to Gender Neutrality? Ideologies in Canadian Child Custody Law', in J. Brophy and C. Smart (eds), *Child Custody and the Politics of Gender*, London: Routledge, 1989.

[47] M. Lamb, *The Role of the Father in Child Development*, New York: John Wiley, 1997; E. Flouri, *Fathering and Child Outcomes*, New York: John Wiley, 2005.

[48] A. J. Dawkins and D. C. Dollahite (eds), *Generative Fathering: Beyond Deficit Perspectives*, London: Sage, 1997.

substantive legal dimensions of which are explored in more detail in the book *Fragmenting Fatherhood*, has several implications for my concern here, the changing relationship between law and masculinity.[49]

Family law: marriage, men and heterosexuality

Ideas about men's responsibilities, place and duties in relation to families have been historically interlinked, we have seen, with normative beliefs about marriage, masculinity and heterosexuality.[50] Legal marriage, the mechanism by which law has sought to attach men to children, has been, and remains, an institution by statute open only to men and women (Matrimonial Causes Act 1973, s. 11). However, social, demographic, cultural and technological changes have profoundly undermined ideas about paternal responsibility and related assumptions about men that, in the past, legally bound fathers to families. Marriage, for example, is no longer the sole vehicle used in family law to safeguard (legal) fatherhood. Other legal concepts and techniques are regularly now used to attach men to children. The legal recognition in law of civil partnerships,[51] of the social parent within same-sex households[52] and of gay couples to adopt,[53] alongside an expansion of the remit of Parental Responsibility (PR), linked to the growing numbers of non-marital births (a 'rolling out' of PR),[54] has reshaped, if not challenged, hetero-normative understandings of family life and, with it, assumptions about marriage as the primary determinant of paternal rights. These developments have generated an increased emphasis within law on biological fatherhood (see below) and the biological and relational bonds between men and children. At the same time, as controversy around the enactment of the Human Fertilisation and Embryology Act 2008 shows, one result of this reframing of parenthood,

---

[49] Collier and Sheldon, op cit, 2008.

[50] R. Collier, '"The Art of Living the Married Life": Representations of Male Heterosexuality in Law', *Social and Legal Studies*, 1992, vol 1, p 543; J. Carabine, 'Heterosexuality and Social Policy' in D. Richardson (ed), *Theorising Heterosexuality: Telling it Straight*, Buckingham: Open University Press, 1996; R. Collier, 'Straight Families, Queer Lives? Heterosexual(izing) Family Law' in D. Herman and C. Stychin (eds), *Sexuality in the Legal Arena*, London: Athlone Press, 2000.

[51] P. Mallender and J. Rayson, *The Civil Partnership Act 2004: A Practical Guide*, Cambridge: Cambridge University Press, 2005.

[52] Pre-dating the Civil Partnership Act 2004 note, for example, the legal depictions of 'family' in *Fitzpatrick v Sterling Housing Association* [2000] 1 FLR 21; *Ghaidan v Godin-Mendoza* (2004) 2 AC 557; *Wilkinson v Kitzinger* [2006] EWHC 2022 *Fam* 121.

[53] Adoption and Children Act 2002.

[54] Collier and Sheldon, op cit, 2008, ch. 6. See further chapter 7. As an example of the strengthening of unmarried fathers' rights and responsibilities, fathers who are named on the birth certificate are no longer dependent on being married to the child's mother or on application to the court to be awarded parental responsibility: such responsibility is automatic. Note also A. Barlow et al, *Cohabitation, Marriage and the Law: Social Change and Legal Reform in the 21st Century*, Oxford: Hart, 2005, chs 1 and 2.

child welfare and heterosexuality has been a heightened debate about whether, indeed, families do now 'need fathers'.[55]

The decline of marriage as a lifelong commitment, the emergence of new ideas of child welfare and an increased political focus on responsibility provide part of the context for the growing debate about men and social policy that I explore in the next section. Rising levels of divorce and cohabitation (with its attendant legal consequences),[56] alongside developments around assisted reproduction,[57] all raise questions about how fathers should, or should not, be recognised in law. The resulting 'fragmentation' of fatherhood in law, as Sally Sheldon and I have termed it, cannot be reduced, however, in Connell's schema (see chapter 1, p 33), to the level of a crisis tendency within a dominant gender order and/or a hegemonic model of masculinity. Rather, the hetero-normative basis of family life in law has itself been reshaped in a number of ways. We have moved towards a position in which law appears increasingly open to both same-sex relations[58] and a 'splitting' of the rights and responsibilities associated with parenthood between different men.[59] At the same time, the increased focus in law on genetic links, bound up with assumptions about the need for the 'Truth' of one's identity,[60] has informed a view in law that a man's relationship with his children should be direct, and not mediated via his relationship with their mother.[61] In short, if it was the case that, in the past, all aspects of fatherhood united in the person of one man (the mother's husband and child's genetic and social father),[62] contemporary law is marked more by a two-fold fragmentation and geneticisation[63] of fatherhood. If law does embody, or reproduce,

---

[55] Collier and Sheldon, op cit, 2008, ch 7; F. MacRae, 'Another Blow to Fatherhood: Now IVF Mothers Can Name ANYONE as "father" on birth certificate – and it doesn't have to be a man', *Daily Mail*, 2 March 2009.

[56] Law Commission, *Cohabitation: The Financial Consequences of Relationship Breakdown*, Consultation Paper, London: Law Com CP No 179, 2006.

[57] Collier and Sheldon, op cit, 2008, ch 3.

[58] Contrast C. Stychin, 'Family Friendly? Rights, Responsibilities and Relationship Recognition' in A. Diduck and K. O'Donovan (eds) *Feminist Perspectives on Family Law*, London: Routledge-Cavendish, 2006.

[59] See further Collier and Sheldon, op cit, 2008.

[60] C. Smart, *Personal Life*, Cambridge: Polity, 2007, ch 5.

[61] See chapter 7.

[62] Although this was itself, of course, to varying degrees, based on a number of social and legal 'presumptions': see C. Smart, '"There is of course a Distinction dictated by Nature": Law and the Problem of Paternity' in M. Stanworth (ed), *Reproductive Technologies: Gender, Motherhood and Medicine* (Feminist Perspectives Series), Cambridge: Polity, 1987.

[63] Whereby there has occurred an enhanced focus on genetic links as grounding the rights and responsibilities associated with fatherhood across law. I have argued elsewhere, with Sally Sheldon (Collier and Sheldon, op cit, 2008), that this genetic link is not by itself necessary or sufficient to claim the rights associated with fatherhood. It has been legally accepted, however, as forming an important basis on which a father may claim the right to develop a relationship with his child. See further Smart, op cit, 2007.

any ideal of hegemonic masculinity, then it is a model that has itself fragmented in complex ways, involving new alignments of interests and gender
relations.

Fragmenting the breadwinner father

We have seen in chapter 1 how ideas about men in families have historically been
constructed via reference to sexual divisions in law and gendered assumptions that
underpinned the cultural legitimacy of men's disengagement from child care and
domestic labour.[64] A model of the father as breadwinner, however, has been
profoundly challenged, not just by economic and demographic political
change,[65] but also by changes in the contours of intimacy[66] and personal life.[67]
Shifting patterns of economic labour market participation on the part of
women and men,[68] linked to the emergence of a new paradigm around the role
of the State in promoting economic competiveness,[69] have driven the emergence of policy agendas that explicitly seek to 'bring fathers in[to] the frame'[70]
and engage fathers in families (see below). A political concern to tackle social
pressures resulting from women's increased participation in the workforce,
that is, has further disturbed the model of father responsibility based on these
earlier assumptions about men's subjective and material disengagement, if not
absence, from child care and domestic labour. It is in the context of a heightened
focus in social policy on developing 'human capital', whereby men and women
might adapt to new economic conditions and social risks,[71] that traditional
ideas about men and masculinity now appear increasingly anachronistic in the era
of the 'new father'. Again, this has significant implications for understanding
how law relates to ideas of masculinity.

In this shift aspects of men's practices and commitments in relation to
their family lives and paid employment have been positioned within social
policy as potential obstacles to the promotion of women's employment and

---

[64] Collier, op cit, 2001: 'A Hard Time'; Collier, op cit, 1995, pp 213–14.

[65] For an excellent account of these changes from a social policy perspective see Featherstone, op
cit, 2009, pp 128–29.

[66] E. Dermott, *Intimate Fatherhood: A Sociological Analysis*, London: Routledge, 2008; L. Jamieson, *Intimacy: Personal Relationships in Modern Society*, Cambridge: Polity, 1998; A. Giddens,
The Transformation of Intimacy, Cambridge: Polity, 1992.

[67] Smart, op cit, 2007.

[68] Equal Opportunities Commission, *Facts About Men and Women in Great Britain 2006*, Manchester: Equal Opportunities Commission, 2007; O'Brien and Shemilt, op cit, 2003; R. Crompton, *Restructuring Gender Relations and Employment: The Decline of the Male Breadwinner*,
Oxford: OUP, 1999.

[69] J. Jenson, 'Changing the Paradigm: Family Responsibility or Investing in Children', *Canadian
Journal of Sociology*, 2004, vol 29(2), p 169. See further below.

[70] O'Brien, op cit, 2004.

[71] G. Bonoli, 'The Politics of the New Social Policies: Providing Coverage Against New Social
Risks in Mature Welfare States', *Policy and Politics*, 2005, vol 33(3), p 431.

functional, balanced family life within a new globalised economy.[72] Accordingly, what politicians, policy-makers and diverse organisations have argued is required, building on a substantial research base about the importance of the involved father, is legal reforms directed at providing a more 'modern' infrastructure of economic and social support that will promote the caring commitments of both parents within, and beyond, families. Engaging fathers will promote child welfare (playing a role in tackling disadvantage and child poverty), facilitate women's employment, advance gender equality and be 'better' for women and men.[73] I will return to the form this policy debate has taken below.

'Acceptable' Masculinities

Finally, bound up with each of the above, significant shifts have occurred in understandings of normative masculinities. An interlinking of economic responsibility with ideas of male violence and authority, prerogative and power has, in a sense, been a significant, and often overlooked, part of the history of fatherhood in law.[74] Concerns about fatherhood, risk and violence remain central to legal policy debates, as we shall see in chapter 7 in relation to post-separation contact. The dualism between the good dad/bad dad[75] continues to be mediated by assumptions about social class, race, ethnicity and sexuality, the nature of 'safe' and 'dangerous' masculinities.[76] At the same time, however, ideas about what constitutes acceptable male behaviour have been subject to considerable cultural change.[77]

This is evident across multifarious aspects of social life, but it is a theme particularly resonant in relation to men's position in families. The increasingly held view at a political and policy level is that a good father is no longer (or certainly not just) a disciplinarian, a remote embodiment of gendered authority. This is not to say (far from it) that men are not violent, that many do not commit to and psychologically invest in ideas of the father as 'head of household' and gendered characteristics associated with that role, nor is it to say that this idea does not remain resonant in other policy contexts. Rather, in terms of the model of

---

[72] See further on these broader developments, J. Hearn, 'Men, Fathers and the State: National and Global Relations' in B. Hobson (ed), op cit, 2002.

[73] Note, for example, W. Hatten, L. Vinter and R. Williams, *Dads on Dads: Needs and Expectations at Home and Work*, Manchester: Equal Opportunities Commission, 2002; J. Warin et al, *Fathers, Work and Family Life*, London: Family Policy Studies Centre, 1999.

[74] J. Hearn, 'Child Abuse and Men's Violence' in Violence Against Women Study Group (ed), *Taking Child Abuse Seriously*, London: Unwin Hyman, 1990, p 76.

[75] F. Furstenberg, 'Good Dads – Bad Dads: Two Faces of Fatherhood' in A. J. Cherlin (ed), *The Changing American Family and Public Policy*, Washington, DC: Urban Institute Press, 1988.

[76] R. Collier, 'Men, Masculinities and Crime' in C. Sumner (ed), *The Blackwell International Companion to Criminology*, Oxford: Blackwell, 2003.

[77] Note here B. Gough, 'Men and the Discursive Reproduction of Sexism: Repertoires and Difference in Equality', *Feminism and Psychology*, 1998, vol 8(1), p 25.

paternal masculinity being deployed in relation to equality agendas in the social investment State (as above), what is now 'expected' of a man, the messages law has sought to radiate about men's responsibility, has changed. In terms of a child's psychological health, future socio-economic status, educational achievement and adolescent development, social policy has been informed by the view that men, like women, have responsibilities, not just rights, a move encapsulated in the concept of parental responsibility enshrined in the 1989 Children Act.[78]

I argue in the next section that each of these three developments around marriage, employment and masculinities/child welfare, taken together, has served to do more than simply reframe ideas about fathers' responsibilities in law. They have reconstituted men and masculinity as a new and particular *kind* of social problem, resulting in a debate about men, law and gender that has taken a further turn in recent years.

Law, policy and the 'problem of men'

There has been a growing view, cutting across political divides, that it is via law reform, at least in part, that a new form of social responsibility on the part of men might be encouraged and facilitated. Two elements of this development are significant for understanding the changing relationship between law, men and gender. First, across diverse fields of law and policy a refiguring of paternal responsibility, as above, has informed legal reforms at the interface of work and family life. Second, underscoring these legal changes has been a conceptualisation of men that has involved ideas about masculinity and about fathers as, simultaneously, both the cause of, and the solution to, social problems. I will address below each of these points in turn.

'Dad-proofing' policy

Over the past decade or so in Britain an explicit attempt has been made to promote, via the use of law, father-inclusive practices across diverse areas of social policy and service delivery.[79] In relation to work-life balance (chapter 6), child support and post-separation contact (chapter 7) there has been a central

---

[78] Section 2(1) of which provides that, in cases where a child's father and mother are married to each other at the time of birth, they shall each have parental responsibility for the child. 'Parental responsibility' encompasses 'all the rights, duties, powers, responsibilities and authority which by law a parent of a child has in relation to the child and his property', including 'the rights, powers and duties which a guardian of the child's estate ... would have had in relation to the child and his property' (s. 3(1)). See further L. Fox Harding, 'Parental Responsibility: The Reassertion of Private Patriarchy?' in E. Silva (ed), op cit, 1996; and since, J. Eekelaar, op cit, 2006.

[79] D. Bartlett, A. Burgess and K. Jones, *A Toolkit for Developing Father-Inclusive Practice*, London: Fathers Direct, 2007; A. Burgess and D. Bartlett, *Working With Fathers*, London: Fathers Direct, 2004.

assumption in law that 'fathers matter'. With regard to engaging fathers in services, the Childcare Act 2006,[80] the Equality Act 2006,[81] documents such as *Every Parent Matters* (2007)[82] and a range of National Service Frameworks, practice guidance and other developments[83] have sought to increase expectations and change the practices of local authority and health care providers, as well as other organisations, around the need to include and engage fathers, regardless of social background, in the delivery of services. Engaging fathers has become a strategic requirement for children's services in England and Wales, with initiatives seeking to develop and support work with men and, in particular, socially vulnerable men.[84] At the time of writing, further attempts have been made to encourage agencies to 'Think Fathers' and for family policies to be 'dad-proofed',[85] with the aim of 'dispelling the myth', in the words of the then Children's Minister, that dads are the 'invisible parent'.[86] Thus, in February 2009, the *Child Health Strategy* was announced, making key recommendations about fathers' involvement in maternity services, including a Fathers' 'Early Years Life Check'.[87] The Equality and Human Rights Commission, in the *Working Better* Report 2009, has proposed reforms allowing fathers to take more paid time off work following the birth of a child, prompting debate about the need for fathers to 'balance' their commitments.[88] Meanwhile, a succession of reports has raised questions about fathers and parenting cultures,[89] with politicians across parties speaking of

---

[80] Requiring Local Authorities in England and Wales to identify parents and prospective parents considered unlikely to use early childhood services (fathers are specifically mentioned) and facilitate access to those services.

[81] Placing upon public bodies a requirement to publish an 'action plan' for promoting gender equality, to undertake a 'gender impact assessment' and to gather information and consult on how services impact on men and women.

[82] Department for Education and Skills, *Every Parent Matters*, London: Department for Education and Skills, 2007, stating that fathers – irrespective of the degree of involvement they have in the care of their children – should be offered routinely the support and opportunities they need to 'play their parental role effectively'.

[83] Department for Education and Skills, *Children's Centre Practice Guidance 2006*, London: DfES, 2006 and Department for Children, Schools and Families, *Planning and Performance Management Guidance 2006*, London: DCSF, 2006 place specific requirements on including fathers; Department of Health and Department for Communities, Schools and Families, *Teenage Parents Next Steps: Guidance for Local Authorities and Primary Care*, London: DH and DCFS, 2007, prioritises the need to work with young fathers in the development of service provision around pregnancy and birth.

[84] See further J. Page and G. Whitting, *A Review of How Fathers Can Be Better Recognised and Supported Through DCSF Policy*, DCSF Research Report DCSF-RR040, London: DCFS, 2008.

[85] P. Curtis, 'Family Policies to be "Dad-Proofed" … ', *The Guardian*, 21 February 2009.

[86] J. Bristow, 'Deconstructing Dads', <http://www.spiked-online.com/index.php?/site/reviewofbooks_printable/6306>, accessed 28 March 2009.

[87] The Fatherhood Institute and their ex-Chief Executive Duncan Fisher can be seen as key in pushing this particular agenda.

[88] Equality and Human Rights Commission (EHRC), *Working Better*, London: EHRC 2009.

[89] Centre For Social Justice, op cit, 2008; Children's Society, *A Good Childhood: Searching for Values in a Competitive Age*, London: Children's Society, 2009, <http://www.childrenssociety.org.uk/all_about_us/how_we_do_it/the_good_childhood_inquiry/1818.html>, accessed 27 March 2009.

the need to support fathers during economic recession.[90] This debate is a now well-established feature of the political landscape and legal policy debate in Britain.

These initiatives have been shaped, however, by more than a rethinking of the effects on children of father involvement. Underscoring these developments have been beliefs about gender and personal responsibility, justice, equality and social cohesion, each integral elements of the commitment to social investment[91] that has informed the economic and social policy agendas of the Labour governments in the years since 1997.[92] These values have fed into legal policy around men's responsibilities in a number of ways; in the promotion, for example, of gender equality;[93] in an attempt to facilitate work-life balance (chapter 6); in a commitment to protect the vulnerable; in the belief that parental responsibilities during subsisting relationships and after separation (chapter 7) must be negotiated, joint and lifelong, regardless of whether men are married or unmarried;[94] in the belief that both parents should be responsible for their children;[95] and in a policy commitment to the idea that to be a responsible citizen, male or female, is to be economically productive.[96] Developments in the law have also drawn on the wider social changes around

---

[90] N. Clegg, 'There's a job at home for out-of-work dads', *The Times*, 17 February 2009.

[91] R. Lister, 'Children (But Not Women) First: New Labour, Child Welfare and Gender', *Critical Social Policy*, 2006, vol 26(2), p 315; B. Featherstone, *Family Life and Family Support: A Feminist Analysis*, London: Palgrave, 2004.

[92] C. Annesley, 'New Labour and Welfare' in S. Ludlam and M. J. Smith (eds), *New Labour in Government*, London: Macmillan, 2001; B. Featherstone and L. Trinder, 'New Labour, Families and Fathers', *Critical Social Policy*, 2001, vol 21(4), p 534; K. Rake, 'Gender and New Labour's Social Policies', *Journal of Social Policy*, 2001, vol 30(2), p 209; Scourfield and Drakeford, op cit, 2002.

[93] The Gender Equality Duty, created by the Equality Act 2006, places a duty on public authorities to eliminate unlawful discrimination and harassment and promote equality of opportunity between men and women. Importantly, this means public authorities need to be proactive and are required to demonstrate that men and women are treated fairly. It encapsulates how issues of gender equality have become mainstream across diverse areas of social policy: J. Lewis, 'Balancing Work and Family: The Nature of the Policy Challenge and Gender Equality', Working Paper for GeNet Project 9: *Tackling Inequalities in Work and Care Policy Initiatives and Actors at the EU and UK Levels, 2007*, <http://www.genet.ac.uk/projects/project9.htm>, accessed 18 October 2008. It also raised the question of whether a 'service deficit' approach means such services are being blamed: Featherstone, op cit, 2009.

[94] Department for Work and Pensions, *Joint Birth Registration: Recording Responsibility*, White Paper, Cm 7293, London: DWP, 2008.

[95] L Koffman, 'Holding Parents to Account: Tough on Children, Tough on the Causes of Children', *Journal of Law and Society*, 2008, vol 35, p 113; C. Piper, 'Feminist Perspectives on Youth Justice' in A. Diduck and K. O'Donovan, op cit, 2006; A. James and A. James, 'Tightening the Net: Children, Community and Control', *British Journal of Sociology*, 2001, vol 52, p 211; C. Piper and S. Day Sclater, 'Remoralising the Family? Family Policy, Family Law and Youth Justice', *Child and Family Law Quarterly*, 2000, vol 12(2), p 135.

[96] R. Plant, 'Citizenship and Social Security', *Fiscal Studies*, 2003, vol 24(2), p 153.

marriage, heterosexuality and parenting discussed above.[97] They have been premised on the ideas of gender difference and gender convergence discussed in chapter 1. Yet there remain significant limits to and inconsistencies in this approach that relate directly to the ways in which ideas about men, masculinities and gender have been understood within these debates.

On the 'problem(s) of men'

A distinctive policy agenda around engaging fathers has, I have suggested, been embedded in law. If we look more closely, however, we find that ideas about fatherhood, and men, are pulled in different directions in these debates. In an insightful analysis of how a 'problem of men' was articulated within an early phase[98] of New Labour social policy, Jonathan Scourfield and Mark Drakeford[99] suggested that there has tended to be a degree of policy optimism about men in debates about fatherhood relating to 'inside the home' and, in contrast, a marked pessimism about men outside it. The reverse, curiously, is true for women. In the home and family, we have seen, attempts have been made to encourage and facilitate men in their role as fathers. There has been an assumption, reflected in numerous Ministerial and policy statements, not only that men are changing but also that men want to change.[100] This perspective highlights the institutional and organisational barriers to change, the cultural and legal obstacles to achieving 'active fathering'.[101] It envisages a key role for law, government and voluntary organisations alike[102] in making men better

---

[97] See further Prime Minister's Strategy Unit, *Building on Progress: Families*, London: Cabinet Office, 2007; M. Kilkey, 'New Labour and Reconciling Work and Family Life: Making it Fathers' Business?', *Social Policy & Society*, 2006, vol 5, p 167; R. Collier, '"Feminising the Workplace"? (Re)constructing the "good parent" in employment law and family policy' in A. Morris and T. O'Donnell (eds), *Feminist Perspectives on Employment Law*, London: Cavendish, 1999.

[98] A distinction can be made, Featherstone suggests (op cit, 2009, p 133), between policy development in the period 1997–2000, focused more on flexibility and *fairness*, and since, where questions of flexibility and *choice* have tended to be stressed. This issue of choice is considered further below. Earlier policy development in relation to fathers must also be seen in the light of debates of the early to mid-1990s around the problem of fatherhood in relation to crime and social order: Collier, op cit, 1998. Note, for example, Home Office, *Supporting Families: A Consultation Document*, London: Home Office, 1998. The legacy of these debates is discussed further below.

[99] Scourfield and Drakeford, op cit, 2002.

[100] Reflected also in much media reporting of the issue: see, for example, D. Campbell, 'Fathers Fight for Family Flexi-Time', *The Observer*, 12 March 2006.

[101] A. Burgess, *The Costs and Benefits of Active Fatherhood: Evidence and Insights to Inform the Development of Policy and Practice*, London: Fathers Direct, 2007; Bartlett et al, op cit, 2007; see further A. Burgess and G. Russell, 'Fatherhood and Public Policy' in G. Barker et al, op cit, 2004. Note A. Burgess and S. Ruxton, *Men and Their Children: Proposals for Public Policy*, London: Institute for Public Policy Research, 1996; K. Stanley, *Daddy Dearest? Active Fatherhood and Public Policy*, London: Institute for Public Policy Research, 2005.

[102] F. Williams and S. Roseneil, 'Public Values of Parenting and Partnering: Voluntary Organizations and Welfare Politics in New Labour's Britain', *Social Politics*, 2004, vol 11(2), p 181.

fathers, linked to a belief that experts and expert knowledge have much to contribute to a debate about parenting cultures.[103] Thus, fathers have, for the first time, a right to take parental leave, to restrict their maximum working hours, to request flexible working and so on.[104] Alongside investment in child care, funding has been provided to develop father-friendly initiatives at national and local levels, with organisations providing information about fatherhood and support for fathers, a development exemplified in the work of the Fatherhood Institute.[105]

Outside the home, however, the debate appears different. Far from finding optimism about changing men, Scourfield and Drakeford suggest that ideas about men and masculinity are positioned in different ways. In the development of law and policy around youth crime and criminality,[106] in debates about anti-social behaviour and the educational underachievement of boys,[107] in questions around men working with children, men's health and illness,[108] child support and the meaning of paternal irresponsibility,[109] we find a deployment of masculinities that contrasts starkly with the figure of the caring new father. If a deficit model of fathering has been rejected inside the home, outside it, across diverse media and academic and political discourse, a problem of men is understood very differently. What marks these latter debates are concerns about men's individual and collective failure and lack (of ability, of commitment) to engage in families, tracking to themes that were a feature of policy debates around child support and the 'feckless father' during the early 1990s.[110] These issues remain resonant in calls to 'shame' 'errant fathers', men who should be made to feel as 'socially unacceptable as drink drivers'.[111] Different ideas about men and masculinity, it would seem, collide at the interface of different areas of law, throwing up a range of beliefs about men's capacity and willingness to care.

---

[103] Although see J. Bristow, *Standing up to Supernanny*, London: Societas, 2009; ESRC Seminar Series, 'Changing Parenting Culture', <http://www.parentingculturestudies.org/seminar-series/index.html>, accessed 28 March 2009.

[104] Discussed in detail in Collier and Sheldon, op cit, 2008, ch. 4.

[105] <http://www.fatherhoodinstitute.org>, accessed 28 March 2009. For discussion, see Featherstone, op cit, 2009, pp 140–42, who notes a policy alignment here with child outcomes rather than gender equality: also Collier and Sheldon, op cit, 2008. Note also <www.dads-space.com>, accessed 29 March 2009.

[106] Piper, op cit, 2006.

[107] D. Epstein et al (eds), *Failing Boys? Issues in Gender and Achievement*, Buckingham: Open University Press, 1998.

[108] B. Featherstone, M. Rivett and J. Scourfield, *Working With Men in Health and Social Care*, London: Sage, 2007; S. Robertson, *Understanding Men's Health: Masculinity, Identity and Well-Being*, Buckingham: Open University Press, 2007.

[109] F. Williams, 'Troubled Masculinities in Social Policy Discourses: Fatherhood' in J. Popay, J. Hearn and J. Edwards (eds), *Men, Gender Divisions and Welfare*, London: Routledge, 1998.

[110] Williams, op cit, 1998.

[111] David Cameron: *BBC News*, 22 February 2007.

That is not the only problem here, however. In accounting for these differences two observations can be made. First, the ideal of the new fatherhood is, as Carol Smart and Bren Neale suggested,[112] an undifferentiated social phenomenon made up of distinct elements in how men and 'what men do' are conceptualised. Second, just like the new fatherhood, the idea of a 'problem of men' is not, Scourfield and Drakeford[113] observe, a unitary discourse. It 'does not arise from a homogenous set of concerns, but comes from several different directions and focuses on a variety of behaviours'.[114] A number of 'fundamentally different' approaches define the identification of fathers as a social problem. In some areas of law, men appear as potential perpetrators of social harm, the 'source of danger and disorder, an anti-social influence'.[115] Boys require 'traditional' masculine values in their socialisation, the presence of the male disciplinarian, the authority figure, the man who will provide something women, alone, it is presumed, cannot. This links to themes within the feminist and masculinities scholarship discussed in chapter 1, as the focus of critical attention becomes how men are empowered in society, how dominant discourses of masculinity, and a dominant gender order, serve to privilege the interests of men.

In debates about crime and social disorder, in particular, tackling fathers' responsibilities has been positioned via reference to such ideas, an engagement with fathers being a key element of policy development aimed at addressing issues of respect, exclusion and social cohesion.[116] Yet, at the same time, we have seen, in other areas of policy the focus is more on the disadvantages that can befall men as a result of present gender relations, attention being paid to the costs and burdens, if not crisis, of contemporary masculinity.[117] In relation to the family policy, it is a more optimistic, progressive model of the father as active participant in family life that has tended to prevail. This theme is also present in strands of the feminist and masculinities work discussed in chapter 1, only aligned to arguments that men too need to be 'freed' from dominant oppressive gender categories.[118]

Each of these perspectives, I suggest, following Scourfield and Drakeford, has informed understandings of men's responsibilities in the legal arena, with contemporary debates about law and parenting marked by a simultaneous cultural devaluing[119] and celebration of fathers, as politicians and policy-makers alike

---

[112] C. Smart and B. Neale, '"I Hadn't Really Thought About it": New Identities/New Fatherhoods' in J. Seymour and O. Bagguley (eds), *Relating Intimacies: Power and Resistance*, Basingstoke: Palgrave Macmillan, 1999.

[113] Scourfield and Drakeford, op cit, 2002.

[114] Scourfield and Drakeford, op cit, 2002, p 621.

[115] Scourfield and Drakeford, op cit, 2002, p 621.

[116] P. Squires, 'New Labour and the Politics of Anti-Social Behaviour', *Critical Social Policy*, 2006, vol 26(1), p 144; Day Sclater and Piper, op cit, 2000.

[117] Contrast S. Faludi, *Stiffed: The Betrayal of the Modern Man*, London: Chatto and Windus, 1999.

[118] F. Ashe, *The New Politics of Masculinity. Men, Power and Resistance* (Routledge Innovations in Political Theory), London: Routledge, 2007, pp63–69; W. Farrell, *The Myth of Male Power*, New York: Simon & Schuster, 1993.

[119] Note, for example, the argument of Burgess, op cit, 1997, esp pp 19–20.

slide between different ideas about men (often in the same speech/report). Thus, 'father absence' and 'father distance' are presented as indicative of men's individual and collective avoidance of their responsibilities[120] whilst, at the same time, they become products of institutional barriers to men spending more time with children.[121] The former view is supported by time-use surveys that point to marginal, rather than significant, shifts in fathering practices.[122] The latter is supported by research indicating that, whilst changes might not be as advanced as many would desire, this does not mean that things have not changed at all; and that many men do want qualitatively different kinds of relationships with their children.[123] What it is so difficult to obtain, however, is an appreciation of how ideas about masculinity can have multiple meanings, deployed in different contexts, in different ways as a particular kind of (inter)discursive construction.

For critics of these developments, this engaging fathers agenda has itself been based more on a moral exhortation to change in the parenting practices of both women and men, rather than a committed engagement to meaningful structural, political reform.[124] It is bound up, in particular, with a re-moralising of parenting in the legal arena, a development that has, in significant respects, served to efface the role and significance of mothers (who, in this model, need to have the importance of the father 'explained' to them) and the needs of children (who appear simply as outcomes of good parenting).[125] As Featherstone has argued, developing the work of Williams, we find – in this debate about men and change – a view, not only that 'men need compensatory policies', but also that 'women [are] to blame for not allowing men to care' in the first place.[126] What

---

[120] A. McMahon, *Taking Care of Men: Sexual Politics in the Public Mind*, Cambridge: Cambridge University Press, 1999; see also B. Campbell, *Goliath: Britain's Dangerous Places*, London: Methuen, London, 1993.

[121] Burgess and Ruxton, op cit, 1996; Stanley, op cit, 2005.

[122] Office for National Statistics, *UK 2000 Time Use Survey: Dataset*, 2nd edn, London; Office for National Statistics, 2002; Office for National Statistics, *Key Statistics for Local Authorities in England and Wales: Census 2001*, London: Office for National Statistics, 2003. See further E. Dermott, 'Time and Labour: Fathers' Perceptions of Employment and Childcare' in L. Pettinger et al (eds), *A New Sociology of Work?* Sociological Review Monographs, Oxford: Blackwell, 2006, p 91.

[123] Cabinet Office Strategy Unit, *Families In Britain: An Evidence Paper*, London: Cabinet Office Strategy Unit, 2008.

[124] Featherstone, op cit, 2008.

[125] Lister, op cit, 2006; Jenson, op cit, 2004. Note, in particular on this issue, Featherstone, op cit, 2009, ch 5.

[126] Featherstone, op cit, 2009, pp 131, 145; Williams, op cit, 1998. This raises the issue of whether women are being blamed for the *failure* to engage the father in services that are largely female dominated. Further, that it is women, and not men, who have been held responsible for a failure to control children, with mothers tending to be made the subject of parenting orders: D. Ghate and M. Ramalla, *Positive Parenting: The National Evaluation of the Youth Justice Board's Parenting Programme*, London: Policy Research Bureau, 2002. More generally, a blaming of all working parents has been identified in these debates: C. Douglas Home, 'Blaming Working Parents Doesn't Help Their Children', *The Herald*, 3 February 2009.

we do not see is an engagement with the kinds of issues being raised within recent feminist legal scholarship, where there has been an attempt to debate and reclaim a place for autonomy in the family and to rethink the value given to care and dependency in advanced capitalist societies.[127] Moreover, a form of gendered authoritarianism[128] has been detected in government initiatives around parenthood, with the rise of intensive parenting cultures marked by a reconstitution of the family as a site for the moral reassessment of the behaviour of parents.[129] In passing over the way many parents do try, as best they can, to put 'family before work',[130] and struggle with often limited resources, a debate has thus emerged about changing men focused on engaging with a particular ideological apparatus around gender, a set of beliefs about men and masculinity, rather than questions of structural change.[131]

Concluding remarks

This chapter has presented a reading of men's responsibilities in one area of contemporary social and legal policy debate. I have unpacked contrasting assumptions about the paternal subject in law. Law, we have seen, has embodied and reproduced conflicting ideas about masculinities and about how fathers work and care for young children. I have traced a shift from 'rights to responsibility' in law, broadly from the late nineteenth to the late twentieth century, and in more recent years a coming together of economic, cultural and political shifts. These changes, taken together, have reframed what being a 'good father' and responsible 'family man' entails in law. On one level this story of men's parenting can be read as a transition from a model of the father as a distant authority figure and breadwinner to a paradigm in which fathers are now viewed as having a central role to fulfil in meeting the day-to-day needs of children.[132] Yet this narrative is, I have argued, far more complex than it may at first seem.

It is certainly tempting, Sally Sheldon and I have suggested, to see this as a linear progression in law, whereby the position of men in families has been subject to changes that occur in identifiable, sequential stages, reflected in legal reforms.[133]

---

127 Fineman, op cit, 2004.

128 Scourfield and Drakeford, op cit, 2002, p 630.

129 'Where New Labour is optimistic, it tends to produce policies that are encouraging and facilitative. This is true of those policies that are designed to assist men as fathers and women as public figures. Where New Labour is pessimistic, it can produce policies that are authoritarian': Scourfield and Drakeford, op cit, 2002, p 623.

130 Cabinet Office Strategy Unit, op cit, 2008: *Families In Britain*; P. Curtis, 'Making Time for the Children: One in Four Parents Now Put their Family before Work', *The Guardian*, 19 December 2008.

131 An argument made, in different ways, by Hearn, op cit, 1996; McMahon, op cit, 1993, p 690; A. Howe, *Sex, Violence and Crime: Foucault and the 'Man' Question*, London: Routledge-Cavendish, 2009.

132 For example, see Stanley, op cit, 2005.

133 Collier and Sheldon, op cit, 2008.

Such a view would, however, be misleading, and the position is more complex than any modernisation thesis would suggest. Class, race, ethnicity and geographical location remain important factors influencing family structures and men's practices within specific locales and communities.[134] The 'micro-political realities of fatherhood', everyday experiences of breadwinning, domesticity and child nurturing, that is, 'occur at the interface of structure and individual agency within specific situated contexts'.[135] Experiences of caring and the social responsibilities associated with fatherhood are themselves mediated by biography and life history in ways that map to the reading of the male subject in chapter 1. A wealth of research suggests that the experience of fatherhood continues to involve, for many if not most men, a significant temporal and spatial trade-off between the domains of work and family,[136] and that many men, women and children continue to view the good father, at least in part, in terms of a breadwinner role.

There are political dangers, therefore, in pitching a policy aimed at changing men in terms of a debate about changing masculinity. The problematic nature of the sex/gender distinction, the materiality of gender in/of bodies and the gendered dimension of ethics of care (chapter 1, pp 46–48) suggest that the realities of the investments women and men can have in gendered categories are more complex. What remains unclear, in particular, is how men's 'choice' to change is socially and structurally constrained, bound up within rationalities and relational networks[137] that are gendered and socially, economically and culturally situated in ways that frame how some men's capabilities and agency, but not others,[138] are understood within this policy promotion of responsibility.[139] At issue is how it might be made possible for all fathers to

---

[134] See V. Gillies, *Marginalised Mothers: Exploring Working Class Experiences of Parenting*, London: Routledge, 2006; V. Gillies, 'Meeting Parents' Needs? Discourses of "Support" and "Inclusion" in Family Policy', *Critical Social Policy*, 2005, vol 25(1), p 70; G. Marks and D. M. Houston, 'Attitudes Towards Work and Motherhood Held by Working and Non-Working Mothers', *Work, Employment and Society*, 2002, vol 16(3), p 523.

[135] Collier and Sheldon, op cit, 2008, p 133.

[136] R. Crompton and C. Lyonette, *Who Does the Housework? The Division of Labour Within the Home: British Social Attitudes 24th Report*, National Centre for Social Research, London: Sage, 2008.

[137] A. Sen, *Development as Freedom*, London: Knopf, 1999; A. Barlow, S. Duncan and G. James, 'New Labour, the Rationality Mistake and Family Policy in Britain' in A. Carling, S. Duncan and R. Edwards (eds), *Analysing Families: Morality and Rationality in Policy and Practice*, London: Routledge, 2002.

[138] A particular criticism, Featherstone suggests (op cit, 2009, p 142), of the heterosexual version of fatherhood represented by the Fatherhood Institute; see n 87.

[139] B. Hobson, A. Z. Duvander and K. Halldén, 'Men's Capabilities and Agency to Create a Work Family Balance: The Gap Between European Norms and Men's Practices', paper presented at conference, *Fatherhood in Late Modernity: Cultural Images, Social Practices, Structural Frames*, April 2007 (copy of paper with authors); J. Lewis and S. Guillari, 'The Adult Worker Model Family, Gender Equality and Care: The Search for New Policy Principles and the Possibilities and Problems of a Capabilities Approach', *Economy & Society*, 2005, vol 34(1), p 76; A. Sen, 'Capability and Well-Being' in M. Nussbaum and A. Sen (eds), *The Quality of Life*, Oxford: OUP, 2003.

make real, genuine choices to work and care in ways that, far from negating the work of mothers, might promote gender equality.[140]

Notwithstanding policies aimed at engaging men in areas such as social and health care provision,[141] fathers' take-up of support is still limited,[142] with significant numbers not seeing themselves as in need of support.[143] Engaging with the barriers that can deter men from accessing services entails recognising, alongside the limits of the present structuring of provision for parental leave in law,[144] the nature of men's and women's complex investments in gendered identities, and the way a policy debate around fathers' responsibilities has been pervaded by mixed messages.[145] This agenda has uncertain aims, encompassing simultaneously concerns about gender equality, child welfare and economic imperatives. Further, it is unclear what is seen as motivating or facilitating change in men. Is it the holding out of legal rights for individuals, or the mobilising of men's collective commitments to gender equality, of the kind espoused in some of the pro-feminist critical writings on masculinity discussed in chapter 1? It may well, of course, be all of the above, but this does not mean that these policy aims are compatible.

As Brid Featherstone has observed, an issue that I shall explore further in chapter 7, it is most unlikely that 'good outcomes for children will ... be promoted by forcing father involvement against the wishes of mothers'.[146] Any expansion of women's choices will itself depend on a significant change in the behaviour of men in the home. This links to the difficult question of what

---

[140] Lewis, op cit, 2007; J. Lewis and M. Campbell, 'UK Work-Family Balance Policies and Gender Equality', *Social Politics*, 2007, vol 14(1), p 4.

[141] Gillies, op cit, 2005; N. Lloyd, M. O'Brien and C. Lewis, *Fathers in Sure Start: The National Evaluation of Sure Start (NESS)*, London: Institute for the Study of Children, Families and Social Issues, Birkbeck, University of London, 2003; F. Williams and H. Churchill, *Empowering Parents in Sure Start Local Programmes*, London: HMSO, 2003.

[142] B. Daniel and J. Taylor, *Engaging with Fathers: Practice Issues for Health and Social Care*, London: Jessica Kingsley Publishers, 2001; D. Ghate, C. Shaw and N. Hazel, *Fathers and Family Centres: Engaging Fathers in Preventative Services*, York: Joseph Rowntree Foundation, 2000.

[143] R. Edwards and V. Gillies, 'Support in Parenting: Values and Consensus Concerning Who to Turn To', *Journal of Social Policy*, 2004, vol 33(4), p 623.

[144] For discussion, see Featherstone op cit, 2009, p 134; M. O'Brien, B. Brandth and E. Kvande, 'Fathers, Work and Family Life: Global Perspectives and New Insights', *Community, Work and Family*, 2007, vol 10(4), p 375.

[145] Lewis, op cit, 2007; note also I. Dey and F. Wasoff, 'Mixed Messages: Parental Responsibilities, Public Opinion and the Reforms of Family Law', *International Journal of Law, Policy and the Family*, 2006, vol 20, p 225.

[146] Featherstone, op cit, 2009, p 131. In relation to parental leave, note R. Ray Seward, D. E. Yeatts, I. Amin and A. Dewitt, 'Employment Leave and Father's Involvement with Children: According to Mothers and Fathers', *Men and Masculinities*, 2006, vol 8(4) p 405.

happens, within a policy debate focused on child outcomes, to the needs and wishes of adults, women and men. There is much force to the argument that men have failed to articulate their own needs. Rather than blame institutions and social convention, however, this might entail 'looking at who holds the real power for change: men'.[147] Further, the gender equality agendas associated with the rise of the democratic social investment state, encapsulated in the Gender Equality Duty (above), can be seen as double-edged resulting in, from one feminist perspective, unforeseen and unwelcome alignments around men, law and equality.[148] The idea of the new caring fatherhood, I have argued, is made up of different assumptions about men, obfuscating as much as it reveals about the complexities of men's parenting and the nature of what Esther Dermott has termed intimate fatherhood.[149] In the light of these confusions, there would appear to be much uncertainty about whether engaging fathers, as set out above, is part *of* the promotion of gender equality or is, in some important respects, oppositional *to* it.

Finally, it is important to recognise how developments in this area have been embedded within broader neo-liberal economic trends and the evolution of intensive parenting cultures.[150] Political concerns to promote the privatisation of economic responsibilities in families over the past thirty years run through these debates around fathers' responsibilities to a considerable, if often unspoken, degree, framing the positioning of fathers as cause of and solution to social problems. Far from displacing men from families, gender relations have been reshaped within a global and mobile economy in ways which cut across traditional gendered class and race divisions. This links to the engagement with global masculinities developed in the work of Connell,[151] questioning the pitching of a debate about men and care solely at a national level. Conceptual issues around sex and gender discussed in chapter 1, meanwhile, further complicate this picture, suggesting limits to the interchanging of women and men in debates about child care. In some respects at least, I have argued, questions about gender neutrality, the economic imperatives of the State[152] and the nature of the gendered investments

---

[147] A. Mann, 'Of fatherhood and health, men need to articulate their needs', Letter to the Editor, *The Independent*, 15 April 2008. Contrast D. Fisher, 'Work "Success" at the Expense of Child Care', *The Independent*, 24 September 2008.

[148] For example, G. Hinsliff, 'Women's refuges told they must admit men: councils say charities could lose funding under new gender equality laws', *The Observer*, 5 April 2009; R. Bennett, 'Cuts in maternity leave to give fathers more time off', *The Times*, 30 March 2009.

[149] Dermott, op cit, 2008.

[150] Boyd, op cit, 2004.

[151] R. W. Connell, 'Globalization, Imperialism and Masculinities' in M. Kimmel, J. Hearn and R. W. Connell (eds), *Handbook of Men and Masculinities* London: Sage, 2005; R. W. Connell, 'Men, Gender and State' in S. Ervo and T. Johansson (eds) *Among Men: Moulding Masculinities*, Aldershot: Ashgate, 2003.

[152] Thus, commenting on the proposed reform to name unmarried fathers on birth certificates, as Greer has succinctly commented: 'The Government doesn't care who the real parent is – it just

both women and men make in diverse family practices continue to be effaced.[153]

It is intriguing how, at the very moment when gender-neutral social care agendas have been expanded in ways that reshape and individualise ideas of paternal responsibility, other, more established, social policies around care have contracted.[154] Economic imperatives and Treasury concerns around public expenditure, significantly heightened at a time of economic recession, frame these debates about men's responsibilities to a considerable degree. More generally, the demands of globalisation and market competition have restructured the labour market and work patterns in the UK in ways that continue to be profoundly 'family-unfriendly' for all parents.[155] At the time of writing, and in a period of severe economic downturn and a heightened surveillance of parents, if not moral panic around parenthood, there is little reason to think that the prospects for significant reform will improve, and every sign that the pressures on both women and men as parents may heighten and intensify.[156]

wants somewhere to send the bill for the upbringing': G. Greer, 'A Father's Role in Bringing up a Child will never equal a mother's', *The Times*, 4 June 2008.

[153] See, for example, W. Hollway, *The Capacity to Care: Gender and Ethical Subjectivity*, London: Routledge, 2006.

[154] Lewis, op cit, 2007.

[155] See further Lewis and Campbell, op cit, 2007.

[156] J. Carvel, 'Mandelson Under Fire Over Flexible Working Proposals', *The Guardian*, 22 October 2008.

Chapter 6

'Please send me evenings and weekends'

Male lawyers, gender and the negotiation of work and family commitments

Economic and social factors have changed greatly in the last decade and the legal sector needs to adapt accordingly. There is a greater need than ever for law firms to attract and retain the most talented people and offering a balanced working culture will enable them to achieve this.[1] When they [the Law Society] actually ... address issues of work/life balance it is to do with women going off to have children, not wishing to return to the profession ... they don't look at men.

(fee-earner)

I think [work-life balance] is extremely important in the profession. Amongst my peer group it's more of a concern than before ... it is a big issue for my generation.

(trainee)

Introduction

This chapter draws upon and develops three themes central to the earlier discussions of law, men and gender in this book. First, it interrogates, in one specific area of the profession, what it means to speak of legal practice as 'masculine' in the light of the social changes and developments detailed in preceding chapters. Second, it addresses the relation between men, parenting and family practices introduced in chapter 5, asking to what extent shifting beliefs around gender, work and masculinity are informing perceptions of career success and understandings of an acceptable workplace performance within the legal profession. Third, it contributes to understandings of gender, law and masculinity by exploring an issue that has, in contrast to the now rich volume of empirical, historical and theoretical research concerned with 'the woman lawyer',[2] been relatively underexplored: that is, the relation between male lawyers and the negotiation of 'work-life' balance. Notwithstanding the well-established nature of questions of gender within studies

---

[1] Sarah Jackson OBE, Chief Executive of Working Families, <http://www.legalweek.com/Navigation/36/Articles/1000155/Addleshaw+Goddard.html>, accessed 1 February 2009.

[2] See further chapter 1, p 11, chapter 2, p 53.

of the legal profession internationally – and noting the profile of present gender equality and diversity agendas in law – there have, to date, been few studies of male lawyers, of men *as men*, in terms of the framework of analysis set out in chapter 1. This chapter seeks to address this absence.

What follows presents the key findings of a research project which sought to investigate how a group of men working in one area of the legal profession in England and Wales seek to negotiate, or otherwise combine, what they experience as work and family commitments. The research involved an empirical study of male solicitors, at various stages of their careers, working within large commercial law practices.[3] This field of employment is widely understood, we have seen in chapter 4, to be marked by a long-hours culture,[4] strong organisational commitment and a 'bottom-line' need to meet client-led demands. I will explore, in the context of this field of legal practice, the views of a group of men towards a series of social changes impacting on the profession, changes that have had implications for issues of recruitment and retention and that have, I shall suggest, reshaped understandings of gender equity. The chapter, in summary, seeks to develop understanding of how male lawyers ascribe meanings to work and family in ways underscored, I argue, by complex and at times contradictory beliefs about gender. In so doing it provides important insights into how ideas about responsibility and dependency, introduced in chapter 5, can mediate men's experience of paid employment as a lawyer and their personal lives.

Three research questions frame this discussion:

- Is there evidence to suggest that a generational shift in attitude is taking place in this area; might new adaptations, forms of attachment and commitment be emerging on the part of men in the legal profession as to what it means to achieve an acceptable work-life balance?
- What insights can be derived from fields of study discussed in chapter 1 (for example, sociology, social theory, feminist and masculinities scholarship) in developing understanding of how ideas of gender difference become socially, politically and ethically significant within a field of legal practice?
- How are arguments for/against change articulated by men themselves, some of whom (for example, Senior Partners in law firms) may be in positions to initiate and direct organisational reform in the future?

To conduct the research twenty-two individuals were interviewed in depth – nineteen men (all solicitors) and three women (all Human Resource Managers/

---

[3] Funded by the British Academy, SG ref 31920. Whilst the following focuses on the experiences of men, in keeping with the framework set out in chapter 1, I do not wish to efface the relational nature of gender in this context; see further P. Yancey Martin, '"Mobilizing Masculinities": Women's Experiences of Men at Work', *Organization*, 2001, vol 8(4), p 587.

[4] See also chapter 5. At the time of writing it appears that the UK will keep the opt-out of the 48-hour working week of the EU Working Time Directive, with the British government continuing to assert the right of workers to determine their own working hours.

Personnel Directors) – employed across eight different law firms located in four British cities. Each of the firms engages primarily in corporate commercial work. Some are established international practices with a home base in the City of London; others are regional commercial firms located within the principal financial centres. All interviews took place in the offices of the firms in which the individuals worked. Interviews were semi-structured in nature with an average length of 45 minutes. Prior to each visit a topic guide was distributed to interviewees along with a consent form outlining the relevant ethical codes of practice which governed the project.[5] Material on the firms was collected from the legal press in advance of each visit and the interviewees were, in keeping with the need to engage with the issue of generational shift, as above, of differing levels of seniority and age.[6] The work was undertaken prior to the economic downturn that gathered pace during 2008 and which has had a profound impact on the legal profession, like many other fields of employment, reshaping the debate about work-life balance.[7] The contemporary profession is facing, at the time of writing, pressures and demands qualitatively different from those that informed perceptions of work-life balance in a period of relative economic upturn.[8] This does not detract, however, from the force of the following findings. Indeed, they are leant greater resonance when it is considered how, in such a short space of time, things can change. Importantly, notwithstanding the very different economic climate, it does not appear that debates in this area are fading away.[9] Rather, perceptions of the issues discussed below may be in the process of being redrawn in unpredictable ways, raising new questions about the nature of individual and collective commitments to career success in the legal profession.

Beyond a central and distinguishing focus on men, gender and work-life balance, this project differed in a number of ways from previous studies in

---

[5] The University of Newcastle Code of Good Practice in Research: the Ethical Code of Practice for Legal Research produced by the Socio-Legal Studies Association (SLSA). All data reported have been provided on an anonymous basis.

[6] Interviews took place with salaried and equity Partners, assistant solicitors (with a varying number of years post-qualification experience (PQE)) and trainees. In addition, HR managers/directors of personnel were interviewed where possible. Two additional interviews took place; one with a representative of the Law Society (Research and Policy Planning Unit) and one, speaking in a personal capacity, with a representative of the Trainee Solicitors Group. In the case of Partner interviews an attempt was made to ascertain broader management perceptions of difficulties arising in this area. Interviews with fee-earners and trainees focused, in contrast, on aspects of work organisation and how this might then impact on perceptions of work-life conflict.

[7] The profession, including the large law firms discussed below, and in chapter 4, has experienced significant redundancies, across all levels, including Partners.

[8] Although pre-dating the recession, see A. M. Francis, 'Out of Touch and Out of Time: Lawyers, Their Leaders and Collective Mobility within the legal profession', *Legal Studies*, 2004, vol 24(3), p 322.

[9] See Addleshaw Goddard, *Legal Lives: Retaining Talent through a Balanced Culture*, London: Addleshaw Goddard, 2008. This firm has itself been listed as one of the 'Top 100 Best Companies to Work For' by the *Sunday Times* newspaper (2008); 'We are about maintaining a balanced culture' (Addleshaw Goddard, advertisement, 2008).

this area.[10] As a relatively small-scale study what follows does not seek to be representative in its findings. In keeping with the qualitative tradition on which the research draws it presents, rather, a flavour of the reality of certain men's working lives within the contemporary legal profession in England and Wales. In so doing it adds a texture and complexity to our knowledge of men's relationship to employment and family life.[11] In recognising the limitations of a study such as this, not least in terms of the size and sample selection,[12] the central aim in what follows is to address social relations in a way which might bring conceptual analyses of what men do closer to the world of everyday experience, a theme in keeping with the personal turn in sociological thought considered in chapter 1. Set against the context of other work on work-life balance in the legal profession,[13] I shall suggest that previous understandings of the gender(ing) of legal practice might, in a number

---

[10] The project can be contrasted, for example, with an earlier study funded by the Law Society through its Research and Policy Planning Unit (RPPU) and conducted by R. G. Lee, *Firm Views: Work of and Work in the Largest Law Firms: Research Study No 35*, London: Law Society, 1999; also, more recently, Addleshaw Goddard, op cit, 2008, *Legal Lives*. The latter was a major study of the state of work-life balance and flexible working opportunities in the legal sector, involving interviews with focus groups and transactional heads in 13 UK law firms: <http://www.legalweek.com/Navigation/36/Articles/1000155/Addleshaw+Goddard. html>, accessed 1 February 2009. Lee's research was larger in scale and scope than the present study and sought to encompass a broader range of issues; for example, it elicited information on the internal management and working structures of the firms; practice development strategies; procedures and practices relating to progression to Partnership; the dynamics and consequences of an 'up or out' policy; see further R. G. Lee, '"Up or out" – Means or Ends? Staff Retention in Large Law Firms' in P. Thomas (ed), *Discriminating Lawyers*, London: Cavendish, 2000. Note also B. Cole, *Solicitors in Private Practice – their Work and Expectations: Findings from the Law Society Omnibus Survey*, Research Study 26, London: Law Society, 1997. Also K. Cunningham, 'Father Time: Flexible Work Arrangements and the Law Firm's Failure of the Family', *Stanford Law Review*, 2001, vol 53, p 967; A. Boon, 'From Public Service to Service Industry: The Impact of Socialization and Work on the Motivation and Values of Lawyers', *International Journal of the Legal Profession*, 2005, vol 12(2), p 229; A. Boon, L. Duff and M. Shiner, 'Career Paths and Choices in a Highly Differentiated Profession: The Position of Newly Qualified Solicitors', *Modern Law Review*, 2001, vol 64(4), p 563; A. Boon, J. Flood and J. Webb, 'Postmodern Professions?: The Fragmentation of Legal Education and the Legal Profession', *Journal of Law and Society*, 2005, vol 32(3), p 473.

[11] The choice of interviewee was theoretically and practically driven, designed to generate a sample that would cover a range of work and family circumstances. As with other close-focus empirical studies, the interview method was seen as ideal in eliciting information about men's views and experiences.

[12] This relates to the essentially self-selecting nature of the interview sample; it is recognised that it is possible that the men interviewed may themselves be individuals who already had some awareness of or degree of personal interest in issues of work-life balance; and that this, in turn, informed their willingness to agree to be interviewed.

[13] Comparisons with the findings of the Addleshaw Goddard study, op cit, 2008, *Legal Lives*, are considered below. Note J. Gaymer, 'Flexible Working – The Individual, The Employer and You' paper presented to *The Woman Lawyer Forum Conference*, London, 5 March 2005 (copy of paper with author).

of respects, need to be rethought in the light of complex changes that have taken place in the lives of men, women and children.

Why male lawyers? Reframing the 'women problem'

Law firms 'losing talent over hours and work-life balance': The culture in City law firms of working long hours is draining talent from the legal profession.[14]

The legal world is changing, and our clients now rightly expect to see a diverse workforce combined with a forward looking and innovative partnership.[15]

Two interrelated contexts inform this investigation of male lawyers. First, the need to address a knowledge gap in the area, the relative absence of studies of male lawyers;[16] and, second, the need to engage with the responses of the legal profession to an increasingly high-profile debate about work-life balance over the past decade or so (see chapter 5). The work-life agenda,[17] as it has been termed, encompasses concerns about gender equity, diversity and business efficiency, issues of importance to law firms within an increasingly globally competitive and market-driven profession. At the organisational level the legal profession has sought, to varying degrees, to address this diversity agenda[18] – one

---

[14] F. Gibb, *The Times*, 13 October 2008, p 19.

[15] Judith Hardy, HR Director of Addleshaw Goddard, <http://www.legalweek.com/Navigation/36/Articles/1000155/Addleshaw+Goddard.html>, accessed 1 February 2009.

[16] Although a larger study, the Addleshaw Goddard, op cit, 2008, *Legal Lives* research did not look at these issues from a perspective framed by the concerns about law and gender as set out in chapter 1 and discussed further below.

[17] The literature on this topic is methodologically, theoretically and politically diverse, and beyond the scope of this book. In brief, the idea of 'work-life' balance has been widely seen as referring to any connection between the work and personal domains of an individual. This involves both structural aspects (time commitment, geographical location, family size) and psychological aspects (job/life satisfaction, stress, general health and well-being). The broader legal and policy framework is discussed in chapter 5. See further, and generally, B. Hayward, B. Fong and A. Thornton, *The Third Work-Life Balance Employer Survey: Main Findings*, London: Department for Business, Enterprise and Regulatory Reform, 2007; T. Hogarth, C. Hasluck and G. Pierre, *Work Life Balance 2000: Results from the Baseline Study*, London: Department for Education and Employment, Research Report 249, 2001; A. R. Hochschild, *The Second Shift: Working Parents and the Revolution at Home*, London: Piatkus, 1989; A. R. Hochschild, *The Time Bind: When Work Becomes Home and Home Becomes Work*, New York: Metropolitan Books, 1997; J. Williams, *Unbending Gender: Why Family and Work Conflict and What To Do About It*, New York: OUP, 2000.

[18] Department for Constitutional Affairs, *Increasing Diversity in the Legal Profession: A Report on Government Proposals*, London: DCA, 2005; Cabinet Office, *Fair Access to the Professions: Good Practice, Phase 2 Report*, London: Cabinet Office, 2009; Cabinet Office, *Fair Access to the Professions: Phase 1 Report, An Analysis of the Trends and Issues Relating to Fair Access to the Professions*, London: Cabinet Office, 2009. In relation to work-life balance issues the Law Society has for some time organised focused events on this subject, for example, 'Comfortably Balancing Work and Life – Is This a Distant Dream for Most of Us?', Debate, Law Society, London, 26 February 2001. See D. Nicolson, 'Demography, Discrimination and Diversity: A New Dawn for the British Legal Profession?', *International Journal of the Legal Profession*, 2005, vol 12, p 201.

which transcends, of course, issues of gender[19] – and, in so doing, rethink many aspects of the working practices of lawyers. It is important to note, in addition, the role of the large commercial law firm within debates around equity, diversity and representation.[20] In conversations about gender and equality, the 'double-bind' of combining work and home commitments, along with the perceived inflexibility of many law firms relative to other fields of work, has been a central feature in studies of women lawyers. Across jurisdictions, research on women and the world's legal profession(s) has highlighted concerns pertaining to the importance of work-life balance; for example, the gendered nature of (visible) commitment and the long hours culture; the impact of women's 'double-shift' on pay differentials, recruitment, retention; the pressing issue, for the law firms and for the Law Society, of the career drift of women from the profession.[21]

The general conclusions of this work on women lawyers are clear. Not simply that women still find it more difficult than men to make progress through to Partnership, but that many aspects of professional practice continue to be gendered in ways that have damaging effects on the career advancement of women, notwithstanding the transformation in the gender ratio of entrants to the profession. What is intriguing, therefore, is how male lawyers have remained, in a sense, an 'invisible presence' in this entire debate, even though the question of what men do has been self-evidently central to the study of woman lawyers. It is in the spirit of reframing this 'women problem', turning it on its head, that the following discussion sets out the views of men themselves.

Finally, what follows is an engagement with the formation of masculinities within a particular local setting (the legal profession and, more specifically,

---

[19] 'Looking at traditional equal opportunities issues such as race and gender [is] no longer sufficient, and matters such as sexual orientation and religious affiliation had to be "put into the melting pot"': John Renz, HR Director for CMS Cameron McKenna, quoted in *Lawyer 2B*, vol 4(2), December 2003, p 1.

[20] See further chapter 4, p 102.

[21] The Law Society of England and Wales has commissioned a number of studies of women who leave the profession, exploring the particular difficulties which can face those seeking to return: see, for example, L. Duff and L. Webley, *Equality and Diversity: Women Solicitors: Research Report 48: Vol II Qualitative Findings and Literature Review* London: Law Society, 2004; J. Siems, *Equality and Diversity: Women Solicitors: Research Report 48: Vol I Quantitative Findings*, London: Law Society, 2004; T. Williams and T. Goriely, *Recruitment and Retention of Solicitors in Small Firms*, London: Law Society, 2003. Note R. McNabb and V. Wass, 'Male-Female Earnings Differentials Among Lawyers in Britain: A Legacy of the Law or a Current Practice?', *Labour Economics*, 2006, vol 13(2), p 219. See further, on the broader employment context, M. Brewer and G. Paull, *Newborns and New Schools: Critical Times in Women's Employment*, London: Department for Work and Pensions, 2005; H. Metcalf and H. Rolfe, *Employment and Earnings in the Finance Sector: A Gender Analysis*, London: EHRC/National Institute for Economic and Social Research, 2009.

certain kinds of law firms) in order to see how men's experiences can be the material for analysis of men's identities and the relationships these identities have with ideas of power.[22] In questioning the relation between power and masculinities in the area of the large law firm this reading, following the work of Connell, can be seen as pitched at four levels: first, the level of the transnational global arena in which these law firms operate; second, the regional level of the specific cultures of the firm itself; third, at the local level of face-to-face interactions in that firm (the 'everyday' nature of lawyers' work); and, finally, in terms of a man's 'bodily reflex practices', the experience of the individual.[23] In different ways, this study of male lawyers engages, as we shall see, with each of these dimensions. At issue in the debate about work-life balance in the legal profession are, I shall argue, questions about how gender politics interact with international trade and global markets,[24] how the gender regime of specific law firms connects to this global gender order and, importantly, how within local contexts these gender relations can be remade, reproduced, resisted.

General perceptions

> We are in the 21st Century and we can't, I think, just talk about it and 'tick the boxes' ... Work-life [balance] is the big issue and the single question that they [trainees at interview] ask about more than anything else ... is the working hours, how long they will have to work ...
>
> (Partner)

A minority of interviewees stated they 'couldn't see the problem' with what one fee-earner described as the 'now fashionable' issue of work-life balance.[25] Long hours would remain 'part and parcel' of the job.[26] Problems were not as pressing as some organisations with 'vested interests' sought to make out. Notwithstanding such views, however, there existed a clear belief amongst the majority that the issue of work-life balance had become a topic of heightened concern within the legal profession; and that it had, in particular, become an issue of importance to women *and* men.

> It's clearly a problem and it will continue to be a problem ...
>
> (fee-earner)

---

[22] See S. Halford and P. Leonard, *Negotiating Identities at Work: Place, Space and Time*, Basingstoke: Palgrave Macmillan, 2006.

[23] R. W. Connell and J. W. Messerschmidt, 'Hegemonic Masculinity: Rethinking the Concept', *Gender and Society*, 2005, vol 19(6), pp 829, 852.

[24] R. W. Connell, 'Globalization, Imperialism and Masculinities' in M. Kimmel, J. Hearn and R. W. Connell (eds), *Handbook of Men and Masculinities*, London: Sage, 2005.

[25] A view expressed by two of the nineteen men interviewed.

[26] 'You have to show that you are dedicated ... you are committed and that you can put ambition before many, many things. *And that's fine*' (fee-earner, my emphasis).

There is this issue over time and people are starting to say that perhaps they wish they had less work so they could spend more time with their family.

(partner)

Trainees and younger lawyers[27] were perceived as being 'more assertive' and concerned with these issues than had been the case with previous generations. Interviewees at all stages of their careers noted a 'new mood' amongst graduates, reflecting what one described as the 'very different relationship ... with employers than they had ten years ago' (HR Director).[28]

At recruitment stage ... there has been quite a shift in what graduates are looking for. Even the most able graduates are definitely talking much more about, yes, wanting a career, but not at any cost ... not being prepared to ... work at any cost to achieve Partnership. I think this is different from even seven or eight years ago.

(HR Director)

Definitely ... attitudes to work and the expectations of firms, particularly amongst junior staff ... have changed dramatically.

(fee-earner)

Some suggested that it was younger men who were expressing these concerns:

I think we've moved on, people do see it more as a male issue, because men have left, because there are more examples ... I mean ... existing staff and also people coming for interview ... they are asking [these] questions.

(Partner)

It is men ... male graduates or undergraduates ... who started asking questions about combining a career with family life, which, you know, we'd never have heard of ... it was presumed that the question was coming from women.

(HR Director)

Frequent reference was made to the way a growing number of law firms, of varying sizes and across locations, make explicit reference to quality of life issues within their recruitment and promotional materials (as discussed in chapter 4).[29] Interviewees also reflected, at times critically, on the initiatives and activities of professional bodies,[30] as well as the broader legislative framework

---

[27] On 'late starters' to the profession, see chapter 4, n 44.

[28] Whether this view will change during an economic recession is, of course, another matter.

[29] 'I know it's in all of the literature; they really sell themselves here as a firm that promotes the work-life balance' (fee-earner).

[30] Reference was made, for example, to how professional associations and organisations such as the Association of Women Solicitors (AWS), the Trainee Solicitors Group (TSG) and the Young Solicitors Group (YSG), as well as the Law Society, have sought to address the issue of work-life balance over recent years.

shaping work-life agendas (chapter 5). It was repeatedly stressed, however, that for law firms the most significant factors underlying this heightened concern were the implications for recruitment and retention of quality staff and the need to address (or at least be seen to address) externally imposed equality and diversity agendas.[31] Common reference was made to individual women and men who had left the profession entirely, or else moved on to another firm, citing work-life balance as a significant factor in their decision to leave:

> Oh, yes, yes ... it becomes an almost clichéd reason for leaving ... They have gone to a smaller law firm, or have moved into the provinces ... specifically because of work-life balance.
>
> (Partner)

Notwithstanding such views, however, there was some uncertainty as to whether significant changes had taken place in the firm in which they worked. The men, including several Partners, appeared unclear, in particular, as to what provision for flexible working (if any) existed;[32] and, equally, about the extent to which firm initiatives such as diversity committees and focus groups had sought to address these concerns.[33] 'We have established a diversity committee, which has taken over from what was, I guess, a female lawyer group. It was a group of three female partners who got together to talk about what might be called "women issues ... " ' (HR director). 'I remember we were doing something about diversity *which presumably was about the idea of women*, making sure that our women staff can stay on, leagues table etc. etc.' (trainee, my emphasis). Illustrations of flexible working in practice tended to be anecdotal and vague, derived from reporting in the legal press or else discussed in terms of other firms:

> Oh, at [names three comparable firms] it's far, far worse. One of my friends at [firm name] is fed up with the hours. I actually was shocked when he told me ... he was very, very keen, loved it and everything. But [same firm name] has almost got quite a brain-washing policy; there is a sort of superiority about them ... they try and put all this into their trainees' heads.
>
> (trainee)

---

[31] Law Society, *The Law Society Equality and Diversity Policy and Strategy*, London: Law Society, 2005.

[32] None of the men in this study were working part-time, although one fee-earner, at the time of interview five years post-qualification, had been in negotiations with his firm as to whether he might revert to part-time work for 'personal reasons'. He described the response of the firm as follows: 'It's clearly not going to happen. I've not had a final confirmation that it is a "no", but I've had a very strong indication that it's a no ... So yes, there we are.'

[33] Described as small groups of solicitors, usually made up of Partners and others in senior personnel or management positions, charged with looking at these and related issues and developing policies and responses accordingly.

I have got to say in most City law firms their diversity performance is atrocious, we are better than most to be frank.

(trainee)

Cases of men working on a flexible basis in their firm were rare. The following comments capture a general theme in this regard:

I don't know [of] any males, I don't know anyone who has put in a flexible working request on the basis of wanting to spend more time with their children.

(HR Director)

I mean ... how many men do you get working part-time in a law firm? None! It's the women that do it.

(Partner)

I don't know of anyone who is doing it, other than a couple of female clerks. I'd be struggling to know any male lawyers who have taken it up ...

(fee-earner)

Examples of flexible working by men, therefore, although referred to on occasion, were seen as exceptional, with what flexibility did exist, the interviews suggest, not being uniformly experienced across the firm and at all levels. There were marked differences between the cultures and practices of departments, with an acceptance that 'different departments demand different types of working': 'For the Mergers and Acquisitions person, it is very difficult to say "I am going to do a three days week and work from home"' (Partner). Corporate finance was seen as a particularly 'driven' area, with the status of the individual significant in having the ability to adapt workloads in such a way as to make time for family commitments (for example, in terms of responsibility for diary arrangements, transaction and caseload management or ability to delegate: see further below).

The impact: managing work, parenthood and 'a normal life'

In the spring who can say?

Please send me evenings and weekends

Shared by with the weeks

Please send me evenings and weekends ('Return the Gift', Gang of Four, 1979)[34]

---

[34] *Entertainment*, EMI Records, 1979: Music and Lyrics Allen, Burnham, Gill, King.

All interviewees made reference to the need for men, as well as women, to have what was referred to as a 'normal life outside the office'. The meaning of this varied considerably, however, according to the individual circumstance and background. The idea of having an imbalance – a life which revolved solely around work – was seen as potentially damaging both for individuals and for society. Such imbalance was, nonetheless, something several trainees perceived as having occurred in the lives of men within their firm, especially at Partner level. These men were described as displaying a range of physical and psychological characteristics associated with significant overwork (reference was made, for example, to premature ageing and frequent ill-temper as visible indicators of high levels of stress). Certain Partners had got 'used to doing these hours and don't really realise how different their lives have become ... a lot of their friends have fallen away [and] they don't really have social lives outside of the law firm' (trainee).

> Lawyers are crap at managing people generally, I must say that ... Their interpersonal skills are atrocious ... You take them out of this empire of theirs, and go and have drinks in a bar with them, or whatever, some of them are completely socially inept. Awful, outside the business context ... this 'chilling out' or whatever, you can tell they find it difficult.
>
> (trainee)

> It's a peculiar profession. It attracts a lot of individuals that are just not really very terribly complete people you know ...
>
> (fee-earner)

In terms of the hours worked, describing a typical day was difficult, notwithstanding the attempt to do just that on the part of the firms in their advertising materials, discussed in chapter 4. The international dimension of the practice area, alongside the cultural norms and expectations of departments, mediated perceptions of what would constitute a desirable level of visible commitment. Further, the often cyclical nature of the work resulted in a tendency for some to move from intensive periods of activity to 'breathing time'. The position and the role of the individual in the firm further resulted in considerable variation in terms of billable targets, informing attitudes towards acceptable working hours and the assessment of whether or not they could be seen (by themselves and others) as delivering what the firm expected of them.

Nonetheless, attempts to describe a typical working day indicated that the average working hours of these men, in many cases exacerbated by lengthy commuting times (in particular, although not exclusively, in London), did have a far-reaching impact on their personal lives.[35] Significance was attached to the

---

[35] Commuting was at times described as 'pretty horrific', adding, for some, a total of around three hours to the average working day.

impact of working hours and commuting times on both men's health and inter-personal relationships with partners, children, wider families and friendship net-works:

> Stress causes a whole range of health issues, you know, whether it is just the fact that you are preoccupied and you can't switch off ... or whether it is actual physical manifestations such as insomnia, or whatever else ... there are big problems ...
>
> (fee-earner)

> Oh, I know lots of people who are utterly miserable ...
>
> (fee-earner)

> A friend of mine called [name], for example, was in another City firm, he is basically miserable, he's a corporate lawyer, he works ridiculous hours.
>
> (fee-earner)

These tensions were particularly acute in the period of the run-up to Partner-ship; a time when, interestingly, it was felt that, increasingly, men in large law firms were becoming fathers for the first time, an observation in keeping with demographic shifts around later parenthood:

> The time when you don't want that [children] to happen is when you are eighteen months prior to partner and you are gunning for it basically, that's the time not to have your children.
>
> (HR Director)

Further concern was expressed about the frequent unpredictability of the work and the difficulties of planning events ahead, with comments made about the impact this could have on holiday time[36] and, for some, child care (see below). The breakdown of marriages and relationships was described on several occasions as commonplace within the legal profession, with the demands of work identified as a significant contributory factor. Whilst it is necessary to treat anecdotal evidence and general assertions of unhappiness with a con-siderable degree of caution, the research suggests that the nature of the com-mitment called for was related directly to feelings of dissatisfaction.[37] Yet on closer examination, the picture appears more complex, revealing a subtle and at times contradictory change taking place in this area. Notwithstanding the above comments, repeated reference was also made to the fact that an indivi-dual man could, if he so desired, 'make it work' in practice:

---

[36] The need to cancel pre-arranged holidays at fairly short notice was referred to on several occasions.
[37] See further J. Monahan and J. Swanson, 'Lawyers at Mid-Career: A 2 Year Longitudinal Study of Job and Life Satisfaction', *University of Virginia Law School: Public Law and Legal Theory Working Paper Series No 104*, 2008.

I had a conversation ... about having to leave the office to do things at school ... well I just left the office, I left at three and went and did it ... this other chap said, well [he] had to take Monday morning off because he was visiting school ... People do it. *It can be done.*

(Partner, my emphasis)

The following section looks more closely at the nature of these changes, and what it means to 'make it work'.

Work, family and the changing role(s) of men

There was general agreement amongst interviewees that the expectations placed on men had increased considerably over the past two decades in relation to both paid employment and family life. Fathers, in particular, were perceived as having experienced change in an acute way. The majority of interviewees with children, regardless of whether the children resided with them, described their family role primarily in terms of being a 'good father', mapping to the themes around gender, men and parenthood discussed in chapter 5. There was less agreement, however, as to what this role actually involved. For some it meant, as far as possible, engaging in 'hands-on' parenting: (physically) being there. Others equated good, active fathering with the traditional model of the male breadwinner, being a good provider. In the majority of accounts, the men appeared to slide between, and struggle with, these two contrasting discourses around fatherhood.

Both the men who were already fathers and the generally younger men who felt that they might, at some point in the future, become a father, sought to distance themselves from the fathering practices of previous generations. Interviewees responded strongly when asked if there were more expectations on men today to be a good father, to 'be there' for their children in a way that, some readily admitted, their own fathers had not been for them:

If I go to [a] school event the expectation is that the dads will all be there ... my son's at a ... very traditional sort of prep school. I am guessing twenty years ago you turn[ed] up for speech day in the summer, but, you know, that's it. Now *you are expected* to turn up to everything, and I think that is a generally held view. There is a pressure I think to do it. I am not sure necessarily everybody's signing up for it gladly but I think there is a pressure to do it

(Partner, my emphasis)

Twenty years ago ... if a man attended the birth of ... [his] child ... well, my father turned up and was presented with the child and you weren't allowed in the hospital [then], to change nappies, all that sort of thing. Now it's as if, if you don't do that it's generally frowned upon ...

(fee-earner)

I mean, my father didn't ... do the housework or cooking or anything like that ... The good old days, you know, you didn't bother with anything. Now ... there are more pressures on us to be a caring parent, as opposed to be just a figurehead who occasionally sort of belts out the discipline.

(trainee)

This pressure was seen as arising from a range of sources – 'society ... the media' but, in particular, 'especially from women':[38]

It's a social pressure, a pressure from partners.

(fee-earner)

There is more of an expectation from the women in our lives that men should take more of an active role.

(Partner)

Women are becoming more demanding of men. I can think of ... examples where wives have been really, really demanding ... the poor guy is now sort of pulled in every direction.

(Partner)[39]

A (female) HR Director described the pressure on many men in the following terms:

When issues arise with children who are unwell, or you know, problem pregnancies, one of the things we are seeing is men finding that their partners ... are more demanding about, you know, you need to be home, to put the children to bed, not working at weekends. You know, and it turns the screws on these guys ... He's got the pressure of the children, and the mother of the children making demands and the pressure of work, and I do see that.

(HR Director)

Another man, echoing these comments, stated:

I wouldn't put it in a sensitive e-mail. At one time when my son was ill when I simply couldn't stay at home and I had to come in here ...

(fee-earner)

Several felt that they 'had it harder' than previous generations of lawyers. This was a time when, it was implied, gender roles were more clear-cut, and there was opportunity for fathers to have both 'dad's time' and a professional career:

---

[38] Echoing themes in A. Giddens, *The Transformation of Intimacy*, Cambridge: Polity, 1992; U. Beck and E. Beck Gernsheim, *The Normal Chaos of Love*, Cambridge: Polity, 1995.

[39] One fee-earner commented on a colleague who 'was criticized at home for not making Partner, and ultimately that led to long-term depression on his part'.

'[my father] was regarded as a workaholic at the time because he came home at a quarter to seven in the evening, you know. The chances of me going home at quarter to seven in the evening are minimal and most people get home much later than that.'

(Partner)

B: You have to be a bit of everything ... You have to be seen to be this 'all-singing, all-dancing' dad.
A. A kind of 'Super dad'?
B. Yes, super dad, it's undoubtedly the case.

(Partner)

This illustrates themes around the idea of intensive parenting cultures, discussed in chapter 5, and ideas of intimate fatherhood considered further in chapter 7 (p 226). Whilst these activities had a deep significance for the 'good father', fathers today, it was suggested, had to be 'on' all the time:

In my childhood ... married fathers still had relationships with their friends, male friends, going out drinking with them at the weekend or going to football without their families and doing things, perhaps playing golf ... none of my friends do that, all my friends are committed to their families at the weekends, it's only at the children's places we do things together.

(trainee)

I think when I have a look back at my own dad, you know ... [there was] very defined [time] ... which was 'dad's time'. You know, to go down to the bowling club on a Friday night ... *We don't have time for that.* I mean if I want to do something, a leisure activity at the weekend, it has to be a leisure activity that fits in with taking the children along.

(Partner, my emphasis)

Several described their fathers as having been good role models, men who had instilled in their sons a respect for family life. This did not necessarily correlate, however, with having a 'hands-on' relationship with their sons. One Partner, who did not see a great deal of his father when growing up, felt his dad had nonetheless contributed to him feeling secure in his sense of 'family life':

Even if I only saw him for, you know, maybe half an hour in the morning, for five minutes at home at night, you know, very little, but somehow we just knew that and that was always there.

(Partner)

Regardless of individual circumstances, these men felt their families were central to their lives, supporting here Esther Dermott's depiction of fatherhood as an intimate relationship in which the aspects of parenting that men view as most significant can include the expression of emotion and affection, and the exclusivity of the reciprocal father-child dyad (see further discussion in chapter 7).[40] The majority of the men with children accepted that they saw 'very little' of their children during a typical working week. It was described as a 'fairly common' arrangement amongst residential fathers with younger children for contact to occur, rather, at 'one end of the day':

> The reality is I see my children in the morning, and that's that. I don't see them in the evening. … yes, it impacts, my wife gets annoyed about it, but it doesn't affect the children.
>
> (Partner)

> They go to sleep by 6.15 and the chance of me getting back at 6.15 is limited … I might manage that once or twice a week. So I only ever see them really when I get them up in the morning and then at weekends … That's just how it is, that's just what my job is going to be like. I have no choice about that.
>
> (Partner)

In some cases, considerable effort was made, by both parents, to ensuring that such contact did take place, and, for the men, to see their children, albeit for a short time, had a great symbolic value in marking an identity as a good father. The weekend, in particular, as noted in comments above, was seen as 'family time', at least to such a degree as work demands allowed. Some, however, were far from content with the quantity and quality of the interaction with their children which resulted; nor with the fact that such contact was often mediated and facilitated by the work of others (notably their partners).[41] The suggestion was made, intriguingly, that child care might function as a 'safety-valve' for the over-worked male lawyer:

> Men are realising that their children and their family are the most effective antidote to the pressure of work. So being able to go home to their children makes it all worthwhile even though they are having an absolutely shit horrible time at work … people are realising that there is nothing quite as good as bathing the kids after an awful day.
>
> (HR Director)

For those men with 'stay at home' wives and partners, or who had access to other networks of support, the interviews suggest that becoming a father did

---

[40] E. Dermott, *Intimate Fatherhood: A Sociological Analysis*, London: Routledge, 2008. In the context of business masculinities (below), see also I. Aaltio-Marjosola and J. Lehtinen, 'Male Managers as Fathers? Contrasting Management, Fatherhood and Masculinity', *Human Relations*, 1998, vol 51(2), p 121.

[41] See further C. Lewis, *A Man's Place in the Home: Fathers and Families in the UK*, York: Joseph Rowntree Foundation Ref 440, 2000; M. O'Brien and I. Shemilt, *Working Fathers: Earning and Caring*, Manchester: Equal Opportunities Commission, 2003.

not, by itself, necessarily entail a major reordering in the man's working life.[42] The difficulties of the transition were, however, more marked in the case of the dual-earner/dual-career household.[43] Men in this group consistently reported that balancing work and home life could, at times, be a source of considerable stress and difficulty (including in their relationship with their partners). For the dual-career lawyer, that is, managing work and family life gave rise to problems that could not always be easily negotiated if a man had to take into account the employment needs of his partner:[44]

> She [name of wife] has actually been working harder than me, and doing crazy hours ... and [I] don't want [to be in a] position where we start not to see each other and not to see the baby, and the baby doesn't know who the parents are anymore ... which is what happens at the moment.
>
> (Partner)

> What I do know is a lot of the female partners, a good number have husbands who run the home and don't work ... having somebody at home running the family is easier ...
>
> (HR Director)

Some felt they had been disadvantaged in the firm, compared to other men, due to the fact that their partners were also in full-time employment:

> I think I am unusual amongst male partners at [firm name] in that I have a wife who works full-time ... most of them don't ... Finding decent childcare provision ... was really, really difficult. It took us three and half months ... we've seen 28 people ...
>
> (Partner)

> [We have men] who ultimately their dream would be to have a little house in the country with their wife and children ... The wife not working, possibly running a charity or something. There are so many people with that kind of mentality ...
>
> (fee-earner)

> Would it be easier? Yes, definitely ... I have to think every day about getting back in good time, whereas [then] I would just kind of, I wouldn't look at my watch and just finish my work and then when I was ready I would go home.
>
> (Partner)

---

[42] One found it difficult to see 'what the fuss was about' (fee-earner).

[43] C. Skinner, *Running Around in Circles: Coordinating Childcare, Education and Work*, London: Policy Press, 2003.

[44] S. Aryee and V. Luk, 'Balancing Two Major Parts of Adult Life Experience: Work and Family Identity Among Dual-Earner Couples', *Human Relations*, 1996, vol 49(4), p 465; cf 'Professional Women "Stress Out" Their Partners At Home', *The Independent*, 6 January 2000: 'When professional couples bring their work home, it is the men who suffer.'

Interestingly, however, even in cases where both the man and woman worked full-time, and engaged in a form of 'relay parenting' (in handing over the children), there appeared marked differences with regard to how child-care commitments were experienced (see chapter 1, chapter 5). Interviewees routinely made reference to situations where, although both partners were employed full-time (often as solicitors), it would be the woman who would, in the majority of cases, take primary responsibility for child care, leaving the man to 'carry on in the race'. The following captures a common observation:

> She is the one ... to leave at 5.30 every night to go home and take over from the nanny and then put the children to bed and log on from home ... even [though] they are both full-time, she takes that responsibility, because their perception was that if they shared that responsibility they'd both be hampering their long-term career prospects. Whereas it was easier for the women to take that responsibility *leaving the man free to be able to carry on in the race*.
>
> (HR Director, my emphasis)

> It's much easier for [a man] to phone up and say to his wife 'look I am going to be late tonight', than it is for her to say the same thing to him. Simply because if he says that to his boss, [the boss] is going to say, 'well I have got two small children as well, and I am still here'.
>
> (fee-earner)

As another man put it:

> It's easier for a man to work late because he knows that, traditionally, you know, the woman is looking after the children and when you get, I suppose, both parents working, I think it still tends to be the woman who will leave work to pick the kids up ...
>
> (fee-earner)

If a man and woman did not prioritise one career, 'they would both be shooting themselves in the foot, whereas [now] just one of them did ... ' (fee-earner). This raises the issue of the gendered cultures of the organisation in which such perceptions were formed and of how these views are themselves grounded in the psychosocial investments in particular gender categories (ideas of, for example, what being a man, and a 'successful lawyer' might entail (chapter 1, pp 39–43).

Partnership, promotion and the idea of the 'weak man'

Diverse views were expressed about the role of Partners in the firm and their impact on organisational cultures and practices. For all the men, trainees, fee-earners or Partners themselves, regardless of status, the view was expressed that individuals who became Partners, men and women, had a key role and responsibility in promoting good practice and a healthy attitude to work-life balance. For some, a number of Partners succeeded in so doing. For a majority of trainees and assistant solicitors, however, male senior figures within the firms were described as those generally more inclined to resist, rather than embrace, change. Whilst the allure of Partnership was seen as strong for many, it was suggested that for a growing number of women *and* men the 'carrot' of Partnership may be waning; and, in particular, the potentially heavy demands of developing a Partnership track lifestyle were a factor in this shift:[45]

> There is beginning to be a ... change in terms of attitudes ... people don't necessarily think that Partnership is the be all and end all anymore.
>
> (fee-earner)

> There's been a real shift and it's partly tied in with the fact that the overall carrot that we have been holding out to people has changed ... people, women and men, are just not prepared to pursue it.
>
> (HR Director)

The well-documented idea that a long-hours culture has become institutionally embedded in many law firms – not least in the understanding that putting in long hours is part of the apprenticeship the trainee and assistant will undertake – was generally accepted.

> When you are young and you are coming in as a trainee ... it shouldn't take you that long to realise that, unless you put in the hours, you don't get anywhere.
>
> (fee-earner)

On closer examination, however, some assumptions about men and gender informed these perceptions of Partnership, commitment and career progression.

The weak man: raising the issue

In ways that echo themes within the study of Podmore and Spencer over twenty years ago,[46] large law firms, whether in the City of London or elsewhere, were routinely described as 'hyper-competitive' (Partner), 'aggressive'

---

[45] It is, of course, difficult to generalise about the experience of Partners, which can vary considerably within and between firms, departments and practice areas, as well as between Salaried and Equity status. Partnership was seen as providing, on the one hand, a greater responsibility to 'be there' and 'take the flak', but on the other, greater potential control over diary commitments and autonomy: 'it's not nearly the same pressure as with an assistant ... you have the ability to control your own time ... ' (Partner).

[46] D. Podmore and A. Spencer, 'Gender in the Labour Process – The Case of Women and Men Lawyers' in D. Knights and H. Wilmott (eds), *Gender and Labour Process*, Aldershot: Gower, 1986.

(fee-earner)[47] and 'macho', 'masculine' environments. The interviews suggest, however, that the ideas about gender informing these perceptions of the masculine culture of law are complex and cannot be reduced to any simplistic association with hegemonic masculinity (chapter 1, pp 33–39). The majority of the interviewees felt that for men, in ways that contrasted to women, it could be 'career suicide' to play, as one put it, the 'quality of life card'. Men who did so would most likely be seen as 'weak' by others. Those men who were described as having 'not coped' were themselves referred to, by one man, as the 'breakdown' cases.[48] It could be a difficult and risky business for individuals on Partnership track, in particular, to 'rock the boat' (fee-earner) by admitting to problems in negotiating the competing demands of work and family commitments:

> It would be perceived as being a weakness. I mean if you were to mention it [wanting more time to be with family] to investment bankers, they would be even more aggressive [than lawyers] ... but yes, it would be tantamount to saying 'I don't really want to work here anymore'.
>
> (Partner)

> We've got an example here of a newly qualified lady solicitor who has left because, I think, the stress of the job ... I don't know ... in the past they might have called [a man] a bit of a wuss.
>
> (Partner)

> If in espousing the philosophy [of work-life balance] you think it is going [to] damage your career, then it's probably not to be ... you want to be carrying on.
>
> (Partner)

> My suspicion is that you are never going to get a male assistant who leaves saying that he wants a better work-life balance. He just wouldn't do it.
>
> (Partner)

Women lawyers, in contrast, found it 'far easier' (fee-earner) to raise problems and concerns around work-life issues with their firms and, if necessary, seek assistance in making suitable arrangements. The following are just a number of comments on this theme:

> My friend has got a baby, his wife is also a lawyer in the City, and although she works full-time, if there is ever any working late, it is always

---

[47] 'Eat what you kill can cause unhealthy behaviour. People will tend to be more selfish and won't share work and will do work that should be done by someone else': Hugh Crisp, Freshfields Bruckhaus Deringer, quoted in *Lawyer 2B*, May 2003, p 31.

[48] Although, on the potential longer-term costs for some of 'managing' things, see J. Goodliffe and D. Brooke, 'Alcoholism in the Legal Profession', *New Law Journal*, 19 January 1996, pp 64–66; 'Stressful Job Linked to Depression', *BBC News*, 1 August 2007.

going to be easier for her to say to her employer, 'actually, I've got to go home for baby'

(fee-earner)

Women have the, have an advantage in that they have a socially acceptable get-out clause; 'Well I am going off to raise a family,' and they can step out 'honour intact', whereas for a man it's 'Well, you just couldn't cut it, could you' and 'You just weren't good enough, you are not Partner, you are not going to make Partner, and if you haven't been made up after X number of years well you should just get the message and leave. Go off and do something ... '

(trainee)

All interviewees felt it would be 'more understandable if a flexible working request came from a women ... than from a male who just wanted to spend more time with his family' (HR Director), a point that connects to the gendered nature of perceptions, above, as to what constitutes acceptable personal commitment to the firm/family in the first place:

In the City, if a 6-, 7-, 8-year qualified solicitor announced that he was taking time out to spend time with his young family ... I think the unspoken question, or perhaps the spoken question, would be sort of, Why? What happened to his career? Is there some negligence claim that we haven't heard of yet?

(trainee)

I really do believe that ... women are more willing to admit defeat than men. When I say defeat I don't mean to be in that, you're a failure. Just that you choose to accept that something hasn't worked out for you ...

(fee-earner)

There is a tension here, however, between, on the one hand, the idea of men being reluctant to 'stand up to' the firm if such an action might be perceived as a sign of weakness; and, on the other, statements expressed in other contexts regarding the individual qualities and confident self-image required of the successful male lawyer (the 'star player'): men, that is, who *are* assertive, willing to 'speak their mind', 'say how things are' and 'stand up for themselves'. The very kinds of attributes, that is, called for in the advertising materials discussed in chapter 4.

Women lawyers and the masculine culture(s) of the firm

The majority of the men expressed a belief that the route to Partnership in their firm was, generally, an open and egalitarian process. At the same time, however, assumptions around gender informed their perceptions of how this process worked in practice and, in particular, around the question of who would, and would not, 'fit' Partnership. This was particularly evident in relation to the men's views of women solicitors and, especially, the female Partners in law firms. The latter were routinely described as 'more aggressive', 'more masculine' than other (implicitly normal?) women:

I use the term female loosely, you know it takes a certain type of female to succeed in this environment ... I think you can only do that by being incredibly robust and making probably greater sacrifices ...

(fee-earner)

Driven and very focused and ultra-competitive, yes, yes.

(Partner)

It tends to be more aggressive women ... you know, acting just like men, potentially or alternatively ... they are acting like propelled women [?], which can mean even more scary creatures than an aggressive man.

(fee-earner)

The majority of the men questioned, at times with force, whether there was any sense of 'feminist solidarity' amongst the women in their firm who had been made up to Partnership. Rather, in ways which, it was accepted, were similar to the majority of male Partners, these women were described as ascribing to a view that all individuals, regardless of gender, should 'pay their dues':

The women lawyers ... are as guilty as the men ... the more ... career-driven women who would have little time for any suggestion that, you know, 'I can [only] work 9–5 because I've got a family'.

(fee-earner)

I think lots of women who do reach ... Partnership ... don't really want to help other women reach the level that they are at. It's very much a 'me and you' kind of culture ... *I've worked like a man* ... to reach the level that I am at and you need to do the same if you want to obtain the same goals.

(fee-earner, my emphasis)

Those women who have made it into Partnership ... I can't see them turning around and saying 'You know what, let's give our sisters the easy route, a leg-up'. I can't see somebody who has spent 15 years of vicious competition suddenly turning around and saying, 'well, you know, I think it's time to make this all a lot easier, I will be the last one to have worked my guts out and not have a life'.

(trainee)

It was generally accepted that female Partners in law firms were more likely than their male counterparts to be women who did not have children:

I suspect that if you took a cross-section of the women Partners [those] that have made Partner relatively young will be the woman who didn't have a family ...

(fee-earner)

For a woman, the combination of having children and being a Partner in a large law firm was seen as, at best, a difficult balancing act:

If you look at the female Partners in most City law firms, this one included, you will find that they tend either not to have children, or to be the sort of people who, are not quite 'sod the children', but who recognise they are driven, and will put the long hours in and then go and see their children.

(fee-earner)

I think quite a lot of [women] have been affected by the need to limit the impact of their families ... they have had to be perhaps a bit more macho, than their male colleagues.

(HR Director)

It would, nonetheless, be misleading to say that these men subscribed in any straightforward way to 'sexist' attitudes that have been associated with the term 'hegemonic masculinity' (chapter 1, p 14), at least as it has been used within some of the literature on gender and the legal profession. It is possible to detect, rather, an appreciation of the contradictory nature of social changes that have impacted on the profession. A minority of the men did believe that women in contemporary law firms 'had it easier' than their male colleagues. Such an advantageous position related to the growing profile of equity, diversity and discrimination agendas within the legal profession and in society as a whole:

Just because they are women, why should they have more privileges than you? You know they want equalities, but equality is equality, they have to work. If they want to be treated like an equal, I was going to say like a man, but if they want to be treated just as a lawyer then they [have to] accept what being a lawyer is, don't they?

(trainee)

B: Everybody has got their eye firmly on sex discrimination to the extent that the experience now almost is that it is becoming impossible to discriminate.

A: What do you mean?

B: ... [in] numerous firms ... women on the Partnership track who have been considering ... having a young family, if they don't make

Partnership, will see it as a reason to challenge [the firm] ... maybe justly or unjustly. They are obviously very clever people.

(fee-earner)

It is an advantage being a woman in the legal profession now ... I mean ... it is a fact that, generally, for the older males in the legal profession, if you are a pretty female they will give you preferential treatment.

(fee-earner)

A complex amalgam of personal injustice, vested interests and distrust of 'fashionable issues' informed the view that it was men, and not women, who had become the victims of equality agendas (see further on this idea, in the context of fathers' rights, chapter 7).

At the same time, however, a significant majority of the interviewees suggested that women in the profession – including those in the firm in which they worked – could face additional hurdles and difficulties compared to men. There was a general acceptance that the gendered cultures of the law firm, in certain circumstances, disadvantaged women and serve to advantage men *as men* in their careers. Indeed, some recognised that they themselves had been advantaged due to the fact they were men:

It's [a world] still prejudiced against them [women]. You had to be very tough, you had to set aside what might traditionally be called some of the softer, maternal things. ... some of the female partners have got far more of a workload sent to them ... [than some of the men].

(Partner)

Of course there is a gender issue, definitely. Of course there is ...

(fee-earner)

I tell you, it's worse for women than it is for blokes.

(fee-earner)

Women have worse pressure ... [there are] more women coming into the legal profession, but they never make it to the top, there just aren't that many that get to Partnership. I suspect they have got to work twice as hard just to get there ...

(Partner)

The men subscribing to these views linked the difficulties facing women lawyers to the double burden (above) of combining employment with primary responsibilities for child care:[49]

---

[49] 'A couple of people got a bit of a bollocking ... the ones happy to leave at 6 o'clock to pick up their child from the nursery or whatever ... and I have no doubt that they are statistically more likely to be women, having to go off to pick up their children ... ' (fee-earner).

An acquaintance ... in a City law firm, she was told, basically, if you have kids you do realise that's going to harm your career, by a Partner, yes.

(trainee)

However, this did not mean that the wider role of men in child care was then factored in to any criticism of such arrangements. Rather, the choice both to have children and to assume responsibility continued to be seen as an essentially individual decision on the part of a woman – a decision beyond the broader social context within which choice was exercised (chapter 5). Choice was set apart from attitudes and practices that, it was also recognised, were deeply embedded in the culture of the firm:

I don't think there are any barriers to women progressing through the profession, other than the barriers that they place on themselves such as having children. *They don't have to have children if they don't want to.*

(fee-earner, my emphasis)

[It's] because *they go and have kids*, they get penalised for it, it's as simple as that.

(trainee, my emphasis)

Even when [name of partner] is not working ... I am expected to share all the responsibilities at home, not only hoovering but all the day-to-day items ... *I opted to feed the baby last night*, and I think that is fair.

(fee-earner, my emphasis)

The nature of the relationship these men had to the idea of a dominant hegemonic masculine culture within the firm, therefore, emerges as problematic and complex (see further below). As noted elsewhere in this book, in particular in chapter 1 and chapter 3, differential access to dominant codes of social, cultural and economic capital, as well as questions of individual biography, are important factors mediating experience within specific discursive and institutional contexts. In these law firms, it was notable that several men made a point of describing themselves as 'a bit different', 'set apart' from what they recognised could be the 'laddish', 'masculine' culture and norms of homosocial bonding and socialising that characterised some sections of the firm:

There would be this mentality that on a Friday ... he [Partner] would rally up all of the guys and take them for a drink. ... the invitation would only be for the guys ... the girls wouldn't be asked, the women wouldn't be asked ...

(fee-earner)

We have assistants who will bugger around all day and then come 6 o'clock go downstairs have dinner in the canteen and then come back and work for 4 hours and then go home at 11 o'clock. Well, you know that's, you know … [pause] I come in, my day, is I come in, do my work, and go home at 6 o'clock.

(Partner)

This view was articulated, in particular, by those men who stated that their 'family came first'. Prioritising family, focusing on work during office hours and not participating in a 'one of the lads' drinking culture, could and at times did, it was felt, bring difficulties, including for those who had already attained Partnership.[50]

'Be successful': work-life balance, consumption and identity

I am not doing this myself, because I want the glory of being Partner, I am doing it for my family, for my children, because I want my children to have the best …

(fee-earner, my emphasis)

As noted above, throughout the interviews repeated reference was made by the men, at all levels of the firm, regardless of their status, to the idea that there existed a distinctive 'lawyer lifestyle' associated with working in the large commercial firms (see further on this idea chapter 4, p 106). This lifestyle was described at times in broadly negative terms. It was inimical, in a number of respects, to having flexibility in work and family lives. Yet, paradoxically, the need to maintain the lifestyle was seen as a central motivational force underscoring the men's commitment to their careers – *why* they did *what* they did. Moreover, intriguingly, as observed in relation to the discussion of images of lawyers in professional advertising and publicity material in chapter 4, this lifestyle was developed as much around the consumption of commodities and the acquisition of cultural experience as through engaging in economic production and/or any sense of public service as a lawyer. The lifestyle, that is, was intimately entwined with 'working hard, rolling your sleeves up and [then] getting the [material] rewards' (fee-earner).

On closer examination, these understandings of lifestyle were mediated by age and stage of life-course in ways that had an impact on the men's perceptions of what might constitute an acceptable work-life balance.[51] Trainees and younger male solicitors, especially, made common reference to the lawyer lifestyle primarily in terms of having a 'work hard, play hard' attitude to life:

For young lawyers and … assistant solicitors in their 20s I think there is this sort of … work hard, play hard type of mentality and I do think the two sides of the equation are quite evenly balanced …

(HR Director)[52]

[50] 'You know, "putting yourself about a bit". It's easier … if you are out five nights a week … I do kind of think, I wish they [other men] would go off and have families and then we can sort something out for our mutual benefit' (Partner).

[51] See Boon et al, op cit, 2001, pp 579–86.

[52] 'There is a macho element to the work part side, you know, "I'm doing thousands of billable hours per week, look how macho I am," and that means I'm going to party all night as well' (HR Director).

> It's a work hard, play hard culture ... we try to be frank with people and they
> do have to work very hard, we all have to, we all have to work very hard ...
>
> (Partner)

This discourse of work hard, play hard, I argued in chapter 4, is framed by an
ethic of 'playful responsibility' interlinked with an appeal to upmarket consumption practices and ideas of social distinction[53] and economic advancement.[54] In relation to younger lawyers and trainees it maps to wider
transitions in cultural identifications amongst young adults (chapter 4, pp 111–
114). Bearing in mind the scale of the facilities and leisure provision now
offered by many large law firms, the negotiation of work and family commitments was, generally, not perceived as a particular problem for younger early-
career lawyers.

In contrast to this view, however, and whilst sharing a concern with high-
end consumption practices and material reward, older lawyers, in particular
those with children, tended to describe the lawyer lifestyle through a very
different lens and, specifically, via reference to ideas of responsibility and
planning that involved rather different ideas of masculinity. For the latter
group, the either already realised or potential financial rewards of a career in a
large law firm were such that they did not just enable participation in distinctive upmarket consumption (housing, private education for their children,
certain kinds of holidays and so forth) and the acquisition of positional
goods,[55] they also embraced a particular *kind* of family responsibility as (male)
breadwinner:

> If you are single, it's not such a big deal. But if you are married and you
> have children, then that's very difficult ...
>
> (fee-earner)

This lawyer lifestyle was seen as facilitating, for some, a potential chance
of 'escape' from the profession:[56] ' ... you know, *this doesn't have to be*

---

[53] 'Like every sort of taste [distinction] unites and separates. Being the product of the conditioning
associated with a particular class of conditions of existence, it unites all those who are the
product of similar conditions while distinguishing them from all others. And it distinguishes in
an essential way, since taste is the basis of all that one has – people and things – and all that
one is for others, whereby one classifies oneself and is classified by others': P. Bordieu, *Distinction: A Social Critique of the Judgment of Taste*, London: Routledge & Kegan Paul, 1984, p
56. Compare B. Longhurst and M. Savage, 'Social Class, Consumption and the Influence of
Bordieu: Some Critical Issues', in S. Edgell, K. Hetherington and A. Warde (eds), *Consumption
Matters: The Production and Experience of Consumption*, Oxford: Blackwell, 1996.

[54] The ability, for example, to 'buy nice things, live in a nice house, that sort of thing' (trainee).

[55] 'Of course that [work] will impact on your family situation, but invariably your children will be
at private schools and have long holidays' (fee-earner).

[56] P. Ghazi and J. Jones, *Downshifting: A Guide to Happier Simpler Living* London: Hodder &
Stoughton, 2004; N. Corder, *Escape from the Rat Race: Downshifting to a Richer Life*, London:
Right Way Plus, 2001; A. Bull, *Downshifting: The Ultimate Handbook*, London: Thorsons, 1998.

forever' (fee-earner, my emphasis). Leaving the profession entirely, or taking early retirement, was seen as viable option. Problems with work-life balance might only exist, that is, for just part of the life-course, with early retirement a potential option during the 'late forties or early fifties' (Partner):

> It's a bit of a trade-off whether you are going to sacrifice your 20s and your early 30s, but you will be reasonably set up by that time ... I think the 40s wouldn't necessarily be an early retirement age in this sort of industry.
>
> (fee-earner)

> We've had a series of partners who have retired early, and when I say early I mean in their 40s, not even their 50s ... So they've been partners for 10–15 years [or] whatever ... so when they get to 48 or something they've decided to go off and do something different – take a degree, go to university or whatever. They haven't gone to other law firms, they have gone completely out because they don't need to work.
>
> (Partner)

In contrast to such views, others were less sanguine about the chances of men leaving law after they had 'become successful'. Rather, the commitments and subjective investments associated with the breadwinner ethic – in particular the need to provide for positional goods at a high level for their families – was seen as 'locking us in' (Partner) to work: 'nursery is nearly 700 pounds a month for three days' (fee-earner); 'I want to send the children to private school ... fund the university education ... be able to go on the good holiday with the family ... to offer [the] family all the finer things in life ... ' (fee-earner).

Retention and downshifting: the 'grass isn't always greener'

In keeping with the above, different views were expressed about the social trend towards downshifting, much discussed over the past decade or so in the media, in particular amongst those working in the financial services sector (at least, that is, prior to the economic recession of 2008 onwards). For these men downshifting in the legal profession was associated with making the move from a large commercial firm to a smaller firm (whether based in London itself or, frequently, in the provinces):

> One of the reasons people choose to come out to the regions is because there is more of a balance and that was part of the main reasons why I didn't apply to train in London because I thought I'd have a better standard of life outside.
>
> (fee-earner)

> The big firms, they ... use their assistant solicitors as sort of work-horses, they work them until they bale out, and they replace them, and then you find if you look at firms outside of London ... they get a lot of the people from City firms who have just had enough. They wait, you know. ... a couple of years, when you stick your head down and you work and you build up some money ...
>
> (fee-earner)

One fee-earner noted how the 'demands [can] become too much in the firm and you find that you are not spending enough time with your family'. Then:

> people just call it a day and they either move in-house, where the perceived hours are less ... or they move to a smaller firm ... I have seen some people 'go intellectual', and on occasion people move away from the law entirely – they have just had enough of it.
>
> (fee-earner)

There was, however, some doubt as to the validity of the argument that 'the grass is greener' elsewhere. Not only, it was suggested, would the financial rewards be less, the support structures within the large firm might, contrary to expectations, offset the supposed advantages of working in a smaller, less prestigious organisation. Equally, commercial pressure, deregulation and heightened competition impacted across the profession as a whole. Both anecdotal evidence and, on occasion, personal experience suggested, rather, that long working hours were endemic to the legal profession and could not be confined just to the larger firms:

> There are a few people who I have kept in touch with who went to a smaller firm thinking it was going to be an easier setup and they actually got the shock of their lives. Because, you know, organisations like this ... have a phenomenal support structure around the lawyers, you know, 24-hour support ...
>
> (Partner)

Regardless of the region or practice area in which the individual worked, the ideas of lifestyle, consumption and the work hard, play hard discourse noted in chapter 4 informed dominant understandings of what being a successful lawyer in the contemporary profession would involve:

> I have a good friend who works in Newcastle and he enjoys his job, but is under extreme pressure from his firm, and is always in the office. I have spoken to him on weekends ... I say, 'Oh, you know, you are at work, what are you doing at work' and this will be on a Sunday afternoon or on a Saturday lunchtime, and 9–9.30pm on a week night, and he's always in the office ...
>
> (fee-earner)

A growing number of firms have sought to introduce initiatives to improve work-life balance. The men appeared, however, ambivalent about the effect of some of the measures introduced. The provision for home and remote working, in particular, was seen as double-edged, bringing about an increase in surveillance of the lawyer and a blurring of what was, for some, a subjectively valuable distinction between the realms of work and a private life away from the firm:

> It means that you are never getting away from the office, because once you have gone home, the Partners are very acutely aware that you do have access to all the systems and there is no excuse for you actually not to get on and do the work while you are at home.
>
> (fee-earner)[57]

> Sometimes if you talk to some of the Partners about flexible working, yes, they are all for it: because they see it as [you] being able to log on wherever you are in the world, and at any time of the day or night, being contactable twenty-four hours a day.
>
> (HR Director)

Some were highly critical of the increasing visibility of 'lifestyle assistant' companies in the legal profession. Whilst liberating them for work, one result was a further negation of autonomy over aspects of their lives. For one interviewee this had 'a real sinister veneer to it because, what they are saying to you is, "You don't need to do your things, your personal life things yourself, we'll help you with those. We will do it for you" ... ' A number of examples were given of how such companies work – 'organising a birthday for your child ... organising a magician, entertainment, a cake ... that kind of thing'.[58] 'They would do all that for you ... it's your father's 50th birthday and, you know, you want to organize a special thing for him, ring us up and we'll come back to you with 20 different ideas, pick one and then just pay by credit card ... ' (fee-earner). At the same time, however, the extensive support structure which surrounded these lawyers was recognised as a fundamental feature of – indeed, as essential to – satisfactorily carrying out the job: 'you can go and get yourself a sandwich at midnight if you wish to ... Silly things like that' (Partner).

---

[57] 'I mean, I regularly worked long hours, but then when I walked out the door I had switched off completely, whereas now I know on my days off that actually I should probably just keep in touch, so it is harder to switch off and I don't think that's ... terribly healthy' (Partner).

[58] These acts were not necessarily perceived of as being burdens; rather, the service was 'taking away those little things that add value to life ... there is a certain value in having done those things yourself, a certain thought that goes into it' (fee-earner).

Concluding remarks: male lawyers, business masculinities and social change

> I think until men probably start saying 'enough is enough' of this ridiculous hours culture we have, well, only then will people listen.
>
> (HR Director)

> In our society, hegemonic masculinity is heterosexual, aggressive and competitive, and homosocial (excluding women from its social networks). It emphasises hierarchy and the capacity to dominate other men.[59]

Studies of work-life balance in the legal profession raise issues that go far beyond, of course, questions of gender. Recent debates have focused, for example, on how law firms can encourage 'smarter working' by changing the culture of the organisation in such a way as to better support 'balanced' lawyering (in the form, for example, of out-of-office working). There has been discussion of the pivotal importance of role models (men and women) in shifting the cultures of law firms, as well as the increasing demands from clients for 'healthier, happier' lawyers (see further below). The 2008 research undertaken by Addleshaw Goddard,[60] on a far larger scale than this focused study of male lawyers, confirms the general conclusions of the present work in noting how a concern about work-life balance, and the need to promote flexible working, has become a pressing issue across the legal profession, notwithstanding the economic downturn:

> The legal world is changing, and our clients now rightly expect to see a diverse workforce combined with a forward looking and innovative partnership.[61]

Of particular importance in shaping this debate, as Law Society research has for some time shown, has been the loss of women lawyers. This remains a key point of concern in the legal profession.[62] Engaging with these issues can be seen, on one level, as questioning the internal working of specific law firms.[63] In these final remarks, and tracking to the themes outlined at the beginning of this chapter, as well throughout this book, I wish to reflect further on what this work can tell us about the changing relationship between law, men and

---

[59] R. W. Connell, 'Men, Masculinities and Feminism', *Social Alternatives*, 1997, vol 16(3), pp 7–8.

[60] Addleshaw Goddard, op cit, 2008, *Legal Lives*.

[61] Judith Hardy, HR Director of Addleshaw Goddard <http://www.legalweek.com/Navigation/36/Articles/1000155/Addleshaw+Goddard.html>, accessed 1 February 2009.

[62] Duff and Webley, op cit, 2004.

[63] The findings of Addleshaw Goddard, op cit, 2008, *Legal Lives* point to the importance of internal deadlines as more of a barrier than client demands, issues around the allocation of resources, the impact of 'presenteeism', and the significance of role models, as above, to communicate flexible working. This research grouped the challenges for private practice into three categories: working practices, culture and out-of-office working.

gender in a more general sense, in reshaping our understandings of the 'man of law' and masculinities discussed in chapter 1.

(Re)gendering the firm (and the client): 'money isn't enough'

> Lawyers look up and see Partners ... continuing to work ridiculous long hours, seeing that the balance in their life is one that they would not want in theirs. So, if that is the prize for making Partnership, then yes, it holds a lot in terms of financial reward, but ... is only achieved whilst putting in a substantial sacrifice on what they see as their work-life balance. So they don't want it. So, you know, *the money isn't enough*.
>
> (HR Director, my emphasis)

This study supports arguments both for and against the view that significant change is taking place in this area. Two themes, in particular, are supportive of the view that change will gather pace as the profession begins to take work-life balance as a matter of increasing seriousness. First, the argument that, as women and men with more family-friendly attitudes work their way through the promotion structures of the firm to Senior Partner level, the result will be a greater move to engage with these issues. For some, the profession was already seeing 'the emergence of men ... with a different attitude' (Partner), men who will, given the chance, seek to push through change: 'When I become a Partner I am going to change this [because] we don't have to work these ridiculous blockbusters' (trainee). Change was a 'necessary and inevitable' reflection of 'the fact that people of my age [mid-thirties] who are now junior Partners tend to have young families' (Partner).[64] The key to such change would be 'the younger Partners who do want a greater balance and are more in touch with the younger generation in terms of their aspirations and values' (HR Director).

Supporting this view, some interviewees noted significant shifts in clients' demands and expectations, as noted above. Reference was made to clients who were, increasingly, seeking a more balanced lawyer. The client base, that is, was becoming increasingly aware of these issues as more women moved into senior positions within companies. The legal profession, unlike some other fields of employment, was mired in 'erroneous assumptions' about caseload management and the nature of what client service could and should be:[65]

> [Clients] ... are asking things like 'what's your diversity policy, what's your policy on flexible working, how many women have you got. ... What

---

[64] 'I think it [the future] will be different. I think you will see more lawyers working part-time, you will see a lot of part-time Partners ... I think as soon as one firm starts doing it, it becomes hard for the others not to seek ways of addressing it' (Partner).

[65] 'They [the Partners] just didn't have the bottle to turn around and say "no" ... so they ended up working on [the deal] on Christmas Day, full flat out at Christmas when they should have been with their families' (trainee).

do you do about parents that work ... ?' Clients love this, because of course it's reflecting their own practices, so increasingly organisations ... want to employ lawyers who share their views ... the client has much more influence in what's happening in law firms.

(HR Director)

Tackling these issues was just part of providing a 'first-class' professional service to clients: 'you are going to get the best service from fundamentally fulfilled people' (Partner), rather than those focused on an 'unrelenting' drive for profit.[66]

PR, policy and professional practice

At [X, firm name] ... *we don't know where all the blokes go.* They were going to the dot.com companies. They probably aren't going to the Investment Banks because [they] ... aren't recruiting. So I think perhaps ... they have decided 'well, actually, no thank you very much this isn't for me,' and it is actually quite extraordinary.

(HR Director, my emphasis)

Second, a further driver for change concerned the economic self-interest of the firms in promoting flexible working practices within a competitive and volatile market for legal services.[67] The specific requirements placed on firms by external organisations (such as the Law Society: chapter 4, p 102) were identified, along with broader public shifts in attitudes, as necessitating a growing recognition that successful competitive firms have no choice but to 'move with the times'. The research data on work-life balance and the business case for efficiency in law present a convincing case that law firms can benefit considerably from addressing the concerns of employees in this area.[68] In recognising the degree to which certain firms have begun to address these issues, therefore, future demographic change, of the kind discussed in chapter 1, alongside cultural and legal shifts around parenting (chapter 5) suggest that there will be a heightened concern over diversity and equity issues in the future. Career drift from the profession, in particular around the retention of women lawyers, alongside issues of recruitment and market profile, were seen as necessitating that law firms urgently tackle problems in this area:

Worse case scenario? I think we have got a real, real problem on our hands, in that the people coming into the profession just don't buy

---

[66] 'I mean, I look somewhere like [Firm X], one of our competitors, now X seem to be pulling out every single stop to try to do nothing other than make their firm as profitable as possible. Their target for the firm is specified in nothing other than profit [terms]' (Partner); 'They [the firms] are greedy. It's just about money' (trainee).

[67] To place these concerns in context see B. Cole, *Trends in the Solicitor's Profession: Annual Statistical Report 2007*, London: Law Society, 2008.

[68] C. McGlynn, 'Strategies for Reforming the English Solicitors' profession: An Analysis of the Business Case for Sex Equality' in U. Schultz and G. Shaw (eds), *Women in the World's Legal Professions*, Oxford: Hart, 2002.

into what they see the senior guys doing ... at some point, it is going to start hitting the firms very tangibly in that ... they are not going to have enough of the good people staying to continue to grow the practice.

(HR Director)

As Lee observed in 1999, for the largest law firms generally:

Disaffection with professional life [is leading] to the departure of talented and trained personnel, leaving shortages of experienced and qualified lawyers. In a situation of short supply, the wage rates for solicitors in these firms are rising rapidly. But this is being paid for by ever-increasing billable hours, leading to yet more disaffection. In short, and in both senses of the word, the result is a vortex.[69]

Writing in a very different economic climate from that facing Lee a decade ago,[70] and notwithstanding the above observations, this research also provides evidence, however, to question whether the work-life agenda will, in fact, make significant inroads into practices of men within this part of the legal profession; or, at the very least, that it will do so in the way that some of its advocates (and some of the men interviewed here) would wish. Again, two reasons suggest themselves, tracking to the complexity of the reconfiguration of gender relations that has taken place in this area.

Cultural resistance

Perceptions aren't changing as much as we might like to think. People do still have very conservative views on things, even women.

(Partner)

I think things are on a downward spiral actually, personally.

(fee-earner)

The interviews suggest that arguments highlighting the pressing nature of problems in this area downplay important issues about personal commitment, ambition and the material, subjective rewards associated with work as a lawyer:

Money motivates, status motivates ... all organisations have competition in amongst them, but some encourage it more of it than others ...

(Partner)

---

[69] R. G. Lee, op cit, 1999, p 200. Compare 'The Pain Barrier: My City Hell', *Lex*, Spring Term 2003, pp 86–88; J. Currie, 'Dead End', *Lawyer 2B*, March 2003, p 25.

[70] A time, notably, of phased redundancies across the sector, impacting primarily on fee-earners and support staff; see for example C. McPartland, 'Redundancy Bloodbath Hits Legal Sector as UK Slides into Recession' *Lawyer 2B*, 2008, vol 7(6), p 1; E. Sadowski, 'Details Emerge of A & O Redundancy Programme', *Legal Week*, 16 March 2009; C. Ruckin, 'Halliwell's Kicks off 4th Redundancy Round', *Legal Week*, 13 March 2009.

Notwithstanding the comments detailed in this chapter, many men (and women) appear to greatly enjoy many aspects of their careers as lawyers, including, for some, the demands and satisfactions which relate directly to the 'buzz ... the excitement' (fee-earner) of intensive periods of labour, working on the 'big deal', seeing something through to completion and working as 'part of a team', at times under intense pressure:

> Partners down, we all work those crazy hours. Yet there was a very good team atmosphere, it was exceptional, it was out of the ordinary ... there was this buzz.
>
> (trainee)

> You know, my deal is on the front page of *The Times* and I have been up five nights without sleep, and had just flown ... to get something signed ... how exciting is that?
>
> (fee-earner)

> I love the job ... I love doing this work.
>
> (fee-earner)

Participating in a highly competitive process of professional socialisation and credentialisation can be seen as bringing with it certain psychological and material seductions, in ways not dissimilar to what criminologists have identified in discussion of the 'seductions of crime'.[71] It is important to recognise the gendered nature of this subjective dimension in accounting for the personal lives of male lawyers. The nature of the work potentially delivers not only economic and symbolic capital, access to the upmarket consumption practices discussed above and in chapter 4, but also a powerful experiential satisfaction which should not be underestimated and may itself have a gendered dimension:[72]

> Oh, I enjoy it – it's one of the good things about the job, travel. A change of scene. I look forward to it.
>
> (Partner)

> I quite like the travel ... I am at home most of the time. I wouldn't want to not have any international travel because it's a change to go on a trip ...
>
> (Partner)

Enmeshed with the observation that these men were committed to a model of intimate fatherhood that, Dermott has suggested,[73] does not base identity as

---

[71] J. Katz, *Seductions of Crime: Moral and Sensual Attractions in Doing Evil*, New York: Basic Books, 1988.

[72] K. Purcell and P. Elias, 'Wanting to "help people" exacerbates the pay gap for young professional women', *Genet Newsletter* 3, February 2008, p 4, available at <http://www.genet.ac.uk/newsletter/newsletter_feb08.pdf>, accessed 18 March 2009.

[73] Dermott, op cit, 2008.

a good father on child care and domestic labour, this points to the complexity of the masculine identifications at play here, the nature of the investments men have in gender and the way 'subjectivity and knowledge are grounded in gender categories';[74] how, that is, ideas about the work as a lawyer[75] in this context were bound up with particular ideas about what it means to *be* a man.

Running through the observations detailed above was an awareness that professional success in the field of law enabled these men to facilitate a differentiation of the self from others – from those who did not 'make the grade', did not 'have what it takes' to succeed.[76] The demands of the job, that is, were interlinked with a psychosocial investment in ideas of superiority and distinction that, the research suggests, has a gendered dimension (in not being the 'weak man' for example). If there were undoubtedly personal and social costs to be managed in terms of family life, such as in meeting the dominant cultural codes of being a good father, these had to be balanced against the subjective rewards in terms of the status and esteem achieved on being (and to be seen to be being, including by women and children) a 'successful man' in law. There appeared a clear gap, that is, between an often ill-defined perception of a problem in this area and a general acceptance of workplace practices and cultures which, it was recognised, also 'make the firm what it is' (Partner).

Such observations suggest that, far from any coming crisis in recruitment and retention – and leaving aside the transformations wrought by severe economic downturn – there is no reason to think that the appeal of these firms will diminish in the future. Indeed, broader structural social and economic shifts relating to youth cultures, the funding of Higher Education in England and Wales and the consequences of high levels of student debt on graduation may, notwithstanding the counter-tendencies noted above, further heighten the appeal of the large law firms for law and other graduates. It is important to remember the wider context of entrenched long working hours in the UK (chapter 5)[77] and how, in comparison with salary levels and working conditions across many other employment sectors, those employed as solicitors in these large commercial organisations have been, and remain, a social group who, even if they are in some senses in the front line of economic recession, continue to be highly rewarded.[78]

---

[74] B. Featherstone, *Contemporary Fathering: Theory, Policy and Practice*, Bristol: Policy Press, 2009, p 136.

[75] H. Sommerlad, 'Researching and Theorizing the Processes of Professional Identity Formation', *Journal of Law and Society*, 2007, vol 34(2), p 190.

[76] Note here A. Adonis and S. Pollard, A Class Act: The Myth of Britain's Classless Society, London: Penguin, 1998, ch 3, 'The Super-Class'.

[77] Chapter 5; A. Gillan, 'Work until you drop: how the long-hours culture is killing us', *The Guardian*, 20 August 2005.

[78] Insecurity is endemic in much of the workforce, particularly at a time of economic downturn. Comparison with the financial circumstances facing the majority of the population is, in this regard, sobering; see S. Arthur, *Money, Choice and Control: The Financial Circumstances of Early Retirement*, London: Policy Press, 2003; S. Lissenburgh and D. Smeaton, *Employment Transitions of Older Workers: The Role of Flexible Employment in Maintaining Labour Market Participation and Promoting Job Equality*, London: Policy Press, 2003.

The 'bottom line': the market, profit and client demands

> When you are young and you are coming in as a trainee ... it shouldn't take you that long to realise that, unless you put in the hours, you don't get anywhere.
>
> (fee-earner)

Finally, despite the fact that the majority of the men interviewed stated that they ideally would like to see a change in the profession, only a minority believed that significant cultural shift within law firms would ever be possible. In a flipside to the recruitment and retention argument, above, some suggested that, paradoxically, work-life issues have a higher profile at a time of market downturn; and, as the market eventually picks up, there is no reason to think a supply of suitably qualified individuals committed to a bottom line of client service satisfaction will cease:[79]

> I've never seen any evidence either generated within the [Law] Society or anywhere else which suggests any really major problems with recruiting into the large firms, it's the smaller ones that struggle and can't get people.
>
> (Law Society representative, personal view)

> Yes, you will lose good people, women and men [because of work/life issues], but there will always be those people who don't have those worries. So you will always be able to operate on the same basis ...
>
> (Partner)

Expending considerable energies and resources on recruitment, and ensuring that the firms employ, as far as possible, the 'right' individuals, meant that the 'kind of people who get on' tended themselves to be 'very much status quo people, they are not people who will rock the boat' (Partner). It is against this context that the realities of client demand/satisfaction and market survival can be seen as key factors militating against any significant change occurring in this area. It was further noted, recognising that the role of men would be crucial in initiating change, that it remained the case, the 'brutal truth'[80] as one man put it, that men continued to be in the more senior positions within

---

79 'With the downturn in M & A [Mergers and Acquisitions] work the last couple [of] years the corporate department has gone very quiet ... People aren't doing deals, people are suing on deals' (fee-earner); see further F. Kay, 'Flight From Law: A Competing Risks Model Of Departures From Law Firms', *Law and Society Review*, 1997, vol 31(2), p 728; Duff and Webley, op cit, 2004.

80 One Partner, generally sympathetic to greater flexibility, recounted how he had recently been asked by a female trainee about her future within the firm, given that she did plan to become a mother; 'What I said to her was, if you want to have a career here and you want to go off and have children there is nothing intrinsically that is going to stop you, but you are going to have to think very carefully how you schedule your commitments and arrange your life and you have to be quite clinical about it, and that's the brutal response I think' (Partner).

the law firms relative to women, and generally, were more resistant to change than women:

> For a lot of women maternity leave stretches out for 2 or 3 years, probably at the time that's crucial to them becoming Partners. So unless you change the ... whole criteria from which we select Partners then you are not going to see that changing and I'm not sure it should. *We are a money-making organisation,* only we sell expertise, we sell commitment *and that's the bottom line.*
>
> (trainee, my emphasis)

Set against the backdrop of the well-documented culture of 'up or out' and an organisational imperative towards profit maximisation that frames the management of attrition within large law firms,[81] losing staff at moments of market downturn, especially those who 'did not have what it takes', should not necessarily be considered a problem in and of itself. There is no reason to think that the supply of suitably qualified individuals will dry up. Nor, from the perspective of those recruited, can it be assumed that the majority will go on to question the view that the bottom line of client service satisfaction and market survival will (and must) prevail:

> I don't know how easy a change can be at the end of the day ... we are primarily a business ... they [Partners] are not going to do anything which is going to make us less profitable ...
>
> (fee-earner)

> We say, well, that's fine, and we'll do everything we can ... but you have to appreciate that the work takes priority, that's what this place is about and if you can't accept that then you shouldn't have come. We are very frank about that ... Now, that doesn't mean they can't have a life, but it does mean that *if there is a conflict your life will come second, it always does.*
>
> (Partner, my emphasis)

Whilst the issues of work-life balance and related diversity agendas undoubtedly have a high profile in the contemporary profession, some of the men saw firm initiatives as little more than paying lip-service to external pressures. At times a stronger degree of cynicism was expressed about the genuine depth of concern to change practice and culture in this area[82]:

---

[81] Lee, op cit, 2000; 'Now, because of the economic conditions the firm has been quite happy to lose people – indeed, some have even had to manage their attrition up a little bit ... ' (HR Director); 'As the market is down people aren't retaining and recruiting as many people as they used to' (trainee).

[82] 'We are trying to compete for good quality candidates ... [so] we try to present something a little bit different, one area where we can score over those competitors is producing a better work-life balance for everybody' (HR Director). 'it's just PR', "[It's about] ... marketing, profile building. It gives a good image that the firm is supportive ... ' (fee-earner).

... lip-service is paid to these things ... [but] the reality [in this firm] is that there was, and I think still is in the organisation ... a growing disrespect for all aspects of work-life balance.

(Partner)

Improved family policies had been introduced ... as a part of a recruitment drive or part of a retention exercise. But as soon as that issue has gone away then the policies have evaporated. It's that sort of like, you know, it's the dress-down thing; then somebody whispers in your ear 'don't throw your suits away'. It's that sort of thing.

(Partner)

For one man there was a profound dishonesty in 'all this talk of diversity':

I struggle with hypocrisy ... I would prefer an organisation which simply said 'we are going to work you to death and treat you like rubbish, and we don't care a damn about you. We will pay you loads and that's the way it is – you can either do it or not.' There is something [worse] ... about an organisation that purports to be all things caring, investors in people and all that goes with it, but actually applies very high levels of pressure.

(Partner)

This reading supports work that suggests, far from seeing a 'feminisation' of the legal profession as a result of the entry of women, it may be more accurate to trace a 'gendered segmentation'[83] whereby resistance to change, a 'defence mechanism' for an embattled profession, connects to an ideology of women's difference in such a way that elite groups maintain their status and rewards. These issues, I argue in the concluding section, relate to how ideas of masculinity have themselves been transformed in this area.

The legal profession: business masculinities and the contradictions of gender

What do you dream of? Age 17: Buy a Suit – Age 35: Buy a Hand-Made suit – Age 52: Burn the Suit.

(Advertisement for American Express Card, 2003)

As noted in chapter 1, it is men, and not women, who have historically been understood to be largely free from family responsibilities and expectations, entitled to act in ways appropriate to such a position. Women's domestic

---

[83] S. Bolton and D. Muzio, 'Can't Live With 'Em; Can't Live Without 'Em; Gendered Segmentation in the Legal Profession', *Sociology*, 2007, vol 41(1), p 47.

labour has, in contrast to men's, been routinely commodified, characterised as the expression of (naturally given) love and commitment. The 'innate characteristics of the sexes', the fact that it is women who tend to remain primary caregivers regardless of their employment status 'and the incontrovertible needs of corporations and of small children' have been seen to merge in a 'complex matrix of gendered beliefs, practices and structural arrangements'.[84] Parenting, in short, like 'working life', remains an activity deeply infused with social relations of gender. It is men, on this view, who have been 'cut' from the inevitable dependencies associated with family life whilst, at the same time, women who do wish to care and nurture children have been devalued.[85]

Yet, we have seen in chapter 5, if not without contradiction and contestation, these ideas about gender may well be shifting in significant respects within a social and legal context marked by ideas of gender neutrality and egalitarianism. This is, we have seen in this book, a context in which men have been encouraged to take on greater responsibility, not just for children but also for their personal lives in a more general sense. This chapter has explored, in the context of the contemporary legal profession, how shifting experiences of work and family practices may be reshaping perceptions of what being a lawyer entails. Far from deploying a monolithic ideal of the masculine culture of law, or of law as a somehow straightforwardly masculine profession, however, the picture painted by these men is far more complex. This reading suggests, importantly, that attitudes are in a state of considerable flux.

Among dominant groups of men, Connell and Messerschmidt have argued, 'circles of social embodiment constantly involve the institutions on which their privileges rest'.[86] Drawing on the work of Donaldson and Poynting,[87] they note the 'everyday' importance of how 'characteristic sports, leisure and eating

---

[84] K. Abrams, 'Cross-Dressing in the Master's Clothes', *Yale Law Journal*, vol 109, p 745; see further Williams, op cit, 2000; M. Selmi, 'Care Work and the Road to Equality: A Commentary on Fineman and Williams', *Chicago-Kent Law Review*, 2001, vol 76, p 1557; M. Selmi, 'The Work-Family Conflict: An Essay on Employers, Men and Responsibility', *University of St Thomas Law Review*, 2007, vol 4, p 573; C. Fuchs-Epstein, C. Seron, B. Oglensky and R. Saute, *The Part-Time Paradox: Time Norms, Professional Life, Family and Gender*, London: Routledge, 1999. Compare C. Hakim, *Key Issues in Women's Work: Female Heterogeneity and the Polarisation of Women's Employment*, London: Routledge-Cavendish, 2004.

[85] C. Albiston, 'Anti-Essentialism and the Work/Family Dilemma', *Berkeley Journal of Gender, Law and Justice*, 2005, vol 20, p 30.

[86] R. W. Connell and J. W. Messerschmidt, 'Hegemonic Masculinity: Rethinking the Concept', *Gender and Society*, 2005, vol 19(6), pp 829 852.

[87] M. Donaldson and S. Poynting, 'The Time of Their Lives: Time, Work and Leisure in the Daily Lives of Ruling Class Men', in N. Hollier (ed), *Ruling Australia: The Power, Privilege and Politics of the New Ruling Class*, Melbourne: Australian Scholarly Press.

practices deploy their wealth and establish relations of distance and dominance over other men's bodies'. This opens up a rich field of research 'especially when we consider how expensive technologies – computer systems, global air travel, secure communications – amplify the physical powers of elite men's bodies'.[88] Aspects of the gendered identifications of male lawyers discussed above illustrate these themes in a particularly clear way. Elsewhere, Connell and Wood have explored the interconnections between globalisation and business masculinities,[89] noting the phenomena of 'transnational business masculinity'. These are described in relation to socially powerful men who are nonetheless marked by gender anxieties (for example, in their role as fathers), who engage in 'intense and stressful' work (much like these male lawyers), who are reflective of the changes they see about them (like these men) and who, importantly, are aware that they are subject to 'mutual scrutiny'.

This study broadly supports, in the context of the field of law, Connell and Woods's reading of business masculinities. We have seen above, as well as in chapter 4, how male lawyers view their life and career as an enterprise or project, who self-consciously manage not just their finances but also their bodies and emotions, often in complex ways in the context of an organisation that calls for contradictory practices (chapter 4). Linking to the depiction of the re-masculinised university in chapter 2, and connected to broader shifts around work and families detailed in chapter 5, social and economic changes have, I suggest, reshaped and remodelled earlier ideas about lawyers and the legal profession. One feature of this has been the move from a model of the 'lawyer as gentlemen' to the very different kind of entrepreneurial, business masculinity depicted in this chapter,[90] marked by a 'tolerance to diversity' and the equality agendas associated with the entry of women into the profession. A form of transnational business masculinity, that is, has replaced 'models of bourgeois masculinity that were embedded more in local organizations', a form of masculinity 'marked by egocentrism, conditional loyalties and a declining sense of responsibility'.[91]

There is, Connell and Wood observe, no one mode of participating in transnational (legal) business, just as there is no one model of transnational business masculinity or gender order that is imposed on the large law firm. Rather, law firms interacting with a range of discourses around gender, produce distinctive configurations of masculinity in specific settings. These masculinities remain, however, centrally related to power. In terms of the framework set out in chapter 1, hegemonic masculinity emerges in the

---

[88] Connell and Messerschmidt, op cit, 2005, p 852.

[89] R. W. Connell and J. Wood, 'Globalization and Business Masculinities', *Men and Masculinities*, 2005, vol 7(4), p 347.

[90] Boon, op cit, 2005; M. Burrage, 'From a Gentleman's to a Public profession: Status and Politics in the History of English Solicitors', *International Journal of the Legal Profession*, 1996, vol 3, p 45.

[91] Ashe, op cit, 2007, p 150.

practices and values of powerful men such as these, even though they may not exhibit it in their everyday behaviour. It is these 'business executives, political executives ... who [still] control dominant institutions'[92] within a global gender order challenged by the entry of women, in this case into the legal profession. As has been noted in other contexts, men in various institutions may find it easier to support gender equality if it fits their agendas of, for example, modernisation; 'they are less likely to change the power structures of their own personal relationships'.[93] However, many aspects of their lives, I have argued, can be seen as indicative of 'crisis tendencies' around gender and economic globalisation that have heightened the insecurity of these men, all the more so in the context of economic recession and widespread redundancies in the legal profession.[94] Recognition of the differential commitments men have to dominant modes of masculinity suggests that any discussion of masculinity and the legal profession must be textured and nuanced. Certainly, it is too simplistic to say that law is 'masculine' without noting how, in this context, the meaning of masculinity has changed significantly.

In light of the above, the experiences of these men appear to be interlinked with still powerful economic and cultural imperatives, as well as subjective investments, around the meaning and value of paid work. However, they indicate that men are negotiating issues of work-life balance in different ways from previous generations. Just as the failure to address questions of gender difference has been described as a rationality mistake[95] within social policy (chapter 5), studies of the legal profession will miss much if they fail to engage with the multi-layered and fragmentary nature of men's gendered experiences. The complicated moral and economic rationalities by which women and men make decisions about and experience work-life balance suggest that the gender-neutral ideal on which policy in this area has rested stands in a complex relation to individual aspirations and practices, a point noted in chapter 5 in relation to the effacing of women within a policy debate focused on engaging fathers in families. Some men, in law as in other fields of work, encounter deeply entrenched institutional, cultural and organisational resistance to taking up what limited provision for leave and flexible working is available. Some experience powerful subjective tensions between their commitments to a breadwinner model of fathering and the ideas of the hands-on, nurturing parent associated with the new father ideal (chapter 5). Others, however, do not (or do not appear to), and the cultural uncertainties

---

[92] Ashe, op cit, 2007, p 150.

[93] Connell, op cit, 1997, p 7. See further Ashe, op cit, 2007, p 150.

[94] Note, for example, R. Susskind, *The End of Lawyers? Rethinking the Nature of Legal Services*, Oxford: OUP, 2008.

[95] A. Barlow, S. Duncan and G. James, 'New Labour, the Rationality Mistake and Family Policy in Britain', in A. Carling, S. Duncan and R. Edwards (eds), *Analysing Families: Morality and Rationality in Policy and Practice*, London: Routledge, 2002.

which have resulted from the dissolving of hitherto normative gendered ideals are considerable, not least around the shifting negotiations of child care and domestic labour. It is here that Dermott's notion of intimate fatherhood provides a useful handle on how these men are able to hold together these contradictory discourses about men, care and work, denoting a gendered parenting ideal that remains powerful and resonant for many men.

What this reading has shown is that discussion of masculinities must be situated within specific socio-cultural and economic contexts. Much of the literature on men, gender and employment has tended to focus on social, political and cultural consequences of the collapse of traditional working-class male jobs. For some time, however, and with a heightened significance in the context of an economic recession, ongoing as I write this, there is evidence to support the claim that many middle-class men have also been profoundly challenged by these reconfigurations of gender. In the case of the legal profession, this is a social context in which lawyers have experienced, across countries, increased competition and growing regulation. In such a process, as the North American writers Kimmel and Kaufman have observed:

> Although ... economic, political and social changes have affected all different groups of men in radically different ways, perhaps the hardest hit *psychologically* were middle-class, straight, white men from their late twenties through their forties. For these were the men who not only inherited a prescription for manhood that included economic autonomy ... public patriarchy ... they were also men who believed themselves entitled to the power that attended upon *the successful demonstration of masculinity*.[96]

This chapter, in looking to the experiences of men at an interpersonal, micro-political level, has told us something of *how* ideas about this successful demonstration of masculinity have shifted. The changes which have taken place in the legal profession in recent years have, it would seem, reshaped, to degrees, understandings of what being a (successful) lawyer entails. These changes are bound up with a broader reconfiguration of the relationship between men, law and gender that is impacting on the legal profession in some at times contradictory ways.

---

[96] M. Kimmel and M. Kaufman, 'Weekend Warriors: The New Men's Movement' in M. Kimmel (ed), *The Politics of Manhood: Pro feminist Men Respond to the Mythopoetic Men's Movement (and the Mythopoetic Leaders Answer)*, Philadelphia, PA: Temple University Press, 1995, p 18, original emphasis. See further B. Martin, 'Knowledge, Identity and the Middle-Class: From Collective to Individualised Class Formation?', *The Sociological Review*, 1998, vol 46 p 653.

Chapter 7

On fathers' rights, law and gender

Recasting the questions about men, masculinities and personal life

Introduction

I began chapter 5 with an observation made by Martha Fineman in her 2004 book *The Autonomy Myth*. What has been missing from policy and reform discussion, she suggested, is a debate about the nature of fatherhood and 'the transformation of the role of the father in response to changing expectations, norms and practices'.[1] 'How', she asked, might a 'desire for gender neutrality and the ideal of egalitarianism have played a role in the creation of a new set of norms for fatherhood'?[2] This chapter, building on the discussion of law, gender and policy in chapter 5, explores these questions in the context of recent debates in England and Wales concerning post-separation contact. More specifically, focusing on contemporary fathers' rights activism, it considers the gendered politics shaping organised claims for recognition of men as 'active fathers' and the interrelationship between gender, rights and responsibility within this high-profile, and politically sensitive, area of law. A growing body of work on fathers' rights politics,[3] troubled by the arguments advanced by and the impact of fathers' organisations,[4] has suggested that there is a pressing need to articulate what significance fathers' adopting a rights-based approach might have had upon the idea of welfare and its practical application

---

[1] M. Fineman, *The Autonomy Myth*, New York: The New Press, 2004, p 195.

[2] Fineman, op cit, 2004.

[3] For example J. Crowley, *Defiant Dads: Fathers' Rights Activism in America*, Ithaca, NY: Cornell University Press, 2008; R. Collier and S. Sheldon (eds), *Fathers Rights' Activism and Legal Reform*, Oxford: Hart, 2006; B. Featherstone, *Contemporary Fathering: Theory, Policy and Practice*, Bristol: Policy Press, 2009, ch 7; E. Dermott, *Intimate Fatherhood: A Sociological Analysis*, London: Routledge, 2008, pp 120–23; A. Gavanas, *Fatherhood Politics in the United States: Masculinity, Sexuality, Race and Marriage*, Chicago, IL: University of Illinois Press, 2004; R Collier, 'Fathers 4 Justice, Law and the New Politics of Fatherhood', *Child and Family Law Quarterly*, 2005, vol 17, p 511.

[4] A. Diduck and F. Kaganas, *Family Law, Gender and the State: Text, Cases and Materials*, Oxford: Hart 2006, 2nd edn, comment that the 'fathers' rights campaigns [do] appear to have had the effect of galvanising the government and the courts into action against mothers whom they see as obstructive', p 561.

in the field of family law.[5] Particular concern has been expressed about the influence of fathers' activism on legal policy and practice, and the implications for women and children especially.[6] Within one strand of literature, the resurgence of fathers' claims in the legal arena has been interpreted as something akin to a backlash to feminism, if not the reassertion of a form of hyper-masculinity then a problematic, troubling and deeply regressive shift in the terrain of family politics.[7]

This chapter questions these ideas, tracing a way through the often highly polarised debates in the area and locating a shifting political terrain around fathers' rights in the context of evolving legal frameworks marked by gender neutrality and formal equality. Drawing on a different literature from that which has informed much discussion to date, I suggest that contemporary debates are characterised, if not by crisis tendencies in relation to gender, then by significant contradictions and tensions around ideas of men, masculinity and the role of law. In a telling observation, Featherstone has noted how 'given the symbolic weight and often the centrality of fathering practices for everyday lives', to some extent 'men and masculinities scholars have vacated the field [of fathers' rights politics] and left a vacuum for the conservatives to fill'.[8] This chapter seeks to address this vacuum, to re-read the political terrain and, in so doing, to provide a deeper understanding of the relationship between law, men and gender in this area.

The structure of the argument is as follows. In the first section I ground the discussion in the context of what is known about men's parenting following separation and a legal framework that has, I suggest, following discussion in chapter 5, redrawn understandings of what a good father entails in law. I proceed, in the second section, to explore the development of fathers' rights politics in the UK since the early 1970s, tracking significant shifts in the arguments advanced by fathers' groups. A distinctive problem of law, I suggest, has been constructed in these debates. In the third section, I consider the critique of fathers' rights advanced within a rich international and interdisciplinary

---

[5] For further comment see J. Herring, S. Choudhry and J. Wallbank (eds), *Rights, Gender and Family Law*, London: Routledge-Cavendish, 2009.

[6] C. Smart, 'Equal Shares: Rights for Fathers or Recognition for Children?', *Critical Social Policy*, 2004, vol 24(4), p 484; C. Smart, 'The Ethic of Justice Strikes Back' in A. Diduck and K. O'Donovan (eds), *Feminist Perspectives On Family Law*, London: Routledge-Cavendish, 2006; C. Smart, 'Losing the Struggle for Another Voice: The Case of Family Law', *Dalhousie Law Journal*, 1995, vol 18(2), p 173. Note also S. Coltrane and N. Hickman, 'The Rhetoric of Rights and Needs: Moral Discourse in the Reform of Child Custody and Support Laws', *Social Problems*, 1992, vol 39, p 400.

[7] M. Flood, 'Backlash: Angry Men's Movements' in S. E. Rossi (ed) *The Battle and Backlash Rage On: Why Feminism Cannot be Obsolete*, Philadelphia, PA: Xlibris Press, 2004. Contrast S. Boyd, 'Backlash and the Construction of Legal Knowledge: The Case of Child Custody Law', *Windsor Year Book of Access to Justice*, 2001, vol 20, p 141; S. Boyd, 'Backlash Against Feminism: Canadian Custody and Access Reform Debates of the Late Twentieth Century', *Canadian Journal of Women and Law*, 2004, vol 16(2), p 255.

[8] Featherstone, op cit, 2009, p 110.

literature, detailing key concerns that have been expressed about the impact and politics of fathers' rights activism. The critique I shall suggest leaves some important questions unanswered and, in the final section, I recast the debate about fathers' rights and law. Focusing on issues of masculinities, intimacy and emotion, and linking to legal and policy frameworks around post-separation parenting, I argue that the increased political and cultural prominence of fathers' rights groups is more complex, and doubled-edged, than might at first seem to be the case. Far from dismissing fathers' rights activism as a minority activity, this chapter suggests that these developments tell us much about changing ideas of the responsibilities and obligations that accrue to that status of father, about parenting cultures and the relationship between law and personal life more generally.[9]

Contextualising the debate: fathers' rights, law and gender

Separated fathers, legal policy and social change

In debates about post-divorce/separation contact, a vocal, visible and increasingly organised fathers' movement[10] has been credited, to varying degrees across jurisdictions,[11] with influencing the direction of family law reform. Fathers' rights groups have been described as seeking to 'refashion and reposition fatherhood in the legal and cultural imaginary'[12] in ways that draw not only on ideas about men, equality and gender neutrality discussed in chapter 5, but also on two seemingly competing narratives about fatherhood. One, aligned with the themes of crisis and fragmentation considered in chapter 1, highlights the fragility of men's relationships with women and children, the contingent, problematic nature of male parenting. Interlinked to the argument

[9] See further C. Smart, *Personal Life*, Cambridge: Polity 2007; J. Eekelaar, *Family Law and Personal Life*, Oxford: Oxford University Press, 2006.

[10] On the idea of a 'movement' see further Collier and Sheldon (eds), op cit, 2006, ch 1; M. Messner, *Politics of Masculinities: Men in Movements*, London: Sage, 1997; K. Clatterbaugh, *Contemporary Perspectives on Masculinity*, Boulder, CO: Westview Press, 2000.

[11] On developments in Canada and Australia note S. Boyd, 'Demonizing Mothers: Fathers' Rights Discourses in Child Custody Law Reform Processes', *Journal of the Association for Research in Mothering*, 2004, vol 6(1), p 52; H. Rhoades, 'The "Non Contact Mother": Reconstructions of Motherhood in the Era of the New Father', *International Journal of Law, Policy and the Family*, 2002, vol 16, p 72; H. Rhoades, 'The Rise of Shared Parenting Laws – a Critical Reflection', *Canadian Journal of Family Law*, 2002, vol 19, p 75; M. Kaye and J. Tolmie, 'Discoursing Dads: The Rhetorical Devices of Fathers' Rights Groups', *Melbourne University Law Review*, 1998, vol 22, p 184; S. Boyd and C. F. Young, 'Who Influences Family Law Reform? Discourses on Motherhood and Fatherhood in Legislative Reform Debates in Canada', *Studies in Law Politics and Society*, 2002, p 43. Specifically on the differences between Canada and Australia, see H. Rhoades and S. Boyd, 'Reforming Custody Laws: A Comparative Study', *International Journal of Law, Policy and the Family*, 2004, vol 18, p 119; Flood, op cit, 2004.

[12] Smart, op cit, 2006, 'The Ethic of Justice', p 123.

that father 'absence'[13] from families is connected to a range of social problems,[14] this maps to the idea, considered below, that fathers have become the new victims of family law.

The other narrative, in contrast, draws on the more optimistic vision of fathering practices discussed in chapter 5, highlighting the extent to which men's practices, aspirations and experiences have changed and are different, in positive ways, from what they were at earlier historical moments. This position, supported by research studies and policy reports,[15] sees the relationship between men and children as having become, not less, but more, enduring. Far from any social and legal acceptance of men's physical and/or emotional distance from children following separation, seen as a further sign of men's 'flight from commitment',[16] separation opens the door to a new *kind* of parenting for men.[17] This approach to post-separation fathering, encapsulated in the concept of parental responsibility in the Children Act 1989, has become increasingly significant in family policy in England and Wales (see below). It draws on two further specific, interrelated ideas about fatherhood. First, notwithstanding the fact that a significant proportion of children stay in contact with their fathers following separation,[18] a growing policy concern is about the numbers who lose touch.[19] This problem is exacerbated in a social context where large numbers of children experience divorce and fathering has become, for many, an activity occurring across households, or is undertaken by men who are not necessarily the genetic fathers of the children with whom they live.[20] Second, recognising that the

---

[13] An idea that should itself be treated with considerable caution: J. Bradshaw et al, *Absent Fathers?* London: Routledge, 1999; R. Collier and S. Sheldon, *Fragmenting Fatherhood: A Socio-Legal Study*, Oxford: Hart 2008, ch 1.

[14] Centre for Social Justice, *The Family Law Review Interim Report*, London: Centre for Social Justice, 2008, on the idea of 'guesting fathers'; I. Duncan Smith, 'Now They Want to Abolish Fatherhood', *Mail on Sunday*, 18 November 2007, News 29; N. Dennis and G. Erdos, *Families Without Fatherhood*, London: Institute of Economic Affairs, 1993.

[15] See the reading in K. Stanley, *Daddy Dearest? Active Fatherhood and Public Policy*, London: Institute for Public Policy Research, 2005. See further chapter 5.

[16] B. Ehrenreich, *The Hearts of Men and the Flight from Commitment*, London: Pluto, 1983.

[17] There has been an explosion of texts, including numerous self-help books, containing advice and information aimed at supporting separated fathers: for example S. Barker and A. Einstein, *How to Be a Great Divorced Dad*, Slough: Foulsham, 2007.

[18] R. Creasey et al, 'Family Networks and Parenting Support in England and Wales' in C. Attwood et al, *2001 Home Office Citizenship Survey: People, Families and Communities* London: Home Office Research, Development and Statistics Directorate, 2003. See M. O'Brien, 'Social Science and Public Policy Perspectives on Fatherhood' in M. E. Lamb (ed), *The Role of the Father in Child Development*, Hoboken, NJ: John Wiley, 2004.

[19] B. Simpson, J. A. Jessop and P. McCarthy, 'Fathers After Divorce' in A. Bainham, B. Lindley and M. Richards (eds), *Children and their Families: Contact, Rights and Welfare*, Oxford: Hart, 2003; B. Simpson, P. McCarthy and J. Walker, *Being There: Fathers After Divorce*, Newcastle: Centre for Family Studies, University of Newcastle upon Tyne, 1995.

[20] Of the 12 million children in the country, it is estimated that more than one in four now have separated parents. About 45% of marriages now end in divorce: Office for National Statistics,

majority of post-separation parenting arrangements, estimated at around 90 per cent, are uncontested,[21] politicians, judges and legal policy-makers alike have become increasingly troubled about the other 10 per cent of cases involving varying degrees of parental conflict and hostility. In these cases, where conflict is often entrenched, some parents (both fathers and mothers), it has been suggested, can be 'vengeful' in their pursuit of justice through the courts.[22] These cases provide one of the main contexts for contemporary disputes in relation to the making and enforcement of contact orders under section 8 of the Children Act 1989 (see further below).

Against this backdrop, tracking to a growing research base highlighting the importance of the role of the father in child development and welfare (chapter 5), increasing attention has been paid to the problems that can follow, for parents, children, wider kin and society,[23] from parental conflict.[24] Set against a literature detailing the negative effects of such conflict on children, whether during subsisting relationships or in the process of separation and divorce,[25] there has been a growing view at policy level that 'fathers matter'.[26] Allied to

Population Trends, London: Palgrave Macmillan, London, 2008, <http://www.statistics.gov.uk/downloads/theme_population/Population_Trends_131_web.pdf>, accessed 30 March 2008. Further, around one in three children in England and Wales will experience parental divorce before the age of 16: J. Hunt with C. Roberts, *Family Policy Briefing 3: Child Contact with Non Resident Parents*, Oxford: Department of Social Policy and Social Work, University of Oxford, 2004; J. Hunt, *Researching Contact*, London: National Council for One Parent Families. See further C. Smart and B. Neale, *Family Fragments?* Cambridge: Polity, 1999.

21 Hunt with Roberts, op cit, 2004.

22 G. Vallance-Webb, 'Child Contact: Vengeful Mothers, Good Fathers and Vice Versa', *Family Law*, 2008, p 678. Also M. Piercy, 'Intractable Contact Disputes', *Family Law*, 2004, p 815.

23 S. Day Sclater and M. Richards, 'How Adults Cope with Divorce – Strategies for Survival', *Family Law*, 1995, p 143; F. Kaganas, 'Grandparents' Rights and Grandparents' Campaigns', *Child and Family Law Quarterly*, 2007, vol 19(1), p 17; F. Kaganas and C. Piper, 'Grandparents and Contact: "Rights vs Welfare" Revisited', *International Journal of Law, Policy and Family*, 2001, vol 15(2), p 250.

24 For an excellent overview of the literature on separated fathers generally, see G. B. Wilson, 'The Non-resident Parental Role For Separated Fathers: A Review', *International Journal of Law*, 2006, *Policy and the Family*, p 1.

25 J. Reynolds (ed), *Not in Front of the Children?: How Conflict Between Parents Affects Children*, London: One Plus One, 2001; B. Rodgers and J. Pryor, *Divorce and Separation: Outcomes for Children*, York: Joseph Rowntree Foundation, 1998; M. L. Sturge-Apple, P. T. Davies and E. M. Cummings, 'The Impact of Hostility and Withdrawal in Interparental Conflict on Parental Emotional Unavailability and Children's Adjustment Difficulties', *Child Development*, 2006, vol 77(5), p 1623.

26 Remembering that, in the vast majority of cases, estimated at around 90 per cent, children living in lone parent families in England and Wales will live with their mothers: A. Blackwell and F. Dawe, *Non-Residential Parental Contact*, London: Lord Chancellor's Office, 2003; Hunt with Roberts, op cit, 2004; J. Pryor and B. Rodgers, *Children in Changing Families: Life after Parental Separation*, Oxford: Blackwell, 2001; P. R. Amato and J. G. Gilbreth, 'Non-Resident Fathers and Children's Wellbeing: A Meta-Analysis', *Journal of Marriage and Family*, 1999, vol 61, p 557; J. Dunn and K. Deater-Deckard, *Children's Views of their Changing Families*, York: York Publishing Services/Joseph Rowntree Foundation, 2001.

greater awareness of the difficulties entailed in establishing and maintaining post-separation relationships between non-resident fathers and their children,[27] how, therefore, has law responded to these dilemmas? How has law been used to promote consensus, reduce conflict and, with it, encourage 'good enough' relationships between fathers and children?

Divorce is widely seen within legal policy debates to be not so much as a one-off event but, rather, as an ongoing process, a continuing dynamic that obliges parents to 'position themselves in relation to a range of often competing discourses (legal, welfare, therapeutic and, more recently, human rights) and to find ways of living alongside them'.[28] Law has moved, that is, from a concern with moral judgement and the determination of fault and, increasingly, towards what has been described by Helen Reece as a model of 'divorcing responsibly'. In this post-liberal visioning of divorce it is assumed that both women and men are (or, at least, should be) committed to a co-parenting ideal, able to act in ways that are rational, settlement minded and altruistic.[29] 'Framed at the intersections of legal practice, social policy, welfare ideology, relationship breakdown and personal pain',[30] the development of law from the mid-1990s onwards has reflected the rethinking of the father figure detailed in chapter 5 and related concerns about conflicted separation discussed above. It has also been enmeshed with this reframing of divorce as a certain kind of social problem.[31]

The repositioning of fatherhood, importantly, has been a central element of this re-visioning of post-separation life.[32] Core beliefs within the new

---

[27] For excellent discussion see M. Maclean (ed), *Parenting After Partnering: Containing Conflict After Separation*, Oxford: Hart, 2007; also J. Lewis and E. Welsh, 'Fathering Practices in Twenty-Six Intact Families and their Implications for Child Contact', *International Journal of Law in Context*, 2005, vol 1(1), p 81.

[28] F. Kaganas and S. Day Sclater, 'Contact Disputes: Narrative Constructions of "Good" Parents', *Feminist Legal Studies*, 2004, vol 12(1), p 2 at p 3; S. Day Sclater and F. Kaganas, 'Contact Mothers: Welfare and Rights' in A. Bainham, B. Lindley and M. Richards (eds), *Children and their Families: Contact, Rights and Welfare*, Oxford: Hart, 2003.

[29] H. Reece, *Divorcing Responsibly*, Oxford: Hart, 2003; C. Piper, *The Responsible Parent*, Brighton: Harvester Wheatsheaf, 1993; J. Dewar, 'The Normal Chaos of Family Law', *Modern Law Review*, 1998, vol 61, p 467. See also S. Boyd, 'Review Essay: Being Responsible in the New Family Law', *International Journal of Law in Context*, 2005, vol 1(2), p 199; R. van Krieken, 'The "Best Interests of the Child" and Parental Separation on the "Civilising of Parents"', *Modern Law Review*, 2005, vol 68(1), p 25; R. Collier, 'The Dashing of a "Liberal Dream"? The Information Meeting, the "New Family" and the Limits of Law', *Child and Family Law Quarterly*, 1999, vol 11, p 257.

[30] Kaganas and Day Sclater, op cit, 2004.

[31] S. Coltrane and M. Adams, 'The Social Construction of the "Divorce Problem"', *Family Relations*, 2003, vol 52, p 363.

[32] See further Smart and Neale, op cit, 1999, *Family Fragments*; C. Smart and B. Neale, '"I Hadn't Really Thought About It": New Identities/New Fatherhoods' in J. Seymour and P. Bagguley (eds), *Relating Intimacies: Power and Resistance*, Basingstoke: Palgrave Macmillan, 1999. C. Smart, 'Wishful Thinking and Harmful Tinkering? Sociological Reflections on Family Policy' *Journal of Social Policy*, 1997, vol 26(3), p 1; B. Neale and C. Smart, 'Experiments with Parenthood?', *Sociology*, 1997, vol 31(2), p 201; C. Smart and B. Neale, 'Good Enough Morality?

welfarism and pro-contact culture have been, first, that children are vulnerable,[33] with the conflicted divorce and separation potentially damaging and, second, that non-resident parents (the majority of whom are fathers) should have contact with their children, provided arrangements are safe and in the best interests of the child.[34] What has occurred, Carol Smart and Bren Neale have suggested,[35] is a clear and determined attempt to effect 'social engineering' in the area of the family by, in Smart's words, 'changing the very nature of post-divorce family life'.[36] Thus, with regard to contact and residence,[37] by 2005 the UK government described as a core belief of family policy their commitment to ensuring that 'both parents should continue to have a meaningful relationship with their children after separation as long as it is safe and in the child's best interests'.[38]

If we look more closely at these developments, however, I have argued elsewhere, with Sally Sheldon, that this policy move involved a reframing of fatherhood that rested on gendered ideas about fathers' responsibilities, most clearly in relation to the provision of child support and the role of the separated father in promoting child welfare and development.[39] Encapsulated in the idea that the non-residential father is 'once a parent, always a parent', the

Divorce and Postmodernity', *Critical Social Policy*, 1997, vol 17(4), p 3; C. Smart, 'The "New" Parenthood: Fathers and Mothers After Divorce' in E. Silva and C. Smart (eds), *The New Family?* London: Sage, 1999; J. Drakich, 'In Search of the Better Parent: The Social Construction of Ideologies of Fatherhood', *Canadian Journal of Women and the Law*, 1989, vol 3, p 69. Compare A. James and M. Richards, 'Sociological Perspectives, Family Policy and Children: Adult Thinking and Sociological tinkering', *Journal of Social Welfare and Family Law*, 1999, vol 21 (1), p 23.

[33] On shifting images of children in this context, see F. Kaganas and A. Diduck, 'Incomplete Citizens: Changing Images of Post-Separation Children', *Modern Law Review*, 2004, vol 67(6), p 959. Also C. Smart, A. Wade and B. Neale, 'Objects of Concern? Children and Divorce', *Child and Family Law Quarterly*, 1999, vol 11(4), p 365; C. Smart, 'From Children's Shoes to Children's Voices', *Family Court Review: An International Journal*, 2002, vol 40(3), p 305; I. Butler et al, *Divorcing Children: Children's Experiences of Their Parents' Divorce*, London: Jessica Kingsley Publishers; C. Piper, 'Divorce Reform and the Image of the Child', *Journal of Law and Society*, 1996, vol 23(3), p 364; B. Neale and C. Smart, 'In Whose Best Interests? Theorising Family Life Following Parental Separation or Divorce' in S. Day Sclater and C. Piper (eds), *Undercurrents of Divorce*, Aldershot: Ashgate, 1999; Kaganas and Diduck, op cit, 2004.

[34] On developments in the US context, and generally, see J. Carbone, *From Partners to Parents: The Second Revolution in Family Law*, Columbia, NY: Columbia University Press, 2000.

[35] Smart and Neale, op cit, 1999, *Family Fragments*.

[36] Smart, op cit, 1997, 'Wishful thinking … '.

[37] Introduced by the Children Act 1989 to replace the language of custody and access.

[38] C. Falconer, R. Kelly and P. Hewitt, 'Ministerial Foreword' in HM Government, *Parental Separation: Children's Needs and Parents' Responsibilities: Next Steps*, Cm 6452, London: HMSO, 2005. See further S. Gilmore, 'Contact/Shared Residence and Child Well-Being: Research Evidence and its Implications for Legal Decision Making', *International Journal of Law, Policy and the Family*, 2006, vol 20, p 344.

[39] Collier and Sheldon, op cit, 2008. For detailed discussion of child support, see N. Wikeley, *Child Support: Law and Policy*, Oxford: Hart, 2006.

desirability of contact has now been embedded within legislation, legal practice and a vast body of relevant case law,[40] as well as being reflected in numerous policy initiatives and Ministerial statements. Set against such a legal policy backdrop, therefore, what have fathers' rights groups themselves argued? What, in their view, is 'wrong' with a legal policy that would seem, on the surface, to have accorded increasing significance to the importance of fathers?

Fathers' rights groups and the problem of law

There exists, in the UK as elsewhere, no *one* fathers' rights perspective or agenda. Rather, within what is at best a loosely based coalition there is a diversity of approaches and political views. The growing international research literature on fathers' rights reveals something of this diversity, the different elements that make up a 'fathers' movement'.[41] It is necessary to differentiate between the views of fathers' rights activists and those of 'fathers' in a more general sense. Significantly, we shall see, many groups eschew the term 'fathers' rights', particularly those who position themselves as social care organisations.[42] Further, national economic, political and cultural contexts pertaining to the substantive law and processes of distinctive legal systems mediate how these debates evolve at particular moments.[43] Fathers' rights politics are culturally specific, situated within grounded contexts (for example, the welfare regimes and political traditions of different countries). The embrace of a rule-based or formal equality claim has been a significant strategy of fathers' rights groups internationally in their resort to law.[44] We should not overstate the significance of this equality claim, however, in considering the broader activities of groups, an issue to which I shall return.

[40] For discussion see J. Herring, *Family Law*, 3rd edn, Harlow: Pearson Longman, 2007, ch 9; A. Diduck and F. Kaganas, *Family Law, Gender and the State: Text, Cases and Materials*, 2nd edn, Oxford: Hart, 2006, ch 14; on shifts in the professional attitudes of lawyers and others, see B. Neale and C. Smart, '"Good" and "Bad"' Lawyers? Struggling in the Shadow of the New Law', *Journal of Social Welfare and Family Law*, 2004, vol 19, p 377.

[41] In addition to work cited above, n 3, see A. Gavanas, 'The Fatherhood Responsibility Movement: The Centrality of Marriage, Work and Male Sexuality in Reconstructions of Masculinity and Fatherhood' in B. Hobson (ed), *Making Men into Fathers: Men, Masculinities and the Social Politics of Fatherhood*, Cambridge: Cambridge University Press, 2002. Compare W. F. Horn, D. Blankenhorn and M. B. Pearlstein, *The Fatherhood Movement: A Call to Action*, Lanham, MD: Lexington Books, 1999.

[42] Thus, whilst I use 'fathers' rights groups' in this chapter, it is important to use the term with caution.

[43] See, for example, M. Eriksson and K. Pringle, 'Gender Equality, Child Welfare and Fathers' Rights in Sweden' in Collier and Sheldon (eds), op cit, 2006; B. Featherstone, op cit, 2009, p 127.

[44] R. Collier and S. Sheldon, 'Fathers' Rights, Fatherhood and Law Reform – International Perspectives' in Collier and Sheldon (eds), op cit, 2006; M. Kaye and J. Tolmie, 'Fathers' Rights Groups in Australia and Their Engagement with issues in Family Law', *Australian Journal of Family Law*, 1998, vol 12 p 12.

In light of the above, what kinds of groups, in the context of England and Wales, are we talking about? Following the enactment of the Divorce Reform Act 1969 (henceforth DRA 1969) and the Matrimonial Causes Act 1973 (henceforth MCA 1973) there was a marked shift in how the effects of divorce on men and women respectively have been understood.[45] This is reflected in popular culture and in relation to specific debates about law. Running alongside the various legal reforms introduced since the early 1970s (below),[46] there has been a growing concern on the part of some men, and women, that fathers have become the victims of injustice in law. I have elsewhere charted this transition in terms of a move from a discourse of 'women's emancipation' to one that has increasingly been shaped by the idea of a 'sex war',[47] a point that requires further clarification here.

The DRA 1969 and MCA 1973 were widely seen at the time of their enactment as examples of broadly permissive legislation of consent marked by a concern to protect women from the consequences of new, liberalised divorce laws. From the early 1970s onwards, however, there has been a heightened focus on the implications of these legal changes on men. This shift rested on two interrelated ideas. First, the embedding in law of formal equality and gender neutrality, noted elsewhere in this book, reflected in the belief that law must be 'just to husbands as well as to wives'.[48] Second, some wider cultural shifts in ideas about men's economic power relative to women, alongside changing beliefs about gender and sexuality, class and propriety.[49] Thus, from a position in which the liberalising of divorce was seen in the late 1960s as a potential 'Casanova's Charter', resulting in 'blameless wives' being repudiated by their husbands and left in economic difficulties, we moved towards a different political terrain by the early 1980s. In the period from the mid-1970s to the mid-1980s, as the economic and social bases of the earlier reforms were, it was argued, undermined by changes in patterns of women's employment, cultural and sexual-political realignments further shifted perceptions of fathers on divorce. The film *Kramer v Kramer*, released in 1979, exemplifies in its cultural impact internationally an emerging debate about a new role for fathers. Far from the 'innocent' wife being the potential victim of divorce law, it is the figure of the divorced father who, increasingly, emerges as the potential object of law's injustice, a theme reflected in numerous cultural texts since concerned with the changing nature of fatherhood, including further films, novels and television programmes.

---

[45] J. Eekelaar, *Family Law and Personal Life*, Oxford: Oxford University Press, 2006, esp pp 141–43.

[46] Legislation such as the Matrimonial and Family Proceedings Act 1984, the Children Act 1989, the Child Support Act 1991 (as amended), and the Family Law Act 1996 (FLA 1996).

[47] R. Collier, 'From "Women's Emancipation" to "Sex War"?: Beyond the Masculinized Discourse of Divorce' in Day Sclater and Piper (eds), op cit, 1999.

[48] Royal Commission on Marriage and Divorce, *Royal Commission on Marriage and Divorce: Report 1951–1955*, Cmd 9678, 1956, p 46.

[49] See further K. O'Donovan, *Family Law Matters*, London: Pluto, 1993, pp 77–79.

In this period the beginnings of contemporary fathers' rights politics can be located, with the emergence of organisations seeking to campaign on diverse issues relating to fathers and law. Of particular significance in the UK has been the pressure group and registered charity Families Need Fathers (henceforth FNF), formed in 1974. This organisation has secured a relatively high public profile and has played an important role as a recognised stakeholder in policy debates about law reform[50] (see below, p 229). By the early 1980s, meanwhile, amidst growing calls for the laws on property and financial provision to be reformed,[51] the early fathers' pressure group Campaign for Justice in Divorce sought to question what it meant to achieve a just, fair, equitable settlement on divorce. An argument at the time was that it had become increasingly unfair for men to have to support a former wife capable of supporting herself (and who, in many cases, would have access to a second partner's finances).[52] These concerns about the substantive outcomes of divorce continue to resonate in law, not least in the area of child support.[53] Debates have shifted, however, in ways that reflect the transformation of the role of the father detailed in chapter 5.

In what way? Controversies in the early 1990s surrounding child support liability, exemplified in a series of protests against the workings of the Child Support Agency (CSA), set up by the Child Support Act 1991,[54] marked a particular political and moral moment in British society, a coming together of concerns about 'family values', absent fathers, a rising social underclass, crime and moral breakdown.[55] The protests against the CSA, however, an object of considerable anger on the part of fathers and their supporters, can in retrospect be seen as a sign of 'things to come' in the development of political agendas around fathers' rights. The campaign against the CSA marked a

---

[50] FNF seeks to provide advice and support to divorced and separated parents, 'irrespective of gender or marital status' on shared parenting issues arising from family breakdown: Families Need Fathers, Charity Profile (January 2000), <http://www.fnf.org.uk/about-us/charity-profile>, accessed 18 December 2007; see <http://www.fnf.org.uk/fnfindex.htm>. See further S. Secker, *For the Sake of the Children: The FNF Guide to Shared Parenting*, London: FNF Publications, 2001.

[51] For detailed discussion of this period, see C. Smart, *The Ties That Bind: Law, Marriage and the Reproduction of Patriarchal Relations*, London: Routledge & Kegan Paul, 1984.

[52] D. Allen, *One Step from the Quagmire*, Aylesbury: Campaign for Justice in Divorce, 1982; P. Alcock, 'Remuneration or Remarriage? The Matrimonial and Family Proceedings Act 1984', *Journal of Law and Society*, 1984, vol 11(3), p 357. See further Eekelaar, op cit, 2006.

[53] Collier and Sheldon, op cit, 2008, ch 5; Featherstone, op cit, 2009, pp 145–49; R. Collier, 'The Campaign Against the Child Support Act, "Errant Fathers" and "Family Men"', *Family Law*, 1994, p 384; J. Wallbank, 'The Campaign for Change of the Child Support Act: Reconstituting the "Absent" Father', *Legal Studies*, 1997, vol 6, p 191.

[54] Wikeley, op cit, 2006.

[55] F. Williams, 'Troubled Masculinities in Social Policy Discourses: Fatherhood' in J. Popay, J. Hearn and J. Edwards (eds), *Men, Gender Divisions and Welfare*, London: Routledge, 1998; R. Collier, 'A Father's "Normal Love"? Masculinities, Criminology and the Family' in R. Dobash and L. Noakes (eds), *Gender and Crime*, Cardiff: University of Wales Press, 1995.

reassertion of fatherhood in the legal arena that has gathered pace in the years since. During the period from the mid- to late 1990s, meanwhile, alongside these developments in law, other cultural and political influences, including the evolution of a broader men's movement,[56] were beginning to inform a view of the divorced father as a different kind of victim of (in)justice in law from that which had existed during the 1970s and 1980s.[57] It is during this time, increasingly, allied to concern about a crisis of masculinity, that the issue of a father's post-separation relationship with his children assumes centre stage in debates about fatherhood. It is against this backdrop of developments in law and popular culture that contemporary fathers' rights groups have sought to focus, following the enactment of the Children Act 1989, on the issue of contact and residence law in a high-profile, visible and politically resonant campaign for justice for fathers on divorce.

So what is wrong with the law? Equality, political strategy and protest

> If you give a father no options, you leave him no choice. Fatherhood is under attack in a way inconceivable thirty years ago.[58]

Fathers' groups in the UK have embraced a claim to equal treatment bolstered by reliance on a rights discourse that has been increasingly resonant following the incorporation into UK law of the European Convention on Human Rights, through the Human Rights Act 1998.[59] Within recent debates in England and Wales, the claim to equality has been manifest most clearly in the call for reform of the law and the introduction of a legal presumption of contact, alongside the related assumption that shared parenting should become, in law, the 'normal arrangement' in cases where there are two fit, capable parents.[60] Allied to this claim is a wide-ranging critique of the present family justice system and the role of law in reproducing injustice for fathers. Key grievances include:

- the lack of any structured, accountable decision-making in the family courts and a failure on the part of successive governments to introduce a statutory legal presumption of contact and equal, shared parenting in law, as above;
- the weak enforcement of court orders that are made, notwithstanding evidence of substantial non-compliance by some resident parents, predominantly, we have seen, mothers;

---

[56] See further F. Ashe, *The New Politics of Masculinity: Men, Power and Resistance*, London: Routledge, 2007; Gavanas, op cit, 2002; Messner, op cit, 1997.

[57] For an excellent, insightful discussion of policy development at this time see Featherstone, op cit, 2009, ch 8.

[58] M. O'Connor, founder of Fathers 4 Justice, quoted in *The Guardian*, 3 February 2004.

[59] J. Herring, 'The Human Rights Act and the Welfare Principle in Family Law – Conflicting or Complementary?', *Child and Family Law Quarterly*, 1999, vol 11, p 223.

[60] Contrast the present 'checklist' in the Children Act 1989, s. 1(3)(c).

- the demand for a more open and accessible court system (the transparency issue)[61] linked to concerns about process and delay, an issue with detrimental consequences for non-resident fathers in giving the residential parent a form of situational power and control over proceedings;
- a dissatisfaction with the amount of contact and residence often awarded by courts to fathers;
- underscoring each of the above, a concern about the resulting power of some mothers to produce a form of 'parental alienation syndrome';[62]
- a concern about the adjudicatory role, perceived pro-mother bias and vested self-interest (in maintaining the status quo) of legal agents, including judges, lawyers and, in particular, employees of the Children and Family Court Advisory and Support Service (CAFCASS), the latter a body with a key role in disputes via their role in welfare reporting;
- a concern with the practices of the CSA and the substantive provisions of the Child Support Act 1991, as amended, and, more recently, the newly introduced C-MEC, the Child Maintenance and Enforcement Commission, in particular in relation to its 'draconian' enforcement measures;[63]
- issues of housing, finance, tax,[64] welfare benefits and legal aid, with high levels of cost impacting significantly on fathers, resulting in many having to represent themselves in court as Litigants in Person;
- a critique of dominant interpretations of domestic violence in the family justice system, notably concerns over the making of false allegations of violence and sexual abuse by some mothers against men (see below); and
- a political failure on the part of government to take seriously the circumstances of separated fathers and commit to, and adequately fund, policy reforms (for example around early interventions and compulsory mediation) that might, were they introduced, begin to address the above concerns.

---

61 J. Baker, 'Open Glory?: Why Transparent Family Justice is Vital for all concerned', *McKenzie: The National Magazine of Families Need Fathers*, 2000, February, no 83, p 9. 'We do not recognise the authority of these secret courts. Whatever it takes, however long it takes and whatever the sacrifice, we will prevail and achieve the reforms that every child and family in this country desperately deserve and need': Matt O'Connor, <http://www.fathers-4-justice.org/f4j>, accessed 14 November 2007.

62 C. Bruch, 'Parental Alienation Syndrome and Alienated Children – Getting it Wrong in Child Custody Cases', *Child and Family Law Quarterly*, 2002, vol 14, p 381; C. Williams, 'Parental Alienation Syndrome', *Family Law*, 2002, vol 32, p 410; S. Maidment, 'Parental Alienation Syndrome – A Judicial Response?', *Family Law*, 1998, p 264; J. Rosenblatt and P. Scragg, 'The Hostile Parent: A Clinical Analysis', *Family Law*, 1995, p 152.

63 With particular concern being expressed about deduction from earnings orders to collect maintenance and the potential seizure, under the new rules, of passports and driving licences as part of the government's laws to make sure that parents pay support.

64 A. Mumford, 'Towards a Fiscal Sociology of Tax Credits and the Father's Rights Movement', *Social and Legal Studies*, 2008, vol 17(2), p 217.

In seeking to advance these objectives, by turning to the campaigning methods of other social movements, several fathers' groups have embraced a form of direct action politics that contrasts with the participatory, stakeholder role of FNF, a development best represented in the UK by the group Fathers 4 Justice (henceforth F4J). Founded in December 2002 by Matt O'Connor, a 'designer, marketing and public relations man by trade', F4J has been described as 'a new civil rights movement campaigning for a child's right to see both parents and grandparents'.[65] F4J has been positioned within a long tradition of 'outsider groups' protesting at the injustices of law, with a membership embracing 'Fathers, Mothers, Grandparents, Teachers, Doctors, Company Directors, Policemen, Barristers – a complete cross section of society'.[66] F4J is, in comparison with FNF, a relatively new organisation. It has attracted considerable national and international media attention, however, critical as well as supportive of its aims, as the result of a series of high-profile demonstrations involving fathers and their supporters.[67]

These protests, diverse in form and the level of their organisation and planning, have attracted the attention of politicians and policy-makers alike, backed, notably, by the public support of Sir Bob Geldof.[68] That politicians should have 'sat up and took notice' is understandable given the high public profile of these protests and the frequent disruption (for example, to traffic) that has on occasion resulted. They have encompassed the civil rights march,[69] physical attacks on government offices, in particular those of CAFCASS, and demonstrations outside the homes of senior politicians, solicitors, barristers and judges

---

[65] '[We] have adopted a twin track strategy based around publicity and press. Raising awareness through publicity "making the injustice visible" and mobilising a "dads army" – applying pressure to the system and MP's to bring around meaningful change and enforce the will of Parliament', <http://www.fathers-4-justice.org/introducing/index.htm>, accessed 5 November 2007. See further *Fathers 4 Justice Blueprint for Family Law in the Twenty First Century* document: <http://www.fathers-4-justice.org/f4j/index.php?option=com_content&task=view&id=18&Itemid=41>, accessed 2 April 2009.

[66] <http://www.fathers-4-justice.org/introducing%20f4j/index.htm>, accessed 7 July 2008.

[67] Reputation Intelligence, *F4J Heralds a New Era in Political Campaigning: Media Report*, London: Reputation Intelligence, 2004. For an example of this reporting, S. Hattenstone, 'We're On a Mission: After Years of Campaigning, Fathers Rights' Groups Are Finally Being Taken Seriously by Politicians', *The Guardian* (Family), 29 October 2005, p 4; C. Jardine, 'Mothers Deserve Justice Too', *Daily Telegraph*, 31 October 2005, p 23; J. Gilchrist, 'Outlaw Fathers fight Back', *The Scotsman*, 29 May 2003; G. Hinsliff, 'Militant Fathers will risk jail over rights to see their children', *The Observer*, 20 April 2003; Press Association, 'Fathers' Rights Protest on Court Roof', Press Association (PA News), 18 May 2004; 'Unholy Fathers in Church', *The Sun*, 12 July 2004; S. Dominus, 'The New Fathers Crusade', *New York Times*, 8 May 2005. Contrast A. Phillips, 'Most Fathers get Justice', *The Guardian*, 13 October 2004.

[68] Transcript of BBC Radio 4 Today programme, 3 April 2004, 'Rights for Fathers – Lord Geoff Filkin and Sir Bob Geldof' (GICS Media Monitoring Unit, London, 2004) (copy of transcript with author); B. Geldof, 'The Real Love that Dare Not Speak Its Name' in A. Bainham, B. Lindley, M. Richards and L. Trinder (eds), *Children and Their Families*, Oxford: Hart, 2003.

[69] For example, 'The Rising: Outlaw Fathers Fight Back' (October 2003) and 'The McDad Day Demo' (planned for June 2005, subsequently cancelled).

(including, in September 2004, the British Royal Family). F4J members have undertaken highly visible public stunts, including the interruption of live television programmes.[70] They have had a succession of confrontations with senior government figures including, in May 2004, an incident involving the throwing of a condom of purple flour at the then British Prime Minister in Parliament.[71] As one activist put it, 'we are going to target solicitors, members of the judiciary and barristers and we have a list of the people we are looking at'.[72] In the words of Matt O'Connor, speaking in 2004:

> We are at war now, and that war will continue until such time as the Government starts taking the crisis in family law seriously. The gloves are off. There is a difficult time ahead, but we are prepared for it.[73]

F4J has become most well known for a series of protests involving men dressed as comic book characters (such as Batman, Spiderman, Superman) scaling a succession of cranes, bridges, courthouses and other public structures and buildings around the country.[74] This image of the protesting father has become the visible public face of fathers' protests in the UK, a representation of fathers' rights used on numerous occasions in the media to accompany more general discussion of the changing nature of contemporary fatherhood.[75] Indeed, in the period 2004–08 much discussion of fathers and fatherhood in the media and popular culture became commonly associated with this debate about fathers' rights.[76]

For all this high visibility, however, what has been the effect of these protests? As social policy literature has demonstrated, tracing the determinants of a specific law reform is notoriously difficult.[77] Nonetheless, the evolution of legal policy around contact and residence, in the years since the formation of F4J in 2002, does suggest that the climate of debate has been informed, to

---

[70] 'Lottery Show delayed by Protest', <http://news.bbc.co.uk/1/hi/uk/5001386.stm>, accessed 7 January 2009.

[71] 'Blair Hit During Commons protest', *BBC News*, 19 May 2004.

[72] Peter Molly, reported in *The Guardian*, 3 February 2004.

[73] M. O'Connor, *The Independent on Sunday*, 8 February 2004.

[74] In the course of these protests Matt O'Connor, Jason Birch and David Chick of F4J received particular prominence. Chick, who held a vigil in a crane over Tower Bridge in London in November 2003, was subsequently voted second in a BBC Radio 4 poll for 'Man of the Year 2003' (reported in the *Independent on Sunday*, 8 February 2004). See further: M. O'Connor, *Fathers 4 Justice*, London: Weidenfeld & Nicolson, 2007; D. Chick, *Denied Access*, London: Pen Press, 2006; M. Harris, *Family Court HELL*, London: Pen Press, 2006.

[75] For example, S. Durrant, 'What are Fathers For? An Interview with Richard Collier', *The Guardian*, 3 January 2009.

[76] It is against this backdrop, for example, that the organisation Fathers Direct changed its name to *The Fatherhood Institute*, signalling a distance from the rights focus of such groups: Featherstone, op cit, 2009, p 141.

[77] See Featherstone op cit, 2009, p 127.

a degree, by the protests of fathers' activists. It is against the backdrop of the F4J campaign that policy-makers and politicians have articulated a view that 'something needs to be done' about the present laws concerning contact.[78] Senior figures in the judiciary expressed serious concern, for example, about the difficulties they face in dealing with contested cases, notably in relation to the limited options they have had in seeking to enforce court orders. Some, on occasion, made public what would normally have been private court rulings, making clear their belief that the family justice system has frequently failed fathers.[79] In April 2004, in the midst of F4J's protests, the government announced its commitment to 'new laws to end the child custody wars'.[80] The resulting Green Paper, *Parental Separation: Children's Needs and Parents' Responsibilities* (2004) outlined proposals aimed at diverting as many divorcing parents as possible from the courts and promoting 'generous parenting' for both.[81] In January 2005, the government published its response to the Green Paper, *Parental Separation: Children's Needs and Parents' Responsibilities, Next Steps*.[82] Part I of the resulting Children and Adoption Act 2006[83] subsequently adopted an approach that, at least to a degree, can be seen to have engaged with key concerns of fathers' rights

---

[78] In July 2004 the then Leader of the Conservative Party announced the commitment of his party to the 'strong presumption' that fathers should have equal rights. In 2005, an Early Day Motion (No 128, 'Parenting Time Presumption', 18 May 2005) was tabled in Parliament, signed by 340 Members of all political parties, urging that separated parents should each have a legal presumption of contact with their children unless it compromises the safety of the child. See also Early Day Motion 2367 (Parenting Time Presumption, No 2), 14 June 2006.

[79] Note, for example, the judgement of Munby J in *Re D (A Child) (Intractable Contact Dispute)* [2004] EWHC Fam 727, [2004] 1 FLR 1226. This development prompted the observation on the part of Matt O'Connor of F4J that 'twelve months ago such judgments would have been unthinkable': F Gibb, 'Judge Apologises as Justice "Fails Fathers"', *The Times*, 2 April 2004, <http://www.timesonline.co.uk/article/0,2–1059953,00.html>, accessed 2 January 2008; 'I have had to send a parent to prison and it doesn't achieve anything. Also it may affect the child who feels to blame if mummy goes to prison': Justice Bracewell, *The Guardian*, 22 October 2003.

[80] C. Dyer, 'New Laws to End Child Custody Wars', *The Guardian*, 3 April 2004, <http://www.guardian.co.uk/society/2004/apr/03/childrensservices.politics>, accessed 2 January 2008.

[81] Department for Education and Skills, Department for Constitutional Affairs and Department for Trade and Industry, *Parental Separation: Children's Needs and Parents' Responsibilities*, London: DfES, DCA and DTI, 2004.

[82] Department for Education and Skills, Department for Constitutional Affairs and Department for Trade and Industry, *Parental Separation: Children's Needs and Parents' Responsibilities, Next Steps*, London: DfES, DCA and DTI, 2005, which sets out a summary of responses received to the consultation and outlines an 'agenda for action'. Over 250 responses were received to the consultation, 'with the majority welcoming the general direction of the Green Paper'.

[83] Preceded by the 2005 Children (Contact) and Adoption Bill: C. Dyer and L. Ward, 'Law to help fathers in child contact cases', *The Guardian*, 19 January 2005; J. Wallbank, 'Clause 106 of the Adoption and Children Bill: Legislation for the "Good Father"?', *Legal Studies*, 2002, vol 22(2), p 276; J. Wallbank, 'Getting Tough on Mothers: Regulating Contact and Residence', *Feminist Legal Studies*, 2005, vol 15(2), p 189; F. Gibb, 'Child Contact Powers "Could Worsen Parent Wars"', *The Times*, 8 December 2008, p 11; Collier and Sheldon, op cit, 2008, ch 5.

activists.[84] The legislation seeks, amongst other things, to facilitate, monitor and promote contact,[85] to address the issue of the weak enforcement of court orders[86] and the need to 'educate' parents via the provision of access to information. At the same time, there has been growing acceptance of the view that the family courts, to a limited degree, should be made more open.[87] The government has recognised, in short, that many aspects of 'the present legal system is inadequate, failing in the way the process deals with contact cases'.[88] In the words of the then Lord Chancellor:

> There needs to be change and there needs to be reform because the system is not working, not because of a campaign of civil disobedience. There is ... a most profound acceptance that in very many cases the system is not working.[89]

I will return to the present direction of reform in this area, since the 2006 Act, and the impact of fathers' groups, below. At this stage, it is necessary to look more closely at the critique that has been advanced of these developments in fathers' rights politics and at the concerns, in particular, raised about the impact of fathers' rights agendas on women and children.

The critique: arguments against fathers' rights

A now considerable body of research has, across jurisdictions, sought to explore diverse aspects of the membership and social impact of fathers' rights groups. A common theme in much of this work has been that these developments have been profoundly problematic for women and children.[90] Within a

---

[84] In particular, s. 5 concerning the introduction of warning notices and provision for compensation for financial loss. The Act's provisions inserted new ss. 11A–11P into the Children Act 1989, amending the latter legislation.

[85] Ss. 1–2 of the 2006 Act.

[86] Ss. 3–4. It is envisaged that it will be in relatively few cases, in which there has been implacable failure to comply with an order, that the courts will find it necessary to impose such a sanction.

[87] New rules introduced in 2009 have ended the blanket prohibition on reporting family law cases in the County Court and High Court, although many details continue to be confidential: for example, A. Hirsch, 'Media Access to Family Courts will Improve Clarity Says Judge', *The Guardian*, 27 April 2009.

[88] As acknowledged in the consultation paper, Children Act Sub-committee of the Advisory Board on Family Law, *Making Contact Work. A Report to the Lord Chancellor on the Facilitation of Arrangements for Contact Between Children and their Non-residential Parents and the Enforcement of Court Orders for Contact*, London: Lord Chancellor's Department, 2001.

[89] Lord Falconer, quoted in Dyer and Ward, op cit, 2005.

[90] In addition to the work cited above note, for example, J. Cohen and N. Gershbain, 'For the Sake of Fathers? Child Custody Reform and the Perils of Maximum Contact', *Canadian Family Law Quarterly*, 2001, vol 19, p 121; H. Rhoades, 'Posing as Reform? The Case of the Family Law Reform Act', *Australian Journal of Family Law*, 2000, vol 14(2), p 142; J. Arditti and K.

wide-ranging critique of fathers' rights activism in socio-legal, social policy and sociological literature a number of themes recur. Critics have challenged, for example, the deployment of formal legal rights (what Carol Smart and Bren Neale characterise as evoking a self-interested, individualised form of power),[91] an appeal to treat fathers equally that aligns the political aims of fathers' organisations with those of other social movements.[92] Work has questioned, notably in the context of reform debates in Australia and Canada, a claim to victim status supported by a highly selective use of statistics and emotionally powerful use of personal anecdotes.[93] Further concern has been expressed over the consequences for women of the enforcement of court orders of the kind sought, and at how the interests of fathers and children become conflated in fathers' rights arguments in such a way that they become one and the same thing.

Particular attention has been paid to the way some fathers' groups seek to protect or defend a model of the (heterosexual) family from the perceived social ills of father-absence. This is aligned with a highly questionable depiction of lone motherhood as a social problem,[94] an argument that links to the negative depiction of women and a virulent strand of anti-feminism, if not misogyny, within

Allen, 'Distressed Fathers' Perceptions of Legal and Relational Inequities Post-Divorce', *Family and Conciliation Courts Review*, 1993, vol 31, p 461; C. Berotia and J. Drakich, 'The Fathers' Rights Movement: Contradictions in Rhetoric and Practice', *Journal of Family Issues*, 1993, vol 14(4), p 592; A. Melville and R. Hunter, 'As Everybody Knows: Countering Myths of Gender Bias in Family Law', *Griffith Law Review*, 2001, vol 1(1), p 124; R. Graycar, 'Equal Rights Versus Fathers' Rights: The Child Custody Debate in Australia' in C. Smart and S. Sevenhuijsen (eds), *Child Custody and the Politics of Gender*, London: Routledge, 1989; C. Berotia, 'An Interpretative Analysis of the Mediation Rhetoric of Fathers' Rightists: Privatization Versus Personalization', *Mediation Quarterly*, 1998, vol 16(1), p 15; L. Neilson, 'Demeaning, Demoralizing and Disenfranchising Divorced Dads: A Review of the Literature', *Journal of Divorce and Remarriage*, 1999, vol 31, p 129; M. Kaye and J. Tolmie, '"Lollies at a Children's Party" and Other Myths: Violence, Protection Orders and Fathers' Rights Groups', *Current Issues in Criminal Justice*, 1998, vol 10(1), p 52.

91 Smart and Neale, op cit, 1999, '"I Hadn't Really Thought About It"'; C. Smart, 'Preface' in Collier and Sheldon (eds), op cit, 2006.

92 J. E. Crowley, 'Adopting "Equality Tools" from the Toolboxes of their Predecessors: the Fathers' Rights Movement in the United States' in Collier and Sheldon (eds), op cit, 2006.

93 R. Graycar, 'Law Reform by Frozen Chook: Family Law Reform for the New Millennium?', *Melbourne University Law Review*, 2000, vol 24, p 737; Melville and Hunter, op cit, 2001.

94 Boyd, op cit, 2001, 'Demonizing Mothers ... '. See, for example, the arguments of D. Blakenhorn, *Fatherless America: Confronting Our Most Urgent Social Problem*, New York: Basic Books, 1995. F4J suggests that 'Fathers have struggled to adapt to a brave new world where they have effectively been replaced by the state as the protector and provider to their children': <http://www.fathers-4-justice.org/legacy/index.htm>, accessed 17 November 2007. The F4J website cites the examples of youth offending, children growing up with 'multiple step-fathers' 'but denied access to their own dads', despair, debt, poverty and childlessness on the part of men, anger, suicide, breakdown and social catastrophe as direct results of such father-absence: <http://www.fathers-4-justice.org/legacy/index.htm>, accessed 17 November 2007.

parts of the fathers' rights movement. Mothers, it has been argued, tend to appear within the fathers' rights discourse as 'alimony drones', 'mendacious and vindictive', 'unruly' and 'irresponsible' figures.[95] In marked contrast, the dominant image of 'father' is of a respectable and socially 'safe'[96] subject, a sharer of responsibilities and an active participant in paid employment, child care and domestic labour.

Turning towards the consequences for family justice systems themselves,[97] theoretical and empirical research has raised concerns about the implications of the new contact culture for mothers. The emergence has been noted in case law in England and Wales during the 1990s of the figure of the 'implacably hostile', bad, selfish mother, attention being drawn to the double standard at play whereby there would appear to be no such figure as the implacably *irresponsible* father. This connects to how, as we have seen in chapter 5, mothers' efforts in supporting the bi-nuclear family tend to be noticed when they are *not* made, their everyday work somehow taken for granted ('that is what mothers do'). Smart and Neale have noted the disjuncture between the equality rhetoric advanced by fathers' rights groups and the continuing (gendered) realities of parenting, both during subsisting relationships and after divorce/separation.[98] It is the resident parent, rather than the non-resident, who would appear to be most bound by the obligations of the co-operative parenting project:

> Good mothers not only refrain from obstructing contact but actively facilitate it. Good fathers, at least for the purposes of contact, take some interest in their children and do not harm them or, generally speaking, behave violently to mothers. Good parents co-operate and do not litigate.[99]

It is significant, critics suggest, that fathers' rights groups focus on issues of divorce and separation via the use of gender-neutral language, rather than engage with, and campaign on, the development of policies around work, care and gender equality in subsisting relationships.[100] Ironically, research suggests it is women, and not men, who tend to suffer disproportionate short- and

---

[95] Berotia and Drakich, op cit, 1993, p 603.

[96] See R. Collier, *Masculinity, Law and the Family*, London: Routledge, 1995.

[97] R. Bailey-Harris, J. Barron and J. Pearce, 'From Utility to Rights? The Presumption of Contact in Practice', *International Journal of Law, Policy and the Family*, 1999, vol 13, p 111; C. Smart and B. Neale, 'Arguments Against Virtue: Must Contact Be Enforced?', *Family Law*, 1997, vol 28, p 332.

[98] Smart and Neale, op cit, 1999, *Family Fragments*.

[99] F. Kaganas and S. Day Sclater, 'Contact Disputes: Narrative Constructions of "Good" Parents', *Feminist Legal Studies*, 2004, vol 12(1), p 2 at p 13.

[100] It should be noted, however, that questions of tax and child benefit, in particular, have been central concerns to some groups, and that arguments about equality in welfare regimes does feature within the fathers' rights discourse.

long-term economic hardship following divorce, with men's incomes more likely to rise in the immediate aftermath of separation.[101]

Helen Rhoades and Susan Boyd, writing of developments in Australia and Canada respectively, have observed further consequences of an ideology of motherhood in family law in the form of new stories about selfish mothers that have troubling implications for women who do wish to raise genuine concerns about the capacity of some fathers to care for their children.[102] This issue has assumed particular importance in relation to violence, where non-resident fathers, it is argued, have been empowered by the new contact order culture in such a way that significant pressures can be placed on some women to agree to contact, notwithstanding concerns about domestic violence.[103] In this context attention has been drawn by Women's Aid to the deaths of children during contact visits.[104] At the same time, critics suggests, questions of men's violence more generally, the scale of which is seen as largely denied by fathers' groups,[105] have been systematically marginalised within much divorce mediation practice, all in the name of promoting the 'harmonious divorce'.[106] In her analysis of the development of case law in England and Wales during the 1990s, Felicity Kaganas[107] suggested that to warrant the description of 'bad father' a man must behave in some exceptionally callous ways. Indeed, it is 'almost impossible to conceive of a father who is harmful to children unless he

[101] S. Jenkins, 'Marital Splits and Income Changes Over the Longer Term', ISER Working Paper, Essex: University of Essex, 2008, available at <http://www.iser.essex.ac.uk/publications/working-papers/iser/2008–07.pdf>, accessed 22 April 2009.

[102] Rhoades and Boyd, op cit, 2004.

[103] The literature on this subject is extensive. For a useful overview of the relation between contact and domestic violence, including the approach of the courts, see Hunt with Roberts, op cit, 2004, at pp 7–9. See further F. Kaganas and C. Piper, 'Contact and Domestic Violence' in Day Sclater and Piper (eds), op cit, 1999; J. Hall, 'Domestic Violence and Contact', Family Law, 1997, p 813; C. Sturge, in consultation with D. Glaser, 'Contact and Domestic Violence – The Expert's Court Report', Family Law, 2000, p 615; H. Reece, 'UK Women's Groups' Child Contact Campaign: "So Long As It Is Safe"', Child and Family Law Quarterly, 2006, vol 18(4), p 538 (presenting a bifurcation of the 'domestic violence victim' and 'unreasonable' mother in these debates); cf B. Featherstone and S. Peckover, 'Letting Them Get Away With it: Fathers, Domestic Violence and Child Welfare', Critical Social Policy, 2007, vol 27(2), p 181.

[104] H. Saunders, Twenty-Nine Child Homicides: Lessons to be Learnt on Domestic Violence and Child Protection, London: Women's Aid, 2004. The British media regularly report the cases of 'family wipe-outs', as it has been termed, where men, often described as devoted to their children, kill children, partners and then themselves: K. Hilpern, 'Ending it All: How Can We Stop "Loving" Fathers Killing Their Children?', The Guardian, 24 September 2008, G2, pp 4–7; R. Jenkins, 'Found Dead on Fathers' Day: Husband in Divorce Battle and the Children He Feared Losing', The Times, 17 June 2008.

[105] Where a distinction is set up, Featherstone suggests, op cit, 2009, p 123, between the safe birth father and the (potentially) violent step-social father.

[106] D. Greatbatch and R. Dingwall, 'The Marginalization of Domestic Violence in Divorce Mediation', International Journal of Law, Policy and the Family, 1999, p 174.

[107] F. Kaganas, 'Contact, Conflict and Risk' in Day Sclater and Piper (eds), op cit, 1999.

inflicts direct violence on them'.[108] In a more recent review of case law and policy, Kaganas and Shelley Day Sclater argue that:

> the dominant welfare discourse [has been] interpreted so as to create so strong an association between contact and welfare that neither risks to mothers' health nor, until recently, serious violence on the part of the non-resident father were regarded as sufficient reason to deny an order.[109]

This critique of fathers' rights arguments can be taken even further, with research suggesting that the reasons for the breakdown of contact arrangements may be more complex than the image of a woman simply refusing or blocking access suggests. Leaving aside the questionable empirical reality of large numbers of mendacious, vengeful mothers acting in this way, far from refusing fathers access, stakeholder groups such as, in the UK, Gingerbread/One Parent Families suggest most women want fathers to have contact, and actively facilitate this end in their negotiations with non-resident fathers. Other studies question whether non-resident parents, as a group, are unreasonably treated by the family courts. Rather, in cases where courts proceed to decide that sole residence is an appropriate course of action, they are also likely, in the majority of cases, to decide a child should have regular contact with the non-resident parent and the degree and nature of such contact.[110] The courts, that is, start from the position that contact is in the interests of the child, and most non-resident parents are successful in getting the type of contact sought. Moreover, far from women deploying a form of uni-directional power, as it has been termed, blocking fathers' contact, some mothers experience a form of 'debilitative power' on the part of fathers, a constraining of their own drive to independency, autonomy and self-development post-separation, with fathers using contact as a way of exerting control over the lives of women.[111]

What has emerged, in short, is a body of research charting what would appear to be, if anything, an empowering of fathers as result of the emergence, embedding and consolidation of the pro-contact culture and new welfare discourse in law and legal practice. Far from seeing fathers as the victims of law, from this perspective a more plausible reading might be to see the interests of mothers as having been downgraded or, in Martha Fineman's term, writing of developments in the United States during the 1990s, 'neutered'.[112] There has

---

[108] F. Kaganas and C. Piper, 'Contact and Domestic Violence: The Winds of Change?' *Family Law*, 2000, p 630.

[109] Kaganas and Day Sclater, op cit, 2004, 'Contact Disputes', p 2 at pp 6–7, footnotes omitted.

[110] J. Hunt and A. Macleod, *Outcomes of Applications to Court for Contact Orders after Parental Separation or Divorce*, London: Ministry of Justice, 2008.

[111] Smart and Neale, op cit, 1999, *Family Fragments*. This theme emerges in some media reporting of F4J activists: 'Jason [Birch] is so busy fighting to see his other kids he spends no time with ours', *The Sun*, 15 September 2004.

[112] M. Fineman, op cit, 1995.

occurred, Carol Smart has suggested, in the UK context, an erasure of a moral discourse of care in relation to motherhood,[113] a 'striking back' of an ethic of justice.[114] A form of strategic self-interest and self-empowerment has been seen as motivating many men's actions, particularly in relation to finances.[115] In terms of the masculinity politics discussed in chapter 1, meanwhile, these developments exemplify an entrenching of men's power, an increase in gender inequalities in law. At a conceptual level, feminist engagements have raised important questions about the political and conceptual limits of gender neutrality and formal equality, key themes of this book. Such work has challenged a failure of imagination at a political and policy level to transcend the legal contours of the private (sexual) family and gendered understandings of care and caring, rights and welfare-based approaches, responsibility and autonomy.[116]

Digging deeper ...

In the 2006 edited book *Fathers' Rights Activism and Law Reform in Comparative Perspective*[117] Sally Sheldon and I sought to explore, within an international context, some of the above concerns about fathers' rights politics. The book reflected in its approach a general reading of fathers' rights from a broadly feminist perspective, one that would see, as noted above, recent events as a potentially troubling move in the field of family policy. The issue of violence, in particular, was seen as especially contested in these debates, a 'toxic' question dividing organisations in the sector and at times polarising discussion between stakeholders.[118] In recognising the force of these arguments, however, we should note that a number of important questions remain unanswered, in particular in the light of the broader themes around law, men and gender discussed in this book.

How are we to make sense of fathers' rights, and what do these developments tell us about the changing relationship between law, men and masculinities, the 'man of law'? Is it to be argued that fathers' rights groups are simply wrong in their assessment of the law? Are their claims without foundation? Are they manifestations, say, of a form of false consciousness that reflects a failure to recognise the material realities of (all?) fathers' structural empowerment *as men*, in keeping with one pro-feminist reading of masculinity

[113] Smart, op cit, 1995, 'Losing the Struggle'.
[114] Smart, op cit, 2006, 'The Ethic of Justice'.
[115] J. Taylor, 'Downturn Triggers Rush to the Divorce Courts', *The Independent*, 2 February 2009.
[116] Fineman, op cit, 2004. Herring, for example, has sought to develop a concept of 'relational autonomy' in taking forward this debate: J. Herring, 'Autonomy and Family Law' in Herring et al, op cit, 2009.
[117] Collier and Sheldon (eds), op cit, 2006.
[118] For further discussion see Featherstone op cit, 2009, pp 120–23.

discussed in chapter 1? Why should seemingly large numbers of men, and some women,[119] feel law *is* deeply unfair in how it treats fathers following separation? What do these developments mean for policy-makers trying to understand how concrete demands become intelligible as a pursuit of justice within the legal arena? Do these arguments represent a move towards responsibility on the part of men? How do they relate to feminist equality claims? And how might they be interconnected to shifts around parenting cultures and changes in the law itself?

Family law reform, feminist legal scholarship has long shown, can be open-ended, contradictory and uncertain in its effects. What has happened around fathers' rights, I want to argue in the remainder of this chapter, is the result of social shifts more complex and intricate than any simple manifestation of 'law's bias' (whether towards mothers or fathers) or 'anti-women' or 'anti-men' sentiment. Such a language is undoubtedly culturally and politically resonant, in particular in much of the media. It may be that a severe economic recession will further intensify this divisive discourse, producing the kind of gender configurations around a crisis of masculinity that was seen during the early to mid-1990s. It is important, moreover, not to downplay the often openly misogynistic sentiment evident within a strand of the fathers' rights discourse, notably in a presence on the Internet, and in arguments aligned to a broader anti-feminist 'men's movement' perspective.[120] However, the idea that what has happened represents little more than a backlash to feminism is, I want to suggest, of limited help in trying to address the complexities of reaction and resistance in the legal field and the very real problems *both* parents and children can face in dealing with separation.[121] Writing in the journal *Family Law* in 2008 Vallance-Webb has observed how, across a series of recent cases, courts have sought to deal with mothers and fathers who appear 'vengeful' in their relations with the other parent.[122] As research by Peacey

---

[119] Several groups note that many members and supporters are women, with both FNF and F4J having established 'sister' organisations: in the case of FNF, note links to MATCH (Mothers Apart From Their Children): <http://www.matchmothers.org/>, accessed 27 April 2009.

[120] See further R. Menzies, 'Virtual Backlash: Representations of Men's "Rights" and Feminist "Wrongs" in Cyberspace' in D. E. Chunn, S. Boyd and H. Lessard (eds), op cit, 2007. In the UK there is no clear correlation between a level of group activity and the sophistication or otherwise of a presence on the Internet. It is necessary, in particular, to distinguish fathers' rights groups primarily focused on issues of family law reform (especially those with charitable status) from other individual-driven Internet-based men's movement organisations. The issue of transient membership raises further questions in this context about the method and logic of collective action in mobilising around law reform, and the strength and durability of fathers' rights groups in terms of whether this constitutes a discernible 'movement'.

[121] In making this argument I do not wish to efface questions and concerns about men's violence, the scale of which has led some to deploy the notion of 'male backlash' and, indeed, a 'war against women' in accounts of 'what men do': K. Cochrane, 'Now, The Backlash', *The Guardian* (G2), 1 July 2008, pp 6–11; 'Female Complacency and the Male Backlash', Letters, *The Guardian*, 3 July 2008.

[122] Vallance-Webb, op cit, 2008.

and Hunt[123] draws out, meanwhile, both resident and non-resident parents can experience problems with contact and if the minority who use the legal system are more likely to be those with problems, this does not mean that the majority of parents who do not may not also face real difficulties.

These are issues that, I want to argue in the next section, have significant implications for understanding fathers' rights politics. The effects of law reform, I have argued elsewhere, cannot be reduced to a zero-sum framework.[124] Male and female interests are not 'locked' in relation to their personal lives in such a way that, as women gain power, so men simply lose it, and vice versa.[125] Indeed, such an approach can be aligned to the essentialist notions of masculinity and forms of categorical thinking, in Connell's terms, that I sought to challenge in chapter 1. It is a perspective that misreads how everyday experiences of family life are bound up with, and constituted through, a diverse set of social practices. It is time, therefore, to chart a way through these debates. So how might we do that?

Recasting the questions: fathers' rights and personal life

As part of an attempt to rethink the idea of the gendered male subject in legal studies, I sought in chapter 1 to highlight, drawing on recent sociological scholarship, the importance of not effacing the 'real lives' of individuals. This issue has particular bearing on fathers' rights where, as Esther Dermott has argued in her book *Intimate Fatherhood*,[126] it is important not to pass over the aspects of men's parenting that fathers themselves view as significant, the deep psychological investments that fathers can have in gendered categories (see below). Further, noting the problematic nature of the sex/gender distinction, discussed in chapter 1, there is, as Wendy Hollway has argued, reason to question the tendency of policy-makers to minimise differences between women and men in relation to the care, and capacity to care, for children.[127] This connects to the problematic nature of social constructionist accounts of gender and the failure therein to adequately address the biological aspects of fatherhood and the psychosocial dimensions of experience within specific and grounded contexts.

---

[123] V. Peacey and J. Hunt, *Problematic Contact after Separation and Divorce? A National Survey of Parents*, London: One Parent Families/Gingerbread, 2008.

[124] Collier, op cit, 1999, 'From Women's Emancipation'. Note, for example, the argument of C. Smart, 'Feminism and Law: Some Problems of Analysis and Strategy', *International Journal of the Sociology of Law*, 1986, vol 14, p 109.

[125] R. Collier, 'Fathers 4 Justice, Law and the New Politics of Fatherhood', *Child and Family Law Quarterly*, 2005, vol 17, p 511.

[126] E. Dermott, *Intimate Fatherhood: A Sociological Analysis*, London: Routledge, 2008.

[127] W. Hollway, *The Capacity to Care: Gender and Ethical Subjectivity*, London: Routledge, 2006: chapter 1, p 46–48; chapter 5, p 146.

A reading of fathers' rights ...

With this in mind, seeking to place these developments in law in a broader social context – and in so doing to connect law to the insights of other disciplines – the following presents one plausible if, I shall suggest, fairly limited and superficial reading of what has happened. The historical development of fathers' protests around law can be located at a nexus of three developments. First, changes in the content, scope and function of family law, as set out above and in chapter 5 (for example, the role of law in radiating messages about responsible behaviour, the balance of rules and discretion and so forth).[128] Second, the rethinking of the role of the father in child welfare and development, and the proliferation of 'expert' knowledge about fatherhood within intensive parenting cultures; and, third, shifting social, political and economic contexts that frame the development of the substantive law itself (such as the embedding of gender neutrality and formal equality in law). Thus, in England and Wales, mapping to all three themes, it is possible to trace the beginnings of the contemporary fathers' movement in the aftermath of the DRA 1969 and the MCA 1973 (with FNF formed in 1974), as set out above.

Shifts in the content and form of the arguments advanced since then map to two further ideas. First, changes in what it means to be a 'good father' following separation, drawing on the debates about engaging fathers in families, discussed in chapter 5. Second, evident in both law and popular culture, a wider reconfiguration of ideas about men and masculinities. Thus, in the period from the mid-1980s to the late 1990s, for example, we see a coming together of a two-fold 'crisis of fatherhood' and 'crisis in families' discourse increasingly informing both legal policy debates, strands of an emerging men's movement and a series of cultural debates about what is happening to men and masculinities. The latter theme remains particularly resonant within one strand of fathers' rights politics on the Internet, drawing on ideas of loss linked, it has been suggested, to a growing phenomenon of 'ressentiment' within advanced capitalist societies, whereby hostility and blame can be directed at the perceived causes of loss.[129] Such arguments, however, I now wish to argue, whilst part of the picture, simply scratch the surface of the many layers of fathers' rights politics in the legal arena. I will here address three points before concluding this discussion of law, men and gender.

Rights, justice, care: (fragmenting) fatherhood, men and masculinities

The historical shift in the focus of fathers' grievances is connected to the way fathers' legal claims have been increasingly articulated, as Carol Smart has suggested, both through a language of rights and justice (a traditional rights model)[130] and via reference to ideas about men's caring and capacity to care and children's welfare.[131] On closer examination, however, this move, and the co-existence of 'rights-talk' and 'care-talk', is not surprising given the broader social changes that have occurred around fatherhood and intimacy, men and children, rights and responsibility, each a key component of the refiguring of fatherhood in legal policy discussed in chapter 5. Nor, of particular importance to this discussion, is it surprising given the kinds of messages that law itself has sought to radiate about what being a good father entails, especially in a context marked by the internalisation of responsible parenting following the development of the new contact culture during the 1990s, as above.[132] These changes in the fathers' rights discourse, that is, are aligned to, and intimately bound up with, wider social and legal developments. Two immediate observations can be made in this respect.

First, interlinked to a refocusing in law on the welfare of the child in which the father-child dyad has been positioned as of equal importance to that of mothers, there has occurred, I have suggested elsewhere, with Sally Sheldon, a 'geneticisation of fatherhood'.[133] This move, evident across diverse legal contexts, has seen a heightened importance ascribed to genetic links in a policy paradigm focused on investment in children (see further chapter 5). Bound up with cultural shifts around the psychological importance of (genetic) Truth,[134] this has reflected a growing belief that fathers do, and should, have a direct, vertical relationship with their children, one that is unmediated by the child's mother. Debates, ongoing at the time of writing, around the reform of the law relating to unmarried fathers and birth registration,[135] as well as developments around sperm donor anonymity in the context of assisted reproduction, exemplify this theme in a particularly clear way.[136] In seeking such a direct relationship fathers' rights activists are, in a sense, attuned to what law itself is saying about the importance of fathers, equality and gender neutrality, as well

---

[130] Contrast T. Arendell, *Fathers and Divorce*, London: Sage, 1999.

[131] Smart, op cit, 2006, 'The Ethic of Justice'; Smart, op cit, 2004, 'Equal Shares'.

[132] By which normative messages about the welfare of the child and 'doing the right thing' have, for both women *and* men, filtered through to the accounts of parents in making sense of their actions: Kaganas and Day Sclater, op cit, 2004, 'Contact Disputes'.

[133] Collier and Sheldon, op cit, 2008, pp 225–26.

[134] Chapter 5, p 137.

[135] Department for Work and Pensions, *Joint Birth Registration: Recording Responsibility*, White Paper, Cm 7293 London: DWP, 2008: <http://www.dwp.gov.uk/jointbirthregistration/>, accessed 25 February 2009; Department for Work and Pensions, *Joint Birth Registration: Promoting Parental Responsibility*, Green Paper, Cm 7160, London: DWP, 2009: <http://www.dwp.gov.uk/jointbirthregistration/>, accessed 25 February 2009; C. Barton, 'Joint Birth Registration: "Recording Responsibility" Responsibly?', *Family Law*, August 2008, p 789.

[136] Collier and Sheldon, op cit, 2008, ch 3; C. O'Donovan, 'Genetics, Fathers and Families: Exploring the Implications of Changing the Law in Favour of Identifying Sperm Donors', *Social and Legal Studies*, 2006, vol 15(4), p 494.

as reflecting the political resonance of rights discourse more generally following the Human Rights Act 1998. In positioning mothers 'blocking' contact as a
form of violence, moreover, Featherstone has noted, fathers' groups are strategically drawing on a wide definition of violence within policy debates, a
definition so broad that, to the concern of some critics, it has come to
encompass a range of behaviour.[137]

Second, there has been a general acceptance on the part of legal policy-
makers and politicians, as well as judges, that law has a profound *symbolic*
power in signalling ratification of the parental role and equality between men
and women. This power is heightened within the context of increasingly therapeutic cultures in which it has been argued, individuals, men and women, can
seek affirmation of their identities through recourse to law.[138] Fathers in particular, it would seem, appear ever more dependent on having identity as a
parent confirmed by the State. The symbolic power of law in relation to
fatherhood is reflected in the birth registration debates, above, where we find
an assumption on the part of policy-makers that giving unmarried fathers
automatic parental responsibility will send a clear message about men's
responsibility. Developments in case law around the allocation of parental
responsibility,[139] meanwhile (chapter 5, p 136), suggest there has also been
acceptance on the part of the courts that the legal arena can be an understandable focus for political frustration and gender equality claims. That some
fathers will, and should, then seek affirmation of their role as a father through
recourse to law is in keeping with the messages communicated within recent
case law in the area. Thus, in relation to Parental Responsibility Orders and
Shared Residence under the Children Act 1989, we find explicit judicial
statements that parental responsibility has an important symbolic element, a
status that any good father might understandably, and perfectly reasonably,
seek to obtain.[140] This raises the issue of how fathers' claims for public
recognition of responsibility, when seen as a status, a label, are occurring
within a social and legal economy increasingly marked by concerns about

---

[137] Featherstone, op cit, 2009, p 123; see also the reading by Reece, op cit, 2006.

[138] Fathers' claims, H. Rhoades, 'Yearning for Law: Fathers' Groups and Family Law Reform in
Australia' in R. Collier and S. Sheldon (eds), *Fathers' Rights Activism and Legal Reform*,
Oxford: Hart, 2006 suggests, can thus be seen more as symbolic demands, rather than as claims
about how children should be parented in practice.

[139] For discussion of the shift from parental authority to parents being 'approved' via the allocation of parental responsibility see further H. Reece, 'The Degradation of Parental Responsibility' in R. Probert, S. Gilmore and J. Herring (eds), *Responsible Parents and Parental
Responsibility*, Oxford: Hart, 2009; *Re D* [2006] EWHC 2.

[140] The issue of the importance of 'labels' to individuals has also been detected in the case law on
shared residence where a drift has been identified towards the making of such orders based on
assumptions about the symbolic power of such an order in relation to granting parental
responsibility to both parents: see *Re F (Shared Residence)* [2003] 2 FLR 397; *Re A (Shared
Residence)* [2008] EWCA Civ 867; B. Neale, J. Flowerdew and C. Smart, 'Drifting Towards
Shared Residence?', *Family Law*, 2003, December, p 904.

respect and recognition,[141] a context, I suggested in chapter 5, that has transformed ideas around the role of law in relation to the promotion of 'active fathering'.

Set against such a legal backdrop, it is not difficult to see how a legal failure to then accord fathers equal contact time with their children can be perceived, if not so much as a practical problem, then as a psychological injury relating to some men's sense of their worth as fathers 'equal' in law to that of mothers. A perception, that is, that they are indeed accorded secondary importance to their children's mothers in this area of law. At a time when a heightened concern with individual responsibility in family policy and a rapidly evolving separation industry and therapy culture communicate powerful messages that parents should 'sort this out' for themselves,[142] moreover, turning to law, and evoking ideas of legal rights, is in keeping with the messages law itself is communicating here. It is also, I argue in the following section, attuned to the structures of feeling in relation to shifting ideas about men and masculinities in these debates.

Men and masculinities, intimacy and fatherhood

The kinds of images about fathers, law and equality that pervade the fathers' rights discourse, are, I suggested above, in certain respects not so different from what can be found in law. This point can be taken further, however, in the context of fathers' rights politics, where a 'desire for gender neutrality and ideal of egalitarianism' maps directly to what I have referred to, with Sally Sheldon, as a significant 'fragmentation' of fatherhood in law.[143] Far from charting any historical displacement of the father from families, as some fathers' activists and theorists of individualisation would have it,[144] it is more accurate to see fatherhood as having been transformed via a refiguring of the assumptions that, I argued in chapter 5, historically constituted fathers as a desirable presence within families in the first place. Fatherhood has been transformed, however, not just by social, demographic and economic shifts, changes in patterns of employment and a cultural problematising of the practices of both sexes,[145] nor simply by changing ideas of children and childhood, notably the increasingly fluid boundaries childhood appears to have with

---

[141] Honneth, for example, suggests that a struggle for recognition is central to contemporary social conflicts, and has sought to distinguish between three types of recognition: love, respect and social esteem: A. Honneth, *The Struggle for Recognition: The Moral Grammar of Social Conflicts*, Oxford: Polity, 1996. See also Smart, op cit, 2007, pp 149–55.

[142] F. Furedi, *Therapy Culture: Cultivating Vulnerability in an Uncertain Age*, London: Routledge, 2003; J. Bristow, *Standing up to Supernanny*, London: Societas, 2009; also C. Honore, *Under Pressure: Rescuing Our Children from the Culture of Hyper-Parenting*, London: Orion, 2009.

[143] Collier and Sheldon, op cit, 2008.

[144] U. Beck and E. Beck-Gernsheim, *Individualization*, London: Sage, 2002.

[145] F. Furedi, *Paranoid Parenting*, London: Allen Lane, 2002.

adulthood, an issue relatively unexplored in the literature on fathers' rights. What also reshaped these debates, I shall now argue, are ideas about men and masculinities, about manhood and about the father as the embodiment of a particular kind of heterosexual masculinity.

The protests of contemporary fathers' groups, in particular F4J, discussed above, both embody and yet simultaneously are the antithesis of traditional ideas of masculinity, not least around what it means to be a rational, responsible and reasonable subject in dealing with separation. In some respects, they are quintessentially masculine involving, in the form of the 'heroic' climbing of public buildings, a deployment of the male body in space enmeshed with appeals to danger, risk, struggles and, in the case of some of the protests, violence or the perceived threat of violence. This can be seen as illustrative of protest masculinity, a particular kind of hyper-masculine performance.[146] The campaign described above can be seen, from this perspective, as a gendered, embodied social practice.[147] At the same time, however, these protests stand in a profoundly ambivalent relation to supposedly hegemonic ideas about masculinity (chapter 1, p 33)[148] and, importantly, dominant ideas about what it now means to 'be responsible' within the new parenting culture. This point requires clarification.

Notions of hysteria, irrationality and a failure to be reasonable have historically tended to be associated with women rather than men, culturally encoded as feminine.[149] Examples of men showing emotion, crying or otherwise, a rich interdisciplinary literature shows, can frequently attract a redemptive value not accorded women. This is evident in both the legal domain and popular culture. Nonetheless, features commonly seen as characteristic of engagement with fathers' right politics – obsession, the tendency to self-represent, being psychologically 'stuck' in conflict, appealing to 'my rights' and so forth – are rooted in a mode of masculinity that ill-fits, in its association with symptoms, mental disorders and cognitive impairment, the model of the reasonable, rational subject contained in law. Ideas of gender neutrality and responsibility underscore the ideal of the new, caring father in law, we have seen in chapter 5. What is evoked by fathers' rights groups, however, is a model of paternal masculinity that sits uneasily with contemporary ideas about responsibility in law where, as John Eekelaar has

---

[146] C. F. G. Broude, 'Protest Masculinity: A Further Look at the Causes and the Concept', *Ethos*, 1990, vol 18(1), p 103.

[147] Intriguingly, and with specific regard to F4J, in keeping with the comic book genre, behind the 'superhero' – Batman, Spiderman, Superman – there is always, of course, the 'darker side'.

[148] Certainly, as a policy engagement much of this is not pitched at the level of rationality and reason demanded by policy-makers and politicians, whereas some children's and women's groups have arguably been more adept at achieving this, for example engaging with research evidence rather than using personal anecdote.

[149] E. Showalter, *The Female Malady: Women, Madness and English Culture 1830–1980*, London: Virago, 1987.

observed in his book *Family Law and Personal Life*, a reconfiguration of rights and responsibilities has resulted in the demand for something more than simply the meeting of legal obligations.[150] In showing an appropriate awareness of the potential consequences of one's actions, the truly responsible subject should 'exercise restraint within their legal rights'.[151] They should desist from the inappropriate pursuit of rights through the courts, a pursuit encapsulated perhaps by the figure of the 'vengeful' parent in the context of post-separation conflict. Being neutral is not enough – being responsible entails seeing what is best for the child and acting appropriately.

On the one hand, therefore, fathers' rights groups appear highly attuned to the messages about fatherhood and the symbolic power of law that the legal system is radiating. They evoke ideas of fatherhood and masculinity aligned to the idea of the new, caring father. On the other hand, however, fathers' rights discourses trade in ideas of masculinity that are not just anachronistic and out of step with the broader cultural reframing of masculinity and fatherhood that has occurred in the light of the embedding of gender neutrality and formal equality in law. They also rest on a notion of the social subject incompatible with the new ideas of responsibility, rationality and gender neutrality that circulate in the legal field. In light of the above, if we look more closely, it is perhaps unsurprising that the moral tales and normative constructions deployed by fathers' rights groups in their representations of fatherhood should reflect some very different ideas about men and masculinity. What we find here, for example, is a projection, if not denial, of men's emotional pain that runs alongside a cultural and legal acceptance that men should deal with feelings of loss and vulnerability by recourse to rights, to action, to 'doing something', to taking control.[152] In some of the more highly visible protests, there is a simultaneous imagery of fathers as 'humorous', playful figures of fun, 'superheroes' to their children,[153] men who dress as comic-book characters, who love, care for and only want to be with their children. And, at the same time, a representation of the very same fathers as men 'doing battle', 'foot soldiers' in a sex war, men who, in publicly visible spectacular displays of grief, can declare their pain at what they have lost by putting a noose around their heads, 'risking everything' for their children.[154] Sliding between different ideas about men and masculinity,

---

[150] Eekelaar, op cit, 2006, p 128.

[151] Featherstone, op cit, 2009, p 144.

[152] For discussion of the complexity of these responses, in the context of debates in the United States, see J. Crowley, 'Organizational Responses to the Fatherhood Crisis: The Case of Fathers' Rights Groups in the United States', *Marriage and Family Review*, 2006, vol 39(1/2), p 99.

[153] 'Who's The Daddy?', *Independent on Sunday*, 16 April 2006.

[154] A representation of suicide has played a significant part within the F4J campaign. For example, in December 2003 a man dressed as Santa Claus tied himself to the gantry above the A40 in London with a rope and put a noose around this neck; he unfurled a banner that read 'Children Need Both Parents This Christmas'. 'Try and arrest me', he was reported as telling police, 'and I'll hang myself': *The Independent*, 5 February 2004; also D. Evans, 'Fathers 4 Suicide: Protester Vows to Hang at Judge's Home', *News of the World*, 28 September 2008.

such discursive shifts are symptomatic of wider contradictions and confusions around contemporary ideas of fatherhood evident, I have argued, in law and popular culture, as well as the experiences of many men.

It would be naive to assume, therefore, that 'new fathers' (whatever that is) are in any unproblematic way somehow better than 'old'.[155] The new father ideal, Smart and Neale have shown, as noted in chapter 5, is made up of different elements in how it conceptualises men,[156] whilst historical work reveals a diversity and richness to men's practices that suggests any idea of a clear generational break with earlier ideas of fatherhood must be treated with extreme caution. Thus, I argued above, when a government minister speaks of 'dispelling the myth' that fathers are 'the invisible parent', it is important to ask who is saying fathers are unimportant or invisible in the first place.[157] The protests and the emotional imperatives which drive them – a profound sense, for example, of injustice, anger, betrayal and loss, each central to the fathers' rights discourse – clash starkly, violently, with an official discourse that suggests that contemporary divorce has evolved into an arena beyond politics, something that feminist critics have of course questioned for some time.[158] In noting how fathers' groups have challenged de-contextualised, gender-neutral assumptions about law, however, it would be misleading to reduce this engagement with law to little more than the manifestation of a chaotic, destructive and alienating masculinity. Rather, what is happening, I shall suggest in the following section, connects not just to changes in the law but also to questions about emotion and realigned social solidarities far more complex than the simple idea of men's gender protest would indicate to be the case.[159]

Emotion, separation and law

These shifts around rights, justice and care in law are, I have argued above, bound up with ideas about men and masculinities. It is also necessary to consider the importance, for adults, children and the legal system, of questioning how the psychological and sociological dynamics of separation are dealt with by family justice processes.[160] Family research has long pointed to a correlation between poor adult psychological well-being and high conflict in the cases that reach court, remembering that both mothers and fathers constitute a potentially vulnerable population in the process of separation. Evidence

---

[155] C. Haywood and M. Mac an Ghaill, *Men and Masculinities: Theory, Research and Social Practice*, Buckingham: Open University Press, 2003.

[156] Smart and Neale, op cit, 1999, 'I Hadn't Really Thought About it'.

[157] J. Bristow, 'Deconstructing Dads', <http://www.spiked-online.com/index.php?/site/reviewofbooks_printable/6306/>, accessed 28 March 2009.

[158] Day Sclater and Piper (eds), op cit, 1999.

[159] Contrast G. Wayne Walker, 'Disciplining Protest Masculinity', *Men and Masculinities*, 2006, vol 9(1), p 5.

[160] Day Sclater and Richards, op cit, 1995.

emerging from research on fathers' rights activists suggests a common experience of depression and other serious health problems amongst many separating fathers who become involved in groups,[161] a finding consistent with what is known about the divorcing population generally. This raises the issue of what it might mean to develop gender-sensitive/gender-aware intervention in addressing the psychosocial aspects of separation for highly conflicted fathers.[162] Tracking to the importance of affect and emotion discussed in chapter 1, and in developing an account of family law that does not miss out on the affective dimensions of social relations,[163] this entails looking more closely at the interconnectedness of the lives of women, children and men in this area. What might it then mean for legal studies to look beyond the surface cultural representations of, say, men's invulnerability and protest masculinity and develop a more psychosocial, relevant account, one grounded in men's, women's and children's experiences of family practices and, indeed, of the legal system?

Experiences of fathering (and of being fathered), research suggests, are mediated by a range of factors such as age, class, geographical location, religion, ethnicity, sexuality, health and disability.[164] What it means to be a father can vary enormously depending on life history and biography, as well as the specific contexts that situate parenting practices. Just as the highly conflicted case cannot be seen as typical of the majority of separations, therefore, and there is no 'one' father, there is no one kind of fathers' rights activist.[165] Fathers are a diverse, heterogeneous group, a point that has been recognised in the development of policies aimed at engaging vulnerable, marginalised fathers (chapter 5, p 140).

---

[161] S. Gouldstone, 'Family Law Survey Update', *McKenzie: The National Magazine of Families Need Fathers*, 2008, December, no 82, p 5. See also Crowley, op cit, 2008, *Defiant Dads*.

[162] Note for example <http://www.puttingchildrenfirst.info/>, accessed 7 May 2009.

[163] Engaging, for example, with the many dimensions, conscious and unconscious, that shape personal action: S. Day Sclater, *Divorce: A Psycho-Social Study*, Aldershot: Ashgate, 1999.

[164] For discussion of this diversity, see Featherstone, op cit, 2009; also B. Featherstone, 'Taking Fathers Seriously', *British Journal of Social Work*, 2003, vol 33(2), p 239.

[165] There are a range of other organisations that, whilst by no means fathers' groups per se, have sought to address related issues about men's rights and, as such, can be seen as a key part of the political landscape in which debates around law have developed. Those mapping to fathers' groups' concerns include, for example, the UK Men's Movement, <http://www.ukmm.org.uk>, accessed 22 December 2008; the Cheltenham Group, <http://www.c-g.org.uk/>, accessed 22 December 2008; the National Association for Child Support Action, <http://www.nacsa.co.uk/>, accessed 22 December 2008; the National Society for Children and Family Contact, <http://www.nscfc.com/>, accessed 22 December 2008; the False Allegations Support Organisation, <http://www.false-allegations.org.uk/>, accessed 22 December 2008. Addressing rather different contexts are organisations such as the Family Rights Group, <http://www.frg.org.uk/index.asp>, accessed 22 December 2008, and the Association for Shared Parenting, <http://www.sharedparenting.f9.co.uk />, accessed 7 January 2009. The division between the service provision and campaigning role of some groups can be far from clear, the former sliding easily into the kind of support for fathers provided by organisations that would not align themselves, directly, with fathers' rights agendas.

These are issues, I now wish to argue, that have a particular bearing on fathers' rights and post-separation parenting. In seeking to address these themes, the work of Esther Dermott contains important insights. Developing an analysis that focuses on fathers' own views, contemporary fatherhood, Dermott suggests, can be usefully understood as an 'intimate relationship':

> Conceptualising contemporary fatherhood as an intimate relationship allows for an emphasis on the aspects of male parenting that fathers themselves view as most significant: emotions, the expression of affection, and the exclusivity of the reciprocal father-child dyad.[166]

Contemporary fatherhood, Dermott argues:

> is centred on a personal connection at the expense of participation in the work of childcare; because caring activities flow from an emotional connection rather than in themselves constituting the fathering role, the practicalities of 'intimate fatherhood' are fluid and open to negotiation ... Understanding this special quality of contemporary fatherhood is necessary in order to move beyond narrow formulations of fathers, either as failing to contribute to, or as sidelined from contemporary family life.[167]

In this analysis it is the relationship with the child, rather than the 'work' of parenting, that appears at the core of a particular model of intimate fathering, and a wide range of behaviour is seen as experientially significant in terms of this emotional connection between father and child. Following Dermott's conceptualisation of fatherhood as an intimate relationship, and in focusing on fathers' own views of fatherhood, this raises the question of whether it may be as significant to acknowledge in the context of a debate about behaving responsibly the importance not just of what fathers *rationally* think in shaping behaviour but also what they *emotionally* feel and desire.[168] This issue then has a particular bearing in reflecting on the gendered dimensions of the process whereby parents may themselves be moving in different directions, in asynchronous ways, in the course of separation, both experiencing complex and possibly contradictory emotions within the context of a significant life transition point.[169] In line with the focus on the 'doing' of family practices in theoretical work,[170]

---

[166] Dermott, op cit, 2008, p 143.

[167] Dermott, op cit, 2008, p 143.

[168] Haywood and Mac an Ghaill, op cit, 2003.

[169] A. Douglas, 'Transitions: The New Norm', paper presented at 'Putting Children First' Conference, London, 16 October 2008, available at: <www.cafcass.gov.uk/idoc.ashx?doc-id=e07ff5e5–9c26–4937-af60-ff10764c1a01&version = -1>, accessed 25 April 2009. Separation is itself a key point of intervention in responsible citizenship for the social investment State: chapter 5, p 142.

[170] D. Morgan, *Family Connections: An Introduction to Family Studies*, Oxford: Polity, 1996.

therefore, and in marked contrast to the assumptions underscoring a 'top-down' engaging-fathers policy agenda (chapter 5), we might then ask, contra several government ministers, a number of different questions. Just who is saying that fathers are 'absent' from children's lives, that they 'don't care' or are somehow unimportant? Not necessarily mothers, where research suggests that the vast majority, if certainly not all, want fathers to have contact, and seek to facilitate this end. Not necessarily children, whose voices are so often absent from these debates. Certainly not many fathers where, to follow Dermott, what are seen as the important aspects of male parenting are precisely these questions of emotion, affection and the exclusivity of the father-child dyad.

In such a context, it is important to recognise the challenge that separation can represent to this model of intimate fatherhood. The nature and quality of fathering 'in the absence of maternal guidance and supervision', parenting research suggests, can be experienced as highly problematic by both women and men. The dominant pattern within heterosexual parenting across many societies, including the UK, remains one in which, whilst 'mothers take overall responsibility for care for children', in many households at least they 'may delegate out certain activities to fathers'.[171] Studies of parenting, including time-use surveys, indicate that many fathers have little experience of co-parenting prior to separation, although this position is certainly changing in significant respects. Rather, they are being expected by law to move towards this ideal within the co-operative post-separation scenario. However, the fact that the practices now associated with being a good father in law and policy might not have been so entwined with their 'day-to-day' caring activities does not mean, Smart has suggested, they do not love their children.[172] Far from it, many men, to adopt Morgan's notion of family practices,[173] perceive themselves – and, importantly are viewed by others, including partners and children – as 'doing' family practices precisely through their participation in, and commitment to, paid employment, the facilitation of leisure activities for children and so forth.[174] These fathers' experiences of love may be perceived at the point of separation, however, 'to be rather superficial (he does all the fun things while she does all the laundry!) and so less weighty or emotionally significant',[175] as result of the way family practices have been gendered in the first place. This does not mean that a man's

---

[171] Smart, op cit, 2006, 'Preface'.
[172] Smart, op cit, 2006, 'Preface'.
[173] Morgan, op cit, 1996.
[174] J. Warin, Y. Solomon, C. Lewis and W. Langford, *Fathers, Work and Family Life*, York: Joseph Rowntree Foundation/Family Policy Studies Centre, 1999; M. O'Brien and I. Shemilt, *Working Fathers: Earning and Caring*, London, Equal Opportunities Commission, 2003; W. Hatten, L. Vinter and R. Williams, *Dads On Dads: Needs and Expectations at Home and at Work*, London, Equal Opportunities Commission, 2002. This point is supported by a Danish study of cohabiting fathers: M. H. Ottosen, 'Legal and Social Ties Between Children and Cohabiting Fathers', *Childhood*, 2001, vol 8(1), p 75.
[175] Smart, op cit, 2006, 'Preface'.

subjective identification with the ideal of the post-separation father as 'hands-on' carer, or his investments in a particular 'package deal' of associations between marriage, work and fatherhood, does not remain experientially powerful.[176] A heightened psychological desire to be an active father, one that meshes, we have seen, with broader cultural shifts, can be undercut in the process of separation where, as a father, he is no longer able to be valued as 'being there'.[177]

The result of these tensions would appear to be, for some, a profound sense of loss, pain, injustice and anger with law and the legal system, an anger that is, I have suggested, bound up with the mixed messages law itself contains about the nature of good fathering. The fact that a realisation of perceived inequality in how law has dealt with gendered relations occurs at the very moment of separation and can then mean, Smart has suggested, that fathers' legal demands 'for more contact or even residence [then] becomes part of the ... conflict that surrounds separation and, indeed, even intensifies this conflict'.[178] It is precisely in the escalation of these conflicted dynamics around gender relations, Smart argues, that the interwoven nature of 'care' and 'love' constitute a 'micro-politics' of contact,[179] a theme that opens out the complexity of these processes around fathers' rights to a reading more complex and textured than any simple focus on the substance of law alone would allow.

How separation is experienced, I have argued, is bound up with changing ideas of masculine identity and culturally normative expectations about fathers, including those held by women and children and reproduced in law. In the process of negotiating these tensions, a move from a situation in which both parents may have colluded in maintaining a belief in gender equality in parenting prior to separation,[180] a potential source of men's anger can be located, anger that, I argue in the next section, finds expression within fathers' rights agendas.

The emotional politics of fathers' rights

In view of the above, it is important to recognise that there is more going on 'under the radar' of contemporary fathers' rights politics than a focus solely on the high-profile protests and collective staking out of rights and equality claims in the legal arena of recent years would indicate. Have we perhaps attributed too much influence to, and paid disproportionate attention to, say, F4J, rather

---

[176] See N. W. Townsend, *The Package Deal: Marriage, Work and Fatherhood*, Philadelphia, PA: Temple University Press, 2002.

[177] See further J. Ives, 'Becoming a Father/Refusing Fatherhood: How Paternal Responsibilities and Rights are Generated' DPhil thesis, University of Birmingham, 2007. Also A. Gavanas, 'Domesticating Masculinity and Masculinizing Domesticity in Contemporary U.S. Fatherhood Politics', *Social Politics*, 2004, vol 11(2), p 247.

[178] Smart, op cit, 2006, 'Preface'.

[179] Smart, op cit, 2006, 'Preface'.

[180] K. Backett 'The Negotiation of Fatherhood' in C. Lewis and M. O'Brien (eds), *Reassessing Fatherhood: New Observations on Fathers and the Modern Family*, London: Sage, 1987.

than look more closely at what else is happening? Some fathers' groups have an important service function, involving a provision of advice and support particularly associated with fathers' and parenting organisations that have charitable status. In the UK, FNF, as above, remains the most obvious example of this kind of body. There are, however, a diverse range of smaller, locally based groups that provide advice and assistance.[181] Participation in such groups can address a significant emotional need for some men, a need that might otherwise not be met. Research suggests that some men, and women, turn to fathers' groups in order to access a range of practical and emotional supports and to benefit from services that might otherwise be unavailable (such as counselling, information provision, discussion of health issues and so forth).[182] Fighting for formal equality is not, necessarily, a primary motivation in becoming or remaining involved. Some organisations have had a limited lifespan, far shorter than that of FNF, reflecting the pivotal role of a small number of individuals in their establishment and day-to-day running. The personal commitment of these individuals in maintaining group activity at local and national levels should also not be underestimated.

It may be of course that for critics this participation in fathers' groups is harmful for men, as well as, in particular, for former partners.[183] The internal dynamics of fathers' organisations can be seen, on one reading, to encourage a problematic kind of collective male bonding and projection of negative feelings onto former partners and/or the legal system, making a father less able to 'move on' from, and to be stuck in, a highly conflicted position.[184] Judged against the new father ideal, there is much force to the argument that aspects of fathers' rights politics reproduce anachronistic ideas of both men's and women's respective gender roles, a vision of family life premised on a model of fatherhood and masculinity whose 'time has gone'. This does not mean, however, that participation, and these ideas about fathers are not subjectively experienced as valuable by some men, connecting to emotional need at a time of distress. Further, as noted, what is positioned as a 'traditional', as opposed to 'new', father discourse (not least in relation to the breadwinner role)

---

181 See further below. Featherstone, op cit, 2009, p 111, noted around 23 such organisations 'of differing statuses intervening in public relations' as of January 2008.

182 Crowley, op cit, 2008, *Defiant Dads*; R. Collier, 'The UK Fathers' Rights Movement and Law: Report to the British Academy', British Academy rlf/SRF/2005/88 (2008) (unpublished). FNF provides for members, for example, a list of telephone contacts of volunteers available to provide support, advice and information and potential referral to a panel of members with in-depth knowledge of relevant topics: <http://www.fnf.org.uk/membership.htm>, accessed 9 February 2008.

183 M. Flood, 'Separated Fathers and the "Fathers' Rights" Movement', *Feminism Law and the Family Workshop*, Law School, University of Melbourne, 24 February 2006 (copy of paper with author).

184 Raising issues about the dynamics of men's friendships: P. M. Nardi (ed), *Men's Friendships*, London: Sage, 1992. Note also on this depiction of women, and feminism in particular, N. Edley and M. Wetherell, 'Jekyll and Hyde: Men's Construction of Feminism and Feminists', *Feminism and Psychology*, 2001, vol 11(4), p 439.

remains significant for considerable numbers of men and women, as well as their children, in their ideas of what being a father entails.

This raises the question of whether a diverse range of national and locally based groups may be, in offering practical and emotional support, information, advice and assistance, addressing a social and legal need that could otherwise be seen as being unmet. This can be viewed as potentially important work going on outside the formal system, something that a top-down policy agenda insensitive to complexity and diversity within fathers' rights politics will miss. There is arguably very limited provision available at present to support and engage non-resident fathers. It is against this context that a limited number of father support workers, at a local level, seek to support and engage non-resident fathers.[185] Yet what might a gendered awareness of the issues facing fathers raise for the role of CAFCASS and other bodies in meeting fathers' needs? How have these questions been addressed – or not been addressed – by relevant bodies in the field (such as The Fatherhood Institute)?[186] How, for example, might the development of relationship-based interventions and child-inclusive family law dispute-resolution initiatives, of the kind developed in other jurisdictions, impact on fathers' perceptions of conflict?[187] A more positive response to the difficulties separated fathers can face might be to recognise the potential double-edged nature of the policies seeking to increase fathers' involvement in the care of children, discussed in chapter 5, whilst also supporting separated fathers through service provision 'oriented towards encouraging positive and ongoing involvements in their children's lives'.[188]

That is broadly, for all its limitations, what the government has sought to do. There is, however, another important issue to note here. Legal policy's focus on co-operative post-separation parenting, in the absence of any developed and gender-sensitive support, critics have suggested, sits uneasily with the recognition of potentially conflicted emotions in the process of divorce. The dominant assumption in family policy has been that consensus between the parties is an a priori social good.[189] It is difficult, on one level, to refute such a claim. However, this does not mean, Shelley Day Sclater has argued, that the psychological ambivalences around loss that can accompany the end of human relationships, for both women and men, including emotions such as anger, may not jar with the powerful rhetoric of the harmonious divorce in a number of ways.[190] This

185 Based, for example, in Contact Centres and dealing directly with the issues and needs of non-resident fathers in ways that seek to promote conflict-free parental communication and co-operation.

186 Featherstone, op cit, 2009, pp 140–42.

187 J. McIntosh, 'Enduring Conflict in Parental Separation: Pathways on Child Development', *Journal of Family Studies*, 2003, vol 9, p 63.

188 Flood, op cit, 2006, p 13.

189 Although see Day Sclater and Piper (eds), op cit, 1999.

190 Day Sclater, op cit, 1999. See also S. Day Sclater, 'Divorce – Coping Strategies, Conflict and Dispute Resolution', *Family Law*, 1998, p 150; S. Day Sclater and C Yates, 'The Psycho-Politics

might take the form of, for example, the negation of the legitimacy of, and a denial of the space to articulate, conflicted feelings of loss, guilt and anger, emotions that, from a psychosocial perspective, accompany the process of separation to varying degrees.[191] This raise the question of whether participation in fathers' rights groups potentially provides a 'safe' social space for some men in which to articulate such feelings, to share with others who may generally be sympathetic and empathise with (gendered) experiences. This argument can be allied to the work of some pro-feminist writers who have suggested, in exploring identities beyond traditional oppressive models, that it is important that men do have space to articulate and question their emotions and feelings, in a dominant culture that has constructed masculinity as unemotional and detached.[192]

It remains difficult to see, however, how this space, by itself, engages with and challenges broader gender relations and questions of power, a point I will return to below. Given the emotionally heightened and toxic context in which these dynamics take place, moreover, the result can easily be a reinforcing of, rather than a challenge to, gendered divisions. Far from reducing conflict, I have argued elsewhere, the ideal of co-parenting supported by law may fuel hostility between some parents where it is perceived, not in terms of any shared ideology or mutual commitment, but as a legal or financial coercion bound up with unresolved tensions and conflicts. Conflicts that, in the case of the men participating in fathers' rights organisations, there is reason to believe might well remain unresolved.[193]

Where does this leave us? The good (divorcing) citizen has been repositioned in law, I have suggested, as a particular kind of rational, reasonable and de-gendered subject, an individual who will – given appropriate information/education – act responsibly.[194] In such a social and legal context, fathers, like mothers, can experience a tension between the *ideals* of desirable parenting contained in law and the *realities* of their own social experiences as gendered subjects, the result being a potential sense of disappointment, frustration and, for some, feelings of anger (with law, the legal system) that needs to be managed emotionally. In the case of men who fail the tests of 'therapeutic correctness',[195] the standards of response

of Post Divorce Parenting' in A. Bainham, S. Day Sclater and M. Richards (eds), *What is a Parent? A Socio-Legal Analysis*, Oxford: Hart, 1999. Note also here I. Craib, *The Importance of Disappointment*, London: Routledge, 1994.

[191] J. Brown and S. Day Sclater, 'Divorce: A Psychodynamic Perspective' in Day Sclater and Piper (eds), op cit, 1999.

[192] V. Seidler, *Man Enough: Embodying Masculinities*, London: Sage, 1997.

[193] Collier, op cit, 2008, 'UK Fathers' Rights Movement'. The very men most active in fathers' groups, that is, may be those who are, from a psychological perspective, 'trapped' or 'stuck' in a stage of anger and conflict; on stages of grief and loss, see E. Kubler-Ross, *On Death and Dying*, London: Tavistock/Routledge, 1989.

[194] Reece, op cit, 2009; van Krieken, op cit, 2005. See further J. Bridgeman, C. Lind and H. Keating (eds), *Responsibility, Law and the Family*, Aldershot: Ashgate Publishing, 2008.

[195] Reece, op cit, 2009.

expected of the good, reasonable father, research suggests that participation in fathers' groups might, for some men at least, provide a meaningful space in which these conflicted emotions can be articulated and expressed. Further, noting the diverse range of commitments to fathers' rights politics that result, we cannot assume that all fathers who participate in groups necessarily 'buy in' to the broader critique of law and the legal system put forward by some. Experience and commitment, as Jocelyn Crowley's important work on fathers' groups in the United States suggests, and as limited work in the UK supports, can be more fluid, with men dipping 'in and out' of involvement. Some participate at particular times, for example in the immediate aftermath of the institution of court proceedings; in terms of organisational development, many fathers' groups remain highly dependent on the commitment of a small core of members,[196] who themselves may have 'moved on' from previous experiences of high conflict. At a more general level, turning to sociological work, the organisational responses of fathers' groups to complex social changes track to wider themes around how men and women can mobilise resources in different ways, for example in relation to ideas of relationality, in a project of self-authorship marked by increased introspection around identity formation.[197]

Impact and politics: a shifting debate

Finally, it is important not to overstate the impact of fathers' groups in shaping policy agendas in England and Wales, notwithstanding the fact that some claims have found a degree of resonance with certain judges, politicians and policy-makers, as noted above. For all the public visibility and high media profile of an organisation such as F4J, legal reform to introduce a presumption of contact and shared equal parenting has been unequivocally rejected by the British government.[198] Illustrating the complex and double-edged nature of feminism's impact on family law,[199] the government's position has been informed by research, including work by law and society scholars[200] that directly counters key arguments advanced by fathers' groups. This political terrain is, at the time of writing, in flux, with the future

---

[196] Crowley, op cit 2008, *Defiant Dads*; Collier, op cit, 2008, 'UK Fathers' Rights Movement'.

[197] A. Giddens, *The Transformation of Intimacy*, Cambridge: Polity, 1992.

[198] 'Some fathers' groups have come to believe that the courts and the law are biased against them. *We do not accept this view*': DfES, DCA and DTI, op cit, 2004, 'Ministerial Foreword' p 1, my emphasis.

[199] A. Diduck and K. O'Donovan, 'Feminism and Families: Plus Ca Change?' in Diduck and O'Donovan (eds), op cit, 2006.

[200] Note, for example, C. Smart, V. May, A. Wade and C. Furniss, *Residence and Contact Disputes in Court: Research Report 6/2003* London: Department for Constitutional Affairs, 2003, a study of disputes over residence and contact brought to three County Courts in England in the year 2000, cited by Margaret Hodge, Hansard, HC Deb, col 67W 5 Jan 2004.

uncertain.[201] Equally, it is difficult to predict how the Human Rights Act 1998 will reshape understandings of 'rights talk' in this context.[202] However, recognising the scale of the distress caused by some fathers' protests,[203] and the fact that legal aid cuts are having a profound impact on already vulnerable women and children (see below), it may be more accurate to view events since 2002 as contradictory, raising the profile of issues yet, at the same time, proving counter-productive in alienating potential support.

It is against this backdrop, therefore, that there appears to have been a recent shift in the terrain of fathers' rights politics, signs of a realignment of organisations and family sector leaders around the need to encourage co-operation based on the shared recognition of the need to support *all* separated families, both mothers and fathers. Internally, meanwhile, there has been a significant development within the terrain of fathers' rights politics itself.[204] It was announced in September 2008, after a turbulent history marked by internal disagreement and several attempts at re-branding,[205] that F4J would be shut down and re-launched as a helpline 'for all parents whose family lives are in crisis'.[206] This move is unlikely to mean the end of direct action protest by fathers and their supporters. It does, however, map to a degree of realignment of organisations around the need to bring together stakeholders and promote debate on national support for separated families. In this move FNF has played a key role, and can be seen to

---

[201] See, for example, 'Avalanche: The Times they are campaigning as the Tories start to turn', *McKenzie: The National Magazine of Families Need Fathers*, 2008, Autumn, no 80, p 1.

[202] Herring et al, op cit, 2009. See also C. Henricson and A.Bainham, *The Child and Family Policy Divide: Tensions, Convergence and Rights*, York: Joseph Rowntree Foundation, 2005.

[203] Targeted in an all too clearly gendered way, as the singling out of certain women ministers shows.

[204] There are also signs of a refocusing on post-separation contact as an object of political concern, with the Equal Parenting Alliance emerging as 'a new UK political party' formed in February 2006, with the explicit aim of promoting 'a system of family justice in the UK that puts the needs and interests of children first', <http://www.equalparentingalliance.org/policy-index.html>, accessed 17 November 2008.

[205] The founder Matt O'Connor had earlier announced in January 2006 that the group would be disbanded following the reporting in the British media of a 'plot' to kidnap the five-year-old son of the Prime Minister Tony Blair (*The Independent*, 19 January 2006; 'Fathers 4 Justice is disbanded over "plot" to kidnap Leo Blair', *The Times*, 19 January 2006). Controversy had also ensued following television reports concerned with the background of several members of the group (ITV, 'Tonight With Trevor MacDonald', 14 November 2005; also The 5Live Report, Julian Warwicker Programme, Sunday 26 March 2006, BBC Radio 5 Live, <http://www.bbc.co.uk/fivelive/programmes/worricker.shtml>, accessed 27 March 2006). The emergence of a splinter group, termed the 'Real Fathers 4 Justice', sought to continue the campaign of F4J: S. Laville, 'Batman and Robin Quit Protest Group', *The Guardian*, 9 June 2005 ('You've Heard of the Real IRA. Now meet Real Fathers4Justice, the caped crusaders who refuse to give up the fight'). It was announced in February 2006 that 'the "heroes" of direct-action group Fathers 4 Justice were to be immortalised in *F4J: The Movie* … ' ('Men in Tights: Movie Debut for Fathers 4 Justice', *The Independent*, 2 February 2006).

[206] E. Dugan, '"Come and Join Us": Fathers 4 Justice Welcomes mums', *Independent on Sunday*, 28 September 2008.

have repositioned itself, to a degree, in the light of the broader developments in fathers' rights politics outlined in this chapter. Thus, in recent years we have seen joint statements on separated family policy principles,[207] co-operative research studies involving leading fathers' groups,[208] a range of conferences aimed at bringing together sector leaders[209] and other initiatives seeking to support and facilitate contact subsequent to the enactment of the 2006 Act.[210] Reflecting on the debate in 2008, Matt O'Connor has himself been quoted as saying:

> We don't want to be misogynistic. Fathers can be equally as bad as mothers. I want something that's not about gender, not about fathers, but about families. F4J polarised people, but we ... want to bring everyone together.[211]

Of particular significance has been 'Kids in the Middle', launched in July 2008 by Relate, One Parent Families, FNF and the Fatherhood Institute, a major cross-charity campaign aimed at improving support for separating families.[212] Whilst the success of such measures depends on the provision of adequate support and funding, and political commitment on the part of government, taken together they are indicative of a terrain that has moved on since the high point of fathers' protests discussed in this chapter.[213] Thus, diverse stakeholders are increasingly stressing the limits of adversarial proceedings in court and highlighting the need to engage with the complexities of transition and the emotional dimensions of separation,[214] recognising that public policy will itself create barriers to communication if it is

---

[207] For example, 'Letter to the Editor: The Government Must Help the Children of Divorcees', *The Times*, 12 June 2007, p 16; signatories to this letter included Families Need Fathers, Women's Aid and Fathers Direct; 'Family Sector Leaders Joint Statement On Separated Family Policy Principles', 1 May 2006, <http://www.fatherhoodinstitute.org/index.php?id=4&cID=468>, accessed 20 April 2009.

[208] For example, Families Need Fathers et al, *Beyond the Nuclear*, London: Families Need Fathers, Grandparent's Association and Family Matters Institute, 2009.

[209] Centre for Separated Families, 'Putting Children First' event in London, October 2008; see further <http://www.separatedfamilies.info/>, accessed 27 March 2009; J. Turner, 'The Feminist Battling or Men's Rights', *The Guardian*, 20 May 2006.

[210] Such as Resolution's (formally the Solicitors Family Law Association) *Parenting After Parting Scheme*, 2008.

[211] In Dugan, op cit, 2008.

[212] See <http://www.fatherhoodinstitute.org/index.php?id=4&cID=766>, accessed 25 March 2009; <http://www.dad.info/b/kids-in-the-middle/>, accessed 25 March 2009. In November 2008 the Secretary for State for Children, Schools and Families hosted a 'Relationship Summit' to discuss government policy on parental conflict, involving a range of 'agony aunts' and sector leaders: J. Malvern, 'Dear Deirdrie, I want to talk about relationships with agony aunts. What can I do next?', *The Times*, 19 December 2008.

[213] See further, and in addition, the Men's Coalition: <http://www.themenscoalition.org.uk/Welcome.html>, accessed 23 March 2009, work including the Fatherhood Institute, Men's Health Forum, Respect, Relate, Action for Children and others.

[214] In terms of research noting this complexity and the need for relationship-based intervention, see for example, L. Trider and J. Kellett, 'The Longer-Term Outcomes of In-Court Conciliation', London: Ministry of Justice, 2007.

informed by increasingly outdated gendered assumptions about the lives of *both* women and men.

Concluding remarks

I have argued in this chapter that the development of organisational politics around fathers' rights is interconnected to changing social, legal and cultural discourses around gender and equality. It is against this backdrop that the issue of how men relate to ideas of justice and rights, responsibilities and care has been refigured in the legal arena. This provides an important part of the grounded social context in which the renegotiation of personal identities in the process of separation now takes place. Progressing an engagement with the significance of emotion and personal life considered in chapter 1, it is important to recognise in this context how individuals encounter law in ways shaped by their life history and biography, 'gendered rationalities'[215] and specific location in relation to peer groups and social networks. Highlighting the importance of the psychosocial dimensions of experience, such an approach seeks to recognise that structures beyond law, such as the messages radiated about parenting in popular culture, shape these ideas of individual responsibility in significant ways.[216] Thus, as noted in this chapter and chapter 5, a particular model of paternal responsibility has come to encapsulate in its scope a broad range of conflicting ideas about fathers in terms of both 'care talk', welfare, justice and rights-based claims. However, what is also becoming clear is that a range of socially contingent and very different ideas circulate in these debates about what it means to be a 'good father' or a 'family man', a breadwinner or a caring father, a partner, a friend and so forth.

Far from simply reproducing ideas of hegemonic masculinity, or evoking an essentialist notion of the (masculine) psyche, I have argued that we are dealing with complex processes whereby particular identities – such as that of the 'angry' fathers' rights activist – are socially constituted and take on meaning for individuals.[217] In the case of fathers' rights politics, this entails asking why it is that some men, but not others, invest in certain subject positions, and others do not. In the light of the above, I wish to make three points by way of general conclusion.

Transforming masculinities: social and legal contexts

First, I have suggested that the heightened political and cultural prominence of fathers' rights groups is bound up with the play of identity politics and the

---

215 A. Barlow, S. Duncan and G. James, 'New Labour, the Rationality Mistake and Family Policy in Britain' in A. Carling, S. Duncan and R. Edwards (eds), *Analysing Families: Morality and Rationality in Policy and Practice*, London: Routledge, 2002.

216 Bridgeman et al, op cit, 2008.

217 On these discursive strategies see M. Wetherell and N. Edley, 'Negotiating Hegemonic Masculinity: Imaginary Positions and Psycho-Discursive Practices', *Feminism and Psychology*, 1999, vol 9(3), p 335; Dermott, op cit, 2008. See further chapter 1.

formation of social movements within advanced capitalist societies, in particular in relation to the emergence of political agendas focused on issues around 'everyday' lives, ways of living and questions of self-identification.[218] Ideas about paternal masculinity, I argued in chapter 5, have been reconstituted in law via an uneasy mix of traditional beliefs about men (for example, of a man's role, male authority) and the values and practices associated with the new fatherhood, beliefs that track to the different strands within both feminism and men's movement politics.[219] Set against this backdrop, a growing body of empirical and theoretical research suggests that men may be dealing with the contradiction between various aspects of gendered identity in a number of different ways.

To reduce these debates to a backlash to feminism, or to see them as little more than a manifestation of anti-women sentiment, however, diverts attention from how emotions and gendered social experiences are dealt with (or not dealt with) in law,[220] the many dimensions, conscious and unconscious, that shape personal action.[221] It is precisely the emotive aspects of separation that, I have argued in this chapter, have been underexplored within much legal and social policy analysis of fathers' rights. The concept of hegemonic masculinity, discussed in chapter 1, as an explanatory ideal, is not strong enough to hold together the complexity of what is happening here. The feminist critique of fathers' rights detailed above, meanwhile, has drawn attention to how a deployment of individualistic rights and equality claims by men can easily divert attention from law's conceptualisation of the private (sexual) family and in so doing efface the gendered dimensions of care and social dependency in ways that are profoundly problematic for women. At the same time, it is important to recognise how social relations and structures beyond 'the family' impact on ideas about parenthood in ways that render the law just part, albeit a significant part, of how rights, responsibilities and family practices come to be experienced and take on subjective meaning. Family lawyers will miss much, therefore, as will

---

[218] On the idea of the new social movement in this context see A. Touraine, 'An Introduction to the Study of New Social Movements', *Social Research*, 1985, vol 52, p 749; Ashe, op cit, 2007; R. Kennedy, *Fathers For Justice: The Rise of a New Social Movement in Canada as a Case Study of Collective Identity*, 2nd edn, Ann Arbor, MI: Caravan Books, 2005, a reading of Canadian fathers' rights groups. See further J. Crowley, 'Fathers' Rights Groups, Domestic Violence, and Political Countermobilization', *Social Forces*, forthcoming; J. Crowley, 'On the Cusp of a Movement: Identity Work and Social Movement Identification Processes within Fathers' Rights Groups', *Sociological Spectrum*, 2008, vol 28(6), p 705.

[219] Ashe, op cit, 2007; Messner, op cit, 1997; Clatterbaugh, op cit, 2000.

[220] See, for an alternative view: S. A. Bandes (ed), *The Passions of Law*, New York: New York University Press, 1999; L. Bentley and L. Flynn (eds), *Law and the Senses*, London: Pluto, 1996; M. Douglas, 'Emotion and Culture in Theories of Justice', *Economy and Society*, 1993, vol 22 (4), p 501; M. Nussbaum, *Hiding From Humanity: Disgust, Shame and the Law*, Princeton, NJ: Princeton University Press, 2004.

[221] Day Sclater, op cit, 1999.

feminism, if the rise of fathers' rights activism is dismissed as no more than a minority activity. It can tell us much about the times in which we live, the structures of feeling that shape our lives. This is why it is important to locate debates in the context of the broader shifts around law, men and gender, as detailed in this book, and engage with the issue of what governments might do to better support all parents. The trouble, however, is that the form this policy has taken has itself rested on problematic ideas about parenting culture.

Parenting cultures

Second, following on from the above, it cannot be assumed that social groups relate to the new responsibility and co-parenting ideal, intensive parenting agendas, an emergent therapy culture[222] or, indeed, an engaging fathers discourse (chapter 5) in the same way. The privatisation of responsibilities within family law and the economic imperatives underscoring a family policy debate ostensibly about promoting responsibility, may, rather, have had a particularly hard impact on *already* vulnerable populations, not least, as the important work of Val Gillies shows, some groups of mothers.[223] In recognising the diversity of fathers' experiences and how different groups of men relate to and seek to assert 'rights talk',[224] therefore, it is open to question to what extent policy debates about fatherhood have themselves been informed by problematic assumptions about class, race and ethnicity and social disadvantage.[225] Moreover, that they have done so in ways that have served to efface the very real vulnerabilities of certain groups of men in contemporary British society, whilst casting others (white? middle-class?) as the embodiments of a normative new father ideal.[226] This is something that much of the British media do consistently in their

[222] Furedi, op cit, 2002; Furedi, op cit, 2003.

[223] V. Gillies, *Marginalised Mothers: Exploring Working Class Experiences of Parenting*, London: Routledge, 2006; also V. Gillies, 'Meeting Parents' Needs? Discourses of "Support" and "Inclusion" in Family Policy', *Critical Social Policy*, 2005, vol 25(1), p 70; R. Lister, 'Children (But Not Women) First: New Labour, Child Welfare and Gender', *Critical Social Policy*, 2006, vol 26(2), p 315; see also R. Crompton and C. Lyonette, 'Family, Class and Gender "Strategies" in Mothers' Employment and Childcare', GeNet Working Paper No 34, 2009, available at <www.genet.ac.uk/workpapers/GeNet2008p34.pdf>, accessed 25 March 2009.

[224] A point made by Featherstone, op cit, 2009, p 118, noting how ideas of rights, and perceptions of a 'feminised' State, play out in different ways in specific contexts; see C. Gatrell, '"Whose Child is it Anyway?" The Negotiation of Paternal Entitlements Within Marriage', *The Sociological Review*, 2007, vol 55, p 352.

[225] Note L. McDowell, *Redundant Masculinities? Employment, Change and White Working Class Youth*, Oxford: Blackwell, 2003.

[226] This raises the question of whether the broader 'engaging father' agenda (chapter 5) may itself represent a reframing of, rather than a challenge to, dominant ideas of hegemonic masculinity, in which negative qualities are projected on some subordinated groups of men (whilst the 'new father', in contrast, embodies virtues in ways others do not): K. Henwood and J. Proctor, 'The "Good Father": Reading Men's Accounts of Paternal Involvement During the Transition to First-time Fatherhood', *British Journal of Social Psychology*, 2003, vol 42(3), p 337. See further Featherstone, op cit, 2009.

portrayal of fatherhood, adopting an individualistic, middle-class vantage point, a theme that tracks to the discussions of class, masculinities and law earlier in this book. So, whilst certain men 'grapple' with and 'juggle' contradictory discourses around masculinity in the area of work-life balance considered in chapter 6, others, notably in the context of crime/criminality, continue to be pathologised by law, and subject to law's surveillance, in rather different ways.[227] How, in this respect, does an appreciation of the moral significance of class,[228] considered in chapter 3, inform fathers' differential access to resources and networks? How do these concerns then shape collective cultural responses and perceptions of the play of masculinities within the field of fathers' rights politics? Who have family policy-makers, and indeed, critics of fathers' groups, seen as acceptable voices here? Who has been included, and excluded, from policy networks, and how are some men's and women's actions constituted as irrational, irresponsible, unreasonable, over-emotional and so forth whilst others are not?

These issues take on a particular resonance in the context of a legal policy debate marked by an increasingly moral tone, what has been described as a re-moralising of parenthood. In this process, far from seeing any sociologically robust engagement with the changes that have taken place around law and fatherhood (including fathers' rights politics), questions of economy, social structure and social power appear to get lost as fathers, like mothers, find themselves repositioned, I argued in chapter 5, as both solution *to* and cause *of* certain social problems. An increased emphasis on private ordering has redrawn debates about power imbalances in law, notably in the area of child support and its links with contact. At the very moment the parental role is positioned as potentially crimogenic, however, that role has itself been practically diminished as the experiences of parents become sidelined within policy debates dominated by the voices of those who 'know better'. Those who claim expertise about such issues, however, it has been suggested, can often be detached from the real lives of those individuals who are constituted as the social problem in the first place, a process involving complex codes of judgement, (dis)identification and exclusion.[229] It is not difficult to see in this how, just as ideas about 'respectable' femininity are mediated by class-based assumptions, class, race and ethnicity can inform cultural representations of

---

[227] S. Hall, 'Daubing the Drudges of Fury: Men, Violence and the Piety of the "Hegemonic Masculinity" Thesis', *Theoretical Criminology*, 2002, vol 6(1), p 35; J. Scourfield and M. Drakeford, 'New Labour and the "Problem of Men"', *Critical Social Policy*, 2002, vol 22, p 619. Collier, op cit, 1998.

[228] A. Sayer, *The Moral Significance of Class*, Cambridge: Cambridge University Press, 2005.

[229] See B. Skeggs, 'Haunted by the Spectre of Judgement: Respectability, Value and Affect in Class Relations', in K. P. Sveinsson (ed), *Who Cares About the White Working Class?* London: Runnymede Trust, 2009.

acceptable masculinities in the context of legal policy debates.[230] At the same time, as Featherstone and others have argued, a conceptual separation of the parent and child within the new child-centred social policy runs the danger of reinforcing social exclusion, in particular that of already vulnerable groups of mothers,[231] leading to a greater colonisation of personal life.

Fathers' rights and the limits of law

> Fatherhood is both of interest in itself, and as a lens through which to examine personal lives more widely.[232]

Third, and finally, to conclude by looking to the 'bigger picture' of the social changes around law, men and gender detailed in this book, and consider, in this discussion of fathers' rights, the impact of political and cultural developments on the personal lives and subjectivities of adults and children. This chapter has charted a way through an often highly polarised debate about fathers' rights, locating a shifting political terrain in relation to changing parenting cultures and social and legal ideas about fatherhood. Some fathers' groups maintain a faith in the ability of legal reform to solve the problems that fathers face. This is a faith much socio-legal research suggests may be misplaced. Law, alone, cannot solve these problems, just as legislation struggles to keep up with social change. The limits of law in the regulation and management of intimate relationships, reflecting the inherent 'normal chaos' of family life, has been well documented within scholarship that has noted the inability of law to take into account the complexities of human behaviour.[233] Moreover, research on fathers' groups suggests that specific legal processes reshape equality claims within the terms of a legal system's own norms and rationalities.[234] From this perspective, the emotionally 'messy', psychologically complex disputes discussed in this chapter, as well as elsewhere in this book, can be seen as normal and inevitable features of what happens when law attempts to regulate human relationships, the ambiguous realities of our personal lives and inevitable dependencies.[235]

This does not mean, however, I have argued in this chapter, that the perception that law might potentially solve these problems is any less real or

---

[230] Note here B. Gough, '"Biting Your Tongue": Negotiating Masculinities in Contemporary Britain', *Journal of Gender Studies*, 2001, vol 10(2), p 169.

[231] Featherstone, op cit, 2009; Gillies, op cit, 2006.

[232] Dermott, op cit, 2008, p 143.

[233] J. Dewar, 'The Normal Chaos of Family Law', *Modern Law Review*, 1998, vol 61, p 467.

[234] Collier and Sheldon (eds), op cit, 2006; Featherstone, op cit, 2009, pp 127–28; S. Boyd, 'Is Equality Enough? Fathers' Rights and Women's Rights Advocacy', in R. Hunter (ed), *Rethinking Equality Projects in Law: Feminist Challenges*, Oxford: Hart, 2008.

[235] M. Fineman, *The Neutered Mother, The Sexual Family, and Other Twentieth Century Tragedies*, New York: Routledge, 1995.

experientially significant, especially in a context where the symbolic power of law (in radiating messages, in signalling equality) is widely accepted in the legal arena. The rise of active father cultures and practices (chapter 5), of formal equality agendas and ideas about gender neutrality (chapter 1), has had implications for how men construct ideas of selfhood. Set against this back-drop, the fathers' rights discourse provides a mode of articulation for the problems that some fathers now face and, as such, is a development under-standable when seen in this broader context. At issue in debates about fathers' rights are questions about the conceptual ambiguity of fatherhood, the rela-tionship between men and children,[236] ideas about masculinities and emotion, rationality and intimacy, as well as the male body. The heightened politicisa-tion of fatherhood in the legal arena reflects, I have argued, the contradictory nature of a reconfiguration of gender relations that has profoundly reshaped understanding of the relationship between men, gender and equality.

The changes detailed above, in summary, tell us much about how a 'trans-formation in the role of the father' has taken place in the slipstream of fem-inism and the women's movement,[237] as well as in the context of the embedding in law, and the heightened cultural salience of, gender neutrality and formal equality. What is taking place around fathers' rights represents a complex social development, part of a transformation of adult-child relations and family life occurring across Western countries, that raises important questions about social life, including the variable, contested and changing meanings that attach to gender. In seeking to make sense of these debates, and develop greater conceptual resources by which to do so, then, as Featherstone has argued:

> We need to continue dialogue on what unites and divides us as parents, as men and women, and stop using the welfare of children as a weapon or shield ... Change in this area requires parents, men and women, to engage with the feelings of pain and loss and the vulnerability thrown up by separation.[238]

The reframing of responsibility in family law, forceful legal imperatives of co-parenting and messages conveyed about active fathering within law and pop-ular culture are reshaping men's expectations of equity and fairness in the process of divorce, as well as in relation to other areas of law. Contemporary gender shifts, that is, are 'throwing up real issues for men about how they live

---

[236] See, for example, J. Hearn and K. Pringle, 'Men, Masculinities and Children: Some European Perspectives', *Critical Social Policy*, 2006, vol 26(2), p 365.

[237] Noting in this context, as in chapter 5, the different strands of feminist thought at play. See further S. Lawrence, 'Feminism, Consequences, Accountability', *Osgoode Hall Law Journal*, 2004, vol 42(4), p 583; Hunter (ed), op cit, 2008.

[238] Featherstone, op cit, 2009, p 125.

their role as fathers', an issue with implications not just for law but also for feminism.[239] Studies of law and gender, I have argued in this book, have much to gain from incorporating a more complex and multi-layered account of the gendered male subject and the interconnected nature of the lives of women, children and men. Equally, public policies based on outmoded stereotypes of both sexes are unlikely to address the problems parents can face. Set against a policy agenda that has sought increasingly to engage fathers in families, the greater prominence of fathers' rights politics can be understood as one aspect of a complex renegotiation of men's role as parents that has occurred in the light of growing uncertainty about what it means to be 'a man' in law and in society.[240]

[239] R. Coward, *Sacred Cows*, London: Harper Collins, 1999, p 147.
[240] Bridgeman et al, op cit, 2008.

References

Aaltio-Marjosola, I. and Lehtinen, J. (1998) 'Male Managers as Fathers? Contrasting Management, Fatherhood and Masculinity' 51(2) *Human Relations* 121.

Abel, R. L. (1988) *The Legal Profession in England and Wales* Oxford: Basil Blackwell.

—— (2003) *English Lawyers Between Market and State: The Politics of Professionalism* Oxford: Oxford University Press.

Abrams, K. (2000) 'Cross-Dressing in the Master's Clothes' 109 *Yale Law Journal* 745.

Acker, J. (1989) 'The Problem with Patriarchy' 23 *Sociology* 235.

Adams, P. (1995) *The Emptiness of the Image: Psychoanalysis and Sexual Differences* London: Routledge.

Adams, R. and Savran, D. (eds) (2002) *The Masculinity Studies Reader* Oxford: Wiley Blackwell.

Addleshaw Goddard (2008) *Legal Lives: Retaining Talent through a Balanced Culture* London: Addleshaw Goddard.

Adkins, L. and Skeggs, B. (eds) (2004) *Feminism After Bordieu* Oxford: Blackwell.

Adler, M. (1991) 'From Symbolic Exchange to Commodity Consumption: Anthropological Notes on Drinking as a Symbolic Practice' in S. Barrows and R. Room (eds) *Drinking Behaviour and Belief in Modern History* Berkeley: University of California Press.

Adonis, A. and Pollard, S. (1988) *A Class Act: The Myth of Britain's Classless Society* London: Penguin.

Albiston, C. (2005) 'Anti-Essentialism and the Work/Family Dilemma' 20 *Berkeley Journal of Gender, Law and Justice* 30.

Alcock, P. (1984) 'Remuneration or Remarriage? The Matrimonial and Family Proceedings Act 1984' 11(3) *Journal of Law and Society* 357.

Allen, S. (1982) *One Step from the Quagmire* Aylesbury: Campaign for Justice in Divorce.

Amato, P. R. and Gilbreth, J. G. (1999) 'Non-Resident Fathers and Children's Well-being: A Meta-Analysis' 61 *Journal of Marriage and Family* 557.

Andrews, M., Day Sclater, S., Squire, C. and Treacher, A. (eds) (2000) *Lines of Narrative: Psychosocial Perspectives* London: Routledge.

—— (eds) (2004) *The Uses of Narrative: Explorations in Sociology, Psychology and Cultural Studies* London: Transaction.

Annesley, C. (2001) 'New Labour and Welfare' in S. Ludlam and M. J. Smith (eds) *New Labour in Government* London: Macmillan.

Archer J. (ed) (1994) *Male Violence* London: Routledge.

Archer, J. and Lloyd, B. (1985) *Sex and Gender* Cambridge: Cambridge University Press.

Archer, L. and Francis, B. (2006) *Understanding Minority Ethnic Achievement: Race, Gender, Class and 'Success'* London: Routledge.

Archer, L., Hutchings, M. and Ross, A. (2002) *Higher Education and Social Class: Issues of Exclusion and Inclusion* London: Routledge Falmer.

Arditti, J. and Allen, K. (1993) 'Distressed Fathers' Perceptions of Legal and Relational Inequities Post-Divorce' 31 *Family and Conciliation Courts Review* 461.

Arendell, T. (1999) *Fathers and Divorce*, London: Sage.

Arthur, S. (2003) *Money, Choice and Control: The Financial Circumstances of Early Retirement* London: Policy Press.

Aryee, S. and Luk, V. (1996) 'Balancing Two Major Parts of Adult Life Experience: Work and Family Identity Among Dual-Earner Couples' 49(4) *Human Relations* 465.

Ashe, F. (2007) *The New Politics of Masculinity Men: Power and Resistance* (Routledge Innovations in Political Theory) London: Routledge.

Atkins, S. and Hoggett, B. (1984) *Women and the Law* Oxford: Blackwell.

Attwood, C., Singh, G., Prime, D., Creasey, R. et al (2003) *2001 Home Office Citizenship Survey: People, Families and Communities* London: Home Office Research, Development and Statistics Directorate.

Attwood, R. (2008) 'Young Academics Striving to Fit in Reveal Anxiety' *Times Higher Education* 7 August.

Auchmuty, R. (2007) 'Unfair Shares for Women: The Rhetoric of Equality and the Reality of Inequality' in A. Bottomley and H. Lim (eds) *Feminist Perspectives on Land Law* London: Routledge-Cavendish.

Backett, K. (1987) 'The Negotiation of Fatherhood' in C. Lewis and M. O'Brien (eds) *Reassessing Fatherhood: New Observations on Fathers and the Modern Family* London: Sage.

Bailey-Harris, R., Barron, J. and Pearce, J. (1999) 'From Utility to Rights? The Presumption of Contact in Practice' 13 *International Journal of Law, Policy and the Family* 111.

Bakan, J. (2004) *The Corporation* Toronto: Viking Canada.

Baker, J. (2009) 'Open Glory?: Why Transparent Family Justice is Vital For All Concerned' *McKenzie: The National Magazine of Families Need Fathers* 83 February.

Ball, S., Maguire, M. and Macrae, S. (2000) *Choice, Pathways and Transitions Post-16: New Youth, New Economies and the Global City* London, Routledge.

Bandes, S.A. (ed) (1999) *The Passions of Law* New York: New York University Press.

Barker, G. et al (2004) *Supporting Fathers: Contributions from the International Fatherhood Summit 2003*, The Hague, Early Childhood Development: Practice and Reflections Series, Bernard van Leer Foundation.

Barker, S. and Einstein, A. (2007) *How to Be a Great Divorced Dad* Slough: Foulsham.

Barlow, A., Duncan, S. and James, G. (2002) 'New Labour, the Rationality Mistake and Family Policy in Britain' in A. Carling, S. Duncan and R. Edwards (eds) *Analysing Families: Morality and Rationality in Policy and Practice* London: Routledge.

Barlow, A. et al (2005) *Cohabitation, Marriage and the Law: Social Change and Legal Reform in the 21st Century* Oxford: Hart.

Barnard, J. (1998) 'Reflections on Britain's Research Assessment Exercise', 48(4) *Journal of Legal Education* 467.

Barnett, R. (2000) *Realizing the University in an Age of Supercomplexity* Buckingham: Open University Press.

Bartlett, D., Burgess, A. and Jones, K. (2007) *A Toolkit for Developing Father-Inclusive Practice* London: Fathers Direct.

Barton, C. (2008) 'Joint Birth Registration: "Recording Responsibility" Responsibly?' *Family Law* 789.

Bassnett, C. (2003) 'Opinion' *The Guardian* 27 May.

Bauman, Z. (2006) *Liquid Times: Living in an Age of Uncertainty*, Oxford: Polity.

—— (2007) *Consuming Life*, Oxford: Polity.

BBC Radio 4 (2004) 'Rights for Fathers – Lord Geoff Filkin and Sir Bob Geldof' Today Programme 3 April London: GICS Media Monitoring Unit (copy of transcript with author).

Beasley, C. (2008) 'Rethinking Hegemonic Masculinity in a Globalising World' 11(1) *Men and Masculinities* 86.

Becher, T. (1989) *Academic Tribes and Territories: Intellectual Enquiry and the Culture of Disciplines* Buckingham: Open University Press.

Becher, T. and Kogan, M. (1992) *Process and Structure in Higher Education* London: Routledge.

Beck, U. (2000) *The Brave New World of Work* Cambridge: Polity.

Beck, U. and Beck-Gernsheim, E. (1995) *The Normal Chaos of Love* Cambridge: Polity.

—— (2002) *Individualization: Institutionalized Individualism And Its Social and Political Consequences* London: Sage.

Bell, C. M. (1995) 'All I Really Need to Know I Learned in Kindergarten (Playing Soccer): A Feminist Parable of Legal Academia' 7 *Yale Journal of Law and Feminism* 133.

Bell, D. and Valentine, G. (1995) 'The Sexed Self: Strategies of Performance, Sites of Resistance' in S. Pile and N. Thrift (eds) *Mapping the Subject: Geographies of Cultural Transformation* London: Routledge.

bell hooks, (1983) *Aint I A Woman: Black Women and Feminism* London: Pluto.

—— (1984) *Feminist Theory: From Margin to Center*, Cambridge, MA: South End Press.

Bem, S. (1976) 'Probing the Promise of Androgyny' in A.G. Kaplan and J.P. Bean (eds) *Beyond Sex Role Stereotypes: Readings Towards a Psychology of Androgyny* Boston, MA: Little Brown.

Bender, L. (1991) 'For Mary Joe Frug: Empowering Women Law Professors' 6 *Wisconsin Women's Law Journal* 1.

Benhabib, S. (1986) *Critique, Norm and Utopia: A Study of the Foundations of Critical Theory* New York: Columbia University Press.

—— (1997) *Situating the Self* London: Routledge.

Bennett, R. (2008) 'Cuts in Maternity Leave to Give Fathers More Time Off' *The Times* 30 March.

Benschop, Y. and Brouns, M. (2003) 'Crumbling Ivory Towers: Academic Organising and its Gender Effects' 10(2) *Gender, Work and Organisation* 194.

Bentley, L. and Flynn, L. (eds) (1996) *Law and the Senses* London: Pluto.

Benwell, B. (ed) (2003) *Masculinity and Men's Lifestyle Magazines: Sociological Review Monographs* Oxford: Blackwell.

Berger, M., Wallis, B. and Watson, S. (eds) (1995) *Constructing Masculinity* New York: Routledge.

Berlant, L. (2000) *Intimacy* Chicago, IL: Chicago University Press.

Berns, S. (2006) 'Musings on The Legal Scene: Law, Populism and the Politics of Ressentiment' 25 *Australian Feminist Law Journal* 19.

Berotia, C. (1998) 'An Interpretative Analysis of the Mediation Rhetoric of Fathers' Rightists: Privatization Versus Personalization' 16(1) *Mediation Quarterly* 15.

Berotia, C. and Drakich, J. (1993) 'The Fathers' Rights Movement: Contradictions in Rhetoric and Practice' 14(4) *Journal of Family Issues* 592.

Beveridge, F., Nott, S. and Stephen, K. (eds) (2000) *Making Women Count: Integrating Gender into Law and Policy-Making* Aldershot: Ashgate.

Bibbings, L. (2000) 'Boys Will be Boys: Masculinity and Offences Against the Person' in J. Bridgman and D. Monk (eds) *Feminist Perspectives on Criminal Law* London: Cavendish.

—— (2003) 'The Future of Higher Education: "Sustainable Research Businesses" and "Exploitable Knowledge"' 40 *Socio-Legal Newsletter* 1.

—— (2006) 'Widening Participation in Higher Education' 33(1) *Journal of Law and Society* 74.

Bird, S. (1996) 'Welcome to the Men's Club: Homosociality and the Maintenance of Hegemonic Masculinity' 10 *Gender and Society* 120.

Blackwell, A. and Dawe, F. (2003) *Non-Residential Parental Contact* London: Lord Chancellor's Office.

Blakenhorn, D. (1995) *Fatherless America: Confronting Our Most Urgent Social Problem* New York: Basic Books.

Blanden, J., Gregg, P. and Machin, S. (2005) *Intergenerational Mobility in Europe and North America* London: Sutton Trust.

Blaxter, L., Hughes, C. and Tight, M. (1998) *The Academic Career Handbook* Buckingham: Open University Press.

Blomley, N. (1997) 'The Properties of Space: History, Geography and Gentrification' 18 (4) *Urban Geographer* 286.

Bocock, R. (1993) *Consumption* London: Routledge.

Bolton, S. and Muzio, D. (2007) 'Can't Live with 'Em: Can't Live Without 'Em: Gendered Segmentation in the Legal Profession' 41(1) *Sociology* 47.

Bonoli, G. (2005) 'The Politics of the New Social Policies: Providing Coverage Against New Social Risks in Mature Welfare States' 33(3) *Policy and Politics* 431.

Boon, A. (2005) 'From Public Service to Service Industry: The Impact of Socialization and Work on the Motivation and Values of Lawyers' 12(2) *International Journal of the Legal Profession* 229.

Boon, A. and Levin, J. (1999) *The Ethics and Conduct of Lawyers in England and Wales* Oxford: Hart.

Boon, A., Duff, E. and Shiner, M. (2001) 'Career Paths and Choices in a Highly Differentiated Profession: The Position of Newly Qualified Solicitors' 64(4) *Modern Law Review* 563.

Boon, A., Flood, J. and Webb, J. (2005) 'Postmodern Professions? The Fragmentation of Legal Education and the Legal Profession' 32(3) *Journal of Law and Society* 473.

Bordieu, P. (1977) *Outline of a Theory of Practice* Cambridge: Cambridge University Press.

—— (1979) 'Symbolic Power' 4 *Critique of Anthropology* 77.

—— (1984) *Homo Academicus* Paris: Editions de Minuit.

—— (1987) 'What Makes a Social Class? On the Theoretical and Practical Existence of Groups' 32 *Berkeley Journal of Sociology* 1.

—— (1989) *Distinction: A Social Critique of the Judgement of Taste* London: Routledge.

Bordo, S. (1994) *The Male Body: A New Look at Men in Public and in Private* New York: Farrar, Straus and Giroux.

Bourke, J. (ed) (1994) *Working Class Cultures in Britain 1890–1960: Gender, Class and Ethnicity* London: Routledge.

Bower, L.C., Goldberg, T. and Musheno, M (eds) (2001) *Between Law and Culture: Relocating Legal Studies* Minneapolis, MN: University of Minnesota Press.

Bowker, L.H. (ed) (1998) *Masculinities and Violence* Thousand Oaks, CA: Sage.

Bowl, M. (2003) *Non-Traditional Entrants to Higher Education: 'They Talk About People Like ME'* Stoke: Trentham Books.

Boyd, S. (1989) 'From Gender Specificity to Gender Neutrality? Ideologies in Canadian Child Custody Law' in J. Brophy and C. Smart (eds) *Child Custody and the Politics of Gender* London: Routledge.

—— (ed) (1997) *Challenging the Public/Private Divide Feminism, Law and Public Policy* Toronto: University of Toronto Press.

—— (2001) 'Backlash and the Construction of Legal Knowledge: The Case of Child Custody Law' 20 *Windsor Year Book of Access to Justice* 141.

—— (2003) *Child Custody, Law and Women's Work* Oxford: Oxford University Press.

—— (2004) 'Backlash Against Feminism: Canadian Custody and Access Reform Debates of the Late Twentieth Century' 16(2) *Canadian Journal of Women and Law* 255.

—— (2004) 'Demonizing Mothers: Fathers' Rights Discourses in Child Custody Law Reform Processes' 6(1) *Journal of the Association for Research in Mothering* 52.

—— (2005) 'Review Essay: Being Responsible in the New Family Law' 1(2) *International Journal of Law in Context* 199.

—— (2008) 'Is Equality Enough? Fathers' Rights and Women's Rights Advocacy', in R. Hunter (ed) *Rethinking Equality Projects in Law: Feminist Challenges* Oxford: Hart.

Boyd, S. and Young, C. F. (2002) 'Who Influences Family Law Reform? Discourses on Motherhood and Fatherhood in Legislative Reform Debates in Canada' 26 *Studies in Law Politics and Society* 43.

Bradney, A. (1998) 'Law as a Parasitic Discipline' 25(1) *Journal of Law and Society* 71.

—— (1999) 'Liberalising Legal Education' in F. Cownie (ed) *The Law School: Global Issues, Local Questions* Aldershot: Ashgate.

—— (2003) *Conversations, Choices and Chances: The Liberal Law School in the Twenty-First Century* Oxford: Hart.

—— (2004) 'Academic Duty' 28 *The Reporter* 1.

—— (2008) 'Elite Values in Twenty-First Century United Kingdom Law Schools' 42 *Law Teacher* 291.

Bradney, A. and Cownie, F. (1998) *The English Legal System in Context* London: Butterworths.

Bradney, A. and Cownie, F. (1998) 'Transformative Visions of Legal Education' 25 *Journal of Law and Society* 1.

Bradney, A. and Cownie, F. (2000) 'British University Law Schools in the 21st Century' in D. Hayton (ed) *Law's Futures* Oxford: Hart.

Bradshaw, J., Stimson, C., Skinner, C. and Williams, J. (1999) *Absent Fathers?* London: Routledge.

Braidotti, R. (1987) 'Envy: Or With My Brains and Your Looks' in A. Jardine and P. Smith (eds) *Men in Feminism* London: Methuen.

Brain, K. (2000) *Youth, Alcohol and the Emergence of the Post-Modern Alcohol Order* London: Institute of Alcohol Studies.

Brannon, R. (1976) 'The Male Sex Role: Our Culture's Blueprint for Manhood and What It's Done for Us Lately' in D. David and R. Brannon (eds) *The Forty-Nine Per Cent Majority: The Male Sex Role* Reading, MA: Addison Wesley.

Brewer, M. and Paull, G. (2005) *Newborns and New Schools: Critical Times in Women's Employment* London: Department for Work and Pensions.

Bridgeman, J. and Millns, S. (eds) (1995) *Law and Body Politics: Regulating the Female Body* Aldershot: Ashgate.

Bridgeman, J., Lind, C. and Keating, H. (2008) (eds) *Responsibility, Law and the Family* Aldershot: Ashgate Publishing.

Bristow, J. (2009) 'Deconstructing Dads' <http://www.spiked-online.com/index.php?/site/reviewofbooks_printable/6306/>, accessed 28 March 2009.

—— (2009) *Standing up to Supernanny* London: Societas.

Brittan, A. (1989) *Masculinity and Power* Oxford: Blackwell.

Brockman, J. (2001) *Gender in the Legal Profession: Fitting or Breaking the Mould?* Vancouver: Univeristy of British Columbia Press.

Brod, H. (1987) *The Making of Masculinities: The New Men's Studies* London: Allen and Unwin.

Brod, H. and Kaufman, M. (eds) (1994) *Theorizing Masculinity* Thousand Oaks, CA: Sage.

Brooks, A. (1997) *Academic Women* Milton Keynes: SRHE/Open University Press.

—— (2001) 'Restructuring Bodies of Knowledge' in A. Brooks and A. Mackinnon (eds) *Gender and the Restructured University* Buckingham: SRHE/Open University Press.

Brooks, A. and Mackinnon, A. (eds) (2001) *Gender and the Restructured University* Buckingham: SRHE/Open University Press.

Broude, C. F. G. (1990) 'Protest Masculinity: A Further Look at the Causes and the Concept' 18(1) *Ethos* 103.

Broughton, T. and Rogers, H. (eds) (2007) *Gender and Fatherhood in the Nineteenth Century* London: Palgrave Macmillan.

Brown, B. (1986) 'Women and Crime: The Dark Figures of Criminology' 15 *Economy and Society* 355.

—— (1990) 'Reassessing the Critique of Biologism' in L. Gelsthorpe and A. Morris (eds) *Feminist Perspectives in Criminology* Buckingham: Open University Press.

Brown, J. and Day Sclater, S. (1999) 'Divorce: A Psychodynamic Perspective' in S. Day Sclater and C. Piper (eds) *Undercurrents of Divorce* Aldershot: Ashgate.

Brownsword, R. (1996) 'Where Are All The Law Schools Going?' 30 *Law Teacher* 6.

Bruch, C. (2002) 'Parental Alienation Syndrome and Alienated Children – Getting it Wrong in Child Custody Cases' 14 *Child and Family Law Quarterly* 381.

Bull, A. (1998) *Downshifting: The Ultimate Handbook* London: Thorsons.

Burgess, A. (1997) *Fatherhood Reclaimed: The Making of the Modern Father* London: Vermillion.

—— (2007) *The Costs and Benefits of Active Fatherhood: Evidence and Insights to Inform the Development of Policy and Practice* London: Fathers Direct.

Burgess, A. and Bartlett, D. (2004) *Working With Fathers* London: Fathers Direct.

Burgess, A. and Russell, G. (2004) 'Fatherhood and Public Policy' in G Barker et al *Supporting Fathers: Contributions From the International Fatherhood Summit 2003* The Hague: Early Childhood Development: Practice and Reflections Series, Bernard van Leer Foundation.

Burgess, A. and Ruxton, S. (1996) *Men and Their Children: Proposals for Public Policy* London: Institute for Public Policy Research.

Burrage, M. (1996) 'From a Gentleman's to a Public Profession: Status and Politics in the History of English Solicitors' 3 *International Journal of the Legal Profession* 45.

Burridge, R. and Webb, J. (2007) 'The Values of Common Law Legal Education: Rethinking Rules, Responsibilities, Relationships and Roles in the Law School' 10 *Legal Ethics* 74.

—— (2008) 'The Values of Common Law Legal Education Reprised' 42(3) *Law Teacher* 265.

Butler, I. et al (2003) *Divorcing Children: Children's Experiences of Their Parents' Divorce* London: Jessica Kingsley Publishers.

Butler, J. (1990) *Gender Trouble: Feminism and the Subversion of Identity* London: Routledge.

—— (1992) 'Contingent Foundations: Feminism and the Question of "Postmodernism"' in J. Butler and J. W. Scott (eds) *Feminists Theorize the Political* New York: Routledge.

—— (1993) *Bodies That Matter: On the Discursive Limits of Sex* London: Routledge.

Butler, T. (ed) (1995) *Social Change and the Middle Classes* London: UCL Press.

—— (1997) *Gentrification and the Middle-Classes*, Aldershot, Ashgate.

Byrne, B. (2006) *White Lives: The Interplay of 'Race', Class and Gender in Everyday Lives* London: Routledge.

Cabinet Office (2008) *Families In Britain: An Evidence Paper* London: Cabinet Office (Strategy Unit).

—— (2009) *Fair Access to the Professions: Good Practice, Phase 2 Report* London: Cabinet Office.

—— (2009) *Fair Access to the Professions: Phase 1 Report, An Analysis of the Trends and Issues Relating to Fair Access to the Professions* London: Law Society.

Campbell, B. (1993) *Goliath: Britain's Dangerous Places* London: Methuen.

Campbell, D. (2006) 'Fathers Fight for Family Flexi-Time' *The Observer* 12 March.

Campbell, K., Vick, D., Murray, A. and Little, G. (1999) 'Journal Publishing, Journal Reputations and the United Kingdom Research Assessment Exercise' 25(4) *Journal of Law and Society* 470.

Canaan, J. E. (1996) '"One Thing Leads to Another": Drinking, Fighting and Working Class Masculinities' in M. Mac an Ghaill (ed) *Understanding Masculinities* Buckingham: Open University Press.

Canaan, J. E. and Griffin, C. (1990) 'The New Men's Studies: Part of the Problem, or Part of the Solution?' in J. Hearn and D. Morgan (eds) *Men, Masculinities and Social Theory* London: Routledge.

Cannadine, D. (1998) *Class in Britain* London: Yale University Press.

Carabine, J. (1996) 'Heterosexuality and Social Policy' in D Richardson (ed) *Theorising Heterosexuality: Telling it Straight* Buckingham: Open University Press.

Carbado, D. (ed) (1999) *Black Men on Race, Gender and Sexuality* New York: New York University Press.

Carbone, J. (2000) *From Partners to Parents: The Second Revolution in Family Law* Columbia, NY: Columbia University Press.

Card, R. (2002) Presidential Address Wed 11 September 2002, Society of Legal Scholars Annual Conference, De Montfort University.

Carlsson, B. and Baier, M. (2002) 'A Visual Self-Image of Legal Authority: "The Temple of Law"' 11 *Social and Legal Studies* 185.

Carrigan, T., Connell, R. W. and Lee, J. (1985) 'Towards a New Sociology of Masculinity' 14 *Theory and Society* 551.

Carvel, J. (2008) 'Mandelson Under Fire Over Flexible Working Proposals' *The Guardian* 22 October.

Carver, T. (1996) '"Public Man" and the Critique of Masculinities' 24 *Political Theory* 673.

Casey, C. (1996) 'Corporate Transformation: Designer Culture, Designer Employees and "Post-Occupational" Solidarity' 3(3) *Organization* 317.

Castells, M. (1994) 'The University System: Engine of Development in the New World Economy' in J. Salmi and A. Verspoor (eds) *Revitalizing Higher Education* London: Pergamon.

Cealey Harrison, W. and Hood-Williams, J. (2002) *Beyond Sex and Gender* London: Sage.

Centre for Social Justice (2008) *The Family Law Review Interim Report*, London, Centre for Social Justice.

Chaney, D. (1996) *Lifestyles* London: Routledge.

Chaplin, E. (1994) *Sociology and Visual Representation* London: Routledge.

Charlesworth, S. (2000) *A Phenomenology of Working Class Experience*, Cambridge: Cambridge University Press.

Chatterton, P. (2005) 'Governing Nightlife: Profit, Fun and (Dis)Order in the Contemporary City' 1(2) *Entertainment and Sports Law* 23.

Chatterton, P. and Hollands, R. (2002) 'Theorising Urban Playscapes: Producing, Regulating and Consuming Youthful Nightlife City Spaces' 39(1) *Urban Studies* 95.

—— (2003) *Urban Nightscapes: Youth Cultures, Pleasure Spaces and Corporate Power* London: Routledge.

Chick, D. (2006) *Denied Access* London: Pen Press.

Children Act Sub-committee of the Advisory Board on Family Law (2001) *Making Contact Work. A Report to the Lord Chancellor on the Facilitation of Arrangements for Contact Between Children and their Non-residential Parents and the Enforcement of Court Orders for Contact* London: Lord Chancellor's Department.

Children's Society (2009) *A Good Childhood: Searching for Values in a Competitive Age* London: Children's Society.

Chodorow, N. (1994) *Femininities, Masculinities, Sexualities: Freud and Beyond* Lexington, KY: Free Association.

Christian, H. (1994) *The Making of Anti-Sexist Men* London: Routledge.

Chunn, D. E., Boyd, S. and Lessard, H. (eds) (2007) *Reaction and Resistance: Feminism, Law and Social Change* Vancouver: University of British Columbia Press.

Clare, A (2000) *On Men: Masculinity in Crisis* London: Chatto & Windus.

Clark, B. (1998) *Creating Entrepreneurial Universities: Organizational Pathways of Transformation* Oxford: Pergamon Press.

Clatterbaugh, K. (1996) *Contemporary Perspectives on Masculinity: Men, Women and Politics in Modern Society* London: Harper Collins.

Clegg, N. (2009) 'There's a Job at Home For Out-of-work Dads' *The Times* 17 February.

Coady, T. (ed) (2000) *Why Universities Matter: A Conversation about Values, Means and Directions* Sydney: Allen and Unwin.

Cochrane, K. (2008) 'Now, The Backlash' *The Guardian* (G2) 1 July.

Coffield, F. and Williamson, D. (eds) (1997) *Repositioning Higher Education* Buckingham: Open University Press.

Cohen, J. and Gershbain, N. (2001) 'For the Sake of Fathers? Child Custody Reform and the Perils of Maximum Contact' 19 *Canadian Family Law Quarterly* 121.

Cohen, N. (2009) 'Why I Blame the Left for Britain's Financial Ruin' *The Observer* 25 January.

Cole, B. (1997) *Solicitors in Private Practice – Their Work and Expectations. Research Study No. 26* London: Law Society (Research and Policy Planning Unit).

Cole, B. (2008) *Trends in the Solicitor's Profession: Annual Statistical Report 2007* London: Law Society.

Collier, R (1991) 'Masculinism, Law and Law Teaching' 19 *International Journal of the Sociology of Law* 427.

—— (1992) '"The Art of Living the Married Life": Representations of Male Heterosexuality in Law' 1 *Social and Legal Studies* 543.

—— (1993) 'A Father's "Normal Love"? Masculinities, Criminology and the Family' in R. Dobash and L. Noakes (eds) *Gender and Crime* Cardiff: University of Wales Press.

—— (1994) 'The Campaign Against the Child Support Act, "Errant Fathers" and "Family Men"' *Family Law* 384.

—— (1995) *Masculinity, Law and the Family* London: Routledge.

—— (1997) 'After Dunblane: Crime, Corporeality and the (Hetero)Sexing of the Bodies of Men' 24(2) *Journal of Law and Society* 177.

—— (1998) *Masculinities, Crime and Criminology: Men, Heterosexuality and the Criminal(ised) Other* London: Sage.

—— (1998) '"Nutty Professors", "Men in Suits" and "New Entrepreneurs": Corporeality, Subjectivity and Change in the Law School and Legal Practice' 7 *Social and Legal Studies* 27.

—— (1999) '"Feminising the Workplace"? (Re)constructing the "Good Parent" in Employment Law and Family Policy' in A. Morris and T. O'Donnell (eds) *Feminist Perspectives on Employment Law* London: Cavendish.

—— (1999) 'The Dashing of a "Liberal Dream"? The Information Meeting, the "New Family" and the Limits of Law' 11 *Child and Family Law Quarterly* 257.

—— (1999) 'From "Women's Emancipation" to "Sex War"?: Beyond the Masculinized Discourse of Divorce' in S. Day Sclater and C. Piper (eds) *Undercurrents of Divorce* Aldershot: Ashgate.

—— (2000) 'Straight Families, Queer Lives? Heterosexual(izing) Family Law' in D. Herman and C. Stychin (eds) *Sexuality in the Legal Arena* London: Athlone Press.

—— (2001) 'A Hard Time to be a Father?: Law, Policy and Family Practices' 28(4) *Journal of Law and Society* 520.

—— (2001) 'In Search of the "Good Father": Law, Family Practices and the Normative Reconstruction of Parenthood' 22 *Studies in Law, Politics and Society* (A. Sarat and P. Ewick (eds)) 133.

—— (2001) 'The Paedophile, the Dangerous Individual and the Criminal Law: Reconfigurations of the Public/Private Divide' in C. Brants and P. Alldridge (eds) *Personal Autonomy, the Private Sphere and the Criminal Law: A Comparative Study* Oxford: Hart.

—— (2002) 'The Changing University and the (Legal) Academic Career – Rethinking the "Private Life" of the Law School' 22(1) *Legal Studies* 1.

—— (2002) 'Male Bodies, Family Practices' in A. Bainham, S. Day Sclater and M. Richards (eds) *Body Lore and Laws* Oxford: Hart.

—— (2002) 'Masculinities' 36 *Sociology* 737.

—— (2003) 'Men, Masculinities and Crime' in C. Sumner (ed) *The Blackwell International Companion to Criminology* Oxford: Blackwell.

—— (2003) '"Useful Knowledge" and the "New Economy": An Uncertain Future for (Critical) Socio-Legal Studies' 39 *Socio Legal Newsletter* 3.

—— (2005) 'Fathers 4 Justice, Law and the New Politics of Fatherhood' 17 *Child and Family Law Quarterly* 511.

—— (2005) 'The Liberal Law School, The Restructured University and the Paradox of Socio-Legal Studies' 68 *Modern Law Review* 475.

—— (2007) 'Peter's Choice: Issues of Identity, Lifestyle and Consumption in Changing Representations of Corporate Lawyers and Legal Academics' in S. Greenfield and G. Osborn (eds) *Readings in Law and Popular Culture: Routledge Research Monographs* London: Routledge.

—— (2008) 'The UK Fathers' Rights Movement and Law: Report to the British Academy', British Academy rlf/SRF/2005/88 (unpublished).

Collier, R. and Sheldon, S. (2006) 'Fathers' Rights, Fatherhood and Law Reform – International Perspectives' in R. Collier and S. Sheldon (eds) (2006) *Fathers' Rights Activism and Legal Reform* Oxford: Hart.

Collier, R. and Sheldon, S. (2008) *Fragmenting Fatherhood: A Socio-Legal Study* Oxford: Hart.

Collier, R. and Sheldon, S. (eds) (2006) *Fathers' Rights Activism and Legal Reform* Oxford: Hart.

Collins, L. H., Chrisler, J. C. and Quina, K. (eds) (1998) *Career Strategies for Women in Academe* London: Sage.

Collins, M. (2004) *The Likes of Us: A Biography of the White Working Class* London: Granta.

Collins, P. H. and Andersen, M. (eds) (2003) *Race, Class and Gender: An Anthology* New York: Wadsworth.

Collins Casey, C. (1996) 'Corporate Transformation: Designer Culture, Designer Employees and "Post-Occupational Solidarity"' 3(3) *Organization* 317.

Collinson, D. and Collinson, M. (1997) 'Delayering Managers: Time-Space Surveillance and its Gendered Effects' 4(3) *Organization* 399.

Collinson, D. and Hearn, J. (eds) (1996) *Men as Managers, Managers as Men: Critical Perspectives on Men, Masculinities and Managements* London: Sage.

Collinson, M. (1996) 'In Search of the High Life: Drugs, Crime, Masculinities and Consumption' 36 *British Journal of Criminology* 428.

Coltrane, S. (1997) *Family Man: Fatherhood, Housework and Gender Equity* Oxford: Oxford University Press.

Coltrane, S. and Adams, M. (2003) 'The Social Construction of the "Divorce Problem"' 52 *Family Relations* 363.

Coltrane, S. and Hickman, N. (1992) 'The Rhetoric of Rights and Needs: Moral Discourse in the Reform of Child Custody and Support Laws' 39 *Social Problems,* 400.

Conaghan, J. (2000) 'Reassessing the Feminist Theoretical Project in Law' 27 *Journal of Law and Society* 351.

Connell, R. W. (1987) *Gender and Power* Cambridge: Polity.

—— (1993) 'The Big Picture: Masculinities in Recent World History' 22 *Theory and Society* 597.

—— (1994) 'Psychoanalysis on Masculinity' in H. Brod and M. Kaufman (eds) *Theorizing Masculinities* Thousand Oaks, CA: Sage.

—— (1995) *Masculinities* Cambridge: Polity.

Connell, R.W. (1997) 'Men, Masculinities and Feminism' 16(3) *Social Alternatives* 7.

—— (1997) '"Arms and the Man": Using the New Research on Masculinity to Understand Violence and Promote Peace in the Contemporary World' Paper for UNESCO expert group meeting on Male Roles and Masculinities in the Perspectives of a Culture of Peace, Oslo.

—— (2000) *The Men and the Boys* Cambridge: Polity.

—— R.W. (2002) 'On Hegemonic Masculinity and Violence: Response to Jefferson and Hall' 6(1) *Theoretical Criminology* 89.

—— (2003) 'Men, Gender and State' in S. Ervo and T. Johansson (eds) *Among Men: Moulding Masculinities* Aldershot: Ashgate.

—— (2005) 'Globalization, Imperialism and Masculinities' in M. Kimmel, J. Hearn and R.W. Connell (eds) *Handbook of Men and Masculinities* London: Sage.

Connell, R. W. and Messerschmidt, J. W. (2005) 'Hegemonic Masculinity: Rethinking the Concept' 19(6) *Gender and Society* 829.

Connell, R. W. and Wood, J. (2005) 'Globalization and Business Masculinities' 7(4) *Men and Masculinities* 347.

Connell, R. W., Hearn, J. and Kimmel, M. (eds) (2004) *The Handbook of Masculinity Studies* London: Sage.

Cooper, S. (1992) 'Post-Intellectuality? Universities and the Knowledge Economy' in S. Cooper, J. Hinkson and G. Sharp (eds) *Scholars and Entrepreneurs: The Universities in Crisis* Melbourne: Arena Publications.

Cooper, S., Hinkson, J. and Sharp, G. (eds) (1992) *Scholars and Entrepreneurs: The Universities in Crisis* Melbourne: Arena Publications.

Corder, N. (2001) *Escape from the Rat Race: Downshifting to a Richer Life* London: Right Way Plus.

Cornell, D. (1991) *Beyond Accommodation: Ethical Feminism, Deconstruction and the Law* New York: Routledge.

—— (1991) 'Sexual Difference, the Feminine and Equivalency: A Critique of Mackinnon's "Toward a Feminist Theory of the State"' 100 *Yale Law Journal* 2247.

Cornwall, A. and Lindisfarne, N. (eds) (1994) *Dislocating Masculinity* London: Routledge.

Cotterrell, R. (2002) 'Subverting Orthodoxy, Making Law Central: A View of Socio-Legal Studies' 29(4) *Journal of Law and Society* 632.

Court, S. (1999) 'Negotiating the Research Imperative: The Views of UK Academics on their Career Opportunities' 53(1) *Higher Education Quarterly* 65.

Coward, R. (1999) *Sacred Cows* London: Harper Collins.

Cownie, F. (1998) 'Women Legal Academics – A New Research Agenda?' 25(1) *Journal of Law and Society* 102.

—— (ed) (1999) *The Law School: Global Issues, Local Questions* Aldershot: Ashgate.

—— (2000) 'Women in the Law School – Shoals of Fish, Starfish or Fish Out of Water?' in P. Thomas (ed) *Discriminating Lawyers* London: Cavendish.

—— (2004) *Legal Academics: Culture and Identities* Oxford: Hart.

—— (2009) (ed) *Stakeholders in the Law School* Oxford: Hart.

Craib, I. (1987) 'Masculinity and Male Dominance' 35 *The Sociological Review* 721.

—— (1994) *The Importance of Disappointment* London: Routledge.

Creasey, R. et al (2003) 'Family Networks and Parenting Support in England and Wales' in C. Attwood et al *2001 Home Office Citizenship Survey: People, Families and Communities* London: Home Office Research, Development and Statistics Directorate.

Crenshaw, K. (1991) 'Mapping the Margins: Intersectionality, Identity Politics and Violence Against Women of Color' 43(6) *Stanford Law Review* 1241.

Cretney, S. (1996) '"What Will Women Want Next?" The Struggle for Power Within the Family 1925–75' 12 *Law Quarterly Review* 110.

Crewe, B. (2005) *Representing Men: Cultural Production and Producers in the Men's Magazine Market* London: Berg.

Crompton, R. (1999) *Restructuring Gender Relations and Employment: The Decline of the Male Breadwinner* Oxford: Oxford University Press.

Crompton, R. and Lyonette, C. (2008) *Who Does the Housework? The Division of Labour Within the Home: British Social Attitudes 24th Report*, London: National Centre for Social Research/Sage.

—— (2009) 'Family, Class and Gender "Strategies" in Mothers' Employment and Childcare' GeNet Working Paper No 34, available at <http://www.genet.ac.uk/workpapers/GeNet2008p34.pdf>, accessed 25 March 2009.

Crompton, R. and Scott, J. (2005) 'Class Analysis: Beyond the Cultural Turn' in F. Devine, M. Savage, J. Scott and R. Crompton (eds) *Rethinking Class: Cultures, Identity and Lifestyle* London: Palgrave Macmillan.

Crowley, J. (2006) 'Adopting "Equality Tools" from the Toolboxes of their Predecessors: the Fathers' Rights Movement in the United States' in R. Collier and S. Sheldon (eds) *Fathers' Rights Activism and Legal Reform* Oxford: Hart.

—— (2006) 'Organizational Responses to the Fatherhood Crisis: The Case of Fathers' Rights Groups in the United States' 39(1/2) *Marriage and Family Review* 99.

—— (2008) *Defiant Dads: Fathers' Rights Activism in America* Ithaca, NY: Cornell University Press.

—— (2008) 'On the Cusp of a Movement: Identity Work and Social Movement Identification Processes within Fathers'Rights Groups' 28(6) *Sociological Spectrum* 705.

—— (forthcoming) 'Fathers' Rights Groups, Domestic Violence, and Political Countermobilization' *Social Forces*.

Cunningham, K. (2001) 'Father Time: Flexible Work Arrangements and the Law Firm's Failure of the Family' 53 *Stanford Law Review* 967.

Currie, J. (1995) 'Restructuring Employment: The Case of Female Academics' 2 *Australian Universities Review* 49.

—— (2002) 'Walking Away' *Lawyer 2B* December 4.

—— (2003) 'Dead End' *Lawyer 2B* March 24.

Currie, J., Thiele, B. and Harris, P. (2002) *Gendered Universities in Globalized Economies: Power, Careers and Sacrifices* Lanham, MD: Lexington Books.

Currie, J. and Newson, J. (eds) (1998) *Universities and Globalization* London: Sage.

Curtis, D. and Resnik, J. (1987) 'Images of Justice' 96 *Yale Law Journal* 1726.

Curtis, P. (2004) 'Competition Time' *The Guardian* 9 March.

—— (2008) 'Making Time for the Children: One in Four Parents Now Put their Family Before Work' *The Guardian* 19 December.

—— (2009) 'Family Policies to be "Dad-Proofed" ... ' *The Guardian* 21 February.

Cuthbert, R. (2002) 'The Impact of National Developments on Institutional Practice' in S. Ketteridge, S. Marshall and H. Fry (eds) *The Effective Academic* London, Kogan Page/THES.

Daly, K. (1997) 'Different Ways of Conceptualising Sex/Gender in Feminist Theory and Their Implications for Criminology' 1 *Theoretical Criminology* 25.

Daly, M. (1984) *Pure Lust: Elemental Feminist Philosophy* London: The Women's Press.

—— (1985) *Beyond God the Father: A Philosophy of Women's Liberation* London: The Women's Press.

Daniel, B. and Taylor, J. (2001) *Engaging with Fathers: Practice Issues for Health and Social Care* London: Jessica Kingsley Publishers.

Daniels, R.R. (ed) (1998) *Lost Fathers: The Politics of Fatherlessness in America* New York: St Martin's Press.

David, M. and Woodward, D. (eds) (1998) *Negotiating the Glass Ceiling: Careers of Senior Women in the Academic World* London: Falmer Press.

Davies, C. and Holloway, P. (1995) 'Troubling Transformations: Gender Regimes and Organizational Culture in the Academy' in L. Morley and V. Walsh (eds) *Feminist Academics* London: Taylor & Francis.

Davies, F. (1992) *Fashion, Culture and Identity* Chicago, IL: University of Chicago Press.

Dawkins, A. J. and Dollahite, D. C. (eds) (1997) *Generative Fathering: Beyond Deficit Perspectives* London: Sage.

Day, G. (2003) 'No Thinking Please, We're New Labour' *Times Higher Education Supplement* 23 May.

Day Sclater, S. (1998) 'Divorce – Coping Strategies, Conflict and Dispute Resolution' *Family Law* 150.

—— (1999) *Divorce: A Psycho-Social Study* Aldershot: Ashgate.

Day Sclater, S. and Kaganas, F. (2003) 'Contact Mothers: Welfare and Rights' in A. Bainham, B. Lindley and M. Richards (eds) *Children and their Families: Contact, Rights and Welfare* Oxford: Hart.

Day Sclater, S. and Richards, M. (1995) 'How Adults Cope with Divorce – Strategies for Survival' *Family Law* 143.

Day Sclater, S. and Yates, C. (1999) 'The Psycho-Politics of Post Divorce Parenting' in A. Bainham, S. Day Sclater and M. Richards (eds) *What is a Parent? A Socio-Legal Analysis* Oxford: Hart.

Day Sclater, S. and Piper, C. (eds) (1999) *Undercurrents of Divorce* Aldershot: Ashgate.

Dearlove, J. (1997) 'The Academic Labour Process: From Collegiality and Professionalism to Managerialism and Proletarianisation?' 30(1) *Higher Education Review* 56.

Deem, R. (1999) 'Power and Resistance in the Academy: The Case of Women Academic Managers' in S. Whitehead and R. Moodley (eds) *Transforming Managers: Engendering Change in the Public Sector* London: UCL Press.

Delamont, S. (1996) 'Just like the Novels? Researching the Occupational Culture(s) of Higher Education' in R. Cuthbert (ed) *Working in Higher Education* Buckingham, SRHE/Open University Press.

Demetrious, D. (2001) 'Connell's Concept of Hegemonic Masculinity: A Critique' 30 *Theory and Society* 337.

Dench, G., Gavron, K. and Young, M. (2006) *The New East End: Kinship, Race and Conflict* London: Profile Books.

Dennis, N. and Erdos, G. (1993) *Families Without Fatherhood* London: Institute of Economic Affairs.

Denshire, S. (2006) 'In Praise of Auto-Ethnography' 53(4) *Australian Occupational Therapy Journal* 346.

Dent, M. and Whitehead, S. (eds) (2001) *Managing Professional Identities: Knowledge, Performativity and the 'New' Professional* London: Routledge.

Department for Children, Schools and Families (2006) *Planning and Performance Management Guidance 2006* London: DCSF.

Department for Constitutional Affairs (2005) *Increasing Diversity in the Legal Profession: A Report on Government Proposals* London: DCA.

Department for Education and Skills (2006) *Children's Centre Practice Guidance 2006* London: DfES.

—— (2007) *Every Parent Matters* London: DfES.

Department for Education and Skills, Department for Constitutional Affairs and Department for Trade and Industry (2004) *Parental Separation: Children's Needs and Parents' Responsibilities* London: DfES, DCA and DTI.

Department for Education and Skills, Department for Constitutional Affairs and Department for Trade and Industry (2005) *Parental Separation: Children's Needs and Parents' Responsibilities, Next Steps* London: DfES, DCA and DTI.

Department for Health and Department for Children, School and Families (2007) *Teenage Parents Next Steps: Guidance for Local Authorities and Primary Care Trusts* London: DH and DCFS.

Department for Work and Pensions (2008) *Joint Birth Registration: Recording Responsibility* White Paper Cm 7293 London: DWP: <http://www.dwp.gov.uk/jointbirthregistration/>, accessed 25 February 2009.

—— (2009) *Joint Birth Registration: Promoting Parental Responsibility* Green Paper Cm 7160 London: DWP.

Dermott, E. (2006) 'Time and Labour: Fathers' Perceptions of Employment and Childcare' in L. Pettinger et al (eds) *A New Sociology of Work?* Sociological Review Monographs, Oxford: Blackwell.

—— (2008) *Intimate Fatherhood: A Sociological Analysis* London: Routledge.

Devine, F. (2005) 'Middle Class Identities in the United States' in F. Devine, M. Savage, J. Scott, and R. Crompton (eds) *Rethinking Class: Cultures, Identity and Lifestyle* London: Palgrave Macmillan.

Devine, F. and Savage, M. (2005) 'The Cultural Turn in Sociology and Class Analysis' in F. Devine, M. Savage, J. Scott, and R. Crompton (eds) *Rethinking Class: Cultures, Identity and Lifestyle* London: Palgrave Macmillan.

Devine, F., Savage, M., Scott, J. and Crompton, R. (eds) (2005) *Rethinking Class: Cultures, Identity and Lifestyle* London: Palgrave Macmillan.

Dewar, J. (1998) 'The Normal Chaos of Family Law' 61 *Modern Law Review* 467.

Dey, I. and Wasoff, F. (2006) 'Mixed Messages: Parental Responsibilities, Public Opinion and the Reforms of Family Law' 20 *International Journal of Law, Policy and the Family* 225.

Diduck, A. (1993) 'Legislating Ideologies of Motherhood' 2 *Social and Legal Studies* 461.

—— (2001) 'Fairness and Justice for All? The House of Lords in *White v White*' 9(2) *Feminist Legal Studies* 173.

Diduck, A. and Kaganas, F. (2006) *Family Law, Gender and the State: Text, Cases and Materials* 2nd edn Oxford: Hart.

Diduck, A. and O'Donovan, K. (2006) 'Feminism and Families: Plus Ca Change?' in A. Diduck and K. O'Donovan (eds) *Feminist Perspectives on Family Law* London: Routledge-Cavendish.

Diduck, A. and O'Donovan, K. (eds) (2006) *Feminist Perspectives on Family Law* London: Routledge-Cavendish.

Digby, T. (ed) (1998) *Men Doing Feminism* New York: Routledge.

Dominus, S. (2005) 'The New Fathers' Crusade' *New York Times* 8 May.

Donaldson, M. (1993) 'What is Hegemonic Masculinity?' 22 *Theory and Society* 643.

Donaldson, M. and Poynting, S. (2004) 'The Time of Their Lives: Time, Work and Leisure in the Daily Lives of Ruling Class Men' in N. Hollier (ed) *Ruling Australia: The Power, Privilege and Politics of the New Ruling Class* Melbourne: Australian Scholarly Press.

Doucet, A. (2006) *Do Men Mother? Fatherhood, Care and Domestic Responsibility* Toronto: University of Toronto Press.

Douglas, A. (2008) 'Transitions: The New Norm', paper presented at 'Putting Children First' Conference, London, 16 October 2008, available at: <http://www.cafcass.gov.uk/idoc. ashx?docid=e07ff5e5–9c26–4937-af60-ff10764c1a01&version=-1>, accessed 25 April 2009.

Douglas, M. (1993) 'Emotion and Culture in Theories of Justice' 22(4) *Economy and Society* 501.

Douglas Home, C. (2009) 'Blaming Working Parents Doesn't Help Their Children' *The Herald* 3 February.

Dowd, N. (2000) *Redefining Fatherhood* New York: New York University Press.

—— (2008) 'Masculinities and Feminist Legal Theory: An Anti-Essentialist Project' *University of Florida Legal Studies Research Paper No 2008–05*, Florida: University of Florida. Also available at 13 *Wisconsin Women's Law Journal* 2009, <http:// papers.ssrn.com/sol3/papers.cfm?abstract_id=1238070>, accessed 17 December 2008.

—— (forthcoming) *The Man Question: Feminist Jurisprudence, Masculinities and Law* New York: New York University Press.

Dowd, N. and Jacobs, M. (eds) (2003) *Feminist Legal Theory: An Anti-Essentialist Reader* New York: New York University Press.

Drakich, J. (1989) 'In Search of the Better Parent: The Social Construction of Ideologies of Fatherhood' 3 *Canadian Journal of Women and the Law* 69.

Duff, L. and Webley, L. (2004) *Equality and Diversity: Women Solicitors, Research Study 48, Vol II: Qualitative Findings and Literature Review* London: Law Society.

Duff, E., Shiner, M. and Boon, A. (2000) *Entry into the Legal Profession: The Law Student Cohort Study Year 6* London: Law Society.

Dugan, E. (2008) '"Come and Join Us': Fathers 4 Justice Welcomes Mums' *Independent on Sunday* 28 September.

Duncan, N. (1996) *Bodyspace: Geographies of Gender and Sexuality* London: Routledge.

Duncan Smith, I. (2007) 'Now They Want to Abolish Fatherhood' *Mail on Sunday* 18 November.

Dunn, J. and Deater-Deckard, K. (2001) *Children's Views of their Changing Families* York: York Publishing Services/Joseph Rowntree Foundation.

Durrant, S. (2008) 'What are Fathers For? An Interview with Richard Collier' *The Guardian* 3 January.

Dworkin, A. (1981) *Pornography: Men Possessing Women* London: The Women's Press.

Dworkin, R. (1993) *Life's Dominion* London: Harper Collins.

Dyer, C. (2004) 'New Laws to End Child Custody Wars' *The Guardian* 3 April.

Dyer, C. and Ward, L. (2005) 'Law to help fathers in child contact cases' *The Guardian* 19 January.

Edensor, T. (2000) 'A Welcome Back to the Working Class' 34 *Sociology* 805.

Edgell, S. (1993) *Class* London: Routledge.

Edley, N. and Wetherell, M. (1995) *Men in Perspective: Practice, Power and Identity* London: Prentice Hall.

Edley, N. and Wetherell, M. (1999) 'Negotiating Hegemonic Masculinity: Imaginary Positions and Psycho-Discursive Practices' 9(3) *Feminism and Psychology* 335.

Edley, N and Wetherell, M. (2001) 'Jekyll and Hyde: Men's Construction of Feminism and Feminists' 11(4) *Feminism and Psychology* 439.

Edwards, R. and Gillies, V. (2004) 'Support in Parenting: Values and Consensus Concerning Who to Turn To' 33(4) *Journal of Social Policy* 627.

Edwards, T. (2000) *Contradictions of Consumption: Concepts, Practices and Politics in Consumer Society* Buckingham: Open University Press.

Eekelaar, J. (2006) *Family Law and Personal Life* Oxford: Oxford University Press.

Ehrenreich, B. (1983) *The Hearts of Men and the Flight from Commitment* London: Pluto.

Elliot, A. (1994) *Psychoanalytic Theory: An Introduction* Oxford: Blackwell.

Elshtain, J. B. (1982) *Public Man, Private Woman* Oxford: Wiley Blackwell.

Emmison, M. and Smith, P. (2000) *Researching the Visual* London: Sage.

Epstein, D., Elwood, J., Hey, V. and Maw, J. (eds) (1999) *Failing Boys: Issues in Gender and Achievement* Buckingham: Open University Press.

Equal Opportunities Commission (2007) *Facts About Men and Women in Great Britain 2006* Manchester: EOC.

Equality and Human Rights Commission (2009) *Working Better* London: EHRC.

Eriksson, M. and Pringle, K. (2006) 'Gender Equality, Child Welfare and Fathers' Rights in Sweden' in R. Collier and S. Sheldon (eds) (2006) *Fathers' Rights Activism and Legal Reform* Oxford: Hart.

Eskridge, W. (1999) *Gaylaw: Challenging the Apartheid of the Closet* Cambridge, MA: Harvard University Press.

Etzkowitz, H. and Leydesdorff, L. (eds) (1997) *Universities and the Global Knowledge Economy: A Triple Helix of University-Industry-Government Relations* London: Pinter Press.

Evans, D. (2008) 'Fathers 4 Suicide: Protester Vows to Hang at Judge's Home' *News of the World* 28 September.

Ewick, P. and Silbey, S. (1998) *The Common Place of Law: Stories From Everyday Life* Chicago, IL: Chicago University Press.

Falconer, C., Kelly, R. and Hewitt, P. (2005) 'Ministerial Foreword' in HM Government, *Parental Separation: Children's Needs and Parents' Responsibilities: Next Steps* Cm 6452 London: HMSO.

Faludi, S. (1999) *Stiffed: The Betrayal of the Modern Man* London: Chatto & Windus.

Families Need Fathers et al (2009) *Beyond the Nuclear* London: Families Need Fathers, Grandparent's Association and Family Matters Institute.

Farley, P. (2006) *Distant Voices, Still Lives: BFI Modern Classics* London: BFI Publishing.

Farrell, W. (1993) *The Myth of Male Power* NewYork: Simon and Schuster.

Fathers 4 Justice (2009) *Fathers 4 Justice Blueprint for Family Law in the Twenty First Century:* <http://www.fathers-4-justice.org/f4j/index.php?option=com_content&-task=view&id = 18&Itemid = 41>, accessed 2 April 2009.

Fearn, H. (2008) 'Funding Focus on Research Elite Set to Split Sector' *Times Higher Education* 27 November.

Featherstone, B. (2003) 'Taking Fathers Seriously' 33(2) *British Journal of Social Work* 239.

—— (2004) *Family Life and Family Support: A Feminist Analysis* London: Palgrave.

—— (2009) *Contemporary Fathering: Theory, Policy and Practice* Bristol: Policy Press.

Featherstone, B. and Peckover, S. (2007) 'Letting Them Get Away With it: Fathers, Domestic Violence and Child Welfare' 27(2) *Critical Social Policy* 181.

Featherstone, B. and Trinder, L. (2001) 'New Labour, Families and Fathers' 21(4) *Critical Social Policy* 534.

Featherstone, B., Rivett, M. and Scourfield, J. (2007) *Working With Men in Health and Social Care* London: Sage.

Featherstone, M. (1991) 'The Body in Consumer Culture' in M. Featherstone, M. Epworth and B.S. Turner (eds) *The Body: Social Process and Cultural Theory* London: Sage.

—— (1991) *Consumer Culture and Postmodernism* London: Sage.

Featherstone, M and Lash, S. (eds) (1999) *Spaces of Culture: City-Nation-World* London: Sage.

Fenstermaker, S., West, C. and Zimmerman, D.H. (1991) 'Gender Inequality: New Conceptual Terrain' in R. L. Blumberg (ed) *Gender, Family and Economy* Newbury Park, CA: Sage.

Fenwick, H. (2004) 'Clashing Rights, the Welfare of the Child and the Human Rights Act' 67(6) *Modern Law Review* 889.

Ferguson, K.E. (1993) *The Man Question: Visions of Subjectivity in Feminist Theory* Berkeley, CA: University of California Press.

Fielding, N. (1994) 'Cop Cantine Culture', in T. Newburn and E.A. Stanko, *Just Boys Doing Business* London: Routledge.

Finch, J. (2003) 'Foreword: Why Be Interested in Women's Position in Academe?' 10(2) *Gender, Work and Organisation* 133.

Fineman, M. (1991) *The Illusion of Equality: The Rhetoric and Reality of Divorce Reform* London: University of Chicago Press.

—— (1995) *The Neutered Mother, The Sexual Family and Other Twentieth Century Tragedies* New York: Routledge.

—— (2004) *The Autonomy Myth* New York: The New Press.

Fineman, M. and Karpin, I. (eds) (1995) *Mothers in Law: Feminist Theory and the Legal Regulation of Motherhood* New York: Columbia University Press.

Finer, M. and McGregor, O. R. (1974) 'History of the Obligation to Maintain' Appendix 5 in Department of Health and Social Security, *One-Parent Families: Report of the Committee on One-parent Families* Cmnd 5629-I London: Department of Health.

Fisher, D. (2008) 'Work "Success" at the Expense of Child Care' *The Independent* 24 September.

Five Live Report (2006) Julian Warwicker Programme, Sunday 26 March, BBC Radio 5 Live, <http://www.bbc.co.uk/fivelive/programmes/worricker.shtml>, accessed 27 March 2006.

Flood, J. (1996) 'Megalawyering in the Global Order: The Cultural, Social and Economic Transformation of Global Legal Practice' 3 *International Journal of the Legal Profession* 169.

—— (2008) 'Globalization and Large Law Firms' in P. Cane and J. Conaghan (eds) *The New Oxford Companion to Law* Oxford: Oxford University Press.

Flood, M. (2004) 'Backlash: Angry Men's Movements' in S.E. Rossi (ed) *The Battle and Backlash Rage On: Why Feminism Cannot be Obsolete* Philadelphia, PA: Xlibris Press.

—— (2006) 'Separated Fathers and the "Fathers' Rights" Movement', Feminism Law and the Family Workshop, Law School, University of Melbourne, 24 February (copy of paper with author).

—— (compiler) (2008) *The Men's Bibliography: A comprehensive bibliography of writing on men, masculinities, gender, and sexualities* 19th edn <http://www.xyonline.net/links.shtml> and <http://mensbiblio.xyonline.net>, accessed 1 October 2008.

Flood, M., Gardiner, J., Pease, K. and Pringle, K. (eds) (2007) *The International Encyclopaedia of Men and Masculinities* London: Routledge.

Flouri, E. (2005) *Fathering and Child Outcomes* New York: John Wiley.

Foucault, M. (1991) 'Governmentality' in G. Burchell, C. Gordon and P. Miller (eds) *The Foucault Effect: Studies in Governmentality* London: Harvester Wheatsheaf.

Fox Harding, L. (1996) 'Parental Responsibility: The Reassertion of Private Patriarchy?' in E. Silva (ed) *Good Enough Mothering? Feminist Perspectives on Lone Motherhood* London: Routledge.

Francis, A. M. (2004) 'Out of Touch and Out of Time: Lawyers, Their Leaders and Collective Mobility Within the Legal Profession' 24(3) *Legal Studies* 322.

Freeman, A. (1987) 'A Critical Look at Corporate Practice' 37 *Journal of Legal Education* 315.

Freeman, M. (ed) (2005) *Law and Popular Culture* Oxford: Oxford University Press.

Frosh, S. (1994) *Sexual Difference: Masculinity and Psychoanalysis* London: Routledge.

—— (2006) *For and Against Psychoanalysis* London: Routledge.

Frug, M.J. (1993) *Postmodern Legal Feminism* New York: Routledge.

Fuchs-Epstein, C., Seron, C., Oglensky, B. and Saute, R. (1999) *The Part-Time Paradox: Time Norms, Professional Life, Family and Gender* London: Routledge.

Furedi, F. (2002) *Paranoid Parenting* London: Allen Lane.

—— (2003) *Therapy Culture: Cultivating Vulnerability in an Uncertain Age* London: Routledge.

Furstenberg, F. (1988) 'Good Dads – Bad Dads: Two Faces of Fatherhood' in A. J. Cherlin (ed) *The Changing American Family and Public Policy* Washington, DC: Urban Institute Press.

Gadd, D. (2000) 'Masculinities, Violence and Defended Psycho-Social Subjects' 4 *Theoretical Criminology* 429.

—— (2002) 'Masculinities and Violence Against Female Partners' 11 *Social and Legal Studies* 61.

Galanter, M. (1998) 'The Faces of Mistrust: The Image of Lawyers in Public Opinion and Political Discourse' 66 *Cincinnati University Law Review* 905.

—— (1999) 'Old and In the Way: The Coming Demographic Transformation of the Legal Profession and its Implications for the Provision of Legal Services' *Wisconsin Law Review* 1081.

Galanter, M. and Palay, T. (1991) *Tournament of Lawyers: Growth and Transformation of the Big Law Firm* Chicago: Chicago University Press.

Gang of Four (1979) *Entertainment*, EMI Records, 1979: Music and Lyrics Allen, Burnham, Gill, King.

Garner, M. and Leon, P. (2002) 'Dumbing Down has Become a Fact of Life!' *Times Higher Education Supplement* 3 May.

Garner, R. (2007) 'Top Schools Monopolise Elite University Places' *The Independent* 20 September.

Gatens, M. (1983) 'A Critique of the Sex/Gender Distinction' in J. Allen and P. Patton (eds) *Beyond Marxism? Interventions After Marx* Sydney: Intervention Publications.

—— (1996) *Imaginary Bodies; Ethics, Power and Corporeality* London: Routledge.

Gatrell, C. (2007) '"Whose Child is it Anyway?" The Negotiation of Paternal Entitlements Within Marriage' 55 *The Sociological Review* 352.

Gavanas, A. (2002) 'The Fatherhood Responsibility Movement: The Centrality of Marriage, Work and Male Sexuality in Reconstructions of Masculinity and Fatherhood' in B. Hobson (ed) *Making Men into Fathers: Men, Masculinities and the Social Politics of Fatherhood* Cambridge: Cambridge University Press.

—— (2004) 'Domesticating Masculinity and Masculinizing Domesticity in Contemporary U.S. Fatherhood Politics' 11(2) *Social Politics* 247.

—— (2004) *Fatherhood Politics in the United States: Masculinity, Sexuality, Race and Marriage* Champaign, IL: University of Illinois Press.

Gaymer, J. (2005) 'Flexible Working – The Individual, The Employer and You' paper presented to The Woman Lawyer Forum Conference, London, 5 March (copy of paper with author).

Geldof, B. (2003) 'The Real Love that Dare Not Speak Its Name' in A. Bainham, B. Lindley, M. Richards and L. Trinder (eds) *Children and Their Families* Oxford: Hart.

Genn, H., Partington, M. and Wheeler, S. (2006) *Law in the Real World: Improving Our Understanding of How Law Works: Final Report and Recommendations* (The Nuffield Enquiry on Empirical Legal Research) London: Nuffield.

Ghate, D. and Ramalla, M. (2002) *Positive Parenting: The National Evaluation of the Youth Justice Board's Parenting Programme* London: Policy Research Bureau.

Ghate, D., Shaw, C. and Hazel, N. (2000) *Fathers and Family Centres: Engaging Fathers in Preventative Services* York: Joseph Rowntree Foundation.

Ghazi, P. and Jones, J. (2004) *Downshifting: A Guide to Happier Simpler Living* London: Hodder & Stoughton.

Gibb, F. (2004) 'Judge Apologises as Justice "Fails Fathers"', *The Times* 2 April.

Gibb, F. (2008) 'Child Contact Powers "Could Worsen Parent Wars"' *The Times* 8 December.

Gibbs, J. T. and Merighi, J. R. (1994) 'Young Black Males: Marginality, Masculinity and Criminality' in T. Newburn and E.A. Stanko *Just Boys Doing Business* London: Routledge.

Giddens, A. (1976) *New Rules of Sociological Method* London: Harper Collins.

—— (1991) *Modernity and Self-Identity: Self and Society in the Late Modern Age* Cambridge: Polity.

—— (1992) *The Transformation of Intimacy* Cambridge: Polity.

Gilchrist, J. (2003) 'Outlaw Fathers Fight Back' *The Scotsman* 29 May.

Gillan, A. (2005) 'Work Until You Drop: How the Long-Hours Culture is Killing Us' *The Guardian* 20 August.

Gillborn, D. (2008) *Racism and Education: Coincidence or Conspiracy?* London: Routledge.

Gillies, V. (2005) 'Meeting Parents' Needs? Discourses of "Support" and "Inclusion" in Family Policy' 25(1) *Critical Social Policy* 70.

Gillies, V. (2006) *Marginalised Mothers: Exploring Working Class Experiences of Parenting* London: Routledge.

Gillies, V. and Lucey, H. (eds) (2007) *Power, Knowledge and the Academy: The Institutional is Political* London: Palgrave Macmillan.

Gillis, J. (1996) *A World of Their Own Making: Myth, Ritual and the Quest for Family Values*, Cambridge, MA: Harvard University Press.

—— (2000) 'Marginalization of Fatherhood in Western Countries' 7(2) *Childhood* 225.

Gilmore, D. (1991) *Manhood in the Making: Cultural Concepts of Masculinity* London: Yale University Press.

Gilmore, S. (2006) 'Contact/Shared Residence and Child Well-Being: Research Evidence and its Implications for Legal Decision Making' 20 *International Journal of Law, Policy and the Family* 344.

Glucksmann, M. (2000) *Cottons and Casuals: The Gendered Organisation of Time and Space* York: Sociologypress.

Goffman, E. (1969) *The Presentation of Self in Everyday life* London: Allen Lane.

—— (1976) *Relations in Public* Harmondsworth: Penguin.

—— (1979) *Gender Advertisements* New York: Harper and Row.

Goldscheider, F. K and Goldscheider, C. (1999) *The Changing Transition to Adulthood: Leaving and Returning Home* London: Sage.

Goldsmith, A. (1999) 'Standing at the Crossroads: Law Schools, Universities, Markets and the Future of Legal Scholarship' in F. Cownie (ed) *The Law School: Global Issues, Local Questions* Aldershot: Ashgate.

Goldthorpe, J. (2003) 'The Myth of Education-Based Meritocracy' 10(4) *New Economy* 234.

Goodey, J, (1997) 'Boys Don't Cry: Masculinities, Fear of Crime and Fearlessness' 37 *British Journal of Criminology* 401.

Goodey, J. (1998) 'Understanding Racism and Masculinity: Drawing on Research with Boys Aged Eight to Sixteen' 26 *International Journal of the Sociology of Law* 393.

—— (2000) 'Biographical Lessons for Criminology' 4 *Theoretical Criminology* 489.

Goodliffe, J. and Brooke, D. (1996) 'Alcoholism in the Legal Profession' 19 *New Law Journal* January 19.

Goodrich, P. (1986) *Reading the Law: A Critical Introduction to Legal Methods and Techniques* Oxford: Blackwell.

—— (1987) *Legal Discourse* Oxford: Blackwell.

—— (1996) 'Of Blackstone's Tower: Metaphors of Distance and Histories of the English Law School' in P. Birks (ed) *Pressing Problems in the Law: What Are Law Schools For?* Oxford: Oxford University Press.

—— (1999) 'The Critic's Love of the Law: Intimate Observations on an Insular Jurisdiction' 10(3) *Law and Critique* 343.

Gough, B. (1998) 'Men and the Discursive Reproduction of Sexism: Repertoires and Difference in Equality' 8(1) *Feminism and Psychology* 25.

—— (2001) '"Biting Your Tongue": Negotiating Masculinities in Contemporary Britain' 10(2) *Journal of Gender Studies* 169.

Gouldstone, S. (2008) 'Family Law Survey Update' 82 *McKenzie: The National Magazine of Families Need Fathers* December 5.

Grabham, E., Cooper, D., Krishnadas, J. and Herman, D. (2008) *Intersectionality and Beyond: Law, Power and the Politics of Location* London: Routledge-Cavendish.

Gramsci, A. (1971) *Selection From the Prison Notebooks* London: Lawrence and Wishart.

Graycar, R. (1989) 'Equal Rights Versus Fathers' Rights: The Child Custody Debate in Australia' in C. Smart and S. Sevenhuijsen (eds) *Child Custody and the Politics of Gender* London: Routledge.

—— (2000) 'Law Reform by Frozen Chook: Family Law Reform for the New Millennium?' 24 *Melbourne University Law Review* 737.

Graycar, R. and Morgan, J. (2002) *The Hidden Gender of Law* 2nd edn Sydney: Federation Press.

Grbich, J. (1991) 'The Body in Legal Theory' in M. Fineman and N. Thomadsen (eds) *At the Boundaries of Law* London: Routledge.

Greatbatch, D. and Dingwall, R. (1999) 'The Marginalization of Domestic Violence in Divorce Mediation' 13 *International Journal of Law, Policy and the Family* 174.

Greenfield, S. and Osborn, G (eds) (2005) *Readings in Law and Popular Culture* London: Routledge.

Greenfield, S., Osborn, G. and Robson, P. (2001) *Film and the Law* London: Cavendish.

Greenhalgh, T., Seyan, K. and Boynton, P. (2004) '"Not a University Type": Focus Group Study of Social Class, Ethnic and Sex Differences in School Pupils' Perceptions about Medical School' 328 *British Medical Journal* 1541.

Greer, G. (2008) 'A Father's Role in Bringing up a Child Will Never Equal a Mother's' *The Times* 4 June.

Groombridge, N. (1998) 'Masculinities and Crimes Against the Environment' 2 *Theoretical Criminology* 248.

Grosz, E. (1990) 'A Note on Essentialism and Difference' in S. Unew (ed) *Feminist Knowledge: Critique and Construct* London: Routledge.

Grosz, E. (1994) *Volatile Bodies: Towards a Corporeal Feminism* St Leonards, NSW: Allen & Unwin.

Grosz, E. and Probyn, E. (eds) (1995) *Sexy Bodies: Strange Carnalities of Feminism* London: Routledge.

Gutterman, D. (2001) 'Postmodernism and the Interrogation of Masculinity' in S. Whitehead and F. Barrett (eds) *The Masculinities Reader* Cambridge: Cambridge University Press.

Hacker, H.M. (1957) 'The New Burdens of Masculinity' 3 *Marriage and Family Living* 227.

Hagan, J. and Kay, F. (1995) *Gender in Practice: A Study of Lawyers' Lives* New York: Oxford University Press.

Hakim, C. (2004) *Key Issues in Women's Work: Female Heterogeneity and the Polarisation of Women's Employment* London: Routledge-Cavendish.

Hale, B. and Hunter, R. (2008) 'A Conversation With Baroness Hale' 16(2) *Feminist Legal Studies* 237.

Halewood, P. (1995) 'White Men Can't Jump: Critical Epistemologies, Embodiment, and the Praxis of Legal Scholarship' 7 *Yale Journal of Law and Feminism* 1.

Halford, S. and Leonard, P. (2006) *Negotiating Identities at Work: Place, Space and Time* Basingstoke: Palgrave Macmillan.

Hall, J. (1997) 'Domestic Violence and Contact' *Family Law* 813.

Hall, S. (2002) 'Daubing the Drudges of Fury: Men, Violence and the Piety of the "Hegemonic Masculinity" Thesis' 6 *Theoretical Criminology* 35.

—— (ed) (1997) *Representation: Cultural Representation and Signifying Practices* London: Sage.

Halley, J. and Clough, P. (2007) *The Affective Turn: Theorizing the Social* Durham, NC: Duke University Press.

Halpern, D. (1994) *Entry into the Legal Professions: The Law Student Cohort Study Years 1 and 2* London: Law Society.

Halsey, A. H. (1995) *Decline of Donnish Dominion: The British Academic Professions in the Twentieth Century* Oxford: Oxford University Press.

Halsey, A. H. and Trow, M. A. (1971) *The British Academics* London: Faber and Faber.

Hannigan, J. (1998) *Fantasy City: Pleasure and Profit in the Postmodern Metropolis* London: Routledge.

Harding, S. (1986) *The Science Question in Feminism* Milton Keynes: Open University Press.

—— (ed) (1987) *Feminism and Methodology* Milton Keynes: Open University Press.

Harris, A. (1990) 'Race and Essentialism in Feminist Legal Theory' 42 *Stanford Law Review* 581.

Harris, M. (2006) *Family Court HELL* London: Pen Press.

Harrison, T. (2007) *Collected Poems* London: Viking.

Hartley, R. E. (1974) 'Sex Role Pressures and the Socialisation of the Male Child' in J. Pleck and J. Sawyer (eds) *Men and Masculinity* Englewood Cliffs, NJ: Prentice Hall.

Hatten, W. Vinter, L. and Williams, R. (2002) *Dads on Dads: Needs and Expectations at Home and Work* Manchester: Equal Opportunities Commission.

Hattenstone, S. (2005) 'We're On a Mission: After Years of Campaigning, Fathers Rights' Groups Are Finally Being Taken Seriously By Politicians' *The Guardian* (Family) 29 October.

Hatty, S. E. (2000) *Masculinity, Violence and Culture* Thousand Oaks, CA: Sage.

Hayward, B. Fong, B. and Thornton, A. (2007) *The Third Work-Life Balance Employer Survey: Main Findings* London: Department for Business, Enterprise and Regulatory Reform.

Haywood, C. and Mac an Ghaill, M. (2003) *Men and Masculinities: Theory, Research and Social Practice* Buckingham: Open University Press.

Hearn, J. (1987) *The Gender of Oppression: Men, Masculinity and the Critique of Marxism* Brighton: Harvester Wheatsheaf.

—— (1990) 'Child Abuse and Men's Violence' in Violence Against Women Study Group (ed) *Taking Child Abuse Seriously* London: Unwin Hyman.

—— (1992) *Men in The Public Eye* London: Routledge.

—— (1994) 'Research in Men and Masculinities: Some Sociological Issues and Possibilities' 30 *The Australian and New Zealand Journal of Sociology* 47.

—— (1996) 'Is Masculinity Dead? A Critique of the Concept of Masculinity' in M. Mac an Ghaill (ed) *Understanding Masculinities* Buckingham: Open University Press.

—— (1997) 'The Implications of Critical Studies on Men' 3(1) *Nora* 48.

—— (1998) *The Violences of Men* London: Sage.

—— (1998) 'Theorizing Men and Men's Theorizing: Varieties of Discursive Practices in Men Theorizing of Men' 27 *Theory and Society* 781.

—— (1999) 'Men, Managers and Management: The Case of Higher Education' in S. Whitehead and R. Moodley (eds) *Transforming Managers: Engendering Change in the Public Sector* London: UCL Press.

—— (2001) 'Academia, Management and Men: Making the Connections' in A. Brooks and A. Mackinnon (eds) *Gender and the Restructured University* Buckingham: SRHE/Open University Press.

—— (2002) 'Men, Fathers and the State: National and Global Relations' in B. Hobson (ed) *Making Men into Fathers: Men, Masculinities and the Social Politics of Fatherhood* Cambridge: Cambridge University Press.

—— (2004) 'From Hegemonic Masculinity to the Hegemony of Men' 5(1) *Feminist Theory* 49.

Hearn, J. and Pringle, K. (2006) *European Perspectives on Men and Masculinities* Basingstoke: Palgrave Macmillan.

Hearn, J. and Pringle, K. (2006) 'Men, Masculinities and Children: Some European Perspectives' 26(2) *Critical Social Policy* 365.

Heins, M. (1995) 'Masculinity, Sexism and Censorship Law' in M. Berger, B. Wallis and S. Watson (eds) *Constructing Masculinity* New York: Routledge.

Henkel, M. (2000) *Academic Identities and Policy Change in Higher Education* London: Jessica Kingsley.

Henley Centre (2001) *Working Class Heroes: Press Release No 5* Henley: The Henley Centre.

Hennessy, R. (1993) *Materialist Feminism* London: Routledge.

Hennessy, R. and Ingraham, C. (eds) (1997) *Materialist Feminism: A Reader in Class, Difference and Women's Lives* London: Routledge.

Henricson, C. and Bainham, A. (2005) *The Child and Family Policy Divide: Tensions, Convergence and Rights* York: Joseph Rowntree Foundation.

Henriques, J., Hollway, W., Urwin, C., Venn, C. and Walkerdine, V. (1984) *Changing the Subject: Psychology, Social Regulation and Subjectivity* London: Methuen.

Henwood, K. and Proctor, J. (2003) 'The "Good Father": Reading Men's Accounts of Paternal Involvement During the Transition to First-time Fatherhood' 42(3) *British Journal of Social Psychology* 337.

Hepple, B. (1996) 'The Renewal of the Liberal Law Degree' 55 *Cambridge Law Review* 471.

Herman, D. (1994) *Rights of Passage: Struggles for Lesbian and Gay Equality* Toronto: University of Toronto Press.

Herman, D. and Stychin, C. (eds) (1995) *Legal Inversions: Lesbians, Gay Men and the Politics of Law* Philadelphia, PA: Temple University Press.

Herring, J. (1999) 'The Human Rights Act and the Welfare Principle in Family Law – Conflicting or Complementary?' 11 *Child and Family Law Quarterly* 223.

—— (2007) *Family Law* 3rd edn Harlow: Pearson Longman.

—— (2009) 'Autonomy and Family Law' in J. Herring, S. Choudhry and J. Wallbank (eds) *Rights, Gender and Family Law* London: Routledge-Cavendish.

Herring, J., Choudhry, S. and Wallbank, J. (eds) (2009) *Rights, Gender and Family Law* London: Routledge-Cavendish.

Hetherington, K. (1998) *Expressions of Identity: Space, Performance, Politics* London: Sage.

Hillyard, P. (2002) 'Invoking Indignation: Reflection on Future Directions of Socio-Legal Studies' 29(4) *Journal of Law and Society* 645.

Hillyard, P. and Sim, J. (1997) 'The Political Economy of Socio-Legal Research' in P. Thomas (ed) *Socio-Legal Studies* Aldershot: Dartmouth.

Hillyard, P., Sim, J., Tombs, S. and Whyte, D. (2004) 'Leaving a "Stain upon the Silence": Contemporary Criminology and the Politics of Dissent' 44 *British Journal of Criminology* 369.

Hilpern, K. (2008) 'Ending it All' *The Guardian* 24 September.

Hinsliff, G. (2003) 'Militant Fathers Will Risk Jail Over Rights to See Their Children' *The Observer* 20 April.

—— (2009) 'Women's refuges told they must admit men: councils say charities could lose funding under new gender equality laws' *The Observer* 5 April.

Hirsch, A. (2009) 'Media Access to Family Courts Will Improve Clarity Says Judge' *The Guardian* 27 April.

Hobbs, D., Lister, S., Hadfield, P. and Hall, S. (2000) 'Receiving Shadows: Governance, Liminality in the Night-Time Economy' 53(1) *British Journal of Sociology* 89.

Hobson, B. (ed) (2002) *Making Men into Fathers: Men, Masculinities and the Social Politics of Fatherhood* Cambridge: Cambridge University Press.

Hobson, B., Duvander, A.Z. and Halldén, K. (2007) 'Men's Capabilities and Agency to Create a Work Family Balance: The Gap Between European Norms and Men's Practices', paper presented to conference Fatherhood in Late Modernity: Cultural Images, Social Practices, Structural Frames April 2007 (copy of paper with author).

Hochschild, A. R. (1989) *The Second Shift: Working Parents and the Revolution at Home* London: Piatkus.

—— (1997) *The Time Bind: When Work Becomes Home and Home Becomes Work* New York: Metropolitan Books.

Hogarth, T., Hasluck, C. and Pierre, G. (2001) *Work Life Balance 2000: Results from the Baseline Study* London: Department for Education and Employment, Research Report 249.

Hoggart, R. (1966) *The Uses of Literacy: Aspects of Working-Class Life with Special Reference to Publications and Entertainments* London: Penguin.

Holcombe, L. (1983) *Wives and Property: Reform of the Married Women's Property Acts* Toronto: University of Toronto Press.

Holland, S. and Scourfield, J. (2000) 'Managing Marginalized Masculinities: Men and Probation' 9 *Journal of Gender Studies* 199.

Hollander, A. (1994) *Sex and Suits: The Evolution of Modern Dress* New York: Alfred A. Knopf.

Hollands, R. (1997) 'From Shipyards to Nightclubs: Restructuring Young Adults' Employment, Household and Consumption Identities in the North-East of England' 41 *Berkeley Journal of Sociology* 41.

Holliday, R. and Thomson, G. (2001) 'A Body of Work' in R. Holliday and J. Hassard (eds) *Contested Bodies* London: Routledge.

Hollway, W. (1989) *Subjectivity and Method in Psychology: Gender, Meaning and Science* London: Sage.

—— (1993) 'Theorising Heterosexuality: A Response' 3 *Feminism and Psychology* 412.

—— (1995) 'Feminist Discourses and Women's Heterosexual Desire' in S. Wilkinson and C. Kitzinger (eds) *Feminism and Discourse* London: Sage.

—— (1996) 'Recognition and Heterosexual Desire' in D. Richardson (ed) *Theorising Heterosexuality: Telling it Straight* Buckingham: Open University Press.

—— (2006) *The Capacity to Care: Gender and Ethical Subjectivity* London: Routledge.

Hollway, W. and Jefferson, T. (2000) *Doing Qualitative Research Differently: Free Association, Narrative and the Interview Method* London: Sage.

Home Office (1998) *Supporting Families: A Consultation Document* London: Home Office.

Honneth, A. (1996) *The Struggle for Recognition: The Moral Grammar of Social Conflicts* Oxford: Polity.

Honore, C. (2009) *Under Pressure: Rescuing Our Children from the Culture of Hyper-Parenting* London: Orion.

Hood-Williams, J. (2001) 'Gender, Masculinities and Crime: From Structures to Psyches' 5 *Theoretical Criminology* 37.

Horn, W.F., Blankenhorn, D. and Pearlstein, M.B. (1999) *The Fatherhood Movement: A Call to Action* Lanham. MD: Lexington Books.

Howe, A. (2009) *Sex, Violence and Crime: Foucault and the 'Man' Question* London: Routledge-Cavendish.

Howell, D. (1992) 'The Clubbable Chaps' *AUTLook* 22 October.

Howson, R. (2005) *Challenging Hegemonic Masculinity* London: Routledge.

Hunt, A. (1994) 'Governing the Socio-Legal Project: Or what Do Research Councils Do?' 21(4) *Journal of Law and Society* 522.

Hunt, J. (2003) *Researching Contact* London, National Council for One Parent Families.

Hunt, J. with Roberts, C. (2004) *Family Policy Briefing 3: Child Contact with Non Resident Parents* Oxford: University of Oxford, Department of Social Policy and Social Work.

Hunt, J. and Macleod, A. (2008) *Outcomes of Applications to Court for Contact Orders After Parental Separation or Divorce* London: Ministry of Justice.

Hunter, R. (ed) (2008) *Rethinking Equality Projects in Law: Feminist Challenges* Oxford: Hart.

Hurstfield, J. and Neathy, F. (2002) *Recruitment and Retention of Academic Staff in UK Higher Education 2001* London: IRS Research.

Hyde, A. (1997) *Bodies of Law* Princeton, NJ: Princeton University Press.

ITV (2005) 'Tonight With Trevor MacDonald' 14 November.

Itzin, C. and Newman, J. (eds) (1995) *Gender, Culture and Organisational Change* London: Routledge.

Ives, J. (2007) 'Becoming a Father/Refusing Fatherhood: How Paternal Responsibilities and Rights are Generated' DPhil thesis: University of Birmingham.

Jack, I. (2007) 'Working class has come to mean beer guts and white vans' *The Guardian* 1 December.

Jackson, B. and Marsden, D. (1962) *Education and the Working Class: Some General-Themes Raised by A Study of 88 Working-Class Children in a Northern Industrial City* London: Routledge & Kegan Paul.

Jackson, D. (1990) *Unmasking Masculinity: A Critical Autobiography* London: Routledge,.

Jackson, E. (1993) 'Catherine Mackinnon and Feminist Jurisprudence: A Critical Reappraisal' 19(2) *Journal of Law and Society* 195.

James, A. and Richards, M. (1999) 'Sociological Perspectives, Family Policy and Children: Adult Thinking and Sociological Tinkering' 21(1) *Journal of Social Welfare and Family Law* 23.

James, A. and James, A. (2001) 'Tightening the Net: Children, Community and Control' 52 *British Journal of Sociology* 211.

Jamieson, L. (1998) *Intimacy: Personal Relationships in Modern Society* Cambridge: Polity.

Jardine, A. (1987) 'Men in Feminism' in A. Jardine and P. Smith (eds) *Men in Feminism* London: Methuen.

Jardine, A. and Smith, P. (eds) (1987) *Men in Feminism* London: Methuen.

Jardine, C. (2005) 'Mothers Deserve Justice Too' *Daily Telegraph* 31 October.

Jefferson, T. (1994) 'Crime, Criminology, Masculinity and Young Men' in A. Coote (ed) *Families. Children and Crime* London: Institute for Public Policy Research.

—— (1994) 'Theorizing Masculine Subjectivity' in T. Newburn and E.A. Stanko *Just Boys Doing Business* London: Routledge.

—— (1997) 'Masculinities and Crimes' in M. Maguire et al (eds) *The Oxford Handboook of Criminology* 2nd edn Oxford: Clarendon.

—— (1997) 'The Tyson Rape Trial: The Law, Feminism and Emotional Truth' 6 *Social and Legal Studies* 281.

—— (1998) '"Muscle", "Hard Men" and "Iron" Mike Tyson: Reflections on Desire, Anxiety and the Embodiment of Masculinity' 4 *Body and Society* 103.

—— (2002) 'For a Psychosocial Criminology' in K. Carrington and R. Hogg (eds) *Critical Criminologies: An Introduction* Cullompton, Devon: Willan.

—— (2002) 'Subordinating Hegemonic Masculinity' 6(1) *Theoretical Criminology* 63.

Jefferson, T. and Carlen, P. (eds) (1996) 36(3) *British Journal of Criminology* (Special Issue).

Jenkins, R. (2008) 'Found Dead on Fathers' Day: Husband in Divorce Battle and the Children He Feared Losing' *The Times* 17 June.

Jenkins, S. (2008) 'Marital Splits and Income Changes Over the Longer Term' ISER Working Paper Essex: University of Essex, 2008, available at <http://www.iser.essex.ac.uk/publications/working-papers/iser/2008–07.pdf>, accessed 22 April 2009.

Jenson, J. (2004) 'Changing the Paradigm: Family Responsibility or Investing in Children' 24(2) *Canadian Journal of Sociology* 169.

Jenson, J. and de Sousa Santos, B. (eds) (2000) *Globalizing Institutions: Case Studies in Social Regulation and Innovation* Dartmouth: Ashgate.

Jessop, B. (1997) 'The Entrepreneurial City: Reimagining Localities, Redesigning Economic Governance or Restructuring Capital' in N. Jewson and S. McGregor (eds) *Transforming Cities* London: Routledge.

Jewkes, Y. (2005) 'Men Behind Bars: Doing Masculinity as an Adaptation to Imprisonment' 8(1) *Men and Masculinities* 44.

Johnson, R. (1997) 'Contested Borders, Contingent Lives' in D. L. Steinberg, D. Epstein and R. Johnson (eds) *Border Patrols: Policing the Boundaries of Heterosexuality* London: Continuum.

Johnston, C. and Thomson, A. (2004) 'Golden Diamond Outshines the Rest' *Times Higher Education Supplement* 23 July.

Jones, S. (2000) *Understanding Violent Crime* Buckingham: Open University Press.

Kaganas, F. (1999) 'Contact, Conflict and Risk' in S. Day Sclater and C. Piper (eds) *Undercurrents of Divorce* Aldershot: Ashgate.

Kaganas, F. (2007) 'Grandparents' Rights and Grandparents' Campaigns' 19(1) *Child and Family Law Quarterly* 17.

Kaganas, F. and Day Sclater, S. (2004) 'Contact Disputes: Narrative Constructions of "Good" Parents' 12(1) *Feminist Legal Studies* 2.

Kaganas, F. and Diduck, A. (2004) 'Incomplete Citizens: Changing Images of Post-Separation Children' 67(6) *Modern Law Review* 959.

Kaganas, F. and Piper, C. (1999) 'Contact and Domestic Violence' in S. Day Sclater and C. Piper (eds) *Undercurrents of Divorce* Aldershot: Ashgate.

—— (2000) 'Contact and Domestic Violence: The Winds of Change?' *Family Law* 630.

—— (2001) 'Grandparents and Contact: "Rights vs Welfare" Revisited' 15(2) *International Journal of Law, Policy and Family* 250.

Kahn, J. S. (2009) *An Introduction to Masculinities* Oxford: Wiley-Blackwell.

Kahn, P. W. (1999) *The Cultural Study of Law: Reconstructing Legal Scholarship* Chicago: University of Chicago Press.

Kahn-Freund, O. (1966) 'Reflections on Legal Education' 29(2) *Modern Law Review* 121.

Kamir, O. (2006) *Framed: Women in Law and Film* Durham: Duke University Press.

Katz, J. (1988) *Seductions of Crime: Moral and Sensual Attractions in Doing Evil* New York: Basic Books.

Kay, F. (1997) 'Flight from Law: A Competing Risks Model of Departures From Law Firms' 31(2) *Law and Society Review* 728.

Kaye, M. and Tolmie, J. (1998) 'Discoursing Dads: The Rhetorical Devices of Fathers' Rights Groups' 22 *Melbourne University Law Review* 184.

—— (1998) 'Fathers' Rights Groups in Australia and Their Engagement With Issues in Family Law' 12(1) *Australian Journal of Family Law* 12.

—— (1998) '"Lollies at a Children's Party" and Other Myths: Violence, Protection Orders and Fathers' Rights Groups' 10(1) *Current Issues in Criminal Justice* 52.

Kelsey, J. (1999) 'Academic Freedom Needed More Than Ever' in R. Crozier (ed) *Troubled Times, Academic Freedom in New Zealand* Palmerston North: Dunmore Press.

Kennedy, R. (2005) *Fathers For Justice: The Rise of a New Social Movement in Canada as a Case Study of Collective Identity* 2nd edn Ann Arbor, MI: Caravan Books.

Kenway, J. and Langmead, D. (1998) 'Governmentality, the "Now" University and the Future of Knowledge Work' 41(2) *Australian Universities Review* 28.

Kerfoot, D. and Knights, D. (1996) 'The Best is Yet to Come? The Quest for Embodiment in Managerial Work' in D. Collinson and J. Hearn (eds) *Men as Managers, Managers as Men: Critical Perspectives on Men, Masculinities and Management* London: Sage.

Kerfoot, D. and Whitehead, S. (1998) 'Boys' Own Stuff: Masculinity and the Management of Further Education' 46(3) *Sociological Review* 436.

Kerr, C. (1995) *The Uses of the University* Cambridge, MA: Harvard University Press.

Kersten, J. (1996) 'Culture, Masculinities and Violence Against Women' 36 *British Journal of Criminology* 381.

Kilkey, M. (2006) 'New Labour and Reconciling Work and Family Life: Making it Fathers' Business?' 5 *Social Policy & Society* 167.

Kimmel, M. (1997) 'Integrating Men into the Curriculum' 4 *Duke Journal of Gender, Law and Policy* 181.

——— (2000) *The Gendered Society* Oxford: Oxford University Press.

Kimmel, M. and Kaufman, M. (1995) 'Weekend Warriors: The New Men's Movement' in M. Kimmel (ed) *The Politics of Manhood: Pro feminist Men Respond to the Mythopoetic Men's Movement (and the Mythopoetic Leaders Answer)* Philadelphia, PA: Temple University Press.

Kimmel, M. and Messner, M. (1997) *Men's Lives* Boston, MA: Allyn and Bacon.

Kitsuse, J. I. and Spector, M. (1973) 'The Definition of Social Problems' 20(4) *Social Problems* 407.

Kitzinger, C. and Wilkinson, S. (1994) 'Re-viewing Heterosexuality' 4 *Feminism and Psychology* 330.

Klein, N. (2000) *No Logo* London: Flamingo.

Knights, D. and Richards, W. (2003) 'Sex Discrimination in UK Academia' 10(2) *Gender, Work and Organisation* 213.

Koffman, L. (2008) 'Holding Parents to Account: Tough on Children, Tough on the Causes of Children' 35(1) *Journal of Law and Society* 113.

Kogan, M. and Hanney, S. (2000) *Reforming Higher Education* London: Jessica Kingsley.

Komarovsky, M. (1950) 'Functional Analysis of Sex Roles' 15 *American Sociological Review* 508.

Kronman, A. T. (1993) *The Lost Lawyer: Failing Ideals of the Legal Profession* Cambridge, MA: Belknap.

Kubler-Ross, E. (1989) *On Death and Dying* London: Tavistock/Routledge.

Kuhn, A. (1995) *Family Secrets: Acts of Memory and Imagination* London: Verso.

Lacey, N. (1998) *Unspeakable Subjects: Feminist Essays in Legal and Social Theory* Oxford: Hart Publications.

Lamb, M. (ed) (1997) *The Role of the Father in Child Development* New York: John Wiley.

Land, H. (1980) 'The Family Wage' 6 *Feminist Review* 55.

LaRossa, R. (1997) *The Modernization of Fatherhood: A Social and Political History* Chicago, IL: University of Chicago Press.

Lash, S. M. and Urry, J. (1993) *Economies of Signs and Space* London: Sage.

Laville, S. (2005) 'Batman and Robin Quit Protest Group', *The Guardian*, 9 June.

Law, S. (1988) 'Homosexuality and the Social Meaning of Gender' 2 *Wisconsin Law Review*, 187.

Law Commission (2006) *Cohabitation: The Financial Consequences of Relationship Breakdown* Consultation Paper 179 London: Law Commission.

Law Society (2005) *The Law Society Equality and Diversity Policy and Strategy* London: Law Society.

—— (2005) *Law Society's Model Anti-Discrimination Policy* (policy issued under Rules 3 and 4 of the Solicitors Anti-Discrimination Rules 2004) London: Law Society.

—— (2006) *Factsheet 2006: Women Solicitors* London: Law Society.

—— (2007) *Trends in the Solicitor's Profession: Law Society Annual Statistical Report 2007* London: Law Society.

Lawrence, S. (2004) 'Feminism, Consequences, Accountability' 42(4) *Osgoode Hall Law Journal* 583.

Lee, R. G. (1992) 'From Profession to Business: The Rise and Rise of the City Law Firm' 19(1) *Journal of Law and Society* 31.

—— (1999) *Firm Views: Work of and Work in the Largest Law Firms: Research Study No 35* London: Law Society.

—— (2000) '"Up or Out" – Means or Ends? Staff Retention in Large Law Firms' in P. Thomas (ed) *Discriminating Lawyers* London: Cavendish.

—— (2004) 'A Finger on the Pulse' *Legal Week* Student Special (Spring edn).

Leighton, P., Mortimer, T. and Whatley, N. (1995) *Today's Law Teachers: Lawyers or Academics?* London: Cavendish.

Levit, N. (1996) 'Feminism for Men: Legal Ideology and the Construction of Maleness' 43(4) *UCLA Law Review* 1037.

Lewis, C. (2000) *A Man's Place in the Home: Fathers and Families in the UK: JRF Foundations 440* York: Joseph Rowntree Foundation.

Lewis, C. and Lamb, M. (2007) *Understanding Fatherhood: A Review of Recent Research* York: Joseph Rowntree Foundation.

Lewis, J. (2007) 'Balancing Work and Family: The Nature of the Policy Challenge and Gender Equality': Working Paper for GeNet Project 9: *Tackling Inequalities in Work and Care Policy Initiatives and Actors at the EU and UK Levels, 2007.* Available at <http://www.genet.ac.uk/projects/project9.htm>, accessed 18 October 2008.

Lewis, J. and Campbell, M. (2007) 'UK Work-Family Balance Policies and Gender Equality' 14(1) *Social Politics* 4.

Lewis, J. and Guillari, S. (2005) 'The Adult Worker Model Family, Gender Equality and Care: The Search for New Policy Principles and the Possibilities and Problems of a Capabilities Approach' 34(1) *Economy & Society* 76.

Lewis, J. and Welsh, E. (2005) 'Fathering Practices in Twenty-Six Intact Families and their Implications for Child Contact' 1(1) *International Journal of Law in Context* 81.

Ley, D. (1996) *The New Middle-Class and the Remaking of the Central City* New York: Oxford University Press.

Liddle, M. (1996) 'State, Masculinity and Law: Some Comments on English Gender and English State Formation' 36 *British Journal of Criminology* 361.

Lissenburgh, S. and Smeaton, D. (2003) *Employment Transitions of Older Workers: The Role of Flexible Employment in Maintaining Labour Market Participation and Promoting Job Equality* London: Policy Press.

Lister, R. (2006) 'Children (But Not Women) First: New Labour, Child Welfare and Gender' 26(2) *Critical Social Policy* 315.

Lithgard, B. and Douglas, P. (1999) *Men Engaging Feminisms* Buckingham: Open University Press.

Lloyd, N., O'Brien, M. and Lewis, C. (2003) *Fathers in Sure Start: The National Evaluation of Sure Start (NESS)* London: Institute for the Study of Children, Families and Social Issues, Birkbeck, University of London.

Longhurst, B. and Savage, M. (1996) 'Social Class, Consumption and the Influence of Bordieu: Some Critical Issues' in S. Edgell, K. Hetherington and A. Warde (eds) *Consumption Matters: The Production and Experience of Consumption* Oxford: Blackwell.

Lupton, D. and Barclay, L. (1997) *Constructing Fatherhood: Discourses and Experiences* London: Sage.

Lyotard, J. F. (1984) *The Postmodern Condition* Manchester: Manchester University Press.

McDowell, L. (1995) 'Body Work: Heterosexual Gender Performances in City Workplaces' in D. Bell and G. Valentine (eds) *Mapping Desire* London: Routledge.

—— (1997) *Capital Culture: Gender at Work in the City* Oxford: Blackwell.

—— (2003) *Redundant Masculinities? Employment, Change and White Working Class Youth* Oxford: Blackwell.

McGlynn, C. (1998) *The Woman Lawyer: Making the Difference* London: Butterworths.

—— (2002) 'Strategies for Reforming the English Solicitors' Profession: An Analysis of the Business Case for Sex Equality' in U. Schultz and G. Shaw (eds) *Women in the World's Legal Professions* Oxford, Hart.

Machura, S. and Robson, P. (2001) *Law and Film: Representing Law in Movies* Oxford: Wiley Blackwell.

McIntosh, J. (2003) 'Enduring Conflict in Parental Separation: Pathways on Child Development' 9 *Journal of Family Studies* 63.

MacKinnon, C. (1983) 'Feminism, Marxism, Method and the State: An Agenda for Theory' 8 *Signs* 635.

MacKinnon, C. (1987) *Feminism Unmodified: Discourses on Life and Law* Cambridge, MA: Harvard University Press.

Maclean, M. (ed) (2007) *Parenting After Partnering: Containing Conflict After Separation* Oxford: Hart.

Macleod, D. (2002) 'A Higher Vision' *The Guardian* 19 March.

McMahon, A. (1999) *Taking Care of Men: Sexual Politics in the Public Mind* Cambridge: Cambridge University Press.

McNabb, R. and Vass, V. (2006) 'Male-Female Earnings Differentials Among Lawyers in Britain: A Legacy of the Law or a Current Practice?' 13(2) *Labour Economics* 219.

McNay, I. (1995) 'From the Collegial Academy to Corporate Enterprise: The Changing Culture of Universities' in T. Schuller (ed) *The Changing University?* Buckingham: Open University Press/SRHE.

MacNeil, W. P. (2007) *Lex Populi: The Jurisprudence of Popular Culture* Stanford, CA: Stanford University Press.

McPartland, C. (2008) 'Redundancy Bloodbath Hits Legal Sector as UK Slides into Recession' 7(6) *Lawyer 2B* 1.

MacRae, F. (2009) 'Another Blow to Fatherhood: Now IVF Mothers Can Name ANYONE As "Father" On Birth Certificate – And it Doesn't Have to be a Man' *Daily Mail* 2 March.

McWilliam, E. (2005) 'Changing the Academic Subject' in R. Hunter and M. Keys (eds.) *Changing Law: Rights, Regulation, Reconciliation* Aldershot: Ashgate.

Maidment, S. (1984) *Child Custody and Divorce: The Law in Social Context* London: Croom Helm.

Maidment, S. (1998) 'Parental Alienation Syndrome – A Judicial Response?' *Family Law*, 264.

Malina, D. and Maslin-Prothers, S. (eds) (1998) *Surviving the Academy: Feminist Perspectives* London: Falmer Press.

Mallender, P. and Rayson, J. (2005) *The Civil Partnership Act 2004: A Practical Guide* Cambridge: Cambridge University Press.

Malvern, J. (2008) 'Dear Deirdrie, I Want to Talk About Relationships With Agony Aunts. What Can I do Next?' *The Times* 19 December.

Mamet, D. (1993) *Oleanna* London: Methuen Royal Court Writers Series.

Mangan, J. and Walvin, J. (eds) (1987) *Manliness and Morality: Middle Class Masculinity in Britain and America 1800–1940* Manchester: Manchester University Press.

Mann, A. (2008) 'Of Fatherhood and Health, Men Need to Articulate Their Needs' Letter to the Editor *The Independent* 15 April.

Marginson, S. and Considine, M. (2000) *The Enterprise University: Power, Governance and Reinvention in Australia* Cambridge: Cambridge University Press.

Marks, G. and Houston, D. M. (2002) 'Attitudes Towards Work and Motherhood Held by Working and Non-Working Mothers' 16(3) *Work, Employment and Society* 523.

Marsiglio, W. (ed) (1995) *Fatherhood: Contemporary Theory, Research and Social Policy* London: Sage.

Marsiglio, W., Roy, K. and Litton Fox, G. (eds) (2005) *Situated Fathering: A Focus on Physical and Social Spaces* Lanham, MD: Rowman and Littlefield.

Martin, B. (1998) 'Knowledge, Identity and the Middle-Class: From Collective to Individualised Class Formation?' 46(4) *The Sociological Review* 653.

Maynard, M. and Purvis, J. (1995) *(Hetero)Sexual Politics* London: Taylor and Francis.

Mazey, S. (2001) *Gender Mainstreaming in the EU: Principles and Practice* London: Kogan Page.

Medhurst, A. (2000) 'If Anywhere: Class Identifications and Cultural Studies Academics,' in S. Munt (ed) *Cultural Studies and the Working Class: Subject to Change* London: Cassell.

Melville, A. and Hunter, R. (2001) 'As Everybody Knows: Countering Myths of Gender Bias in Family Law' 1(1) *Griffith Law Review* 124.

Meneley, A. and Young, D. J. (eds) (2005) *Auto-Ethnographies: The Anthropology of Academic Practices* Peterborough, Ontario: Broadview Press.

Menzies, R. (2007) 'Virtual Backlash: Representations of Men's "Rights" and Feminist "Wrongs" in Cyberspace' in D. E. Chunn, S. Boyd and H. Lessard (eds) *Reaction and Resistance: Feminism, Law and Social Change* Vancouver: University of British Columbia Press.

Messerschmidt, J.W. (1993) *Masculinities and Crime: Critique, and Reconceptualization of Theory* Lanham: Rowman and Littlefield.

Messner, M. (1997) *Politics of Masculinities: Men in Movements*, London: Sage.

Metcalf, A. and Humphries, M. (eds) (1985) *The Sexuality of Men* London: Pluto.

Metcalf, H. and Rolfe, H. (2009) *Employment and Earnings in the Finance Sector: A Gender Analysis* London: EHRC/National Institute for Economic and Social Research.

Middlehurst, R. (2002) 'The International Context For UK Higher Education' in S. Ketteridge, S. Marshall and H. Fry (eds) *The Effective Academic* London, Kogan Page/THES.

Middleton, P. (1992) *The Inward Gaze: Masculinity and Subjectivity in Modern Culture* London: Routledge.

Miles, S. (2000) *Youth Lifestyles in a Changing World* Buckingham: Open University Press.

Miller, H. (1995) *Management of Change in Universities: Universities, State and Economy in Australia, Canada and the United Kingdom* Buckingham: SRHE/Open University Press.

Milner, A. (1999) *Core Cultural Concepts: Class* London: Sage.

Mintel, (2000) *Nightclubs and Discotheques* (Mintel, *Pre-Family Leisure Trends*) London: Leisure Intelligence.

Monahan, J. and Swanson, J. (2008) 'Lawyers at Mid-Career: A 2 Year Longitudinal Study of Job and Life Satisfaction' *University of Virginia Law School: Public Law and Legal Theory Working Paper Series No 104*, available at <http://www.law.berkeley.edu/files/manuscandtablesMonahanandSwanson.pdf>, accessed 3 May 2009.

Mooney Marini, M., Fan, P., Finley, E. and Beutel, A.M. (1996) 'Gender and Job Values' 69 *Sociology of Education* 49.

Moran, L. (1990) 'A Study of the History of Male Sexuality in Law: Non-Consummation' 1 *Law and Critique* 155.

—— (1996) *The Homosexual(ity) of Law* London: Routledge.

Morgan, D. (1981) 'Men, Masculinity and the Process of Sociological Enquiry' in H. Roberts, *Doing Feminist Research* London: Routledge & Kegan Paul.

—— (1992) *Discovering Men: Sociology and Masculinities* London: Routledge.

—— (1996) *Family Connections: An Introduction to Family Studies* Oxford: Polity.

Morley, L. (1999) *Organising Feminisms: The Micro politics of the Academy* London: Macmillan.

Morley, L. and Walsh, V. (eds) (1996) *Breaking Boundaries: Women in Higher Education* London: Taylor and Francis.

Morrison, W. (2002) 'Legal Education and Globalisation' *Academic Reporter* (Summer) 4–5 London: Cavendish.

Mort, F. (1996) *Cultures of Consumption* London: Routledge.

Mossman, M.J. (2006) *The First Women Lawyers: A Comparative Study of Gender, Law and the Legal Professions* Oxford: Hart.

Mourad, R.P. (1997) *Postmodern Philosophical Critique and the Pursuit of Knowledge in Higher Education* Westport, CT: Bergin and Garvey.

Mulvey, L. (1989) *The Visual and Other Pleasures* London: Macmillan.

Mumford, A. (2008) 'Towards a Fiscal Sociology of Tax Credits and the Father's Rights Movement' 17 *Social and Legal Studies* 217.

Munt, S (ed) (2000) *Cultural Studies and the Working Class: Subject to Change* London: Cassell.

—— (2007) *Queer Attachments: The Cultural Politics of Shame* Aldershot: Ashgate.

Murray, C. (1990) *The Emerging British Underclass* London: IEA.

Naffine, N. (1985) 'The Masculinity-Femininity Hypothesis' 25 *British Journal of Sociology* 365.

—— (1987) *Female Crime: The Construction of Women in Criminology* Sydney: Allen and Unwin.

—— (1990) *Law and the Sexes: Explorations in Feminist Jurisprudence* Sydney: Allen and Unwin.

—— (1994) 'Possession: Erotic Love in the Law of Rape' 57(1) *Modern Law Review* 10.

—— (1997) *Feminism and Criminology* Cambridge: Polity.

—— (2002) 'In Praise of Legal Feminism' 202 *Legal Studies* 71.

Nardi, P. M. (ed) (1992) *Men's Friendships* London: Sage.

Nayak, A. (2006) 'Displaced Masculinities: Chavs, Youth and Class in the Post-Industrial City' 40(5) *Sociology* 813.

Neale, B. and Smart, C. (1997) 'Experiments with Parenthood?' 31(2) *Sociology* 201.

—— (1999) 'In Whose Best Interests? Theorising Family Life Following Parental Separation or Divorce' in S. Day Sclater and C. Piper (eds) *Undercurrents of Divorce* Aldershot: Ashgate.

—— (2004) '"Good" and "Bad" Lawyers? Struggling in the Shadow of the New Law' 19 *Journal of Social Welfare and Family Law* 377.

Neale, B., Flowerdew, J. and Smart, C. (2003) 'Drifting Towards Shared Residence?' *Family Law* 904.

Neilson, L. (1999) 'Demeaning, Demoralizing and Disenfranchising Divorced Dads: A Review of the Literature' 31 *Journal of Divorce and Remarriage* 129.

Newburn, T. and Shiner, M. (2001) *Teenage Kicks? Young People and Alcohol – A Review of the Literature* York: Joseph Rowntree Foundation.

Newburn, T. and Stanko, E.A. (1994) *Just Boys Doing Business* London: Routledge.

Newman, J. H. (1960) *The Idea of a University* New York: Holt, Rinehart and Winston.

Newson, J. (1992) 'The Decline of Faculty Influence: Confronting the Corporate Agenda' in W. Carroll, L. Christiansen-Rufman, R. Currie and D. Harrison (eds) *Fragile Truths: 25 Years of Sociology and Anthropology in Canada* Ottawa: Carleton University Press.

Newson, J. (1998) 'Conclusion: Repositioning the Local Through Alternative Responses to Globalization' in J. Currie and J. Newson (eds.) (1998) *Universities and Globalization* London: Sage.

Newton, C. (1994) 'Gender Theory and Prison Sociology: Using Theories of Masculinities to Interpret the Sociology of Prisons for Men' 33 *Howard Journal of Criminal Justice* 193.

Nicolson, D. (2005) 'Demography, Discrimination and Diversity: A New Dawn for the British Legal Profession?' 12 *International Journal of the Legal Profession* 201.

Nixon, S. (1996) *Hard Looks: Masculinities, Spectatorship and Contemporary Consumption* London: UCL Press.

Norman, L. (2004) *Career Choices in Law: A Survey of Law Students* (Research Study 50) London: Law Society.

Nussbaum, M. (2004) *Hiding From Humanity: Disgust, Shame and the Law* Princeton, NJ: Princeton University Press.

Nussbaum, N. (1997) *Cultivating Humanity: A Classical Defense of Reform in Legal Education* Cambridge, MA: Harvard University Press.

Oakley, A. (2001) 'Foreword' in A. Brooks and A. Mackinnon (eds) *Gender and the Restructured University* Buckingham: SRHE/Open University Press.

O'Brien, M. (2004) 'Social Science and Public Policy Perspectives on Fatherhood' in M. E. Lamb (ed) *The Role of the Father in Child Development* Hoboken, NJ: John Wiley.

—— (2005) *Shared Caring: Bringing Fathers into the Frame* Manchester: Equal Opportunities Commission.

O'Brien, M. and Shemilt, I. (2003) *Working Fathers: Earning and Caring* Manchester: Equal Opportunities Commission.

O'Brien, M., Brandth, B. and Kvande, E. (2007) 'Fathers, Work and Family Life: Global Perspectives and New Insights' 10(4) *Community, Work and Family* 375.

O'Connor, M. (2007) *Fathers 4 Justice* London: Weidenfeld & Nicolson.

O'Donnell, M. and Sharpe, S. (2000) *Uncertain Masculinities: Youth, Ethnicity and Class in Contemporary Britain* London: Routledge.

O'Donovan, C. (2006) 'Genetics, Fathers and Families: Exploring the Implications of Changing the Law in Favour of Identifying Sperm Donors' 15 *Social and Legal Studies* 494.

O'Donovan, K. (1985) *Sexual Divisions in Law* London: Weidenfeld & Nicolson.

—— (1993) *Family Law Matters* London: Pluto.

O'Malley, P. (2004) *Risk, Uncertainty and Government* London: The Glasshouse Press.

Of Time and the City: A Love Song and A Eulogy (2008) London: HanWay/BBC films.

Office for National Statistics (2002) *UK 2000 Time Use Survey: Dataset* 2nd edn London: Office for National Statistics.

—— (2003) *Key Statistics for Local Authorities in England and Wales: Census 2001* London: Office for National Statistics.

—— (2008) *Population Trends* London: Office for National Statistics. Available at: <http://www.statistics.gov.uk/downloads/theme_population/Population_-Trends_131_web.pdf>, accessed 30 March 2008.

Olsen, F. (1985) 'The Myth of State Intervention in the Family' 18 *University of Michigan Journal of Law Reform* 835.

Ottosen, M. H. (2001) 'Legal and Social Ties Between Children and Cohabiting Fathers' 8(1) *Childhood* 75.

Page, J. and Whitting, G. (2008) *A Review of How Fathers Can Be Better Recognised and Supported Through DCSF Policy* DCSF Research Report DCSF-RRO40, London: DCFS.

Pahl, R. (1995) *After Success* Oxford: Blackwell.

Parker, M. and Jary, D. (1995) 'The McUniversity: Organization, Management and Academic Subjectivity' 2(2) *Organization* 319.

Parker, S. (1992) 'Rights and Utility in Anglo-Australian Law' 55 *Modern Law Review* 311.

Parsons, T. and Bales, F. (1955) *Family Socialization and Interaction Process*, Glencoe, IL: Free Press.

Pateman, C. (1988) *The Sexual Contract* Stanford, CA: Stanford University Press.

Paton, G. (2008) 'Number of Working Class Students Has Barely Increased' *Daily Telegraph* 25 June.

Paton, G. (2008) 'Fewer Poor Students Attend University in England' *Daily Telegraph* 4 December.

Peacey, V. and Hunt, J. (2008) *Problematic Contact after Separation and Divorce? A National Survey of Parents* London: One Parent Families/Gingerbread.

Pease, B. (2000) *Recreating Men: Postmodern Masculinity Politics* London: Sage.

Pease, B. and Pringle, K. (eds) (2002) *A Man's World: Changing Men's Practices in a Globalized World* London: Zed Books.

Petersen, A. (1999) *Unmasking the Masculine: Men and Identity in a Sceptical Age* London: Sage.

—— (2003) 'Research on Men and Masculinities: Some Implications of Recent Theory for Future Work' 6(1) *Men and Masculinities* 54.

Phillips, A. (2004) 'Most Fathers get Justice' *The Guardian* 13 October.

Pickering, M. (1997) *History, Experience and Cultural Studies* London: Macmillan.

Piercy, M. (2004) 'Intractable Contact Disputes' *Family Law* 815.

Piper, C. (1993) *The Responsible Parent* Brighton: Harvester Wheatsheaf.

—— (1996) 'Divorce Reform and the Image of the Child' 23(3) *Journal of Law and Society* 364.

—— (2006) 'Feminist Perspectives on Youth Justice' in A. Diduck and K. O'Donovan (eds) *Feminist Perspectives on Family Law* London: Routledge-Cavendish.

Piper, C. and Day Sclater, S. (2000) 'Remoralising the Family? Family Policy, Family Law and Youth Justice' 12(2) *Child and Family Law Quarterly* 135.

Plant, R. (2003) 'Citizenship and Social Security' 24(2) *Fiscal Studies* 153.

Pleck, J.H. (1976) 'The Male Sex Role: Problems, Definitions and Sources of Change' 32 *Journal of Social Issues* 55.

Plummer, K. (2003) *Intimate Citizenship: Personal Decision and Public Dialogues* Washington DC: University of Washington Press.

—— (2005) 'Intimate Inequalities' in M. Romero and J. Howard (eds) *The Blackwell Companion of Social Inequalities* Oxford: Blackwell.

Podmore, D. and Spencer, A. (1986) 'Gender in the Labour Process – The Case of Women and Men Lawyers' in D. Knights and H. Wilmott (eds) *Gender and Labour Process* Aldershot: Gower.

Pollitt, C. (1990) *Managerialism and the Public Services: The Anglo-American Experience* Oxford: Blackwell.

Polster, C. (1996) 'Dismantling the Liberal University: The State's New Approach to Academic Research' in R. Brecher, O. Fleischman and J. Halliday (eds) *Universities in a Liberal State* Aldershot: Avebury.

—— (2000) 'The Advantages and Disadvantages of Corporate/University Links: What's Wrong with this Question?' D. Doherty-Delorme and E. Shaker (eds), *Missing Pieces II: An Alternative Guide to Canadian Post-Secondary Education* Ottawa: Canadian Centre for Policy Alternatives.

Polster, C. and Newson, J. (1998) 'Don't Count Your Blessings: The Social Accomplishments of Performance Indicators' in J. Currie and J. Newson (eds) *Universities and Globalization* London: Sage.

Porter, D. (ed) (1992) *Between Men and Feminism* London: Routledge.

Press Association (2004) 'Fathers' Rights Protest on Court Roof' London: Press Association (*PA News*) 18 May.

Prime Minister's Strategy Unit (2007) *Building on Progress: Families* London: Cabinet Office.

Pritchard, C. (1996) 'Managing Universities: Is It Men's Work?' in D. Collinson and J. Hearn *Men as Managers, Managers as Men* London: Sage.

—— (2000) 'Know, Learn and Share! The Knowledge Phenomena and the Construction of a Consumptive-Communicative Body' in C. Pritchard, R. Hull, M. Chumer and H. Willmott (eds) *Managing Knowledge: Critical Investigations of Work and Learning* Basingstoke: Macmillan.

—— (2000) 'The Body Topographies of Education Management' in J. Hassard, R. Holliday and H. Willmott (eds) *Organization and the Body* London: Sage.

Pryor, J. and Rodgers, B. (2001) *Children in Changing Families: Life after Parental Separation* Oxford: Blackwell.

Puchalska, B. (2004) 'Legal Education: Professional, Academic or Vocational?' 4 *European Journal of Legal Education* 19.

Pue, W. (2008) 'Legal Education's Mission' 42 *Law Teacher* 275.

Purcell, K. and Elias, P. (2008) 'Wanting to "help people" exacerbates the pay gap for young professional women' Genet Newsletter 3, February, available at <http://www.genet.ac.uk/newsletter/newsletter_feb08.pdf>, accessed 18 March 2009.

Quinn, J. et al (2005) *From Life Crisis to Lifelong Learning: Rethinking Working-Class 'Drop-Out' From Higher Education* York: Joseph Rowntree Foundation.

Rake, K. (2001) 'Gender and New Labour's Social Policies' 30(2) *Journal of Social Policy* 209.

Ray Seward, R., Yeatts, D. E., Amin, I. and Dewitt, A. (2006) 'Employment Leave and Father's Involvement with Children: According to Mothers and Fathers' 8(4) *Men and Masculinities* 405.

Raz, J. (1986) *The Morality of Freedom* Oxford: Oxford University Press.

Readings, B. (1996) *The University in Ruins* Cambridge, MA: Harvard University Press.

Reay, D., David, M. and Ball, S. (2005) *Degrees of Choice: Social Class, Race and Gender in Higher Education* Stoke: Trentham Books.

Redman, P. and Mac an Ghaill, M. (1997) 'Educating Peter: The Making of a History Man' in D. Steinberg et al (eds) *Border Patrols: Policing the Boundaries of Heterosexuality* London: Cassell.

Reece, H. (1996) 'The Paramountcy Principle: Consensus or Construct?' 49 *Current Legal Problems* 267.

—— (2003) *Divorcing Responsibly* Oxford: Hart.

—— (2006) 'UK Women's Groups' Child Contact Campaign: "So Long As It Is Safe"' 18(4) *Child and Family Law Quarterly* 538.

—— (2009) 'The Degradation of Parental Responsibility' in R. Probert, S. Gilmore and J. Herring (eds) *Responsible Parents and Parental Responsibility* Oxford: Hart.

Reed-Danahay, D. (ed) (1997) *Auto-Ethnography: Rewriting the Self and the Social* London: Berg.

Reputation Intelligence (2004) *F4J Heralds a New Era in Political Campaigning: Media Report* London: Reputation Intelligence.

Reynaud, E. (1983) *Holy Virility: The Social Construction of Masculinity* London: Pluto.

Reynolds, J. (ed) (2001) *Not in Front of the Children?: How Conflict Between Parents Affects Children* London: One Plus One.

Rhoades, H. (2000) 'Posing as Reform? The Case of the Family Law Reform Act' 14(2) *Australian Journal of Family Law* 142.

—— (2002) 'The "Non Contact Mother": Reconstructions of Motherhood in the Era of the New Father' 16 *International Journal of Law, Policy and the Family* 72.

—— (2002) 'The Rise of Shared Parenting Laws – a Critical Reflection' 19 *Canadian Journal of Family Law* 75.

—— (2006) 'Yearning for Law: Fathers' Groups and Family Law Reform in Australia' in R. Collier and S. Sheldon (eds) *Fathers' Rights Activism and Legal Reform* Oxford: Hart.

Rhoades, H. and Boyd, S. (2004) 'Reforming Custody Laws: A Comparative Study' 18 *International Journal of Law, Policy and the Family* 119.

Rich, A. (1981) *Compulsory Heterosexuality and Lesbian Existence* London: Onlywomen Press.

Richards, M. (1987) 'Fatherhood, Marriage and Sexuality: Some Speculations on the English Middle-class Family' in C. Lewis and M. O'Brien (eds) *Reassessing Fatherhood: New Observations on Fathers and the Modern Family* London: Sage.

Richardson, D. (ed) (1996) *Theorising Heterosexuality: Telling it Straight* Buckingham: Open University Press.

Richardson, H. (2008) 'Universities "May Face Deficit"' *BBC News* 10 December.

Robertson, R. (1992) *Globalization* London: Sage.

Robertson, S. (2007) *Understanding Men's Health: Masculinity, Identity and Well-being* Buckingham: Open University Press.

Robson, R. (1998) *Sappho Goes to Law School* New York: Columbia University Press.

Rodgers, B. and Pryor, J. (1998) *Divorce and Separation: Outcomes for Children* York: Joseph Rowntree Foundation.

Rolfe, H. and Anderson, T. (2002) *A Firm Decision: The Recruitment of Trainee Solicitors* London: Law Society.

Roper, M. (1994) *Masculinity and the British Organization Man Since 1945* Oxford: Oxford University Press.

Roper, M. and Tosh, J. (eds) (1991) *Manful Assertions: Masculinity in Britain Since 1800* London: Routledge.

Rose, G. (2000) *Visual Methodologies* London: Sage.

Rose, N. (1987) 'Transcending the Public/Private' 14(1) *Journal of Law and Society* 61.

—— (1994) 'Expertise and the Government of Conduct' 14 *Studies in Law, Politics and Society* 359.

—— (1995) *Governing the Soul* London: Routledge.

Rose, N. and Valverde, M. (1998) 'Governed by Law?' 7(4) *Social and Legal Studies* 541.

Rosenblatt, J. and Scragg, P. (1995) 'The Hostile Parent: A Clinical Analysis' *Family Law* 152.

Royal Commission on Marriage and Divorce (1956) *Royal Commission on Marriage and Divorce: Report 1951–1955*, Cmd 9678 London: HMSO.

Ruckin, C. (2009) 'Halliwell's Kicks off 4th Redundancy Round' *Legal Week* 13 March.

Ryan, J. and Sackrey, C. (1984) *Strangers in Paradise: Academics from the Working-Class* Boston, MA: South End Press.

Ryder, R. (1991) 'The Cult of Machismo' 9 *Criminal Justice* 12.

Sabo, D., Kupers, T. and London, W. (eds) (2001) *Prison Masculinities* Philadelphia, PA: Temple University Press.

Sachs, A. and Wilson, J. H. (1978) *Sexism and the Law: A Study of Male Beliefs and Judicial Bias* Oxford: Martin Robertson.

Sadowski, E. (2009) 'Details Emerge of A & O Redundancy Programme' *Legal Week* 16 March.

Sanderson, P. and Sommerlad, H. (2000) 'Professionalism, Discrimination, Difference and Choice in Women's Experience in Law Jobs' in P. Thomas (ed) *Discriminating Lawyers* London: Cavendish.

Sandland, R. (1995) 'Between "Truth" and "Difference": Poststructuralism, Law and the Power of Feminism' 3(1) *Feminist Legal Studies* 3.

Sarat, A. and Kearns, T. (eds) (2000) *Law in the Domains of Culture* Ann Arbor, MI: University of Michigan Press.

Sarat, A. and Simon, J. (eds) (2003) *Cultural Analysis, Cultural Studies and the Law* Durham, NC: Duke University Press.

Sassen, S. (1998) *Globalisation and Its Discontents: Essays on the New Mobility of People and Money* New York: The New Press.

Saunders, H. (2004) *Twenty-Nine Child Homicides: Lessons to be Learnt on Domestic Violence and Child Protection* London: Women's Aid.

Savage, M. (2000) *Class Analysis and Social Transformation* Buckingham: Open University Press.

Savage, M. and Butler, T. (eds) (1995) *Social Change and the Middle Classes* London: UCL Press.

Savage, M., Dickens, P. and Fielding, T. (1992) *Property, Bureaucracy and Culture: Middle Class Formation in Contemporary Britain* London: Routledge.

Sayer, A. (2005) *The Moral Significance of Class* Cambridge: Cambridge University Press.

Saville, P. (2003) *Designed by Peter Saville* Princeton, NJ: Princeton Arch.

Schleef, D. (2000) 'That's a Good Question! Exploring Motivations for Law and Business School Choice' 73 *Sociology of Education* 155.

Schmidt, V. (2005) *Gender Mainstreaming: An Innovation in Europe? The Institutionalisation of Gender Mainstreaming in the European Commission* Leverkusen Opladen: Barbara Burich.

Schultz, U. and Shaw, G. (eds) (2003) *Women in the World's Legal Professions* Oxford: Hart.

Scott, A. (2000) *The Cultural Economy of Cities* London: Sage.

Scourfield, J. (2003) *Gender and Child Protection* London: Palgrave Macmillan.

Scourfield, J. and Drakeford, M. (2002) 'New Labour and the "Problem of Men"' 22 *Critical Social Policy* 619.

Seabrook, J. (1985) *A World Still to Win: Reconstruction of the Post War Working Class,* London: Faber and Faber.

Secker, S. (2001) *For the Sake of the Children: The FNF Guide to Shared Parenting* London: FNF Publications.

Sedgwick, E. (1990) *Epistemology of the Closet* New York: Penguin.

Sedgwick, E. and Frank, A. (2003) *Touching Feeling: Affect, Pedagogy, Performativity* Durham, NC: Duke University Press.

Segal, L. (1990) *Slow Motion: Changing Masculinities Changing Men* London: Virago.

—— (1994) *Is the Future Female? Troubled Thoughts On Contemporary Feminism* London: Virago.

—— (1994) *Straight Sex: Rethinking the Politics of Pleasure* London: Virago.

—— (1997) 'Feminist Sexual Politics and the Heterosexual Predicament' in L. Segal (ed) *New Sexual Agendas* New York: New York University Press.

—— (2001) 'Opinion' *The Guardian* 13 February.

Seidler, V. (1989) *Rediscovering Masculinity: Reason, Language and Sexuality* London: Routledge.

—— (1994) *Unreasonable Men: Masculinity and Social Theory* London: Routledge.

—— (1995) 'Men, Heterosexualities and Emotional Life' in S. Pile and N. Thrift (eds) *Mapping the Subject: Geographies of Cultural Transformation* London: Routledge.

—— (1997) *Man Enough: Embodying Masculinities* London: Sage.

—— (ed) (1991) *The Achilles Heel Reader: Men, Sexual Politics and Socialism* London: Routledge.

Seligman, M. E. P., Verkuil, P. R. and Kang, T. H. (2002) 'Why Lawyers Are Unhappy' 23(1) *Cardozo Law Review* 33.

Selmi, M. (2001) 'Care Work and the Road to Equality: A Commentary on Fineman and Williams' 76 *Chicago-Kent Law Review* 1557.

Selmi, M. (2007) 'The Work-Family Conflict: An Essay on Employers, Men and Responsibility' 4 *University of St Thomas Law Review* 573.

Sen, A (1999) *Development as Freedom* London: Knopf.

—— (2003) 'Capability and Well-Being' in M. Nussbaum and A. Sen (eds) *The Quality of Life* Oxford: Oxford University Press.

Sennett, R. (1998) *The Corrosion of Character: The Personal Consequences of Work in the New Capitalism* New York: W. W. Norton.

Sharpe, A. (2002) *Transgender Jurisprudence: Dysphoric Bodies of Law* London: Cavendish.

Sheldon, S. (1999) '*Re*Conceiving Masculinity: Imagining Men's Reproductive Bodies in Law' 26(2) *Journal of Law and Society* 129.

Sheldon, S. (2001) 'Sperm Bandits: Birth Control Fraud and the Battle of the Sexes' 21 *Legal Studies* 460.

Shepherd, J. (2008) 'Poor Students forced to stay close to home' *The Guardian* 25 November.

—— (2009) 'White, middle class families dominate university places' *The Guardian* 3 February.

Sherman, J. and Frean, A. (2009) 'Thousands of jobs to go at universities as budgets slashed' *The Times* 7 May.

Sherr, A. (1995) 'Superheroes and Slaves: Images and Work of the Legal Professional' 48 (2) *Current Legal Problems* 327.

Sherr, A. and Webb, J. (1989) 'Law Students, the External Market and Socialization: Do We Make Them Turn to the City?' 16(2) *Journal of Law and Society* 225.

Sherwin, R. K. (2000) *When Law Goes Pop: The Vanishing Line Between Law and Popular Culture* Chicago, IL: Chicago University Press.

—— (2004) 'Law in Popular Culture' in A. Sarat (ed) *Blackwell Companion to Law and Society* Oxford: Oxford University Press.

—— (ed) (2006) *Popular Culture and Law* Aldershot: Ashgate.

Shields, R. (ed) (1992) *Lifestyle Shopping: The Subject of Consumption* London: Routledge.

Shiner, M. (1999) *Entry into the Legal Profession: Law Student Cohort Study Year 5* London: Law Society.

Shiner, M. (2000) 'Young, Gifted and Blocked! Entry to the Solicitor's Profession' in P. Thomas (ed) *Discriminating Lawyers* London: Cavendish.

Showalter, E. (1987) *The Female Malady: Women, Madness and English Culture 1830–1980* London: Virago.

Siems, J. (2004) *Equality and Diversity: Women Solicitors: Research Report 48: Vol 1 Quantitative Findings* London: Law Society.

Siltanen, J. and Doucet, A. (2008) *Gender Relations in Canada: Intersectionality and Beyond* Oxford: Oxford University Press.

Silva, E. (ed) (1996) *Good Enough Mothering? Feminist Perspectives on Lone Motherhood* London: Routledge.

Sim, J. (1996) '"Tougher Than the Rest?" Men in Prison' in T. Newburn and E. A. Stanko *Just Boys Doing Business* London: Routledge.

Simpson, B., Jessop, J. A. and McCarthy, P. (2003) 'Fathers After Divorce' in A. Bainham, B. Lindley and M. Richards (eds) *Children and their Families: Contact, Rights and Welfare* Oxford: Hart.

Simpson, B., McCarthy, P. and Walker, J. (1995) *Being There: Fathers After Divorce* Newcastle: Centre for Family Studies, University of Newcastle upon Tyne.

Sinclair, A. (1998) *Doing Leadership Differently: Gender, Power and Sexuality in a Changing Business Culture* Melbourne: Melbourne University Press.

Skeggs, B. (1997) *Formations of Class and Gender: Becoming Respectable* London: Sage.

—— (2000) 'The Appearance of Class: Challenges in Gay Space' in S. Munt (ed) *Cultural Studies and the Working Class: Subject to Change* London: Cassell.

—— (2003) *Class, Self, Culture* London: Routledge.

—— (2005) 'The Making of Class and Gender Through Visualising Moral Subject' 39 (5) *Sociology* 965.

—— (2005) 'The Rebranding of Class: Propertising Culture' in F. Devine, M. Savage, J. Scott and R. Crompton (eds) *Rethinking Class: Cultures, Identity and Lifestyle* London: Palgrave Macmillan.

—— (2009) 'Haunted by the Spectre of Judgement: Respectability, Value and Affect in Class Relations' in K. P. Sveinsson (ed) *Who Cares About the White Working Class?* London: Runnymede Trust.

Skinner, C. (2003) *Running Around in Circles: Coordinating Childcare, Education and Work* London: Policy Press.

Skordaki, E. (1996) 'Glass Slippers and Glass Ceilings: Women in the Legal Profession' 3 *International Journal of the Legal Profession* 7.

Slater, D. (1997) *Consumer Culture* Oxford: Polity Press.

Slaughter, S. (2002) 'National Higher Education Policy in a Global Economy' in J. Currie and J. Newson (eds) (1998) *Universities and Globalization* London: Sage.

Slaughter, S. and Leslie, L. (1997) *Academic Capitalism: Politics, Policies and the Entrepreneurial University* Baltimore, MD: Johns Hopkins University Press.

Smart, C. (1984) *The Ties That Bind: Law, Marriage and the Reproduction of Patriarchal Relations* London: Routledge & Kegan Paul.

—— (1986) 'Feminism and Law: Some Problems of Analysis and Strategy' 14 *International Journal of the Sociology of Law* 109.

—— (1987) '"There is of course a Distinction dictated by Nature": Law and the Problem of Paternity' in M. Stanworth (ed) *Reproductive Technologies: Gender, Motherhood and Medicine* (Feminist Perspectives Series) Cambridge: Polity.

—— (1989) *Feminism and the Power of Law* London: Routledge.

—— (1990) 'Feminist Approaches to Criminology or Postmodern Woman meets Atavistic Man' in L. Gelsthorpe and A. Morris (eds) *Feminist Perspectives in Criminology* Buckingham: Open University Press.

—— (1992) 'The Woman of Legal Discourse' 1 *Social and Legal Studies* 29.

—— (1995) 'Losing the Struggle for Another Voice: The Case of Family Law' 18(2) *Dalhousie Law Journal* 173.

—— (1996) 'Collusion, Collaboration and Confession on Moving Beyond the Heterosexuality Debate' in D. Richardson (ed) *Theorising Heterosexuality: Telling it Straight* Buckingham: Open University Press.

—— (1996) 'Desperately Seeking Post-Heterosexual Woman' in J. Holland and L. Adkins (eds) *Sex, Sensibility and the Gendered Body* London: St Martins Press.

—— (1997) 'Wishful Thinking and Harmful Tinkering? Sociological Reflections on Family Policy' 26(3) *Journal of Social Policy* 1.

—— (1999) 'The "New" Parenthood: Fathers and Mothers After Divorce' in E. Silva and C. Smart (eds) *The New Family?* London: Sage.

—— (2002) 'From Children's Shoes to Children's Voices' 40(3) *Family Court Review: An International Journal* 305.

—— (2004) 'Equal Shares: Rights for Fathers or Recognition for Children?' 24(4) *Critical Social Policy* 484.

—— (2006) 'The Ethic of Justice Strikes Back', in A. Diduck and K. O'Donovan (eds) *Feminist Perspectives On Family Law* London: Routledge-Cavendish.

—— (2006) 'Preface' in R. Collier and S. Sheldon (eds) (2006) *Fathers Rights Activism and Legal Reform,* Oxford: Hart.

—— (2007) *Personal Life: New Directions in Sociological Thinking,* Oxford: Polity.

Smart, C. and Neale, B. (1997) 'Arguments Against Virtue: Must Contact Be Enforced?' *Family Law* 332.

—— (1997) 'Good Enough Morality? Divorce and Postmodernity' 17(4) *Critical Social Policy* 3.

—— (1999) *Family Fragments?* Cambridge: Polity.

—— (1999) '"I Hadn't Really Thought About it": New Identities/New Fatherhoods' in J. Seymour and O. Bagguley (eds) *Relating Intimacies: Power and Resistance,* Basingstoke: Palgrave Macmillan.

Smart, C. and Sevenhujsen, S. (eds) (1989) *Child Custody and the Politics of Gender* London: Routledge.

Smart, C., Wade, A. and Neale, B. (1999) 'Objects of Concern? Children and Divorce' 11(4) *Child and Family Law Quarterly* 365.

Smart, C., May, V., Wade, A. and Furniss, C. (2003) *Residence and Contact Disputes in Court: Research Report 6/2003* London: Department for Constitutional Affairs.

Smith, A. (2006) 'Vicious (Magic) Circle' 9(2) *Legal Ethics* 152.

Smith, A. and Webster, F. (eds) (1998) *The Postmodern University? Contested Visions of Higher Education in Society* Buckingham: SRHE/Open University Press.

Sommerlad, H. (1994) 'The Myth of Feminisation: Women and Cultural Change in the Legal Profession' 1 *International Journal of the Legal Profession* 31.

—— (2002) 'Women Solicitors in a Fractured Profession' 9(3) *International Journal of the Legal Profession* 213.

—— (2006) 'Becoming a Lawyer: Gender and the Processes of Professional Socialization', in S. McIntyre and E. Sheehy (eds) *Calling for Change: Women, Law and the Legal Profession* Ottawa: University of Ottawa Press.

—— (2007) 'Researching and Theorizing the Processes of Professional Identity Formation' 34(2) *Journal of Law and Society* 190.

—— (2008) 'That Obscure Object of Desire: Sex Equality and the Legal Profession' in R. Hunter (ed) *Rethinking Equality* Oxford: Hart.

Sommerlad, H. and Sanderson, P. (1997) 'The Legal Labour Market and the Training Needs of Women Returners in the United Kingdom' 29(1) *Journal of Vocational Education and Training* 45.

Sommerlad, H. and Sanderson, P. (1998) *Gender Choice and Commitment: Women Solicitors in England and Wales and the Struggle for Equal Status* Aldershot: Ashgate.

Spector-Mersel, G. (2006) 'Never-Aging Stories; Western Hegemonic Masculinity Scripts' 15(1) *Journal of Gender Studies* 67.

Spelman, E. (1988) *Inessential Woman: Problems of Exclusion in Feminist Thought* London: The Women's Press.

Squires, P. (2006) 'New Labour and the Politics of Anti-Social Behaviour' 26(1) *Critical Social Policy* 144.

Stanley, K. (2005) *Daddy Dearest? Active Fatherhood and Public Policy* London: Institute For Public Policy Research.

Stevenson, N., Jackson, P. and Brooks, K. (2001) *Making Sense of Men's Magazines* Cambridge: Polity.

Stoller, R. (1984) *Sex and Gender Vol 1: On the Development of Masculinity and Femininity* London: Karnac Books.

Stoltenberg, J. (1990) *Refusing to Be a Man: Essays on Sex and Justice* (revised edition) London: UCL Press.

—— (2000) *The End of Manhood: A Book for Men of Conscience* New York: Dutton.

Sturge, C. in consultation with Glaser, D. (2000) 'Contact and Domestic Violence – The Expert's Court Report' *Family Law* 615.

Sturge-Apple, M. L., Davies, P. T. and Cummings, E. M. (2006) 'The Impact of Hostility and Withdrawal in Interparental Conflict on Parental Emotional Unavailability and Children's Adjustment Difficulties' 77(5) *Child Development* 1623.

Stychin, C. (1996) *Law's Desire* London: Routledge.

—— (2006) 'Family Friendly? Rights, Responsibilities and Relationship Recognition' in A. Diduck and K. O'Donovan (eds) *Feminist Perspectives on Family Law* London: Routledge-Cavendish.

Stychin, C. and Herman, D. (eds) (2000) *Sexuality in the Legal Arena* London: Athlone Press.

Subotnik, D. and Lazar, G. (1999) 'Deconstructing the Rejection Letter: A Look at Elitism in Article Selection' 49 *Journal of Legal Education* 601.

Susskind, R. (2008) *The End of Lawyers? Rethinking the Nature of Legal Services* Oxford: Oxford University Press.

Sveinsson, K. P. (ed) (2009) *Who Cares About the White Working Class?* London: Runnymede Trust.

Symes, C. and McIntryre, J. (eds) (2000) *Working Knowledge: The New Vocationalism and Higher Education* Buckingham: Open University Press.

Talib, A. (2001) 'The Continuing Behavioural Modification of Academics Since the 1992 RAE' 33 *Higher Education Review* 30.

Taylor, I. (1994) 'The Political Economy of Crime' in M. Maguire, R. Morgan and R. Reiner (eds) *The Oxford Handbook of Criminology* Oxford: Oxford University Press.

Taylor, I., Evans, K. and Fraser, P. (1996) *A Tale of Two Cities: Global Change, Local Feeling and Everyday Life in the North of England: A Study in Manchester and Sheffield* London: Routledge.

Taylor, J. (2009) 'Downturn Triggers Rush to the Divorce Courts' *The Independent* 2 February.

Thomas, K. (1995) '"Masculinity", "The Rule of Law" and Other Legal Fictions' in M. Berger, B. Wallis and S. Watson (eds) *Constructing Masculinity* New York: Routledge.

Thomas, P. and Rees, A. (2000) 'Law Students – Getting in and getting on' in P. Thomas (ed) *Discriminating Lawyers* London: Cavendish.

Thompson, E. P. (1970) 'The Business University' *New Society* 19 February.

—— (1970) *Warwick University Ltd: Industry, Management and the Universities* Harmondsworth: Penguin.

Thomson, M. (2006) 'Viagra Nation: Sex and the Prescribing of Familial Masculinity' 2 *Law, Culture, Humanities* 259.

—— (2007) *Endowed: Regulating the Male Sexed Body* New York: Routledge.

Thornton, M. (1989) 'Hegemonic Masculinity and the Academy' 17 *International Journal of the Sociology of Law* 115.

—— (1996) *Dissonance and Distrust: Women in the Legal Profession* Oxford: Oxford University Press.

—— (1998) 'Authority and Corporeality: The Conundrum for Women in Law' 6(2) *Feminist Legal Studies* 147.

—— (1998) 'Technocentrism and the Law School' 36(2) *Osgoode Hall Law Journal* 1369.

—— (2001) 'Among the Ruins: Law in the Neo-Liberal Academy' 20 *Windsor Yearbook of Access to Justice* 3.

—— (2001) 'The Demise of Diversity in Legal Education: Globalisation and the New Knowledge Economy' 8(1) *International Journal of the Legal Profession* 37.

—— (2004) 'Neoliberal Melancholia: The Case of Feminist Legal Scholarship' 20 *Australian Feminist Law Journal* 7.

—— (ed) (1995) *Public and Private: Feminist Legal Debates* Melbourne: Oxford University Press.

—— (ed) (2002) *Romancing the Tomes: Popular Culture Law and Feminism* London: Routledge-Cavendish.

Thrift, N. (1989) 'Images of Social Change' in C. V. Hamnett, L. McDowell and P. Sarre (eds) *The Changing Social Structure* London: Sage.

—— (1997) '"Us" and "Them": Re-imagining Identities' in H. Mackay (ed) *Consumption and Everyday Life* London: Sage.

—— (2007) *Non-Representational Theory: Space, Politics, Affect* London: Routledge.

Thurston, R. (1996) 'Are You Sitting Comfortably? Men's Storytellings, Masculinities, Prison Culture and Violence', in M. Mac an Ghaill (ed) *Understanding Masculinities* Buckingham: Open University Press.

Tolson, A. (1977) *The Limits of Masculinity* London: Tavistock.

Tombs, S. and Whyte, D. (2003) 'Shining a Light on Power? Reflections on British Criminology and the Future of Critical Social Science' 41 *Socio-Legal Newsletter* 1.

Tosh, J. (1999) *A Man's Place: Masculinity and the Middle-class Home in Victorian England* London: Yale University Press.

Touraine, A. (1985) 'An Introduction to the Study of New Social Movements' 52 *Social Research* 749.

Townsend, N. W. (2002) *The Package Deal: Marriage, Work and Fatherhood* Philadelphia, PA: Temple University Press.

Treasury, HM (2003) *Lambert Review of Business-University Collaboration: Final Report* London: HMSO. Available at <http://www.hm-treasury.gov.uk/media/EA556/lambert_review_final_450.pdf>, accessed 14 July 2008.

Trentmann, F. (ed) (2005) *The Making of the Consumer: Knowledge, Power and Identity in the Modern World* London: Berg.

Trider, L. and Kellett, J. (2007) *The Longer-Term Outcomes of In-Court Conciliation* London: Ministry of Justice.

Trowler, P. (1998) *Academics Responding to Change: New Higher Education Frameworks and Academic Cultures* Buckingham: Open University Press/SRHE.

Tudor, A. (1995) 'Culture, Mass Communication and Social Agency' 12 *Theory, Culture and Society* 81.

Turner, D. (2009) 'Extra £120m education savings sought' *Financial Times* 8 May.

—— (2009) 'Universities Slow to Widen Social Mix' *Financial Times* 26 February.

—— (2009) 'Warning on Student Numbers in England', *Financial Times* 9 May.

Turner, J. (2006) 'The Feminist Battling or Men's Rights' *The Guardian* 20 May.

Twining, W. (1994) *Blackstone's Tower: The English Law School* London: Sweet & Maxwell.

—— (1995) 'Remember 1972: The Oxford Centre in the Context of Developments in Higher Education and the Discipline of Law' in D. Galligan (ed) *Socio-Legal Studies in Context: The Oxford Centre Part and Future* Oxford: Blackwell.

—— (1997) *Law in Context: Enlarging a Discipline* Oxford: Clarendon Press.

—— (1998) 'Thinking About Law Schools: Rutland Reviewed' 25(1) *Journal of Law and Society* 1.

Tysome, T. (2004) 'Sector Caught in Parent Trap' *Times Higher Education Supplement* 30 July.

Urry, J. (1995) *Consuming Places* London: Routledge.

Utley, A. (2001) 'Outbreak of '"New Managerialism"' Infects Faculties' *Times Higher Education Supplement* 20 July.

Valentine, G., Skelton, T. and Chambers, D. (1998) *Cool Places: An Introduction to Youth and Youth Cultures* London: Routledge.

Vallance-Webb, G. (2008) 'Child Contact: Vengeful Mothers, Good Fathers and Vice Versa' *Family Law* 678.

Valverde, M. (2003) *Law's Dream of a Common Knowledge* Princeton, NJ: Princeton University Press.

Van Krieken, R. (2001) 'Legal Informalism, Power and Liberal Governance' 19(1) *Social and Legal Studies* 5.

—— (2005) 'The "Best Interests of the Child" and Parental Separation on the "Civilising of Parents"' 68(1) *Modern Law Review* 25.

Varnava, T. (2002) 'Building Research Capacity in Legal Education' 38 *Socio-Legal Newsletter* 4.

Vick, D., Murray, A., Little, G. and Campbell, K. (1998) 'The Perceptions of Academic Lawyers Concerning the Effects of the United Kingdom's Research Assessment Exercise' 24(4) *Journal of Law and Society* 536.

Vignaendra, S. (2001) *Social Class and Entry into the Solicitor's Profession: Research Study 41* London: Law Society.

Vignaendra, S., Williams, M. and Gavey, J. (2000) 'Hearing Black and Asian Voices – An Exploration of Identity' in P. Thomas (ed) *Discriminating Lawyers* London: Cavendish.

Wajcman, J. (1998) *Managing Like A Man: Women and Men in Corporate Management* Cambridge: Polity Press.

Waldby, C. (1995) 'Destruction: Boundary Erotics and Refigurations of the Heterosexual Male' in E. Grosz and E. Probyn (eds) *Sexy Bodies: Strange Carnalities of Feminism* London: Routledge.

Walker, G. (2001) 'Born Again Lawyers' *The Lawyer* 5 March.

Walker, M. (2006) *Higher Education Pedagogies* Buckingham: Open University Press.

Walkerdine, V. (1991) *Schoolgirl Fictions* London: Verso.

—— (1995) 'Subject to Change Without Notice: Psychology, Post-Modernity and the Popular' in S. Pile and N. Thrift (eds) *Mapping the Subject: Geographies of Cultural Transformation* London: Routledge.

—— (ed) (2002) *Challenging Subjects: Critical Psychology for a New Millenium* London: Palgrave.

—— (2003) 'Reclassifying Upward Mobility: Femininity and the Neo-Liberal Subject' 15(3) *Gender and Education* 237.

Walklate, S. (1995) *Gender and Crime: An Introduction* Hemel Hempstead: Prentice Hall/Harvester Wheatsheaf.

Wallbank, J. (1997) 'The Campaign for Change of the Child Support Act: Reconstituting the "Absent" Father' 6 *Legal Studies* 191.

—— (2002) 'Clause 106 of the Adoption and Children Bill: Legislation for the "Good Father"?' 22(2) *Legal Studies* 276.

—— (2005) 'Getting Tough on Mothers: Regulating Contact and Residence' 15(2) *Feminist Legal Studies* 189.

Walters, R. (2003) 'New Modes of Governance and the Commodification of Criminological Knowledge' 12 *Social and Legal Studies* 5.

Warin, J., Solomon, Y., Lewis, C. and Langford, W. (1999) *Fathers, Work and Family Life* York: Joseph Rowntree Foundation/Family Policy Studies Centre.

Waters, M. (1995) *Globalization* London: Routledge.

Wayne Walker, G. (2006) 'Disciplining Protest Masculinity' 9(1) *Men and Masculinities* 5.

Weedon, C. (1987) *Feminist Practice and Poststructuralist Theory* Oxford: Blackwell.

Wells, C. (2002) 'Women Law Professors – Negotiating and Transcending Gender Identity at Work' 10(1) *Feminist Legal Studies* 1.

Wells, C. (2004) 'Working Out Women in Law Schools' 21(1) *Legal Studies* 116.

West, C. and Zimmerman, D. H. (1987) 'Doing Gender' 1 *Gender and Society* 125.

West, J. and Lyon, K. (1995) 'The Trouble with Equal Opportunities: The Case of Women Academics' 7 *Gender and Education* 51.

West, R. (1988) 'Jurisprudence and Gender' 55 *University of Chicago Law Review* 1.

Wetherell, M. and Edley, N. (1999) 'Negotiating Hegemonic Masculinity: Imaginary Positions and Psycho-Discursive Practices' 9(3) *Feminism and Psychology* 335.

Whitehead, S. (1996) 'Men, Managers and the Shifting Discourses of Post-Compulsory Education' 1(2) *Research in Post-Compulsory Education* 151.

—— (1999) 'From Paternalism to Entrepreneurialism: the Experience of Men Managers in UK Post-Compulsory Education' 20(1) *Discourse: Studies in the Cultural Politics of Education* 57.

—— (1999) 'Hegemonic Masculinity Revisited' 6(1) *Gender, Work and Organisation* 58.

—— (2000) 'Masculinity: Shutting Out the Nasty Bits' 7(2) *Gender, Work and Organisation* 133.

—— (2001) 'Man – The Invisible Gendered Subject' in S. Whitehead and F. Barrett (eds) *The Masculinities Reader* Cambridge: Polity.

—— (2002) *Men and Masculinities: Key Themes and New Directions* Cambridge: Polity.

—— (2003) 'Identifying the Professional "Man"ager: Masculinity, Professionalism and the Search for Legitimacy' in J. Barry, M. Dent and M. O'Neill (eds) *Gender, Professionalism and Managerial Change: An International Perspective* London: Macmillan.

Whitehead, S. and Barrett, F. (eds) (2001) *The Masculinities Reader* Cambridge: Polity.

Whitehead, S. and Moodley, R. (eds) (1999) *Transforming Managers: Engendering Change in the Public Sector* London: UCL Press.

Wikeley, N. (2006) *Child Support: Law and Policy* Oxford: Hart.

Wilkins, D. (1998) 'Fragmenting Professionalism: Racial Identity and the Ideology of Blacked Out Lawyering' 5 *International Journal of the Legal Profession* 141.

Williams, C. (2002) 'Parental Alienation Syndrome' *Family Law* 410.

Williams, F. (1998) 'Troubled Masculinities in Social Policy Discourses: Fatherhood' in J. Popay, J. Hearn and J. Edwards (eds) *Men, Gender Divisions and Welfare* London: Routledge.

Williams, F. and Churchill, H. (2003) *Empowering Parents in Sure Start Local Programmes* London: HMSO.

Williams, F. and Roseneil, S. (2004) 'Public Values of Parenting and Partnering: Voluntary Organizations and Welfare Politics in New Labour's Britain' 11(2) *Social Politics* 181.

Williams, G. (ed) (2003) *The Enterprising University: Reform, Excellence and Equity* Buckingham: Open University Press.

Williams, J. (2000) *Unbending Gender: Why Family and Work Conflict and What To Do About It* New York: Oxford University Press.

Williams, P. (1995) 'Meditations on Masculinity' in M. Berger, B. Wallis and S. Watson (eds) *Constructing Masculinity* New York: Routledge.

Williams, R. (1997) *Marxism and Literature* Oxford: Oxford University Press.

Williams, T. and Goriely, T. (2003) *Recruitment and Retention of Solicitors in Small Firms* London: Law Society.

Willis, P. (1977) *Learning to Labour: How Working Class Kids Get Working Class Jobs* Westmead: Saxon House.

Willmott, H. (1993) 'Managing the Academics: Commodification and Control in the Development of University Education' 48(9) *Human Relations* 993.

Wilson, G.B. (2006) 'The Non-Resident Parental Role For Separated Fathers: A Review' 20(3) *International Journal of Law, Policy and the Family* 286.

Witherspoon, S. (2002) 'Research Capacity: A Crisis in Waiting?' 37 *Socio-Legal Newsletter* 1.

Wittig, M. (1992) *The Straight Mind* Boston: Beacon Press.

Witz, A., Halford, S. and Savage, M. (1996) 'Organized Bodies: Gender, Sexuality and Embodiment in Contemporary Organizations' in L. Adkins and V. Merchant (eds) *Sexualising the Social: Power and the Organization of Sexuality* Basingstoke: Macmillan.

Wrigley, N. and Lowe, M. (1996) *Retailing, Consumption and Capital: Towards the New Retail Geography* Harlow: Longman.

Wynne, D. (1990) 'Leisure, Lifestyle and the Construction of Social Position' 9 *Leisure Studies* 21.

Yancey Martin, P. (2001) '"Mobilizing Masculinities": Women's Experiences of Men at Work' 8(4) *Organization* 587.

Yeatman, A. (1993) 'Corporate Managerialism and the Shift from the Welfare to the Competitive State' 13(2) *Discourse* 3.

—— (1995) 'The New Contractualism and the Politics of Quality Management' paper presented at Women, Culture and Universities: A Chilly Climate? National Conference on the Effects of Organizational Culture on Women in Universities, Conference Proceedings 19–20 April, Sydney: University of Technology.

Young, M. and Wilmott, P. (1957) *Family and Kinship in East London* Harmondsworth: Pelican.

—— (1973) *The Symmetrical Family* Harmondsworth: Penguin.

Index